Joy in the Struggle

Author's mother, front left, with servants' strike committee,

Byelorussia, 1905

Joy in the Struggle

My Life and Love

Beatrice Lumpkin

INTERNATIONAL PUBLISHERS
New York

ISBN 10: 0-7178-0762-2   ISBN-13 978-07178-0762-8
Typeset by AarkMany Media, Chennai, India

To the young people
fighting for a world that puts
people before profit

Contents

Frank and Beatrice Lumpkin at Washington D.C. peace rally, 2002

Foreword

Joy in the Struggle is social history at its best; a moving and inspiring account of one activist's lifelong struggle for worker and civil rights. Beatrice Shapiro Lumpkin has spent the last eight decades on the frontlines of some of the most important battles for economic and social justice in the U.S., including the fight to secure union rights and Social Security in the 1930s, the movement to end Jim Crow segregation and racism in the 1950s and 1960s, the fight against U.S. imperialism during the Cold War, and the more recent battle to secure affordable health care for Americans. I had the honor of meeting Bea in 2007 when I was finishing my Ph.D. dissertation on laundry workers at the University of Toronto. I discovered Bea through an article she had written for the *People's Weekly World* chronicling how she and her comrades had helped organize New York City's laundry workers during the Great Depression. Through phone conversations and e-mail exchanges (often into the wee hours of the night), Bea generously shared her memories of this important union campaign with me. By the time we met in person a year later, I knew that Bea was the real deal, that rare breed of person who practices what they preach. Bea has spent most of her life on picket lines, in union halls, at the state capitol and in Washington, D.C. fighting for workers and their families to be treated with dignity and respect. Her life reveals that the great march towards a more inclusive and egalitarian society has been led by people of conviction, people whose passion for social justice inspires those around them to recognize the power of collective action and unity.

Bea's activism has been nurtured and sustained by her deep commitment to working-class solidarity. Born in 1918 in the East Bronx, Bea joined the Young Communist League (YCL) in 1933 after they supported a free speech campaign at her James Monroe High School. Since joining the YCL eighty years ago, Bea explains that she "never had a moment when I had nothing to do." In the 1930s, she participated in the student strikes against fascism, the National Hunger Protest that helped secure a relief program for unemployed Americans, and the struggle to free the Scottsboro Nine, the nine black youths framed on rape charges in 1931. She was part of the great labor upsurge precipitated by the emergence of the Congress of Industrial Organizations, the 1935 Wagner Act and the grassroots activism of workers who were mobilizing at the shop-floor level. *Joy in the Struggle* offers a rare first-hand account of the epic labor struggles that brought four out of every five manufacturing workers into the union movement.

As a defense worker during WWII, Bea moved to Buffalo, New York where she met her soul mate, Frank Lumpkin. The Lumpkins, who spent their early married years in Chicago and Gary, Indiana, were a formidable team. They led protests against discriminatory housing practices and segregation, mobilized their neighbors to demand access to clean drinking water, participated in the campaign that brought Harold Washington, Chicago's first African American mayor into power in 1983, and of course continued to fight for worker rights. In 1965, at the height of the Black Power Movement, Bea began her career in education, working as a Chicago public school mathematics teacher and later as a professor at Malcolm X, a Chicago City College. When Bea discovered that textbooks omitted the multicultural history of mathematics, she started doing her own research and over the next several decades published widely on the multicultural roots of mathematics and science. Bea was active in the Chicago Teachers Union and participated in the 1974 founding of the Coalition of Labor Union Women through which she continues to mentor young trade unionist women. When Wisconsin Steel—the steel plant where Frank worked—suddenly closed in 1980, she helped launch what would become a 17-year battle, chronicled in her *"Always Bring A Crowd!": The Story of Frank Lumpkin, Steelworker*, that culminated in a 19 million dollar settlement for the workers.

Now, Bea is more committed than ever to the struggle to create a more just society. She campaigned for Barack Obama in 2008 and once again in 2012. She attends rallies in Washington to protest the neoliberal-inspired proposal to privatize Social Security, joined Wisconsin public sector workers fighting to preserve the collective bargaining rights that she and other activists helped secure in the 1930s, and most recently could be found on the picket lines in support of Chicago public school teachers. An examination of Bea's more than eighty-year journey deepens our understanding of the great labor and civil rights struggles of the twentieth and early twenty-first centuries and demonstrates how one person can help shape the course of history. Academics and activists alike will learn much from reading about the extraordinary life and times of Beatrice Lumpkin.

Jenny Carson, Assistant Professor, Department of History Ryerson University, Toronto, 2012

Acknowledgements

I thank the many friends who helped me produce *Joy in the Struggle*, my attempt to share the wonderful experiences I have enjoyed in the workers' struggle. Many realize that struggle is hard. But more need to know that fighting for justice fills our lives with joy.

Special thanks go to: Doris Strieter and now-deceased Rev. Tom Strieter, also historian Jenny Carson for their help in editing; Peggy Lipschutz for wonderful cartoons; Scott Marshall, Warren (Sam) Lumpkin and Soren Kyale for photos. Hearty thanks also go to Betty Smith and Gary Bono of International Publishers for their invaluable help in publishing *Joy in the Struggle*.

Preface

In the mid-1950s, Frank and I were driving in upper New York State. We saw a small stream flowing into a cave. A sign invited "good swimmers" to swim through the cave. I decided to try.

The water was not deep, but the stream plunged into darkness. Only a tiny pin-point of light could be seen. It was far downstream, maybe a mile. Cautiously, I pulled myself through the water, towards the light. I was scared and there was no turning back.

For a long time I swam but the light was still tiny and faint. After a while, it got a little larger, as though someone was holding a small flashlight, a long ways away. "At least it's not getting smaller," I thought.

"I am headed the right way."

Ten minutes later, the light was definitely larger and I picked up speed. I was swimming freely, no longer touching the bottom of the stream. It was easier going because the light got bigger and bigger until it became the size of a small room.

At last, I emerged from the cave into broad sunlight. A lot of people were swimming in the river and I was no longer alone. My love was waiting for me on the river bank. That was an experience I never forgot.

I feel very lucky to have joined the workers' movement at a young age. They showed me that there is a light at the end of the tunnel. Put people before profits!

Part 1
(1918-1943)

Chapter 1

Born in East Bronx

*Mostly, our play was vertical, up and down
the fire escapes.*

I was born in 1918 in a very unionized and class conscious neighborhood of the East Bronx. Nearly all of our neighbors were East European Jews who worked in the garment industry. Many were active unionists. Some were Communists and a number were Socialists. My parents were among the few who were not factory workers.

My mother had worked in the Triangle Shirtwaist Factory before I was born. Fortunately, pregnancy forced her to leave that job before the fire broke out. Just months after she left Triangle Shirtwaist, the terrible fire of 1911 killed 146 of the young, mostly women workers.

Perhaps that fire was a factor in my father's decision to "go into business," a decision they regretted 20 years later. The "business" was a hand laundry. My mother did the ironing, and my father ran around on foot, picking up and delivering laundry. They did harder physical work and made less money than if they had stayed in the factory. Over the years, they retained their pro-worker, leftist socialist outlook. I can say that I was born knowing "which side I was on."

Fire Escape Playgrounds

All children like active play. But there really wasn't room in the overcrowded apartments. That did not stop me from turning my parents' bed into a trampoline. I loved to jump off the dresser top and bounce on the bed. I realized vaguely that sooner or later the bed frame would break. But it was soooh... much fun that I could not restrain myself. I also enjoyed swinging on the towel bar on the bathroom door. That was fun until my younger brother Lenny tried it. The glass bar broke and cut his hands. I felt his pain, so I gave up swinging on that door.

Bronx Intercom, by Peggy Lipschutz

We found a way to play in the crowded streets of the East Bronx. Mostly, our play was vertical, up and down the fire escapes. Nobody bothered us there. The iron fire escapes zigzagged from apartment to apartment. The ladders gave us a handy way to visit friends, or play "house," or other games. A few families had turned the horizontal stretch of the "zigzag" into a miniature garden, with beautiful plants and pillow seats.

On a hot summer day, they sat in relative comfort on their fire escape and tried to catch a breeze.

The modern air conditioner had been invented but was still a "downtown" luxury. The stuffy tenements did not cool off at night. Whole families would drag their bedding to nearby parks to sleep. Sometimes we slept on "tar beach," the flat tenement roof.

Windows were another wonderful opening to the world. In good weather, bedding was hung out of the window to "air." There was no need for an intercom system, or a "house" telephone. Anyway, that was years before we got our first telephone. All you had to do in the old neighborhood was throw up the bottom window, stick your head out and holler for your neighbor. Every subject was fair game from, "What are you cooking for dinner tonight?" to advice about raising children, to complaints about husbands who came home late, causing the dinner to get cold.

Strangely, I don't remember any talk about husbands who did not come home at all. All the children seemed to have two parents. We did not know then how lucky we were. Of course there were divorces, but not in my small world.

The Merry-go-round

A child could yell up from the street, "Mama!" And the right mother would open the window. "Throw me two pennies for the merry-go-round." Two pennies would be wrapped in newspaper and accurately aimed to hit the sidewalk near the right child. Two pennies bought a short ride on the hand-cranked, traveling merry-go-round. The small merry-go-round was pulled by a horse from street to street. The ride was long enough for me because I always got motion-sick. Still, when I heard the music as they came to my street, I always wanted to ride.

One of our summer treats was ice off the ice wagon. The iceman came every few days. His cries would bring a rush of orders, shouted down the stairs or out the window. Orders were for 10-cent or 15-cent blocks. We kids marveled at how exactly the iceman scored and split each order from the huge blocks of ice in his wagon. Then he hauled the ice up the stairs and placed it in the oak ice boxes. The iceman's job was seasonal because we used an outside window box in winter. There was an ice-making plant near our house. It was a wondrous place to visit. Sheets of water flowed down the side of the ice building and miraculously turned to ice. I watched for a while but never figured out how it worked.

Most of our active play was outdoors. That was especially true on humid summer days when apartments became stifling hot. On weekends, parents sat outside on chairs near the curb, giving us kids the rest of the pavement for play. Strangely enough, the old English group games hung on in New York, even for our East European immigrant community.

We kids lined up in two opposing rows. Then we marched towards each other chanting, "Walking on the green grass, green grass, green grass/ Walking on the green grass, all on a summer day." Sometimes we played, "Rover, red rover/ Why don't you come over?" It was fun to bounce a rubber ball with one hand, twirling an outstretched leg around each bounce, saying, "Hello, hello, hello Sir/ Meet me at the grocer/ No Sir/ Why Sir/ because I have a cold, Sir." In school we played "London Bridge is falling down/My fair lady," "Bluebird, bluebird, through my window," "Ring around the rosy/ Pocket full of posies/ Ashes, ashes/ All fall down," and more. I liked the lines, "Ashes, ashes/All fall down," because it was fun to fall down on the floor.

Instead of Halloween, we kids dressed in costumes and went begging on Thanksgiving. We asked for money, and got two or three pennies. The threat was indeed, "tricks." Some of us carried stockings with chalk dust or even stones that we swung to show how tough we were. It had something to do with the British Guy Fawkes Day. After my time, Halloween began to take over. That was a good thing. Better to beg for candy than for money.

I don't remember how we survived the winters indoors. There was no television, not even radio. Of course there were card games and board games such as checkers and Parcheesi. That was even before Parker brought out the first Monopoly game in 1934. Better-off families had hand-wound, spring-loaded Victrolas and player pianos. I don't remember those luxury items in our tenement house. After I learned to read, my preferred indoor sport was reading books. I do not remember that we did any chores. I am afraid we left all the housework to my mother.

Before I was old enough for school, my vertical play brought me to grief. One day, I was climbing up an iron gate. Across the top were iron points. Somehow I lost my footing, slipped and was impaled on one of the points. Someone pulled me off and rushed me to the doctor across the street. Doctors had offices on the street in those days (1923). The up side to the accident was that it made me a star attraction. I was able to satisfy my nearly insatiable sweet tooth. For two licks of candy, I unwrapped my bandage and displayed the stitches in my neck. Anyway, the tear healed nicely. Years later I would have to explain that the stitch marks were not thyroid surgery, just a lack of safe recreation.

Almost all of the adults on my block had children. But my mother's friend above us did not. That meant I got some extra attention that I did not always appreciate. Maybe that attention was necessary because my mother always worked. She and my father were small "business people," with emphasis on the "small." Their hand-laundry store required long hours of hard labor.

Hand Laundry

My father pushed a covered cart in which he picked up the wash and delivered the finished bundles. He also used a pen and laundry-proof ink to mark identifying numbers on the dirty clothes before they were sent in bulk to the wholesale steam laundry. Everything was cash and carry. My mother ironed shirts and washed and stretched curtains. That meant standing on her feet long hours. Her legs were thick with swollen veins. It hurt my heart, watching my mother stand on swollen legs every day. But that's the way it was.

In fact, the laundry store is my earliest memory. While my mother starched and ironed clothes, a babysitter would push me around in a carriage. Her name was Gladys. I was in training pants, perhaps prematurely. I remember one day when I had a big problem of wetting my pants. Gladys took me to the laundry store where my mother gave me dry pants. Near the ceiling, a long wood board hung with rows of pegs on both sides. Hand washed items hung on these pegs to dry. Pairs of my just-washed panties filled a long row of the pegs. "Please don't wet this one, too," my mother pleaded. "It's the last pair."

You guessed it. I could not help it and wet the last pair too.

When I was almost four, my baby brother was born. I remember being so lonely while my mother was in the hospital. The neighbors upstairs took care of me until my mother returned. Everybody said my brother Lenny (Leon) was such a beautiful baby. People would "ooh" and "ah" about how cute he was when we rode the subway train. Jealousy dug its evil fangs deep into my soul. I felt left out when my mother rocked the baby on her lap. "Mama, pick me up," I begged. She laughed, reached over and scooped me up so she could rock both of us. That made me feel good and I thought my mother was wonderful. As she was.

"This used to be such a nice neighborhood," some women complained as they sat on chairs near the curb to allow people to pass on the sidewalk. Later in life, it seemed to me I was always moving into neighborhoods that "used to be so nice." It wasn't clear to me who or what had "spoiled" the neighborhood. Did we do it?

The block had a few landlords, a candy store, a doctor's apartment-office, a barber shop, a shoemaker shop, a kosher butcher shop and "Shapiro, the laundry man." Everybody else was a unionized clothing worker. Most had come from "the old country," some part of the old Czarist Empire.

With one exception, everyone I knew was just surviving, if not downright poor. The exception was my friend Eli. His father was the landlord and his brother went to medical school and became a doctor. Then his family moved and invited me to visit. I did that two or three times. You couldn't just run up to his apartment door and ring the bell as I had done when he lived in our building. His new house had a doorman. You had to give your name, and the doorman would call the apartment. Then, if you were accepted, you could go up and visit.

I didn't like that at all. Emotionally, I felt I was being singled out for being poor. Of course, intellectually I knew that all visitors had to be approved. I quit going to see Eli and he did not come back to the old neighborhood anymore.

Speak English

Except for the janitors, everyone who lived on my crowded block was Jewish, mostly from Russia. In fact, my parents were from Byelorussia, but I was not aware of that fine point. Yiddish was spoken everywhere. Russian was used when parents didn't want the children to understand. Usually the children replied in English. "You're in America, speak English," my parents told me. So the children lost the richness of the old culture and a language barrier sprang up between parents and children. I was lucky to be sent to an after-school class where I learned to read and write Yiddish and learned something about the rich literature. But I never became really fluent. I did learn something about antisemitism in Czarist Russia. The teacher in our Jewish school wanted us to understand the impact of antisemitism in those times. She told us a story about a Jewish boy in old Russia.

The boy was told, "There are many, many Russians."

"How many?" he asked.

"So many that each time you draw a breath, a Russian dies."

"Really?" Then the boy began to breathe as rapidly as he could.

As a child I heard many stories of attacks on Jewish ghettoes. Some stories were very bloody. But the story I remember most was about that little boy who breathed faster to make more Russians die. How bad the oppression must have been to have provoked such hate!

Actually, I did not have to go that far to see fear turned into hate. I remember a shameful incident on my street. The daughter of a janitor was wearing a cross on a chain. She was the only Christian in the group of children on the street. The Jewish children began to jeer and taunt her about the cross until she began to cry and run home. I was there and I did nothing. I was only six but I knew it was wrong. I just stood there, silent, and did not know what to do. Still, I could not forget it. I think that shameful memory helped push me into speaking out against injustice.

Why did my friends do such a horrible thing? I still don't fully understand it. I know that in our community in the 1920s, memories of East European pogroms were fresh and painful. Pogroms were murderous attacks on Jewish ghettos. They were often carried out by Czarist troops under cover of religion, under cover of "the cross." It was something like the fearsome image of the flaming cross of the Ku Klux Klan. That's not an excuse for hurtful behavior. These children were acting out another form of prejudice that they had been taught.

Hebrew was the language of the religion, but not used in the community except for prayers. There were a number of synagogues in the neighborhood that were crowded on the high holidays. Many in our community, including my parents, were not believers. Still, they were part and parcel of Jewish culture. That was certainly true of our food. Although my mother did not follow the religious laws, she neither bought nor cooked pork, shellfish or other *treif* (non-kosher) foods. In later years, she would sometimes fry bacon for us. But she never ate it.

Smells and Sounds of Home

Pickle juice ran in the street creating an always-present sour smell. It wasn't too bad because we were used to it. By the age of eight I was old enough to be sent to the store to get a *schmaltz* (fat) pickled herring. Proud that I had been entrusted with this important task, I plunged my arm into the herring barrel. Then I squeezed the herrings in the pickling juice until I felt a thick one. That was it. "Get a fat one," my mother had said.

I, myself, never cared for the pickled or smoked stuff. I did drink the *kvass*, sold by the glass from barrels on the street. It was all right but not my favorite. I did not taste kvass again until I visited the Soviet Union in 1965. Then I loved the kvass, for old times' sake. Only late in life, did I look it up on the Internet and learn that kvass is made from fermented rye bread. In some countries kvass is fermented mare's milk.

Many a time I turned up my nose at lox and bagels, food I now gobble up at $20 a pound. Nor did I care for the sweet and sour stews or the mushroom barley soup that I now find exotic. My taste went to the sweets in which my neighborhood excelled. Tall vendors, who I thought were Turks, came through our street carrying trays on their heads. The trays were covered with clean white cloths and held sesame candy bars, sold by the piece. Halvah, another sesame treat, I found irresistible. Also, the candy store had a glass shelf full of charlotte russe, sponge cake topped with rich, thick whipped cream swirls and a red candied cherry. About the only part of my mother's cooking that I appreciated were her cakes. But then nobody ever begged me to eat the cakes. Her sponge cakes and almond breads were superb.

Early in life I found out that I could gain power through food. As a child, I was normally thin. My sallow complexion and dark rings under my eyes made me look sickly. My parents begged me to eat their good food. I usually refused, even though they reminded me that children were starving in Europe. Calorie-wise, I more than made up for skipping meals by stuffing myself with cake and gulping down a pint of milk.

When I became a mother, I remembered the bad food habits I acquired so young. I also remembered the misery I put my parents through, begging me to eat. That memory made me stick to a "take it or leave it" policy at my own dinner table. It worked, although I am sure I made every other possible mistake in child-rearing.

Along with the smells and the tastes of my neighborhood were the sounds. First in the morning was the milkman. We could hear the thud of the horse's hooves, the creak of the wagon and the milkman's quick steps up three flights of stairs. Later, we heard the cries of the peddler with his horse-drawn vegetable wagon, advertising his wares. On some days the "second-hand" man called out for old clothes or other used goods. The back-yard violinists and opera singers often poured out their song. From their apartment windows, appreciative women tossed down coins, wrapped in newspaper. The musicians, playing in the back yard for food money, made me sad. I thought such talented people should have a more secure way to earn a living. Added to the music was the occasional organ grinder, advertising his hand-cranked carousel. In all, I did not mind the symphony of sounds because I never felt alone. The sounds of human activity were all around.

When the snows came to the East Bronx, I took my sled to Prospect Park. There was a steep hill that emptied into a traffic artery. The thrill was to go down the hill at top speed and avoid being hit by a car at the bottom of the hill. It was wonderful fun. But on my way home a much larger child grabbed my sled and ran away with it. I was utterly miserable when I arrived home. My fingers hurt with frostbite, and my sled was gone. My mother, too, was upset when I told her what happened. For once I did not get the comforting I could normally count on. "You'll just have to learn to hold onto your things if you want to have anything," she told me. There was no money to buy another sled. So that's the way it was.

Learning to Read

I am sure I was the only child who was expelled from kindergarten. Somehow, the kindergarten teacher and I had a difference of opinion. I came home visibly scratched. Perhaps my mother thought I was being mistreated and maybe I was. No doubt Mama took me out of school, but I thought that I was kicked out. I had plenty of time to cool my heels at home. All my friends were in school, and I was very lonely. So I was ready, more than ready, when the new school year began. I plunged into my lessons and quickly learned to read.

I can remember learning to read because it made a big change in my life. Reading was my main entertainment. We did not have one of the new crystal radios. Television was in the realm of science fiction. We did enjoy the silent movies, especially in the summer when an outdoor theater was used. A real, live pianist sat at a piano, up front, and provided the musical background. But that was only on the weekend.

My first reader was easy to memorize. "Dickey Dare was going to school. On the way he met a cow. 'Good morning cow,' said Dickey Dare. 'Moo, moo,' said the cow. Said Dickey Dare, 'I am going to school.' And Dickey Dare walked on. On the way he met a horse, pig, dog, cat ...." After I had learned it by heart, which did not take too long, there was nothing left to read in school.

Learning to read unlocked the world of imagination for me, but it brought its own problems. I borrowed books from the public library. Unfortunately, children were only allowed to borrow two books at a time. They were small books, and the library was about a half mile from my apartment. I would start reading the books as I walked home. By the time I reached my tenement building, I had finished the two books and once again had nothing to read.

It was very frustrating. I tried to save the books to read until after I got home. But I had no self-control. It was as bad as being sent to the store for a "glass" of sweet cream. I knew that I should not sip the cream. But I thought if I took just a little, nobody would know and it wouldn't make any difference. But I could never quit after just one sip. Fortunately, we were only one block from the store so I didn't have time to consume the whole glass of cream. We supplied our own containers; Mama was always sure to give me a large glass when I went to the store.

First grade was a challenge. We called our school, "the chicken coop," it was so old. The building probably predated the Civil War. P.S. 20 continued to use that building for another 50 years after I left. Some of us were doubled up, two to a seat. The teacher had a very large class. The slogan on the front page of the *Daily News*, or perhaps the *Daily Mirror*, called for a "seat for every school child."

I wanted so much to do well, to show what I could do. But I failed abysmally on my first homework assignment. I had to copy all of the capital letters and numbers one through nine. The first time I drew a letter it was not quite right. So I erased and erased until it looked like the model. It was a big mess. I guess the erasers weren't very good in those days. Finally, I was ready. The next day I brought my grubby homework page into class. All around me, I saw lovely clean sheets with beautifully formed letters, especially on the desks of the Shirley Temple look-alikes. These little girls had their hair curled to hang perfectly, just like our movie idol, Shirley Temple. In contrast, my hair was cut in the practical "Buster Brown" style with straight bangs; nothing glamorous there. It didn't occur to me at the time that the beautiful clean homework I saw may have been done by parents. The schools were so crowded that they would often move up half a class to a higher grade. Such mass emergency promotions were common at P.S. 20 in 1924. When the principal came into our class, she called out the names of all the "better" students, the ones with the neat homework. They were instantly promoted, or skipped, to second grade. My name was not called. I thought that was an injustice. Perhaps if I had been selected, I would have escaped one of the most traumatic experiences of my childhood.

Psycho-terror in First Grade

To control the large class, or for whatever other reason, our teacher did not hesitate to use terror tactics. She did not try to mask her contempt of us, the children of Jewish immigrants. In later years I learned that female teachers in New York City had been forbidden to marry. Those who married secretly lived in constant fear of being found out and fired. That inhumane pressure on female teachers may have contributed to the hostility we felt in the school. Still, nothing excuses the mental torture we suffered in my first grade class.

Our teacher told us that she had eyes in the back of her head so we had better not try to talk when she turned her back. We didn't know whether to believe that or not. Sure enough, some children began to talk while Miss F's back was turned. She grabbed two boys and hauled them up to the front. That's when the torture began. Miss F put a slip knot in a length of the stout red cord that we used for craft projects. Then she said she would slip the knot over the boys' tongues and pull out their tongues so they couldn't talk any more. Each boy could save himself from this horrible fate by saying he was sorry and promising never to talk when her back was turned. One of the boys immediately said he would never talk in class again. The other boy stood speechless, struck dumb by fear.

"Well then," Miss F said, "I'll just have to pull out his tongue." And she told him to stick out his tongue so she could adjust the slip knot to the right size. We sat there, horrified, as she slipped the cord over his tongue to adjust the knot. We did not know what to believe. After all, if Miss F had eyes in the back of her head, anything could happen.

"I'll give you one more chance," Miss F sneered. "Say you're sorry you talked and I won't pull out your tongue." The frightened child still stood there, silent. "What's the matter with you? Don't you understand English?" Miss F persisted. The child shook his head, "No." What do you talk, Jewish?" She pronounced the word Jewish with a derisive sneer. Then Miss F turned to the class and asked, "Who will come up here and explain it to him in Jewish?"

None of the children were very fluent in Yiddish. With the rest of the class, I sat there paralyzed. Finally one brave boy stepped forward and went through the charade. He asked, in his broken Yiddish, "Do you want your tongue pulled out?" The poor child shook his head to say, "No!"

"All right," Miss F said. "Now, you can sit down."

It never occurred to me to tell my parents what had happened. Probably none of the other kids did either.

In second grade I finally got my first "promotion." One day, the principal came in to our class and instantly promoted a third of us to third grade. We "skipped" a semester. Still, the pace of instruction seemed slow but I did not complain. In fact, I did not realize the pace was slow until I had to miss a few weeks. I was crossing Southern Boulevard with my father and saw my mother on the other side of the street. "Mama!" I shouted and broke out of my father's grasp. I ran into the path of a car that bruised my leg badly. It took some weeks for the leg to heal. When I returned to school, it was as though time had stood still. Nothing was new; I had not missed a thing.

My Brother Maxie

My older brother, Maxie, was seven years older than I was. We were in the same house and same family. But we lived in different worlds, with little chance to interact. He did "all right" in his classes. But in sports, Maxie was outstanding. His name was often in the newspaper because high school basketball was big in New York. He liked to hang out at garages and mess around with cars. All of this was alien to our Old World, East European Jewish culture. Maxie had adopted early twentieth century technology with enthusiasm.

There had been another brother born between us who died in the hospital during the 1918–1919 flu epidemic. I could not remember him because I was only a year old when he died. But I often thought we could have been playmates. So, I asked my mother about him, more than once. That made her cry and my father told me not to talk about the dead brother. Once again, I had done something wrong.

My Older Brother, Max Shapiro

My Brother Lenny

I did have a chance to play with my younger brother, but Lenny was almost four years younger. I am sure that I bossed him around. He loved animals and was always bringing stray dogs to our apartment. But they were never allowed to stay. However, there were uninvited animals that did stay. In fact you could not get rid of them. Our old tenement building was infested with vermin of all types.

Author, 12, and Brother Leon, 8, on Dickie Estate

One day I stepped on a bump in the linoleum. The bump was a mouse that had made its way under the loosened floor covering. It was one of the mice that had evaded my mother's traps. I am afraid that my step was not very delicate. Somehow, Lenny and I dragged the carcass out and discovered that the mouse was quite dead. There was nothing left to do but give the creature a proper funeral. We put the remains on some heavy paper and walked around the block in our funeral procession. The ceremony done, we flushed the carcass down the toilet, the same way Mama disposed of the rodents she trapped.

The animals that co-habited our apartment did not bother my brother and me. But even at a young age I was conscious of the less-than-ideal layout of the apartment. The kitchen was in the back of the apartment. Behind the kitchen and projecting into it was the toilet and bath. The bathroom had no exterior window, just a window that vented into the kitchen. Perhaps I was so conscious of it because the grownups were always making jokes about that unsavory arrangement. I guess in the "old country" there was plenty of space between toilet and kitchen because toilets were outside. That memory helped me appreciate an old European joke about customs in the United States. "They like to cook outside and go to the toilet inside."

The "Old Country"

Our parents had been in New York more than ten years when I was born. Once in a while, I heard them talk about the "old country." "It was so cold, we had to have double windows," my mother told me. I could not imagine anything that cold. Our ancient Bronx tenement house had single panes. And that seemed enough for New York. I had no way of knowing then that most of my life would be spent in places just as cold as Byelorussia in winter. Putting up and taking down storm windows in Buffalo, Gary, and Chicago would be just another chore. Put the storm windows up by October. Take them down by June.

Byelorussia sounded like a hard but wonderful place. "One day a wolf came and I ran home terrified," my mother told us. "Mama could have been Red Riding Hood," I thought. But instead of visiting her grandmother, my mother was picking mushrooms in the woods. When my mother cooked mushrooms in Byelorussia, she took precautions. Even in New York, she took the same precautions. "Throw a quarter in the frying pan with the cooking mushrooms. If the silver of the quarter turns green, don't eat the mushrooms. They are poisonous!" I have not researched this practice and cannot recommend it to the reader.

Her friends called my father, Avrom, although Morris was his legal name. My mother was Ruhd-eh. The Ellis Island record of August 17, 1907 listed her as "Roda." Some clerk read that as, "Dora," and that became her English name. Her father was a building contractor, much better off than most of the Jews in the ghetto of Bobruisk, Minsk Province. Young Avrom was a brilliant student from a poor family. He earned his living by teaching Jewish youths how to read and write Russian. Jewish students were not allowed to attend the Russian schools.

Ruhd-eh wanted to become a nurse, so her family hired Avrom to teach her Russian reading and writing. But my mother's ambition was never realized. She could not get a permit to go to the big city to attend nursing school. The Czar's government controlled all travel, and few Jews from Bobruisk were allowed to go to the big city. In general, Jews were confined to a ghetto.

The Flame of Revolution

Father was afire with the revolution. Mother caught the flame. Not necessarily from father because the tinder was everywhere in Czarist Russia. A much treasured picture shows Mama sitting in a strike committee meeting, about the year 1905. Many strikes were political, not only for economic needs but for political freedom. Jews, as a whole, wanted to get rid of the Czar and his feudal/capitalist dictatorship.

Many of the young Jewish youth wanted to go further. They wanted to do more than just replace feudal with capitalist rule. They wanted to get rid of all exploitation. These radical youth sympathized with Lenin and the Bolshevik majority that had just split away from the Social Democrats on the issue of revolution. My parents belonged to the more revolutionary sector of the Jewish Socialist *Bund*.

The people of the Russian Empire rose up in 1905 against the Czar. But their revolution was suppressed in blood. After the Czar suffered a humiliating defeat in the Russo-Japanese war, he unleashed a series of pogroms against the Jews. A pogrom was a murderous raid on a Jewish ghetto. Typically, Cossack cavalry conducted the pogroms. Jews were made the scapegoat to divert people's anger away from the corrupt government.

Both of my parents were active participants in the anti-Czarist Revolution of 1905. "I brought ammunition to our fighters," Mama proudly told me. "I went out through the snow and the mud, and dodged the bullets. I hid the ammunition in my long skirt. When our fighters sent me a note to bring them 'bread,' I knew that meant ammunition."

Avrom was among the thousands taken prisoner by the Czar's army. Not until I was grown did I learn that Papa was actually a hero to the Jews of Bobruisk in 1905. But more on that later. From my parents, I picked up the idea of revolution to end exploitation. They wanted to build socialism, a society free of exploitation. As far back as I can remember, I knew that there was something wrong with the system under which we lived. I saw how hard Mama and Papa worked and had nothing to show for it. I knew that was not right.

When I was about eight, my mother's father left Soviet Byelorussia and came to New York City. He lived with us for a few months. It was my job to take him to the synagogue, two blocks away, for his daily prayers. It was a rare opportunity for me to step inside the synagogue, a building not frequented by my parents. There was a main floor where my grandfather (*zaydeh* in Yiddish) joined the other men. Around the main floor were balconies, shielded by curtains from the men. That was where the women prayed.

The second-class status of women in the synagogue was strange and repulsive to me. I was glad to leave after I delivered Grandpa. Other synagogue-goers would make sure that he got home safely. I had heard that pious married women shaved their heads and wore a wig. There was also something about monthly baths for a ritual cleansing after menstruation. That made no sense at all when I was eight. Now that

I am over 90, it still makes no sense to me. I do respect other people's religious beliefs. But please don't put women down.

At 70, Grandpa was a tall, strong-looking man with a light step. Zaydeh was a building contractor and had prospered under the Soviet Union's New Economic Policy. But he left all that behind after Grandma died and he came to "America" to be with his daughters in New York City. No longer working and with nothing to do but pray at the synagogue, grandpa began to shrink. Every day he seemed a little weaker. I began to wonder if Grandpa would have been better off if he had stayed in Byelorussia. Now that I am old, I look around and see many old people who shrank. All I have to do is look in the mirror.

Author, 1928, with essay contest medal.

Chapter 2

My Public Schools
The YCL provided a free (no charge) group social life.

When I was nine, we moved a few blocks away from 165th and Tiffany Streets to Hunts Point. Our new apartment was across the street from my parents' hand laundry. It was a slight move up. The school and tenement buildings in Hunts Point were somewhat newer than in the old neighborhood. The culture was the same. Neighbors were typically unionized needle-trades factory workers, mostly East European Jewish immigrants. My new school also resorted to "skipping" as many students as possible. I skipped another semester and moved up to fifth grade. That put me a year ahead of my age at school.

The Young Pioneers

A year after we moved, I joined the Young Pioneers. They were a left-wing movement for children. In later years, my two younger children became active Boy Scouts. But in the 1920s, my parents thought the Scouts looked too much like a junior army. Instead of the Scout slogan of "Be Prepared," the Young Pioneers said, "Always Ready." I guess that meant, "Always Ready to Help the Working Class." Our "uniform" was almost the same as my junior high school uniform, a white middy blouse and dark skirt. The only difference was that Pioneers wore red instead of black ties with the middy blouse. There was a lot of discussion at our Pioneer meetings, none of which I remember. I remember only two experiences from my Young Pioneers days, one good and one bad.

I remember a wonderful Young Pioneers train trip to New Jersey. The trip was in solidarity with striking textile workers in Passaic, or was it Patterson or Trenton? What I remember clearly is the train itself. It was my first train ride. Of course I rode the subway train many times. But that wasn't a "real" train that went out to the "country." Subway train seats were wood, not upholstered, something like the streetcars of the '20s. But wonder to behold, real trains had toilets right in the cars and a sink where you could wash your hands. The toilet was flushed right on to the tracks in those days. The bottom of the toilet opened and you could see right down to the tracks. Even at the tender age of ten, I wondered about the sanitary aspect of that. I understood and approved when the conductors locked the toilets as we approached a station.

The train ride helped me realize that "America" was a big country. I stared and stared at the passing scenery until I became quite motion-sick. All in all it was a wonderful experience. Unfortunately, I don't remember a thing about the solidarity action itself except some of the songs we sang. At the time I thought they were such brave songs. We certainly got the attention of all who heard these unusual lyrics:

> One two three
> Young Pioneers are free,
> We're fighting for the working class
> Against the bourgeoisie
>
> Four, five, six
> We're happy Bolsheviks,
> We're fighting for the working class
> Against the dirty dicks [cop/detectives].

A bad experience cut short my time with the Pioneers. Their meetings took place after dark, at least in the winter time. There was a well-lit route from the meeting to my apartment. Instead, I took a much shorter route along a hilly street that was deserted at night. On one side of the street was the American Banknote Company, locked up tight at night. The monastery on the other side was surrounded by a high brick wall.

For all I knew, it was always deserted because it never showed any sign of life.

I had almost made it up the dark hill when I heard a man walking behind me, I picked up speed. The man started to run. I did too, but not fast enough. He grabbed me and ripped my middy blouse. By this time I had reached the corner of a neighborhood hospital. Fortunately, some people came out of the hospital just then and the man ran away. The hospital visitors came up to me and asked if I was all right. I was shaken but I said, "Yes, I'm all right." I never took that short cut at night again.

Of course, I did not tell my parents about my narrow escape. That was probably the last time that I attended a meeting of that children's group. But it was not the last time that I was physically attacked. Although I did not escape the later attacks unharmed, at least I was fully grown and could overcome the emotional damage.

Junior High School 60—A School for Girls

At eleven, I entered Junior High School (JHS) 60 in the East Bronx. I gained (or lost depending on how you look at it) another year. I was in a "rapid advance" class that completed seventh, eighth and ninth grades in two years. That made me a high school sophomore at barely 13. JHS 60 was a school for girls. There was a lot of "girl talk" and that included talking about sex. An older girl had already told me some facts of human reproduction, including monthly menses. She described the menses in a way that made no sense to me. Probably it made no sense to her either. My brother's biology textbook did not explain such subjects. In the old neighborhood, I felt sorry for poor Miss Smith who was disrespected by most of the other women. I could not understand their reasoning. It was not her fault if God sent her a baby when she wasn't married.

At JHS 60, I was with older girls. Some were, as we called it then, boy-crazy. The year before, I had been in a coed sixth grade class. In my class, there was a boy I really liked. If I saw him on the other side of the street, I would cross over in hopes that he would notice me. But that's as far as it went. At JHS 60, I barely thought about "boys." But I did care how I looked. I realized that I would never meet the Hollywood standard for beauty. No matter how I turned my profile, my nose was too big. That bothered me. Of course, my skin was way too dark for Hollywood. That did not bother me. I liked being dark enough to stay in the sun and not get sunburned.

The junior high school dress code was a white "middy" blouse with a big, dark middy tie, a dark skirt *and* black cotton stockings. The girls thought the black stockings were very unsexy. Those who "cared about boys" did not want to be seen in black stockings. So they wore normal, beige-colored stockings on their way to school. Before entering the school, they changed to the required black. I was not among them although I, too, resented the dress code.

Unfortunately, in 1928 pants were only for males. So the choice for females was bare legs, bobby sox or some kind of stockings. My preferred dress was bobby sox, winter and summer. Girls/women who could afford it wore silk stockings; nylon had not yet been invented. Silk was imported from Japan and expensive. After the 1933 bombing of Chinese cities by Japan, silk stockings were boycotted by progressive women. The slogan was, "You don't get nott'in, unless you wear cotton."

The junior high academic work was on a higher level and there were extracurricular activities. I became editor of the school paper and a member of Arista, an honor society. For each edition of the school paper, I wrote an episode of a science fiction story. I also won an award for excellence in French. That achievement I blush to mention because I retain so little of what I had learned. All of these positions and awards came to an abrupt end on International Workers Day, May First, 1931.

May First, International Workers Day

For workers all over the world, May First is a holiday. Workers put down their tools, and demonstrate to demand their rights. The day had its origin in Chicago. In 1886, McCormick Reaper workers in Chicago went on strike for an eight-hour day.

Police attacked the strikers and one striker was killed. On May 4, 1886, a rally was held at Haymarket Square to protest the killing. Someone threw a bomb and the police shot wildly, into the crowd and at each other. The massacre was followed by the legal frame-up and hanging of four Haymarket Martyrs. May First became a legal holiday in many countries to remember the Haymarket Martyrs and the fight for a shorter work day. But in the United States, the May First march was red-baited. In 1931, attending the march was not accepted as an excuse for a school absence.

Many children did attend the big May Day march in New York. Their absence from school was excused because their parents gave them a note saying they had been ill. But it was considered more loyal to the cause to stand up for your beliefs and say: "I was absent May First because it is a worker's holiday." I had not done that because I did not have the nerve. Sadie Nussbaum was responsible for shaming me into being more courageous. Sadie Nussbaum was my role model, except that I knew I could never be great like her.

As a child, Sadie had already been to the Soviet Union. She made brilliant speeches about the evils of capitalism. In the school play, Sadie had the main role of Abraham Lincoln. My role was the mother of a young soldier sentenced to death for falling asleep on sentry duty. I had only one line, but on stage, I could not remember the line. Sadie saved me and whispered the line to me. My voice showed real anguish as I said, "President Lincoln, please spare my son." So I could not refuse when Sadie challenged me to do the right thing and tell my teacher I had marched on May Day. Somehow I gathered up enough courage to tell my division teacher, "I was absent May First because it is a worker's holiday."

Stripped of My Honors

Poor Mrs. DuBois! She reacted as though I had just said, "I have just killed my mother!" Real tears rolled down her face as she sent me to the principal's office. I really felt sorry for her. The school authorities sent for my parents who were unable to save me. Punishment was swift and harsh. I felt like Dreyfuss, the French Jewish officer who was court-martialed and stripped of his epaulets. I was expelled from the Arista Honor Society and removed as editor of the school paper. Completing my "continued" science-fiction story was a little bit of a challenge for the school authorities. Given the turn of events, I wrote a class struggle ending for the story. The school authorities had the nerve to write another ending and publish it over my name. Where was the First Amendment when I needed it? But of course, I was only a child so I had no rights. In any case, there was no great work of fiction involved. Years later, looking over the copy, I ran across a sentence that was unintentionally hilarious. In the story, I had created a Frankenstein-type robot. I wanted to say that the robot looked at the floor. What I wrote was, "His eye fell on the floor."

I survived the last year at Junior High School 60. Just before I left, Miss Nice, my English teacher, wished me luck and added, "Come back and tell me about socialism." I never returned. Teenagers are so busy. At 13, I became a sophomore at James Monroe High School Annex. The Annex was close to our apartment. I had some time on my hands. That allowed me to chase around after butterflies with a cousin who was a graduate student in biology. I think she did the studying and I did the legwork, catching butterflies and other winged insects.

A little knowledge can be a dangerous thing. With the materials my cousin gave me I decided to make my own insect collection. Catching them was not bad but I must have goofed when I terminated them with carbon tetrachloride. I caught all kinds of insects, including fat bugs, and mounted them on a board with long, sharp pins. All was well for the first day or two. Then the bugs began to move. Seems I had only put them into a stupor and they were not terminated at all. Mercifully, I don't remember how I solved that gruesome problem. Humanely, I hope.

High School and Free Speech

In 1933, I became a high school junior and moved to the main building of James Monroe. It was a long walk to school but seemed shorter when I kicked a can all the way. James Monroe had 10,000 students, including an evening high school and adult classes at night. The school had a swimming pool and a biology lab. I joined the swimming team and loved the biology lab. I was in heaven! Science had been my love since I was nine years old and read my brother Maxie's high school biology book. I wanted to be a scientist when I grew up. Our school did not have science fairs but New York City had wonderful museums and zoos. For the five-cent fare, I could and did travel everywhere. Museum, zoo and aquarium admissions were free. It was a great crime against working class children when museums and zoos put dollar signs on their doors in recent years. Their high admission fees now bar many children from visiting at will.

Monroe High School offered two years of biology. Mrs. Sweet, the advanced biology teacher, let me work in the lab after school. My cousin, the biologist, got me mutant strains of fruit flies, *Drosophila melanogaster*. I felt very important as I peered into microscopes and decided who could mate with whom (flies of course). Swimming practice also took a lot of time because I was on the team for backstroke. All that changed the next year when the whole school was convulsed by a free speech fight.

One day I saw hundreds of students running down the steps. "What's going on?" I asked Anita, my swimming team buddy. "Oh, you wouldn't be interested," she said. "How do you know?" I demanded. "Tell me, what's happening?" I learned that the International Club's guest speaker had been forcibly removed from the school. The speaker, a rabbi, had urged that the United States recognize the Soviet Union! Word of the speaker's "radical" position spread to the principal. He ran up to the club meeting and ordered the rabbi out of the building. There was so much tension, perhaps because of the Depression, that the school exploded.

Then everybody was running. International Club members ran through the building alerting students. The coach was running to get the football squad out to stop the radical students by a show of force. Thousands of students massed to protest the violation of free speech. At one of our later rallies, Norman Thomas, presidential candidate of the Socialist Party, came to speak to the students. J.B. Matthews of the War Resisters League was another noted outside speaker.

The Young Communist League

Things began to move very fast for me. I joined the free speech fight led by the National Student League. I was ready to go further. I wanted to work to change the system. Should I join the Young Peoples Socialist League (Yipsels) or the Young Communist League (YCL)? I looked them both over and followed my original leaning to the YCL. I saw that the best organizers of the free speech fight were Communists so I wanted to be one of them.

From the moment I joined the YCL, and for the next 85 plus years, I can truly say that I have never had a moment when I had nothing to do. There were always picket lines for workers on strike, demonstrations to demand food for a hungry family, knocking on doors to sell the *Daily Worker* or bringing people out to vote. There were many meetings, parties, dances and dinners to attend or plan. We worked to bring people together and raised the money to organize. There were also books to read and articles to write. All of that, of course, was in addition to the basic need to work for a living and the joy and work of raising a family.

Membership in the YCL was a time of commitment, comradeship and exploration. I must admit that our high school YCL meetings went on for hours. We kept getting off the subject. It could take four hours to decide the date for a protest rally because most of the time we were playing around and not getting down to business. We hung out together but did not pair off although we kind of knew who had a "crush" on whom. Our high school YCL provided a group social life for us teenagers that required no money. It was depression times (1933), and we were all short of money, really short. My friends' parents were low-paid factory workers, often unemployed. I was among the poorest because my family was on Relief and my parents were ill.

That was the time of the rule of the nickel, one-twentieth of a dollar. The dollar has lost so much of its value, there is now talk of discontinuing the penny. The nickel may be next. But in 1933, the nickel was "king." It got you on the subway train, made a phone call and paid for a big candy bar that substituted for lunch. Candy bars are much smaller nowadays. I had to laugh at myself one night when I tried to open my apartment door lock with a nickel. Using the pay phones was itself a challenge. My family could not afford phone service so we did everything face to face. After I became a student activist, I could not avoid making phone calls. At first I was nervous. Would I handle the technology correctly? Would I know how to talk into a phone?

As a busy member of the YCL, I somehow found time to attend classes at The Workers School downtown. I remember how fascinated I was when I ran across Frederick Douglas's autobiography in The Workers School Library. I could not leave until I finished the whole book. Of course, I got hungry. But there was a candy machine in the hallway. I put a nickel in and the machine emptied itself in my arms. What to do? I must have solved that moral dilemma in the right way, because it is not on my conscience. I remember only the bonanza of all that good eating. No wonder I lost my teeth in later years.

Classes in the Park

We YCLers also organized some classes for ourselves. In good weather, we met in the park. In between playing ball and just running around, we studied Marx and Lenin. We took turns reading out loud. After each page, we would stop for a discussion. Everybody had something to say. In recent years, we tried that with four or five working women. It is still a good way to learn and probably had its origin in the nineteenth century workers' reading circles.

One of the ways we spread our message was to hold outdoor meetings on streets with heavy pedestrian traffic. We also used these meetings to raise money for our YCL work. Instead of a soapbox, we carried a short ladder and a U.S.

flag. We believed that the display of the flag made our public meeting "legal." In a short time a curious crowd gathered. The challenge was to capture and hold their interest. If the speaker fumbled, the crowd would leave. One approach was to talk about the Nazi takeover of Germany. Workers were very nervous about fascism. Could it happen here? Word of Nazi atrocities and death camps for Jews was trickling through. I, myself, had many nightmares of Nazis chasing me in Europe. I used to wake up in a sweat but happy to realize it was only a nightmare.

At our street-corner meetings, I talked about how Hitler won over many frustrated youth in Germany. These young people had never had a chance to work and to learn the lessons of unity on a job. Millions of young Americans, too, I warned, had no chance to work and to learn about labor solidarity. The Young Communist League, I said, was bringing unemployed youth the message of unity and the need to fight racism and fascism. Then we passed the hat with good results. Periodically, an elevated train would pass overhead. If I stopped talking, the crowd would leave. So I out-yelled the train.

A reliable resource for my YCL group was the Communist Party club in my neighborhood. We turned to them when we needed money to buy paper for a leaflet. It was a thrill for us kids to attend the grownups' meeting and explain why we needed a leaflet. In no time, a collection was made and they raised a whole dollar. A dollar bought a lot of paper in 1933! The serious atmosphere at the Party meetings impressed us. We looked forward to growing up and joining the Party, the "big league." We also had the help of one of our high school teachers, Isadore Begun. To write this page, I did a Google search for Begun. No wonder he was so helpful. About the time we were fighting for free speech, Begun was leading a fight for democracy in the teachers union. But that went over our heads at the time.

In April 1933, our YCL led hundreds of Monroe High School students in the National Student Strike for Peace. Things continued to move quickly. By June, I was among the student leaders who were removed from the school against our will. We were transferred to Morris High School some distance away. It was a smaller school without a swimming pool and they did not even teach French! Everything at Morris High School was on a smaller scale than at Monroe. But Morris High did have one resource that Monroe High School did not have. Morris had a wonderful physics teacher, Irving Mossbacher.

Death in the Bronx

Mr. Mossbacher let our YCL leaders, mostly good physics students, hang out at his house. It was a real house, not a tenement flat. He let us eat all the candy we wanted and did not kick us out at 8 p.m. We were in heaven! We stayed as long as we liked, discussing heady subjects. That included the stuff the universe was made of. And we dreamed of socialism and how we could win it. I changed my passion from biology to physics. But first we had to win the revolution because that was more urgent. That summer, we all graduated. Then Mr. Mossbacher took a cruise to Europe on a well-deserved vacation. He came back in a box. Only 34, he suffered a fatal heart attack on board the cruise ship. He had no children and had never married. He remained single, as the story went, because he knew about the heart condition. But in a way, we were his children.

For many of us, it was the first death that struck so close. Years before, I had seen my eight-year-old friend crying as I walked to school. Her eyes were blood shot and she looked so sad. "My sister died last night," she told me. I knew her sister and I was sad, too. There had also been a death in the family above us in my old apartment building. "Shhh! Be quiet," we were told. Our parents stopped us from playing and laughing for fear we would disturb the grieving family. "They are sitting shiva," we were warned. That meant they sat on the floor, tore their clothes and smeared ashes on their face. And then, of course, there was the baby brother who had died when I was an infant. My mother had cried when I asked about him. Death was hard to accept and we did not believe in life after death. But over the years, we learned to see our immortality in a better future for humanity.

Hunter College

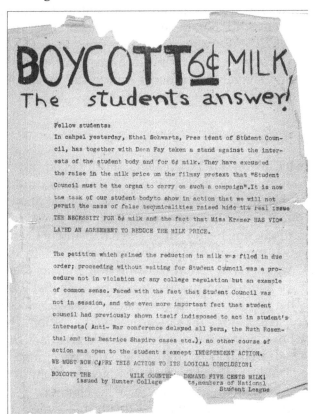

Our physics/YCL group scattered to different places. In 1934, the Bronx and Manhattan city colleges were free of tuition. They even issued free textbooks that we returned at the end of the semester. Only those with higher grades on statewide "Regents" exams were admitted. City College of New York (CCNY) was for men only; Hunter College was for women only. So I had to attend Hunter even though they did not have the engineering classes or the advanced physics classes offered at CCNY.

I had classes at 32nd Street and the main building at 68th Street. I had a nickel to take the subway between classes but no money for lunch. It was an easy decision. I spent the nickel for a big candy bar and walked from 32nd to 68th Street.

In the freshmen school lunchroom, a half-pint of milk cost five cents. To our dismay, a sign went up warning that milk was going up to six cents. Students, coming from depression-struck homes, were outraged. The price for a whole quart of milk was then nine cents. Our YCL club decided to organize a boycott. We stayed up all night producing a leaflet to announce our boycott. First, we had to write the leaflet. That wasn't too hard because BOYCOTT SIX-CENT MILK took up much of the page. Then we had to make 500 copies. That was hard. Wet-ink mimeograph duplicators seldom worked right and we ended up putting in the sheets one at a time. In the process, we got ink over everything. The next morning we weren't sleepy because excitement kept our adrenaline flowing.

The boycott was a huge success. Students massed around our table. I had to climb on top of the table to be heard. I did not realize that the dean of students had come into the lunchroom. The first I knew of her presence, she was standing on a table, too, trying to break up our protest. It was too late to be diplomatic; I am afraid that I had already called her a fascist. We were saved by the bell because it was time for class.

The next day, milk was back to five cents. That was "joy in the struggle." More than saving a penny, we had proved that students, united, had the power to change things for the better. As for the dean, I suspect that she was not really a fascist. She was best known for insisting on proper dress for "ladies." "Only Communists or prostitutes would be seen in public without a hat," was one of her pearls of wisdom.

Student Strike for Peace

Miraculously, none of the milk boycott organizers was disciplined. I was not that lucky in the spring when we organized for the National Student Strike for Peace. This was not a one-cent issue limited to the freshman campus. The strike was college-wide, citywide and nationwide. The strike leaders at Hunter College, four juniors and me, a freshman, were called into the dean's office. We were told that we would have to bring our parents in for a conference about our "behavior." We refused as a matter of principle. As college students, we said we were adults and responsible for our own behavior. We condemned the dean's tactics as intimidation for the purpose of breaking up our student organization. We stuck to our guns and the school administration stuck to theirs. The five of us were suspended from school and allowed to cool our heels for seven weeks. In addition, I lost my state scholarship—money that was paying my family's rent. With no classes to attend, I had a lot of time on my hands. I put some of that time to use by producing an eight-page newsletter for the Hunter College Freshman YCL Club. I am afraid that I wrote all of the articles myself. It was a lot of work. Then, when it came time to distribute the newsletter, I was in for a shock. Nobody was interested. No one volunteered. I had done it all myself and ended up having to distribute it by myself. It was a lesson I tried to remember always.

The next year I moved on with my class to the Bronx campus of Hunter College. Next door was a high school, and I was an advisor to the YCL club there. Indirectly, that advisorship led me to drop my chemistry major. I was following the lab "cookbook" in my qualitative analysis class. For two weeks, off and on, I had been working with an unknown solution. I was in the final stages of heating the solution in an evaporating dish. Just then a high school YCL member came into the lab for advice on their latest "emergency." By the time I returned, the dish had cracked and my unknown solution was lost. Two weeks' work was gone. I would have to start all over. That was the last straw, the one that broke the camel's back.

Much as I liked chemical theory, I decided to change my major. During the Depression, job prospects in chemistry were dim. They were practically zero for Jewish women. Why put in long hours in a chemistry lab if it was not going to lead to a job? That same year I had started studying physics which was much more to my taste. Not that there were more jobs in physics. But for me, it was more fun. Sadly, Hunter College did not offer a physics major. CCNY did, but did not admit women. And that is how I ended up as a history major and political science-economics minor. I decided to try to get a general education, even if it did not lead to a job. Of course, 30 years later I began to give young people different advice. My mature advice was, "Get as much education as you can. It will be useful later."

From Picket Line to Jail, a Short Walk

1935 was a year of heightened working class struggle. Calls for help in strikes or demonstrations came frequently. Our YCL responded to as many as we could. One call for strike support brought me to a familiar street, 14th Street near Union Square. Union Square was the site of the big rallies that climaxed the May Day parades. To support striking clerks at Ohrbach's Department Store, we formed a mass picket line in front of the store. It was peaceful, even dull. Along came a bunch of police wagons. They herded the whole mass picket line into the vans and drove us to the police lockup. Neither I nor most of my fellow arrestees had ever seen the inside of a jail cell before, except in movies. One non-smoker was so nervous that she begged a cigarette. Turned out she did not know how to smoke it. After a few hours, they let us all go. I learned that a common tactic used to break a strike was to call in the police to break up the picket lines. Later, the police dropped the charges. Meanwhile, the picket line had been broken.

Author marching May 1, 1936 with Hunter College YCL

I was lucky enough to avoid jail in some other demonstrations where large numbers were arrested. The Wall Street clerks were on strike and called for mass picketing. In the narrow streets of the Wall Street district, the police horses pinned people in against doorways, holding them there until the police wagons took them away. There are few things more humiliating than to be herded off the scene of a demonstration by a horse's rump. I was pinned by a horse into a doorway until some kind-hearted soul opened the door and let me in. A few of us escaped that way. Everyone else who was pinned in by the horses was arrested.

It was not for nothing that East European immigrants hated the mounted police whose horses had been trained for "crowd control." "Mulrooney's Cossacks," they called them. Edward Mulrooney was the New York City Police Commissioner in 1930. Workers charged him with using tactics that the Czar's Cossacks used in pogroms against Jews.

Pulling Down the Nazi Flag

I was present at another large confrontation with New York's mounted police in the SS Bremen protest. The SS Bremen was a German ship that took passengers between New York and Hamburg. In 1935 she was arrogantly flying a swastika flag. Word had reached us of the Nazi atrocities against Jews, Communists and trade unionists. A number of Communist seamen decided they would not let the swastika fly over New York City. They were determined to pull it down. With 10,000 other demonstrators, I stood along the dock, shouting slogans against fascism. We demonstrators were peaceful, and not aware of the seamen's plan. At least I wasn't. Then the mounted police swung into action. With their horses, they ran us down one street, away from the dock. Then they ran us down another street. It seemed they did it just because they could. They pushed us this way; then they pushed us that way, as though we were a herd of cattle. It was humiliating as well as frightening. People can get trampled in a stampede.

Suddenly the huge crowd let out a roar. The swastika had been pulled down! We all rejoiced, not knowing that six of our heroes were still aboard, being beaten by the police. Goebbels blamed Mayor Fiorello La Guardia for not sending enough police. La Guardia responded to the request for guards at the German consulate by sending ten Jewish police and detectives. When the seamen who pulled down the swastika came to trial, Congressman Vito Marcantonio, the progressive, defended them in court. I heard both Mayor La Guardia and Marcantonio speak many times. They had similar styles. They started out in low, slow tones and ended up in rapid, fiery deliveries. I was always afraid they would have a heart attack as they wound up their speeches, waving their hands, getting red in the face and almost frothing at the mouth. I loved them both.

The last time I sustained a movement arrest, I was all by myself. In the summers I often sold the *Daily Worker* in public places. One likely spot was the entrance to the main New York Public Library. Talking to a potential reader one day, I walked up the steps with him to the library entrance. One of New York's finest came rushing over and arrested me for "peddling on park property." This time I did not see the inside of a jail cell; I just posted my ten dollar bond. It seemed too small a case to bother the International Labor Defense (ILD). I could have just paid the fine, but I wanted to defend the principal of free speech. So I showed up for the "trial." Case was dismissed and I got my bond back.

Bus Girl at the Automat

In the summer of 1936, I worked as a bus girl in the automat, also known as Horn and Hardart. "A coin-operated glass-and-chrome wonder," was the description I found on the Internet. You put in your coins, turned the lever, opened the glass door and removed your fresh meal. That eliminated waiting time but it also eliminated waiters. However, low-paid labor, like me, was still needed to clear the tables and "bus" the dirty dishes.

I have a vivid memory of being unable to sleep all night after coming home from my first day's work at the automat. After my first day at the Eby Factory, I kept assembling radio tube sockets in my sleep. It was much the same after day one at the automat. I got into bed at night and fell asleep. It was an uneasy sleep. I had vivid dreams of carrying glasses of water to the tables and of carrying away the dirty dishes. And it has been the same for me on every one of the many jobs I had after the automat. After the first day at a new job, scenes from the job kept floating through my dreams. Probably the reader has had similar experiences.

Busing dishes was a simple job; no college education needed. However, I did receive some useful on-the-job instruction. "Your legs are stronger than your arms," I was told. "Don't load up your trays too high. Just make more trips." I disregarded that good advice one day when the pressure became extra-heavy. We were always understaffed.

I could not see over my tray because it was stacked sky-high with dishes and glasses. So I did not see the watermelon seed under my foot. Or perhaps it was a piece of watermelon. As I stepped on the mess, my foot slipped back. The dishes and glasses, however, kept moving forward. They made the loudest crash. A sudden hush silenced the lunchtime crowd. No, I had not dropped my tray. In fact, two dishes were still on the tray. Devastated by the catastrophe, I thought, "What's the use!" and let the tray and the two dishes drop. My supervisor came running out. To my surprise, he gently led me to the back. The lunchtime din quickly resumed.

No, I was not fired. Perhaps I would have been better off. I probably gained ten pounds that summer eating all the free pie and ice cream I could stuff. By the end of the summer, my feet broke down at their weak point, my arches. And ever since, I have looked like an orphan around the feet, to use my husband Frank's expression. That was his apt description of my orthopedic shoes. On the good side, however, that job allowed me to hear the only compliment about my looks I ever heard—except, of course, from boyfriends or husbands. And they were prejudiced. As I was bustling about, I heard an older female customer say, "They have such beautiful girls here." She did make that plural but I chose to take it personally.

The other good thing that I learned was to carry several glasses of water to a table without putting my fingers into the glasses. It was a customer, not a supervisor, who taught me that. I proudly brought him four tall glasses of water, carrying two in each hand. To hold them by the rims, I had a thumb inside one glass and two fingers in the other glass. "Now that you've put your fingers in them," he said, "you might as well take a bath in it." Well, there are all kinds of sanitation standards. My standards were instantly elevated. Someone had to teach me.

Langston Hughes

My last years at Hunter College were in the big time, the main campus at 68th Street and Park Avenue. I fondly remember the glorious experience of hearing a lecture by the poet, Langston Hughes. What I remember of his talk are his funny stories, his contagious smile and his dashing good looks. Hughes had just returned from a writers' conference in Republican Spain. That was during the Spanish Civil War. We hung on every word of his report. Hughes had also visited and worked in the Soviet Union. That was in their early days of building socialism. In 1953, Hughes was hauled before the Senate Permanent Subcommittee on Investigations, chaired by Senator Joseph McCarthy. He told them that he was not a Communist. I bet Hughes, like Galileo, never gave up his beliefs. Galileo is said to have affirmed on his death bed, "But the earth does turn!" I think Hughes knew that capitalism does not work for us and that socialism is the future of humanity.

I was able to pass my social science courses at Hunter with a minimum outlay of time. Thanks to the Marxism I had studied, my classes were easy. I am afraid that I provoked a lot of discussion. Unfortunately, a couple of my professors took the heated debate personally. My economics teacher became very upset. I was sorry because I truly respected her. I knew my grade would be either an A or an F. It was an A.

One physics teacher, in a course misnamed "Modern Physics," was sadly out of date. She was describing the vacuum far out in space; a vacuum she said was "truly devoid of matter." Marxists are materialists and believe matter/energy in motion or change is fundamental. So I raised my hand to ask, "Could you have the hole in the doughnut without the doughnut around the hole?" My teacher shouted her reply. "I will not have the existence of God questioned in my class!" I was flabbergasted. To her credit, my teacher knew exactly where I was going. Of course, today we know that space is chock full of radiation, magnetic fields and other cosmic stuff. Although I never cut class, my academic work was just a sideshow to the social activism that stirred the student body. Since 1933, the Nazis had controlled Germany. War clouds gathered and hung low as Mussolini's troops invaded Ethiopia in 1935. I remember walking in a huge protest march in Harlem. "Hands off Ethiopia!" we shouted. The next year, fascist generals began a war against the elected government of Spain. On campus, we organized a Conference against War and Fascism to rally support for Ethiopia and Republican Spain. At that time, Hunter College was restricted to women. It was hard not to notice the small army of male detectives who invaded our campus. The police showing was probably intended to intimidate students, not ferret out information. Everything we did was public. We issued the slogan, "Keep the dicks off campus." The conference itself was very successful and well attended. However, it was followed by the usual repression. Once again, I was kicked out of school, suspended. My crime? Organizing a Conference against War and Fascism!

Make Madrid the Tomb of Fascism!

The plight of democratic Spain had grabbed our hearts. We hung on the reports of each town that was in the headlines, Guernica, Madrid, Teruel. If I had been a boy, I would probably have gone to Spain to fight. Over 3,000 from the United States went to Spain as volunteers to stop the fascist tide. They joined the Abraham Lincoln Brigade, a part of the international brigades of anti-fascist volunteers. Half never came back. They lie buried in the soil of Spain, including some of my best friends.

It was hard to bear the loss of my buddy, Jack Freeman, a mathematics whiz on the New York citywide mathematics team. As high school students, Jack and I spent a lot of time together, solving really hard geometry problems. Sometimes we rode the subway line from end to end, absorbed in a problem. At 17, Jack went to fight against fascism in Spain. I never saw him again. Jack was one of the 1500 Abraham Lincoln Brigade volunteers who fell to fascist fire.

I remember walking with Paul Siegel one evening long ago. I can still smell the fragrance of the privet hedges, then in bloom. Paul had just graduated from New York University with an engineering degree. "What are your plans, now?" I asked. "I'm going to Spain to fight the fascists," he replied. He went to Spain in June 1937 and was killed four months later.

I had a lot of respect for Wilfred Mendelson, a young Communist leader of the National Student League. At 21, four years older than me, he was a brilliant leader. The day he arrived in Spain, he got a rifle and went to the front lines. That was also the day he died. He had never held a gun before in his life.

My friends died in the noblest of causes. I truly believe that World War II could have been prevented had the U.S. allowed the legally elected government of Spain to buy arms. Instead, the U.S., Britain and France clapped an arms embargo against the Spanish government when General Franco attacked. While the legitimate government of Spain was not allowed to buy arms to defend itself, the Nazis shipped huge quantities of arms to Franco. With the aid of the German Nazis and the Italian fascists, Franco won the war in Spain.

I think the Western Powers bear some of the responsibility for the victory of fascism in Spain. Soviet ships tried to bring military supplies to the Spanish government. But German and Italian bombers blew most of the ships out of the water. Franco's victory paved the way for World War II with its frightful loss of 100 million lives. We would be living in a much, much better world today if the United States, France and England had supported the elected Republican government of Spain. But they were blinded to the fascist danger by anti-Communism and the desire to overthrow Socialism in the USSR.

The summer after the Hunter College Conference against War and Fascism, I went to work as a volunteer organizer for the laundry workers and left school. That was a turning point in my life, as I will describe later. But I was still just 19, and the weekends were mostly free. The union had dances, and the athletic lindy-hop was in fashion. I burned up a lot of nervous energy on the dance floor. And whenever I got the chance, I hit the hiking trails.

After the laundry workers' organizing drive, I went back to school. But my interests were elsewhere. I was never intensely active in the student movement again. I finished my degree (history/political science) and retained my interest in science. When jobs opened for military production for World War II, I began to work in electronics. To get more background for the job, I took an electrical engineering course in "AC Circuit Analysis" at a city college. Women were allowed to take evening courses there although the day program remained off limits to females. Had women been allowed to enroll, I would have gone there in the first place.

The rest of my formal education, scattered over the years as a part-time student, was in mathematics and science. My informal education, gained in the workers' struggle has been most valuable. A lot of what I learned I must credit to my husband Frank. He did not get past ninth grade. But self-study, reading the Marxist classics and a world of experience gave him a broad education.

This poem describes what life was like for many workers before the unions gained strength. It was written by martyred Ella May Wiggins (1900-1929), murdered on her way to the picket line. A sister textile striker sang it at her funeral.

The Mill Mothers' Song

We leave our home in the morning,
We kiss our children good bye,
While we slave for the bosses,
Our children scream and cry.

And when we draw our money,
Our grocery bills to pay,
Not a cent to spend for clothing,
Not a cent to lay away.

And on that very evening,
Our little son will say,
"I need some shoes, dear mother
And so does sister May."

How it grieves the heart of a mother,
You every one must know,
But we can't buy for our children,
Our wages are too low.

Now listen to the workers
Both women and you men
Let's win for them the victory
I'm sure 'twill be no sin.

Chapter **3**

Mama, Laundry Worker and Poet

Mother invested some of her dreams in me.

My Parents, Dora (Ruhdeh) and Morris (Avrom) Shapiro

MY mother was substantial. She was short, heavy and with a lap and arms big enough to hold my baby brother and me. She had large black eyes, ample black hair and a face that was pale, as I remember. Relatives told me that she had been a beauty in her youth. No doubt she once had glowing cheeks. I think of her pale face and the slightly mocking, deeply tragic song about the immigrant girl, "My Cousin, the Greenhorn."

According to the song, this young, East European Jewish immigrant came to New York expecting to find "gold in the streets." She arrived with "cheeks red as an apple and feet that loved to dance." Instead of gold, she found poverty and killing labor in the garment sweatshops. The roses faded from her cheeks, and her feet lost their spring as she prematurely aged. The song ends, "Well my green cousin, how do you like this golden country now?"

In Yiddish it rhymes. It sounded something like, "Meine greene koozineh, vee gleichst du die goldene medineh?"

Always Working

My mother always worked, as did many of the women in our working class neighborhood of Southern Boulevard in the East Bronx. Most of our neighbors worked in the garment district of New York City. By the time I was born (1918), they had won union protection. Mama started working in the needle trades soon after coming to the United States in 1906. That was before the union. As described earlier, Mama left her job at Triangle Shirtwaist just a few months before the horrible fire of March 25, 1911. No doubt she had friends among the 146 women who were killed, either burned in the fire or jumped to their death from eighth floor windows. The company owners had locked the exit doors. I had heard it was to keep the union organizers out.

As a child, I never knew a time when my mother was not working. After my brother Max was born, my mother did not go back to work in the factory. Instead, my parents opened a small store, a hand laundry. She did the hand wash, starched and stretched curtains, and hand ironed, especially dress shirts. The store also had a small mangle to iron small, flat pieces. All of this work required standing. I was dismayed and felt helpless when I watched my mother do her daily routine of wrapping her swollen legs with a long, continuous bandage. The varicose veins would pop up and look as though they might burst. I believed my mother's swollen legs were painful, but I never heard her complain. It was just something she felt she had to do: stand all day on her feet, iron shirts and ignore the pain.

Mother invested some of her dreams in me. "You will be a writer," she urged, and gave me a notebook to carry around so I could record my pearls of wisdom, if any. My mother had to give up on her first choice for my career, music. My mother loved to sing and had a very pleasant voice. Later, as a cancer patient, she cheered up the whole ward by singing as she lay in bed. As it turned out, I inherited my father's voice.

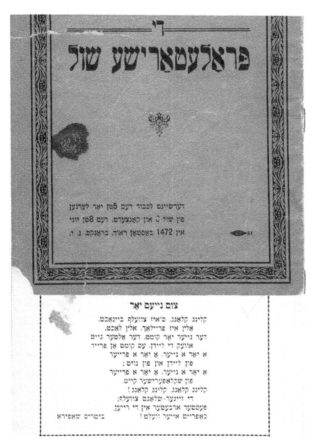

Author's New Year Poem. 1928

I had no strong feelings either way about becoming a writer. I entered essay contests and actually won a medal. It was something about "Safeguarding the Home against Fire." Writing essays was OK but it did not move me. Science moved me. What I really wanted was a microscope. After a while the seldom-used piano disappeared from our apartment, but I never did get that microscope. Over these many years, I never lost my passion for science. But I did not become a scientist. The Great Depression made that almost impossible. Besides, my urgent commitment to the labor movement took precedence.

Mama, the Poet

My mother's influence left me with a deep respect for culture. She wrote poetry in Yiddish and encouraged me to write. Under her influence, I did write some Yiddish poems. As for music, the public schools convinced me that I could never sing and that everybody else would be better off if I did not try. Starting with third or fourth grade, the class was divided into "singers" and "listeners." There were about two rows of listeners, 30%–40% of the class. We were instructed to move our lips in sync with the words of the songs but never, never, to let a sound escape from our throats. Years later, I picked up courage to sing our movement songs in large crowds. There, the roar of many voices could drown out my out-of-tune notes. It was a personal loss to me when mass public singing went out of style. I suspect it was also a great loss to the movement. Nothing else boosts morale like a militant song voiced by the multitude.

Yiddish was my parents' first language. They often spoke to us in Yiddish, but we replied in English. If they did not want us to understand, they spoke in Russian. I was the only child in my family who was sent to an after-school Yiddish school to learn to read and write. But I was never really fluent. Still, two of my earliest poems were in Yiddish. I believe my mother inspired these poems, to say the least. The thoughts may have been a bit mature for a nine-year old. They went something like this, roughly translated:

Ring In the New Year
Cling Clang, Cling Clang,
Ring in the New Year
A year that is new, a year that is free
From war and slavery

Sacco and Vanzetti
Sacco and Vanzetti are dead,
We sing at their gravesides,
They hear us! We promise them
To take revenge for their deaths.

The tone was a bit different from the English language poem
I wrote, at age nine, for a newspaper column called, "Cousin
Eleanor's Corner." I suspect my mother did not help me with
this one:

Once I saw a little house
And in it was a little mouse
Then I saw a butterfly's wing
And I heard a blue bird sing.

Independent Thinking

Mama taught me to think for myself and not to believe everything I heard or read. I grew up believing there were two sides
to most issues. On one side there were working people like us.
On the other side were rich people who lived off the workers'
labor, just as kings of old lived off the serfs. My parents never
became U.S. citizens and were not members of any political
party. However, they supported all the progressive causes of
their day. My mother was active in the Jewish section of the
International Workers Order (IWO), a secular left-wing, fraternal organization that provided burial insurance. Sometimes
she would go door to door and solicit more members for the
IWO. I went along and got my first experience in doorbell
ringing for a cause.
    One Saturday, on the Jewish Sabbath, I was chalking a hop-
scotch game on the sidewalk. Some children from Orthodox

Jewish families came over and began to taunt me. Orthodox Jews believe that work of any kind, even writing or lighting a fire, is forbidden on the Sabbath. "That's a sin," the children squealed, each time I drew a line on the sidewalk. But I had already started to draw the boxes so I continued. "It's a sin! It's a sin!" my little tormenters yelled with each of my strokes. After I accumulated about twenty such sins, I could take it no longer and ran inside to Mama. "When I grow up I'm going to be very religious!" I declared. "All right," Mama replied in a calm even tone. Her willingness to accept my decision took the wind out of my sails and I lost interest in the subject.

There were books in our apartment, even some in English. I often saw my parents read. I grew up thinking that reading was a normal way to spend time. If I was deep into a book, I did not want to quit at bedtime but did turn off my reading light. Then, when I thought everyone was asleep, I would pick up my book and creep out into the hallway. There, crouched under a dim night light, I would finish the book. One night my mother caught me in the act and told me that she did that, too, as a child. "That's what ruined my eyes," she said, pointing to her glasses. I did not want to ruin my eyes. But once in a while, when the book was too fascinating, I could not resist the temptation. "Just this once," I would think, and went back to my old ways of reading under the dim hall light.

Traditional Meals

After a hard day's work, my mother would return home to cook and clean. The only part of housework that she was spared was the laundry. Sunday was her only day off. I should say, "Off from the laundry." In fact, my mother spent half of Sunday cooking the dinner. The meal always included soup, even though we kids used to turn up our nose and pass on the soup. Today these soups are considered gourmet fare such as beet borscht with sour cream, *stchav* (sour spinach soup) with sour cream, mushroom barley soup, sweet and sour cabbage soup, chicken and matzo balls and more.

The traditional meat and side dishes came next. It may have been brisket of beef or roast chicken or lamb chops with kasha (buckwheat), potatoes, tsimmes (sweet sticky carrot hash) and salad. This was all topped off with homemade bread pudding or noodle pudding and of course, my mother's wonderful almond "bread" and sponge cakes.

Sometimes Mama asked me to mix the sponge cake batter. I usually had the job of mixing the egg yolks and sugar. This was in the days before electric mixers. It was beat, beat, beat, for many minutes until I thought it was ready. "No, beat it some more," was her usual answer. I thought I was beating forever until Mama gave me the OK. I thought of that the other day when my electric beaters burned out. Then I remembered that we used to mix by hand. Forget it! After a couple minutes I asked my grandson to take over. I will admit that was the last cake I baked until I got another electric mixer.

Memories of my mother are intertwined with all the little comforts of life. First of all was warmth. Besides the reassuring warmth of her plump embrace, the warmth she created helped me survive when the landlord turned off the heat at night. Mama put bricks to heat in the oven for us. When they were good and hot, she took them out, wrapped one in a blanket and put it under the covers at the foot of my bed. That, and thick quilts kept us warm at night. In the morning, it was still cold in the apartment when it was time to get dressed for school. Mama let me get dressed under the covers. Somehow I managed to put on one piece after the other, while still under the blankets in the warmth of my bed.

I never succeeded in convincing my mother to skip cooking a big Sunday dinner. I wanted to go to the beach for the whole day, instead of just a few hours in the afternoon. I am sure that my dislike of housework goes back to those days. I probably was only of marginal help to my mother. Of course, the boys were not expected to do any housework.

Sick and Poor

When I was 14, my life changed; the whole family was thrust into crisis. It was 1932, the bottom of the Great Depression. The Depression was pushing my parent's laundry store to extinction. Fewer and fewer people could afford to send their laundry out. Papa quarreled with Mama about the bills. Instead of paying the bills owed to the big commercial laundries, Mama used the small remaining income to buy food for the family. To my father, it was a matter of honor to pay his bills. For my mother, feeding her kids came first.

One day at the kitchen table my father had a stroke. We were all at the table when it happened. At first we thought he was joking as he often did. Then he quit acting funny and fell. Mama jumped up and ran to his side. I realized that something terrible had happened. The next things I remember are the visits to the hospital and Papa talking funny. One side of his face was twisted and he could not talk right. He had another stroke a few days later. Then he began the slow process of recovery. The strokes put the finishing touches to the laundry store. Or perhaps the store closed first and the strokes soon followed. Either way, I was sure that stress, brought on by the Great Depression, caused my father's illness. Nothing in the family was ever the same after my father's stroke.

My family went on "Home Relief." In the years that followed, deepening poverty, fencing with social workers and visits to hospital wards became my way of life. After his strokes, my father became hard to deal with, at least for my mother. I don't remember that it spilled over to his dealings with us kids. My mother was very patient but it did bother her. At that time I had been reading feminist literature and was very sensitive to the suffering of women. "Why don't you leave him?" I asked Mama. "He was never like this before he got sick," she replied. That made me back down a bit from my militant feminist stance. Many years later I learned that strokes often create personality changes, at least in the short term.

As time went by, Papa got better. By that time, Mama was very sick. After radical surgery for colorectal cancer, she had a period of recovery. Then the cancer spread to her lungs. With both parents sick, I had to fill in as household manager and a sometime cook and cleaning woman. My father's strokes were sudden and severe. But he did not spend many days in the hospital, at most two weeks. The slow-killing cancer that took my mother's life was different.

I made daily visits to her hospital ward over a period of months for each recurrence of the cancer. As far as I know, she got decent care. No doubt there was better treatment available to those who had money. Near the end, Mama told me that the bird of death sat in the tree, waiting for her. She was not afraid, she said. She added that she was not worried about me because I was so independent. But she was worried about my brother Lenny who was only 15 at the time.

I was 19 when my mother died. I took it very bravely, but I never got over it. In later years, as I earned more, I felt bad that I had not been able to "do anything" for my mother. But my father lived to be 92, and I did not do that much for him. Now that I am old, I realize that is the way of life. The greatest thing children can "do" for parents is to stand on their own feet and to live a good life.

Our Family Fell Apart

After Mama's death, our family fell apart. As soon as my younger brother became 16, he joined the Civilian Conservation Corps (CCC). They sent him out west to work in the woods. My father moved to a furnished room. My older brother, Max, had moved out of our apartment before Mama died. He moved out because our apartment door was never locked. I think the key had been lost, and my parents were not well enough to manage to get another key. Except for Max's clothing, we did not have anything anyone would want to steal. Max got tired of thieves stealing his clothes so he moved to our aunt's apartment. Max was the only member of the family with a wardrobe worth anything. Whatever he could earn from odd jobs went on his back. You could say it was an investment in his future. Max did become a respected salesman of men's clothes.

When my father gave up our apartment, I moved to an apartment that I shared with my boyfriend, Butch. For forty years after my mother's death I continued to have "wish-ful-fillment" dreams. In these dreams, my mother was still alive and I was so happy because I was able to help her. Mama did a lot for me and set me on a path that brought me a lot of joy, struggle and fulfillment. But I could not be as unselfish as she had been in total dedication to her family, with no thought of her own welfare.

Somehow, I think that my mother wanted me to chart a different course. I did not become a singer as she had hoped. As Paul Lawrence Dunbar's poem put it:
> You ain't got the natural organs
> For to make the sound come right.

Nor did I become a nurse, as Mama had wanted for herself. But I did have the chance to spend many joyful years raising a family and in the workers' struggles for peace and justice.

Leaving the Ghetto

It was not easy to leave the old neighborhood. I suppose the process started when I dated Butch (Kenneth), my first boyfriend. He came from a German-Irish Catholic family, or perhaps I should say, Irish-German. He and I were conscious of our cultural differences. Probably part of the difference was between immigrant and native-born backgrounds of our parents. These differences did not affect our relationship. We had too much in common as supporters of the labor and the Communist movements. But I felt that I did not know "how to act" in the "Christian" world. In that sense, I felt "inferior."

For example, Butch and I were seated with some of his fellow commercial artists. He introduced me and the men stood up. So I stood up, too. Later Butch informed me that men, but not women, needed to stand for an introduction. That sounds funny, even as I write it today. I also learned that men are supposed to walk on the street side of the sidewalk, women on the inner side. Nobody seemed to know the origin of that custom. Some suggested it was to shield the woman from garbage thrown out of the window, a practice of the "olden" days. Or was the man acting as a shield against mud splattered from the street? Of course we were used to different foods, but that was no problem. I had failed to appreciate my family's ethnic food and did not come to love it until later years. His family's leg of lamb and white potatoes were OK, but just OK. Food was not a big issue for me then.

Looking back, I think I understand now what I lost when I left the ghetto. Inside the ghetto, everybody had the same cultural and class background. There was protection in that sameness. It was not a matter of religion because many were non-believers. Still, leaving the ghetto meant going out into the unknown "Christian-majority world." In the 1920s and 30s, memories of the Russian Czar's pogroms against the Jews were still strong in my neighborhood. Persecution of the Jews was associated with the Christians' religion and their symbol, the cross. Because of this history, it was years before I could feel comfortable in a Christian church.

Of course, I often left the confines of the ghetto when I took my long walks as a pre-teen and early teenager. But I could always return to the safety of the ghetto. Some of my walks took me to a Turkic neighborhood. I was pleased when a food vendor spoke to me in Turkish, or at least I thought it was Turkish. In other areas, more than one woman came up to me asking for directions in Italian. I wish I could have replied in their language. But when I walked south to an Irish neighborhood, I never thought I was taken to be local. I have one hurtful memory when I had to literally run back to my neighborhood to get away from my tormenters.

On that day, on what was probably my last solo walk to the South Bronx, a group of boys my age began to follow me. They yelled anti-Semitic slurs. I quickened my pace and they quickened theirs. I was afraid to break into a run for fear of showing my fear. Then one, or another, ran up to me, stuck their finger into my dress to my rectum. I was more humiliated than scared. Although I walked very, very fast, I could not shake my tormenters. This torture went on for several blocks, until I was close to my own neighborhood. I was so humiliated, that I never mentioned the assault, not for 80 years. Now that I have survived nine decades, I can express my anger on my own behalf. But I also feel anguished for that little girl of long ago who was harassed by my friends for wearing a cross as I stood by and said nothing.

In our community, there was some divisive thinking that I learned to reject. I had not been raised to think of Jews as "chosen people" in a religious sense. My parents were not believers or Zionists. But many of our neighbors swallowed the falsehood that Jewish students were "smarter." It was something like the current claim that East Asian students are more gifted in mathematics. Any claim for superiority went counter to my mother's teaching of equality. I have long been convinced that there is no difference in natural ability among communities. Rather, more opportunities and higher expectations produce higher student scores.

On the positive side, I remember that most in the East Bronx ghetto of the 1930s were progressive. A significant number were revolutionaries who supported the Communist Party or the Socialist Party. The big split over Zionism came later, when the State of Israel was established in Palestine in 1948.

Chapter 4

Papa in the Revolution of 1905
Where Mama was cautious, Papa was daring.

My Father, Morris (Avrom) Shapiro

There is a famous scene in the classic Eisenstein movie, *Potemkin*. It takes place in the Ukrainian city of Odessa during the 1905 Russian Revolution. Czarist soldiers fire into a peaceful crowd of protesters. As the workers flee with their wounded, a baby carriage starts rolling down a long series of steps to the sea. The carriage picks up speed, and the baby inside the carriage begins to scream. The scene tears your heart out.

My father was there! At least he was in that struggle. Papa took part in the 1905 Revolution in Odessa and in his hometown of Bobruisk in Byelorussia. The 1905 Revolution was defeated. Papa ended up in a Czarist jail. Both he and my mother had been members of the Jewish *Bund*, a socialist organization. At that time, they were engaged. An older cousin told me the story after I was grown. My father confirmed the story but had never seen a reason to share it with his children.

It was rare for East European Jews to own firearms. My father, Avrom Hirschenhorn, owned two pistols. He was also ready to use them. To illustrate how daring a man my father was, my cousin said that Papa fired through the kitchen door for target practice. It was never clear to me whether the door was open or closed. I also learned that my father had taken an unthinkable step to avoid the Russian Army draft. He deliberately punctured his ear drum, or otherwise destroyed most of the hearing in one ear. That seemed like an extreme measure, to me. I assumed that the draft was for two or three years, perhaps not worth a loss of hearing. I have since learned that a soldier drafted into the Czarist Army could be gone for as long as 25 years. That was like losing a lifetime of work. No wonder people rose up in revolution.

During the Russian Revolution of 1905, the Czar used mounted Cossacks to put down the workers. My father was among a group of Jewish revolutionaries who were meeting inside a synagogue. The Cossacks broke into the synagogue on horseback and began shooting. Avrom (my father) returned the fire. He was knocked down and a horse stepped on his mouth. My father was left with a mouthful of broken teeth. All the survivors of the raid, including my father, were thrown into jail.

Every week, the prisoners were hauled before the judge. Some were sentenced. Others, like my father, were sent back to the holding jail. This went on week after week. When Avrom Hirschenhorn came before the judge, the judge said, "Throw that one back." He was never charged or tried and it was clear that the judge intended to let him rot in jail. Meanwhile, the Bund had reorganized and worked underground. They decided to save Avrom by busting him out of jail. That's where my mother, then father's fiancée, played a big role. She baked a cake containing a note giving my father the details of the escape plan. The plan involved Papa's regular trip from the jail to the town's dentist. During the night, the outhouse in the dentist's yard, was lifted up and moved against the fence of the neighbor's yard. Then the wood slats of the outhouse and the touching slats of the neighbor's fence were loosened. My father was to ask to use the outhouse, remove the loosened slats and escape through the neighbor's yard.

The next day, my father was taken to the dentist for treatment of his broken teeth. Many spectators came out to watch the "big" military operation. It took six soldiers to safeguard the "desperado." Two soldiers marched on either side of my father; another marched in front and one in back. When they reached the dentist's house, my father declared an urgent need to use the outhouse. Two soldiers escorted him to the outhouse but kept the door open. "I can't go with the door open," my father told them. "All right, close the door but be quick," the soldiers replied. The door closed, my father removed the loose slats, slipped out into the neighbor's yard and ran to the street. A *droshky* (horse-drawn cab) was waiting and whisked my father to a safe house. Some days later, my father started on his trip to the port city. He had a boat ticket to America and a passport in the name of Morris Shapiro. Avrom Hirschenhorn was going to the New World, to a new life with a new name!

The New Shapiro Family

Soon after his arrival in New York, the Socialist Labor Party contacted Avrom Hirschenhorn, known as Morris Shapiro in New York. They offered him a job as an organizer. My father declined. Now that he was in America, his plan was to start a business and make money. On April 17, 1907, my mother rejoined her sweetheart and they married in New York City. At first, both he and my mother worked in needle trades factories. Then my father went into "business." Unfortunately, the trade he chose was laundry. It was hard physical work for little money. Avrom, as he was still called by his friends, remained an intellectual force in the leftist Jewish community. It was my mother who was willing to do the "Jane Higgins" work for progressive organizations. (Jimmy Higgins was the typical rank and file worker who did the "grunt" work.) Mama worked with the Jewish section of the International Workers Order (IWO) and remained active in community work.

My father was always a very big influence in my life. But in some ways, he was unapproachable. In my early school days, I did a lot of erasing. That was partly due to the trouble I had trying to learn to write neatly. (I never did learn.) In arithmetic I just kept making errors and had to erase until I found the "correct" answer. As I remember it clearly, my father lived to a higher standard.

"See the eraser on my pencil?" he said, one day. The eraser looked new, unused and perfectly clean. "That's because I don't make mistakes," he added. I don't remember that he laughed when he said that. If it was a joke, I missed it. The eraser on my pencil was worn down from frequent use and smudged. I tried to turn over a new leaf and follow my father's example. But I had to give that up. I kept making mistakes and had to use my eraser again and again. I had to accept that I just did not have the same intellectual gifts Papa took for granted. So I stayed away from the games in which he excelled: checkers and various card games. Plenty of other pursuits interested me, even some of my schoolwork. When I won various awards my father was very proud. He even kissed me when I received a medal for scholarship. I was moved because he was not given to shows of affection.

On another level, Papa was a lot of fun. He sent us into spasms of laughter by dressing up as a monster with face full of shaving cream and chasing us around the house. We knew the monster was really Papa. Still it was fun and a little scary too, like monsters are supposed to be. If we wanted to swim, he would go with us. I remember that he stayed with me in the shallow water while I played and splashed around. Then he asked if I minded if he went out into the deep water to swim. I realized then that he had stayed in the shallow water, just for me. I appreciated and remembered his sacrifice.

Papa, the Risk Taker

Where Mama was cautious, Papa was daring. I always admired my father for his willingness to take risks, even if it put us in danger more than once. Thanks to Papa's daring spirit, I had my first vehicle crash at the age of ten. We lived in a hilly area of the Bronx. A series of hills, all nicely paved of course, provided extra thrills for us roller skaters and sled riders. One day I was standing at the top of one of these hills when my father came along with a loaded pushcart full of finished laundry. I was on my roller skates and begged to be allowed to push the cart. "I'll be careful," I promised, at the top of the hill. Well, gravity took over. With minimal rolling friction to slow us down, the cart and I were accelerating, picking up momentum. I was panicking but I did not let go of the cart as we neared the corner. At the corner, on the street side of the walk, mothers were sitting with their baby carriages. I had to stop somehow. There were store windows on the other side of the walk. I made a quick choice and headed for the glass. A huge plate glass window (or two) shattered with a horrible noise. I felt shattered, too. Who was going to pay for the window(s)?

I was never scolded for the accident, maybe because it was so horrible. Hopefully there was insurance to cover the cost of replacing the glass. Much as I loved science, it was a hard lesson in the laws of mechanics.

Papa, the Brain

Papa had the reputation in the community, or at least in the extended family, of being a "brain." In the "old country," he had studied in rabbinical school. That was the only higher education open to a Jew in a small town in Czarist Russia. Papa quit before he graduated. I think he realized that he did not believe in the supernatural. Neither he nor my mother practiced the religion. But he was well versed in the Hebrew language of the Bible. I noticed the contradiction when he was called to read the Bible at family Seders on the Jewish Passover. He read the Hebrew text so well. It brought tears into the eyes of the older people. Yet he was at the table bareheaded and would not wear a yarmulke (skullcap), as required by religious custom.

My brothers and I also sat at the Passover table with our parents and relatives. What we children believed in terms of religion was left up to us. I remember some of us dropping off to sleep because on this special occasion we were allowed to sip the wine. As much as I tried, I could not keep my eyelids open after drinking half a cup of sweet wine.

I had some fear of the supernatural, even though I did not really believe in ghosts. A glass of wine was set on the Passover table for the prophet Elijah. Some swore they saw the wine level drop in Elijah's glass. Others felt the touch of the angel's wings as he passed. I certainly accepted the official story of the Exodus and rejoiced in the Jewish escape from slavery. I still rejoice in any story with an anti-slavery theme. In later years I learned a different view of the Jewish residence in Egypt. For this view, I must credit an Egyptologist friend, Frank Yurco. As he put it, the Jews came into Egypt as small bands of shepherds, poor, hungry and mostly illiterate. They left a few hundred years later numbering in the thousands, prosperous, well fed and educated.

Religion

Religion was not a big issue for us as I was growing up. Most in my neighborhood were Orthodox Jews. But my parents were not unique in not believing. Many others, especially among the Socialist or Communist sympathizers, were no longer practicing the Jewish religion. I believe that split took place in Russia. Some of my parents' friends were militant atheists. On some high holidays, such as Passover, they would hold an "anti-holiday," such as an "anti-Seder." One friend told me her father would send her out with a ham sandwich, to mock those who were strictly kosher. Also, some of my mother's friends talked about a woman who *bencht licht*, prayed over candles on a Menorah. They pitied her as lost to superstition. Happily for me, that was not my parents' attitude. They thought religion was a private matter. In later years, I rejected the idea of holding an "anti-Seder" as repulsively sectarian. But then, I never suffered in the "old country" at the hands of a Czar who murdered Jews in the name of religion. Besides, I never met a holiday that I did not like. I stayed out of school on Jewish holidays and every other possible holiday.

Back to the story of my father: One aspect of my father's "braininess" was his ability to solve mathematical puzzles. I regret that I never found out how he solved the puzzles. Papa never had a class in algebra. He solved puzzles without "algebra" and without using paper and pencil. Once or twice he explained his method but I did not get it. I could solve the puzzles only by writing and solving a lot of equations. Papa just "talked it through."

Hand Laundry Store Owners

Before I entered high school and became "too busy," my father took me to a lot of places. He even let me go with him to his business meetings. The hand laundry storeowners had an association. Perhaps they negotiated prices with the big steam laundries. All I remember of the meetings is that the attendance was mostly, if not entirely, men. The sessions always lasted longer than I wanted to stay. The meetings were held at night, after store hours. Looking back, it was probably an educational experience for me. If nothing else, it gave me the idea that people faced with similar problems could pool their strength and organize.

In reality, the store "owners" were little more than employees of the large steam laundries. The large laundry owners made all the money and the small store owners and laundry workers did all the work. After many years, I heard my parents calculate how much they would have earned if they had worked at a factory job for the same number of years. It was more money than they had made in their "business," doing hard, physical labor. That family experience instilled in me a lasting fear of starting a small business. Many workers still have the dream of starting their own business to escape from the exploitation and insecurity of working for a boss. Whenever that issue came up with Frank and me in later years, I did my best to kill it. It did not matter whether the proposal was for a gas station and car repair, or a tavern. However, my middle son did not "listen" and went ahead to build a small, environmental science company. On the books, he is a big success. Still, I wonder. If he made the calculation that my parents made, would the results be similar?

Since that time, I have changed my thinking to a more positive view of small business. For some time, I have looked to small business for allies on progressive issues. Now I believe that small businesses will play an important role in the building of future socialist societies.

May Day in New York

As a child, small enough to be hoisted up on my father's shoulders, Papa took me to the big May Day marches in New York. I grew up thinking that May First, International Workers Day, was the most important holiday of the year. It was fun to look at the thousands of happy marchers dressed in their best clothes. I remember a sea of signs, the hat-makers, the dress-makers, the pocketbook makers, the men's clothing workers, the printers, on and on. Everyone was a maker, a worker. Then it began to rain. "It's raining, Papa," I said, "Let's go home." "Wait just a while," he answered. The rain kept coming down and the marchers continued to march. Their hair got wet and the paint on their signs began to run. I did not fully understand what was going on but I was impressed. "This must be very, very important." I thought. "Otherwise people would never march in the rain."

The influence of "the old country" loomed large in my life. I kept hearing all the Yiddish songs about suffering and struggle. Some were obviously translations of Russian songs. One, I translated from the Yiddish as, "Many songs have I heard in my homeland/ of love, suffering and victory/

but one song remains in my memory/ It is the song of the workers' struggle." The refrain, "*O, dubinishke*," was set to a work rhythm. I could picture the boatmen, wearing homespun Russian shirts, towing the boat up the Volga River. The lyrics were in Yiddish but the refrain was sung in the original Russian. Others were songs of the Russian revolution and the Red Army. Another, a Yiddish folk song, had the refrain "Poverty is not good, poverty is not good, but one must not be ashamed with one's own blood (relatives)." It was sung by an old woman, a poor relative. She had not been invited to the wedding. But she went anyway and proved to be the best dancer there.

The songs were not 100% progressive. There was a nationalist, reactionary ditty that rhymed in Yiddish: "He is drunk. He must drink. Because he is a Goy (Christian)." In all fairness, I do not remember that my parents ever sang it but I heard the song many times in the community. I know my parents disapproved of the "Green Cousin" song because it mocked the naiveté and the bitter disillusionment of new immigrants.

I do remember my father singing on a few occasions. He did not really have the voice for it but it sounded like a merry tune to me. "What do the words mean?" I asked. His translation from the Russian went something like this: "I have just lost my job, I have no money and I'm going to be put out of my house." I asked no more questions. Another sad song he sang was in Yiddish. I needed no translation. It was a father's lament that he left for work early, before his children were up. And he returned late at night, after his children went to bed. He never saw his children and did not really know them.

These songs reinforced the vague picture I had of the "old country." It was a place that was very cold, where most people were poor and fighting the Czar for their freedom. I also knew that my father and mother belonged to the Jewish Bund, the section that sympathized with the Bolsheviks. At that time, I had no idea that my father had been a dashing hero of the 1905 Revolution. He did tell me, not until later years, that he had hung a red flag out of our window in 1917 to celebrate the Russian Revolution. Everyone said, "Shapiro is a Socialist," he proudly added.

I grew up knowing that the use of tobacco was self-destructive. Perhaps the reason it never tempted me was the example of my father. He was a chain smoker, seldom without a cigarette between his lips. Two doors from his laundry was a candy store which sold individual cigarettes. My father made frequent trips to the candy store to buy another cigarette. He said he bought them one at a time to cut down on the amount he smoked. As a child, that was my only close experience with an addiction. The part that bothered me the most was that a demon, tobacco, was stronger than a person. My father wanted to quit but could not. The alcohol he drank, I think was for show. He demonstrated a he-man, macho breakfast one morning. He ate a crust of black bread, rubbed with raw garlic and washed it down with a shot of strong schnapps. But we seldom had alcoholic drinks at home and my father never went to taverns. In fact, I don't remember any taverns in my neighborhood.

At family parties, the men went into a separate room to play cards as soon as we finished eating. Women and children remained in the dining room as the women cleaned up. I often became bored and begged my mother to take us home.

"Go in and tell Papa you want to go home," Mama told me. Clearly, she was not going to interrupt the men's game. I didn't want to either. But after asking my mother four or five times and getting the same reply, I often did enter the smoke-filled room to tell Papa that I wanted to go home. "Wait just a few more minutes," he always said. I resented the whole scene of men in one room and women and children in another. Most of all I disliked the fact that Mama did not feel free to tell Papa that it was time to go home. That experience did prejudice me against card games. Sometimes we kids played card games such as gin rummy. But, as a grownup, I stayed away from playing cards.

Recovering from Stroke

The year of my father's stroke, 1932, was the bottom of the long Depression. About twelve years later, when World War II created a real shortage of labor, my father went back to work. Among other duties, he pushed racks of clothing to various delivery points. He continued this heavy labor into his 70s. When I last visited him in 1967, he was 92 years old. We decided to go downtown for a movie. On the way to the subway, I thought he had some difficulty walking. So I hailed a cab. That upset him, "wasting money on a cab!" I rarely "wasted" money on cabs either, but that seemed the right time. Once at the station, Papa climbed the many steps up to the train platform. Thinking back, that was an impressive feat for a 92-year-old man

The last time I saw my father was 35 years after his first stroke. He was fine. Three months later, he had another, final stroke and died the next day. Some said that Papa was not harmed by smoking because he lived to 92. For those people I have a ready answer. Papa's father was said to have lived to 110. Smoking could have robbed my father of 18 years of life.

Papa always maintained his keen interest in politics and international affairs. In 1943, he read *Teheran*, a book by Earl Browder, then general secretary of the Communist Party USA. Teheran, capital of Iran, had been the site of a Roosevelt-Churchill-Stalin meeting during World War II. Browder thought the alliance against fascism meant the end of class war. He claimed that intelligent capitalists would understand that they should stop exploiting workers. Then workers and capitalists would cooperate for their mutual benefit. I was struggling to "understand" how that could be. It was contrary to everything I had learned and observed. When I discussed the issue with my father, he was not trying to "understand" it at all. Better stated, he understood it very well. He told me he was so upset when he read *Teheran* that he couldn't sleep all night. Papa never moved away from his basic belief in the necessity of socialism.

In 1945, the French leader, Jacques Duclos, wrote a letter that challenged the Browder thesis. Heated discussion followed among Communists in the U.S. The big majority supported the class struggle approach and re-established the Communist Party. I think my father was right. Capitalism will never work for the benefit of workers.

In 1943, I left New York City to venture into the big world outside the Big Apple. I never returned except to visit family or to attend national meetings. Papa visited me about once a year, whether in Buffalo, Chicago, Gary or Broadview. More often, I visited him in New York City. My four children never had a chance to meet my mother, but they did get to know Grandpa Shapiro.

Chapter 5

Surviving the Great Depression
Don't Starve! Black and White, Unite and Fight!

They call it the "Great Depression." It was long, deep and worldwide. Only the young Soviet Union escaped the mass unemployment that devastated the rest of the world. The Depression was big, but there was nothing "great" about it. When the stock market crashed in 1929, I was 11 years old. I did not understand why Wall Street investors were jumping out of skyscraper windows just because they lost their fortunes. It was even harder to understand those who threw themselves in front of approaching subway trains. The panic came a little closer to home when nervous depositors began runs on banks.

Actually, I did not know anyone who had money to lose in a bank. Nor did I know anyone who owned stock. I guess I did not know the whole story. On our block, a woman did jump off a fifth story roof. Then the mother of one of my friends threw herself in front of a subway train. Horrible! Everything was falling apart. Our Bronx neighborhood felt bombed out. Workers laid off or reduced to part time could not buy clothes. So the garment factories closed. Many of our neighbors lost their jobs; others went down to two days a week. With no income and no government program of welfare, hunger was widespread. President Herbert Hoover said each block should take care of its own. The later "1000 points of light" program of President Bush the First had a similar theme. But there was no way the hungry could feed each other.

There were some ups and downs in the economy after the 1929 stock market crash. For my family it was all down. The

Depression never really ended for us until twelve years later when World War II orders kept the factories working overtime. My teen age years and my early working experiences were all in the shadow of the Depression. As mentioned above, it was impossible to keep our laundry store open. Few could afford to send their laundry out.

National Hunger Marches

The Communist Party and some left-led unions organized national hunger marches on March 6, 1930. Their slogan was, "Don't starve. Fight!" Another very important slogan was, "Black and White, Unite and Fight!" My parents were talking about marching. In my classroom I heard a different story. The teacher was urging us to stay off the streets on that day. "The Bolsheviks are going to throw bombs, and you may be hurt," she said. But I knew my parents would never hurt anybody. And they wanted to join the march. I realized, once again, that there were two different sides. My family was on one side and the school was on the other side.

In New York City 110,000 marched. Detroit had 100,000 hunger marchers and Chicago had 50,000. Many Communist leaders were arrested and some were brutally beaten. Later, I learned that my parents had been right to support the hunger marchers. After millions joined the protests, we won a relief program for poor families like ours. That experience made me very skeptical about the "official" propaganda I heard at school or read in the papers.

Soon after the hunger marches, on July 4, 1930, 1,320 delegates from unemployed groups around the country met in Chicago. Communists played a key role in organizing that conference. The conference decided to organize unemployed councils nationwide. These councils and the later "workers alliances" launched the struggles that won the New Deal safety net. Included in the safety net were Social Security and Unemployment Compensation (Insurance). Many of the unemployed organizers went on to help organize workers in the CIO (Committee for Industrial Organization) in 1935, which in 1938 became the Congress of Industrial Organizations.

A good number of Communists were among these organizers. I can understand why friends asked me, years later, "Is it true that there were only 100,000 Communist Party members in the 1930s? They could not believe that so much was accomplished by just 100,000. I tried to explain that Communists were like the yeast used to make bread. A little goes a long way and makes the whole batch of dough rise. However, if you want to make a lot of bread, you do need more than a little yeast.

In the spring of 1934, as I remember it, half the people on my block were still unemployed. The U.S. Census Bureau said the national figure showed 23% were jobless. Either that figure was too low or my Bronx neighborhood was worse off than average. My family, like some others on the block, was on Relief. Relief allowed our family of five about $11 a week for food and all expenses other than rent. My school carfare had to come out of that and any clothes we bought. So we did not buy any clothes. After my mother had cancer surgery, I was in charge of buying groceries and cooking. First I took my school carfare and other necessities out of the $11. That left about $9 a week for my family's food budget.

We ate a lot of lentils, stuff like that. Occasionally, I indulged the family in *concleten*, Russian-style beef patties. My mother had never trusted the butcher and used to grind her own. That was more work than I was willing to do. I bought the already-ground beef at the kosher butcher shop on the block. As time went on, the Relief began to hand out some free food. I remember canned beef from Argentina. The only meat I knew how to cook was ground kosher beef. I didn't know what to do with canned meat. So we ate it, straight out of the cans. I still remember the taste. I did not like it.

Nobody liked the Relief. I remember marching with the Hunter College YCL, a couple hundred of us. The slogan we shouted was, "Give the bankers Home Relief, we want jobs!" Still Relief, or Welfare, was a big victory, won only after a hard struggle. Relief paid the rent and kept families from starving to death. Before we won government welfare, many people did starve and many died from the diseases of starvation. Without government welfare, there was no one to help the unemployed, except family or church. But if those couldn't help, what was there to do but starve or steal? Stealing wasn't easy, either, because no one around you had anything. A few blocks from our Hunts Point apartment, a "Hooverville" appeared. It seemed to spring up overnight, in the wasteland near the gas works. The Hoovervilles were named after Herbert Hoover, the Republican president, who was letting people starve. Hooverville residents were unemployed workers who had been evicted from their homes. They lived in little shacks they built from whatever scraps they could find. It was a sad sight. People in the Hoovervilles had lost everything. Much as my family suffered, we were well off compared to the Hooverville squatters. Hoover's policies inflicted pain on those already wounded. Little wonder that voters kicked him out. In 1932, Franklin Delano Roosevelt, FDR, was elected with a mandate to make big changes.

Unemployed Councils

An economist could draw a line graph that would show ups and downs of the 1930s: low in 1930, lower in 1932, up a bit in 1935 and down again in 1937. As a teenager, I did not notice these fluctuations. It was all Depression and my family never felt the slight upturns. Paying the rent was always a struggle for my parents. The Relief allowance did not cover the full rent. I really don't know how my parents managed.

From the time I was 14, I became very concerned about the lack of money. I demanded to be included in their financial discussions. I wanted to know what came in and what bills had to be paid. They refused to include me "in the loop." Fortunately, I won a New York state scholarship on graduation from high school in 1934. That money went for the rent. My mother apologized. "In the future," she promised me, "we will save your scholarship money for your Master's degree." I was just as happy to help with the rent. A Master's degree, whatever that was, was a low priority for me and easily put off to the dim future. As indeed it was, for 30 years.

Many families could not pay their rent and were evicted from their apartments. Furniture dumped on the street was a common sight. Local "unemployed councils" became very expert at putting furniture back, restoring the evicted family to their apartment. Usually something was worked out and the family stayed. Others were not so lucky. What happened to them? Sometimes they moved in with relatives, two or three families in one apartment. Others moved to Hoovervilles and some took to the road, including 200,000 children.[1]

There was also a lot of hidden homelessness. When children married, they often remained in their parents' apartment. One spouse moved in with the other spouse's family. Families doubled up, even unrelated families, each paying half the rent. It is not surprising that the country's birth rate dropped.

Although conditions were desperate, we managed to keep our sense of humor. We laughed at the punch line of a story about an eviction scenario. This story may or may not be true. Unemployed council members saw a man standing with his furniture on the street. They knew what to do. They notified the unemployed council and they sent a team to the site. The council members restored the furniture to the man's apartment, over his objections. They overlooked his objections because evicted tenants were often grateful later, although fearful at first. The very next day, the same man was out on the street again with his furniture. A repeat eviction was not usual but it happened. Once again, the unemployed council members restored the furniture. The third day the council stalwarts went back to the street just to check. To their surprise, the man and his furniture were out on the street again. "That landlord is really persistent!" the council members exclaimed. "Well, we are going to make sure that this time is the last time this poor family is evicted." So with that "can-do" spirit, they began to pick up the furniture again. "Please don't put my furniture back," pleaded the tenant. "I'm trying to move!"

The unemployed councils were ready to take quick action when needed. Their demonstrations were always multiracial, a new experience for me. As a teenager, I took part in some of these actions. For example, a family that had not eaten for two

---

[1] *Highlights of a Fighting History–60 Years of the Communist Party USA*, Ed. Philip Bart (New York: International Publishers, 1979), 62.

days came to the council for help. The Relief office was supposed to issue food vouchers for such emergencies. But before they granted the vouchers, the family had to schedule an interview and fill out many forms. Meanwhile family members could starve to death. So we set up a mass picket line in front of the Relief office to demand food *now* for the hungry family. We marched round and round and refused to leave until the family got food. After a few hours of our protest, Relief officials found emergency funds for the family. We went home feeling justified. There was "joy in the struggle."

Other family emergencies were caused by companies who turned off gas and electric service for non-payment of bills. In winter, more than one person was found frozen stiff in an unheated house. In response to the cutoffs, unemployed councils demonstrated in front of utility companies to demand that service be restored. Sometimes, neighbors did not wait for mass action. Unknown friends turned electric service back on by using a wire to bypass the meter.

Winter is the worst time for demonstrations and an even worse time to go hungry. I vividly remember a cold day seventy-five years ago. Like me, the other demonstrators were not warmly dressed. Still, we stayed until the hungry family got food. It was not hard to keep our bodies warm but our hands and feet really suffered. One of the women demonstrators was stout, perhaps a size 40. An unsympathetic passerby shouted at us, "Look at that fat woman. You're not hungry." Even as a kid I thought that was very unfair. The low-cost foods of that day were fattening: rice, pasta, potatoes, lard and bread. At 15, I was the family cook and well aware that the small Relief allowance did not buy non-fattening foods. On our small food allowance, I could buy little besides bread, lentils and milk. Perhaps drinking milk made up for all the other foods I could not buy.

The Depression in the South

In later years, I asked my husband Frank about his Depression experiences. I never got much information. Still, I knew that the Depression had an extra-harsh impact on the people in southern states. Frank lived out the Great Depression just outside of Orlando, Florida. One-fourth of the people in the state were on Relief. To keep more poor people from coming into Florida, where at least they would not freeze to death, the state police were stationed at the state line. People without money or a job were not allowed to drive into Florida.

Frank's family of 12 lived in a three-room company house in the orange groves where they worked. Although their small pay was cut even lower, the family was not evicted because they were still needed to cultivate and pick the fruit. As Frank said, "The kids didn't know the difference between Depression and not-Depression. It was all the same." Friends my age who grew up in the rural or semi-rural South have similar memories. "We didn't know there was a Depression," they said. "It was always Depression times.'"

Demanding Unemployment Insurance

By the spring of 1934, the movement for unemployment insurance was gaining strength. As a member of the high school debating team, I took part in a debate on unemployment insurance. The topic was: "Resolved, unemployment insurance is Communistic." If you proved that something was Communistic, that was supposed to be automatic proof it was bad. That kind of red-baiting backfired. Since everyone who fought for unemployment insurance was labeled "Communist," thousands decided they were Communists, too.

The great, historic struggle for unemployment insurance was launched by the unemployed councils and won the support of the American Federation of Labor (AFL). According to the *Daily Worker*, the issue was placed before the AFL convention by Louis Weinstock, at the risk of his own life. Weinstock was a painter unionist, a leader of the campaign for unemployment insurance. Since he could not get on the agenda, he found another way to get the delegates' attention.

Weinstock jumped from a high balcony onto a chandelier, swaying over the heads of the AFL delegates. From that high perch, he presented the case for unemployment insurance. By the time the firemen were able to get him down, he had completed his speech. Of course, Weinstock was young, still in his 20s. That's one reason I believe that winning movements must be led by young people. You never know when you may have to jump on a swinging chandelier.

Of course there were some who did not support the idea of unemployment compensation. "Pay people for not working?" they sneered. But there were not enough of them to stop the movement. In August 1935, the Social Security bill became law. The Social Security law included unemployment compensation. Payment levels were to be set by the states. Winning unemployment insurance was a great victory. Nobody gave it to us. We won it through struggle.

City Hospital

The city hospital wards are part of my Depression memories. Some would call them the charity wards. Of necessity, I became well acquainted with the city hospitals. That's where my parents received medical care after both became seriously ill. Before the Depression, we had a family doctor. In the East 165th Street neighborhood, we even had a doctor with a home office on our street. Even some serious injuries, such as the tear wound in my throat, were treated in his office. He saved many of us a trip to the hospital emergency room. I hope he was not one of the family doctors who had to give up their practice because patients could not pay. Some doctors in New York City even drove taxi cabs to survive the Depression.

I visited my dying mother in her hospital room every day. It was a very sad time for me. It was especially hard in the drab surroundings of the city hospital. The hospital looked just the way I felt: down at the mouth. I think everything was clean enough, as clean as plenty of bleach could make it. Mama's meals looked good enough, much better than the food we had at home. Mama had no appetite and urged me to eat the food she hadn't touched. Sometimes I did taste it, but I did not have much appetite either. Hospitals used to keep patients like my mother for months. Now they would be sent someplace else to die.

At least New York City did have city hospitals that maintained some minimum standard of care. In many parts of the country, poor families had no access to health care. New York City also had free dental clinics. No doubt, my poor diet accelerated tooth decay. I went to the free clinic when I had a toothache. The free clinic pulled out teeth but did not fill cavities. So they pulled the offending tooth and also the one next to it that was not aching. I heard the dentist say, "Might as well pull the adjacent tooth because it has a big filling." For one tooth, you got novocaine. For two teeth they used gas and you felt no pain. So I let them pull the two. That was the beginning of losing my teeth, one or two at a time.

The worst part of the Depression is that it lasted so long. Home Relief did not replace household items as they wore out. When the sheets wore out, you slept on the pieces that were left. Sheets generally wear out in the middle. They can be repaired by cutting them down the center and sewing the sides together. When the mattress wore out, you slept on the bare springs with a little paper padding. When the bedstead wore out, you placed the spring on four piles of bricks. Broken dishes and burned pots were never replaced. We did not have, so perhaps did not miss, some items considered necessities today. In my neighborhood, few had radios or telephones.

My First Factory Job

I went to work in the summer of 1933, at the end of my junior year at Monroe High School. In August, I was going to be 15. My family desperately needed money because Home Relief did not cover the full rent payment. I heard they were hiring at Eby, a radio parts plant on the lower East Side. I did not have a work permit. Anyway, the minimum legal age for factory work was 18 in New York. So I dressed "old," put on a hat with a big brim to hide my face and decided to lie about my age. I had heard many stories about sweatshops. The factory I pictured was dimly lit and crowded with workers bent over their work. In poor light, I thought I could pass for 18.

To my shock, the Eby factory was well-lit with fluorescent light. My less-than-15-year-old face was in full view. Still, I had nothing to lose so I went ahead, applied and got the job. They did not seem to care about my age. My next big challenge was to get up at 5 a.m. so I could make it to work on time. The job was at the southern tip of Manhattan, far south of the downtown area. We did not own an alarm clock. I don't think we owned a clock. So I lay down to sleep on the floor, next to the apartment door. There I could hear the clomp, clomp, clomp of the milkman's horse, and hear the milkman's quick tread on the stairway. He made his deliveries before 5 a.m.

I showed up to work with little sleep, but that did not matter. I noticed that the plant was full of underage women workers. On the work tables were shimmering piles of small silvery metal parts. Those were the "contacts." It was a simple job. Pick up the contacts and push them through a pre-punched plastic socket, one at a time. Then the sockets were sent to another department, to be used in making radio tubes.

By the end of the 10-hour day, my thumb was sore. It ached all night, but there was another reason that I did not sleep well. All night, I relived the experience of my first day's work in a factory. All night, I heard the voices ringing out, "Contacts!" so our work table could be re-supplied. And all night I was surrounded by my co-workers, pushing metal contacts into radio sockets, fast as we could.

My first pay envelope had three dollars and some change. That was not a full week because I remember the pay as 15 cents an hour. That same summer, the National Industrial Recovery Act (NIRA) put in a minimum wage that doubled our pay. Eby complied, but they doubled our quota of sockets. The job became truly unbearable. I was inspired by the YCL to try to organize the factory. The Metal Workers Industrial Union, affiliated with the Trade Union Educational League, was organizing radio parts plants.

I stepped up my agitation for a union. In two days, I led 50 young women, about half of the workers on my floor, to the nearby union hall. It was a medium-sized hall, with open space in the center. The walls were lined with seated women members. Perhaps they were waiting for a meeting. As we marched in they looked at us with great interest. I will admit to a moment of revolutionary pride. Then I heard the comments. "Child labor!" the women exclaimed. For some reason I felt deflated, as though calling us children took away from

WORKERS OF THE EBY—

Are you satisfied with the low wages?

Do you know that food prices have
risen by 8% while wages remain low?

What is to be done about conditions?

Conditions at the EBY are far from satisfactory. Wages of from $5
to $11 a week. One has to work very fast in order to make anything.
This has resulted in many accidents in the place. At the same time,
prices of food and clothing are rising daily- but the wages remain
as low as ever.

It is said that the owner of the EBY may operate soon on the basis
of the National Recovery Act. One thing should be clear— all that
the owner is interested in is more profits for himself and not in
the conditions of the workers. No doubt, the owner of the EBY will
use the NRA as an excuse for speeding up all workers to turn out
more, of firing those that can't keep up with the speed. This will also result in more accidents.

What should be done? Don't rely on the bosses' code. The workers
of the EBY should set up their own workers' code of demands—
for higher wages; for a definite minimum wage based on straight
time and no piece work; for sanitary conditions. Workers in other
shops are organizing and winning improved conditions. The EBY workers can do likewise!

How? Speak to those of your fellow workers whom you feel you can
trust. Arrange a meeting in one of your or some workers home. Ther
take up the question of higher wages, shorter hours of work, and
other kicks and complaints. Get in touch with the METAL WORKERS IN-
DUSTRIAL UNION, located at 35 E.19 Street, NYC., the union that will
help you to improve your conditions. Remember— If all stick together, better conditions can be won!

                    -- METAL WORKERS INDUSTRIAL UNION,
                       35 East 19 Street
                       New York, N.Y.

the importance of our action. We talked to the organizer who
gave us union cards. A few of my co-workers joined me in
signing. We had an organizing committee!

The New York City YCL leadership agreed that our organizing start was very important. But the fall semester was
opening soon. I regretted leaving my co-workers, but I had to go
back to finish high school. "Don't go back," a YCL leader urged
me. "Look at me," he said. "I never finished high school." I did

look at him and I admired him a lot. He knew so much and spoke so well. He certainly seemed none the worse for having dropped out of high school. But I did not see myself becoming a great leader like him. In my case, I thought it best to finish high school. From there, I planned to go to Hunter College, then tuition-free.

Fighting Racism—the Scottsboro Nine

The need for unity may be the most valuable lesson the Communist Party taught me during the Depression. The biggest barrier to uniting workers was, and still is, racism. So it was natural that Communists made the fight against racism a part of every struggle. Fortunately, by the late 1920s the CPUSA had placed the fight against racism as central to all other struggles. Earlier socialists did not understand this centrality. They thought it was enough to fight for the liberation of all workers, without a special emphasis on fighting racism.

Around 1929, the CPUSA started an intense educational campaign to root out any racist remnants among its own members. It was just in time, just before the Great Depression. Faced with mass hunger and homelessness, Communists put out the slogan, "Black and White, Unite and Fight!" This slogan was adopted by the unemployed councils, the workers alliances and many unions. Multiracial unity was the heart of the coalition that won the New Deal and organized the CIO. That work in the 1930s laid the foundation for every civil rights movement that followed.

The Party sent some of its most talented organizers to help southern sharecroppers organize in the early 1930s. They organized African American and white sharecroppers together. A special part of CPUSA dues was set aside for organizing in the South. We called it, "Southern Solidarity." In 1934, the 8,000-strong Alabama Share Croppers Union won higher prices for cotton pickers. This amazing victory was won despite intense, violent repression by local authorities and business. That inspiring story is dramatized in a wonderful book by labor historian Robin Kelley, *The Hammer and the Hoe.*[2]

---

[2] Robin D.G. Kelley, *The Hammer and the Hoe: Alabama Communists During the Great Depression* (University of North Carolina Press, 1990).

Peggy Lipschutz, Labor Today

Black and white unity was also the basic guide for Communists who organized Southern miners and textile workers. I was inspired by Ann Burlak, an organizer of the National Textile Workers Union. She became known as the "Red Flame of Patterson" (NJ). In 1930, in Georgia, she had been charged with sedition against the state of Georgia. Her supposed crime was daring to speak to an interracial audience. That charge carried the death penalty. Years later, the Supreme Court threw the case out. I met Ann in 1934 in New York when she was sharing an apartment with Fanny Hartman. Both Ann and Fanny were very kind to an eager 16-year-old who talked a dry jargon. They gave me some very good advice that I discuss later. I had the good luck to meet Fanny Hartman again, in Gary, in the

1950s. She was married to my husband Frank's good friend, Joe Norrick. Fanny and I became close friends.

Racism was also challenged when Kentucky miners went on strike. The miners' union included African American and white. In 1931, some family friends went to help the strikers in "Bloody Harlan County, Kentucky." Some were beaten by company thugs in Harlan County. I was sorry that I was too young to go. Anyway, I could not have qualified for that particular trip. My friends were in a musical group that went to sing for the strikers. As I have lamented more than once in these notes, singing for an audience was not one of my skills.

More than any other national campaign, the defense of the Scottsboro "Boys" raised the level of the fight against racism. To give proper respect to the nine young defendants, I will modify the slogan of "Free the Scottsboro Boys" to "Free the Scottsboro Nine." This slogan was heard in every part of our country and around the world. The story behind the slogan was all too common in Alabama in the 1930s. Nine African American youths had been taken from different box cars of a freight train and arrested in Scottsboro, Alabama. Two were only 12 and 13 years old. They were part of the large army of unemployed who rode the rails, looking for work.

Two white women had been taken off the same train. The women were subject to arrest because they had a record of prostitution in Tennessee. They falsely charged the nine youths with rape. In that time, such a charge could give rise to a lynch mob. Lynch mobs sometimes broke into jails and murdered the accused before any trial was held. The nine teenagers were quickly sentenced to death. What made this case different was the Communist Party.

Communist organizers in Chattanooga and Birmingham heard about the arrests and visited the defendants in jail. With the International Labor Defense (ILD), they initiated a legal and political campaign to win their freedom. Attorney William Patterson, able head of the ILD, led the defense. After an international campaign that lasted many years, they did win their freedom. Communist support for the Scottsboro Nine attracted many African Americans to the Communist Party in the 1930s.

In working on local issues, we always included "Free the Scottsboro Nine" in our demands. One example made us smile. A landlord had raised rents and failed to make repairs. The tenants' council decided to withhold rents until their demands were met. They picketed their building with signs demanding repairs, no rent hikes, and "Free the Scottsboro Nine!" The landlord gave in. He said, "OK, I'll make the repairs and cancel the rent increase. But how can I free the Scottsboro Boys?" Actually, if I remember correctly, the demands of the rent strike were even more extensive. It was not only freedom for the Scottsboro Nine but also freedom for Angelo Herndon. Who was Angelo Herndon?

Angelo Herndon

Angelo Herndon was a 19-year-old African American Communist organizer. Charged with "inciting insurrection" in Atlanta, Georgia, he was sentenced to 20 years on the chain gang. His crime? Herndon had led a racially integrated march of the unemployed council, demanding "Jobs or Relief." An interesting sideline of the Herndon trial was his defense by the Atlanta lawyer, Ben Davis. Davis was the son of a prominent African American Republican. Just to remind those younger than this writer, most African Americans voted Republican before the time of Franklin D. Roosevelt. (The Republican Party used to be the party of Abraham Lincoln.)

To prepare for his client's defense, Attorney Davis read the literature found in Herndon's room. The literature convinced Davis that he was a Communist too. After serving some time in Georgia prisons, Herndon's conviction was thrown out by the Supreme Court. Ben Davis joined the Communist Party and became a prominent national leader of the Party. As the Harlem organizer of the Communist Party, Davis became a close associate of Councilman Adam Clayton Powell. When Powell was elected to the U.S. Congress in 1943, Davis was elected to Powell's seat on the New York City Council.

There he joined his Communist comrade, Peter V. Cacchione, who had been elected to a second term as a city councilman. I was in faraway Buffalo so I could not work on Ben

Davis's election. I did work in an earlier campaign to elect Cacchione. The Board of Election had removed him from the ballot. So he ran a write-in campaign. Thousands of voters, including immigrant workers from Italy, learned to draw a box, put in a cross, and then carefully spell, Peter V. C - a - c - c - h - i - o - n - e. I was impressed.

In 1945, Davis was re-elected with an even larger vote. He lost his council seat during the evil days of McCarthy repression. In 1951, Davis was convicted of violating the Smith Act and sentenced to five years in federal prison. In the same trial, ten other Communist leaders were sentenced to long prison terms. They were convicted of "conspiring to teach the overthrow of the U.S. government." A few years after they served their prison terms, that section of the Smith Act was declared unconstitutional by the U.S. Supreme Court. It was too late to restore the eyesight of Henry Winston, a loss that resulted from the prison's refusal to allow competent medical care. Not a penny of compensation was ever paid to these wrongly imprisoned men.

The pioneering work of the Communist Party during the Depression years shaped history for years to come. But the story I sketched above has been kept out of most history books, including labor history. I know about this history because I lived through it. Much has been wiped out of the collective memory of people in the United States. Can this history remain hidden forever? I doubt it. I think it will be hard to chart a path to a better future until we learn the truth of our past,

Joy in the Struggle

All was not grim and joyless during the Depression. I had a very rich cultural life in the mid-1930s, although my family was poor, and my parents were sick. As part of the New Deal program to reduce unemployment, the federal government launched the Works Progress Administration (WPA). WPA jobs projects employed artists, writers and actors as well as construction workers. The WPA built many public buildings. WPA Theater was affordable, enjoyable and high quality. The museums were free, and it was possible to enjoy good concerts while seated among great works of art.

The YCL and the labor movement in general were another source of rich culture. In the summer, our group would often spend Saturday night on the roof of a tenement building. We called it "tar beach." We talked, laughed and sang movement songs until the sun came up. No alcohol was involved; there was no money for that. The next morning, we made the rounds of our *Daily Worker* newspaper route. Our duty done, we were free to take the train to the beach, and we did. When I was young, going without sleep did not dim my enthusiasm for a good swim.

Perhaps the greatest personal benefit of my YCL membership was that it showed me an escape route from the misery of the Depression. First I learned that it was not the worker's fault. Too many still believed that it was the breadwinner's fault if he/she could not put food on the table. Blaming oneself for not having a job was self-destructive and paralyzing. Once the millions of unemployed organized, we won four million public works jobs. That taught us that it paid to fight. There was "joy in the struggle."

It was still deep Depression when I started college in 1934. Some kind teacher gave me a pink sweater blouse and brown wool skirt. They must have been made of good material because I wore that outfit every day for many months that year. I would wash the two pieces every night and dry them on a hot radiator. Sometimes they would not be completely dry because the material was thick and heat was turned off at night. But I would wear them anyway, and they would dry on my body. One day another sympathetic teacher stopped me in the hallway and asked if I would be offended if she gave me some clothes. I was glad to get her castoffs.

That winter I went without an overcoat. Anyway, I had the habit of running from place to place. So I ran a little faster that winter. I claimed that I was not cold. There was a way to get a coat from the Relief, but I did not want to go through all that red tape. The application would have to go through the social service workers who worked for the Relief agency. As I understood it, the main function of these social workers was to find an excuse to throw your family off Relief. I formed a deep distaste for social work as a result of my family's experience with welfare. In later years, I met Communists and many others who were sincere social workers. That did not totally erase the memory of my teen age experience with social workers. Eating out was never an option for my family. We did have family gatherings and movement events where we ate at someone's home or at a workers club. Even before the Depression hit in 1929, we never went to restaurants. That changed for me when I started college. Students often gathered in cafeterias. We students did not order meals because we could not afford it. Occasionally we could buy a bowl of soup or dish of rice pudding for a dime. We knew how to enrich the soup with the freebies from the relish table: ketchup, sliced onions, sauerkraut, grated cheese and other goodies. There were other freebies for the taking. Better-fed diners often left corn muffins untouched. Just as soon as they left their table, we quickly retrieved such edibles. Then we could stay for hours, reviewing and solving all the problems of the world. Late as we stayed, it was not too often that we had to leave because a restaurant was closing. They must have kept even later hours than we did.

People Are Good

In the Depression year of 1937, I had an experience that I remembered with gratitude the rest of my life. Arches in my feet had broken down after a summer job working as a busgirl at Horn & Hardart Restaurant, the "automat." To get some arch supports made, I visited a free clinic attached to a school of podiatry. I carried my total personal fortune with me, $20. At the time, I did not know where or when or how I would ever get more money.

On my way home, I realized that I had dropped the $20. The huge loss devastated me. I went home and went to sleep although it was broad daylight. What else could I do? The next day, after sleeping the clock around, I decided to go back to the clinic and look for my $20. I knew it was stupid but did not know what else to do. So I returned to the clinic and asked if anyone found my $20. To my amazement, they said, "Yes." One of the podiatry students had picked it up! He did not know me, but he knew I needed that money badly. Only poor people came to that clinic. The student doctor's act of kindness lit a warm spot of hope in my heart. I never forgot it. Some 46 years later I had a similar, wonderful experience.

It was Election Day in Chicago, and I was working for Rudy Lozano, people's candidate for alderman. Votes were being stolen left and right and the cop on duty looked the other way. I had to go outside to call Rudy's office and complain. On my return, I missed my wallet. I began a frantic search to find the lost wallet. No, it was not in the phone booth, not on the pavement. Just then, a driver honked his horn. He had seen me searching the streets for something. "Did you lose something?" he asked. "Yes, my wallet." "Is this it?" he asked. And I got my wallet back. There are so many good people!

Winning Social Security

In 1935, we won a lot of social programs. Passage of the Social Security Act (SSA) in 1935 was a major victory for working people. It set up a national pension fund for retired persons, the same fund that is now under attack by Republicans and right-wing Democrats. The SSA also included an unemployment insurance system and public assistance programs for low income mothers, children and the disabled.

Soon after SSA began to pay unemployment compensation, people who were laid off rushed to collect their checks. I was one of them. And who did I see standing up in front, ready to get their unemployment checks? Some of the very same people who had sneered, "What, pay people for not working?" I could not help but smile when I saw them on the line. Still, I was glad that they could collect checks when they were unemployed. "We fought for you, too," I told them. Some smiled. I hoped that they had learned that if you fight, you have a chance to win. And if you don't fight, you are sure to lose. I heard that put more dramatically in later years as "Fight or die!" That's what my husband, Frank Lumpkin, told fellow workers when Wisconsin Steel closed without warning.

The Roosevelt government did some great things in record speed. Where there was political will, there was a way. A good example was the speed with which the New Deal government put the unemployed to work in 1933–34. In just ten weeks, over four million unemployed workers were hired and put to work on thousands of projects. Many worked at rebuilding the country's infrastructure. I helped fight for unemployment compensation. Still I did not realize that we were changing our country forever. In the '70s, Frank and I had the good fortune to meet Ruth Norrick. In the 1930s she had worked with Harry Hopkins, a chief architect of Roosevelt's New Deal. Norrick reported in Labor Today that, "16 days after November 9, 1933, when the money was made available for the Civilian Works Administration, 814,511 unemployed were put to work. Two weeks later, that number reached nearly 2,000.000 and by mid-January, 4,263,644."[3]

The CCC Camps

Thanks to public works job projects, economic conditions improved somewhat around 1935. Wages from WPA jobs pumped money back into the community. Workers spent that money for family needs, creating a demand for more production. My parents were not physically able to take advantage of WPA. But as soon as my younger brother Lenny reached 16, he left for the Civilian Conservation Corps (CCC), a program for young people. The CCC helped build dams, fight forest fires and improve public lands in the West. In later years, Frank and I and our children often camped out West where we saw the work that CCC had done. We may have been looking at work that Lenny did.

For the first time in his adolescent life, Lenny had enough to eat. His outdoor experiences helped prepare him for his life's work as a ship's engineer. As he told the story, one night he got hungry and went to the camp kitchen. At the refrigerator, Lenny met a bear who had the same idea. "What did you do?" I asked my brother. "I turned my back and walked away," he answered.

"And what did the bear do?"

"The same thing!"

---

[3] Ruth Norrick, Labor Today, January, 1983.

The fresh air and physical exercise were hugely benefi-
cial. Lenny went to the CCC an underfed, skinny teenager and
came back looking healthy and muscular. But the CCC was
run by the army on racist and military lines. An officer told
the young men, "Men, line up on the right! Jews on the left!"
The antisemitism and military discipline angered my brother.
Unlike the army, there was an honorable way to quit the CCC.
Lenny asked us to send a letter with the magical three-letter
word, "job." We wrote and said, "Come home. We have a job
for you." That won him his release. Then he shipped out of the
Port of New York and joined the National Maritime Union.

At least our family was never evicted. By whatever means,
my parents managed to pay the rent. In general, there was a
severe shortage of affordable housing. People marched and
protested in such large numbers that the federal government
agreed to build affordable public housing. Winning public
housing was a great victory for the unemployed movement.
The new public housing, when first constructed, was decent
housing. It was only after years of federal underfunding, and
deliberate neglect, that so many housing projects became slums.

No matter how bad things were in the big city, they were
even worse in some rural areas. We read about the "Okies,"
farmers forced off their land by a combination of drought in
Oklahoma and banks calling in their mortgages. A few made
their way to New York City. One couple touched my heart
in a way I cannot forget. It was Easter Sunday. Crowds were
walking on Fifth Avenue to see people wearing their Easter
finery. Many, like me, had nothing new to wear. Then I saw
this couple, dressed in faded blue denim, walking hand-in-
hand. Faded blue denim was not an urban fashion then. More
than their clothes, it was their faces that set them apart. Their
skin was so weather-beaten, I could not guess their age. Their
expression was one of total weariness. They looked as though
they had walked all the way from Oklahoma. I wondered
where their walk would end.

Frances Perkins and the American Labor Party

I had the pleasure of meeting Frances Perkins, FDR's Secretary
of Labor. She was the first woman ever appointed to a Cabinet

position and an architect of the Social Security legislation. Perkins joined the American Labor Party (ALP) in 1936. That year she spoke at a small ALP meeting. I had the good luck of sitting in center front row of the school room where she talked from the teacher's desk. I thought she was wonderful, and I hung on her every word. Her next newsletter mentioned an eager young woman who had listened so intently. I felt sure she had noticed me.

More to the point, the ALP was the kind of party that I wish we had today. It was formed in 1936 by labor leaders, including Sidney Hillman of the Amalgamated Clothing Workers. The ALP had two purposes. Rally support for the New Deal, and press the Roosevelt administration for more workers' benefits. Under New York State law, a candidate could run on more than one party ticket. Unfortunately most states do not allow political parties to form coalitions and run the same candidate on two or more party lines.

It is hard to find a time worse for working people than the "Great Depression." In Chicago, for example, the unemployment rate was 25%. But the drop in total wages paid was 50%. Still, in one way conditions are worse now. (And I recorded these lines *before* the financial meltdown of October 2008!) In the '30s, mills and machine shops and auto plants may have cut back or even closed. But they were not torn down. The idled plants of the 1930s returned to production some years later. In contrast, our plants in South Chicago, and thousands like them around the country, are gone forever. Where the big Chicago steel mills stood, there is now nothing but prairies. But I am not pessimistic about our future. As long as the people are here, we can find a way out.

Chapter 6

"*Country*" *and Ocean*
The sound of the foghorns made me want to travel.

MY 165th Street Bronx neighborhood was in one of the most urban of urban settings. There were no trees or lawns on our streets, just old, brick tenement houses built in the nineteenth century. Some of the adults, including my mother, longed for the green spaces of the villages in the "old country." They put handfuls of earth into window boxes and grew everything from small roses to tomatoes.

Growing up in tenement buildings, I still wanted to put my hands into earth and see open spaces around me. Somehow, I grew up with a love for the "country" and watching things grow. I was eight when we took a memorable trip to the "country." Here's how I described this trip 55 years ago.

A New Spring Story

This spring day was to be different from any other day of my eight years. Mr. Goldberg was coming with his fancy car to take us out to the country. I knew Mr. Goldberg was rich because he had a car and a chauffeur. Nobody else I knew had a car and certainly none had a chauffeur.

You could feel spring in the gentle heat reflected from the pavements and the subtle intensification of all the ghetto smells—the tart pickle juice in the gutters, the ripe fruit on the peddlers' carts, the sweet milk ices at two cents a cup, the baked sweet potatoes in the portable charcoal ovens—all mingled with the smell of manure dropped by the milkman's horse. But on this day there was just a wisp of a scent of green from some faraway park or meadow. The sun seemed to paint away the dirt rather than point a finger at all the sore spots. It was full morning. The tall Turk was already making his rounds, carrying a white-cloth-covered tray high above his head. The cloth fluttered to show glimpses of diamond-shaped sesame seed candy, one cent a slice, sticky with honey, chewy and sweet. I had been in a highly excited state since the night before when Mama said we were going to ride in a car out to the "country." This was one morning when she did not have to coax me out of bed.

After what seemed hours of waiting, Mr. Goldberg's chariot threaded its way among the pushcarts and rattled up to the curb near our apartment building. In we piled, me first in the back seat, next to Mr. Goldberg, then my mother next to me. Up front with the "chauffeur," rode my father and kid brother, Lenny. Maxie, my older brother, was off on his mysterious doings. At 15 there are better things to do than follow your family.

The interior of Mr. Goldberg's car was not lined with gold. In fact the stuffing of the upholstery was coming through. Nor did Mr. Goldberg look any richer than his chauffeur. But the car ran nicely and my fairytale mood persisted.

The tenements rolled by until we were out in the "better" neighborhood. The streets, the air, even the people seemed cleaner, not crowded so closely together. All the foodstuffs in the stores were neatly tucked away behind plate glass windows; not a pushcart was to be seen. And it was quieter too, but somehow not so lively, a watered-down strange type of life. The signs saying kosher-kosher were no longer on the butcher shops. Soon the signs said we were out of the city.

The open road turned out to be a canyon, walled in on either side by high cliffs of signboards. These were very interesting, with clever rhymes and brightly colored figures. In between the signs were brief glimpses of green. Somehow this was not what I expected the "country" to look like. It was not like the picture books.

Then we turned into a side road and a different world. "Cows, Mama, cows," I shrieked. "Can't you see them, Mr. Goldberg?" Mama's strong arm pulled me back in the seat.

"Be quiet," she said, in a strangely strained voice. But I was like mercury, hard to grab and slipping about with a mind of my own. What was wrong with my mother? She wasn't usually like that.

The meadow fragrance went to my head—a million fruit blossoms, earth freshly washed by last night's rain. City stinks were far away. The marvelous birds we saw had splashes of red or yellow or blue or orange. They were so different from the drab English Sparrows on our home street, quarreling over the occasional manure piles left by the milk wagon horses.

"What do you see, my child?" Mr. Goldberg seemed as eager as I was. But my mother seemed most uncomfortable as I shouted with delight, "Look, look at that tree. It's all pink with flowers!"

"Cherry tree," Mama said.

"And these pink and white trees. What are they, Mr. Goldberg?"

"Apple trees," Mama answered.

"And these plants with feathery white flowers like little umbrellas?"

"Just weeds."

"Just weeds? But they're so pretty! Don't you think so, Mr. Goldberg?"

"What else do you see?" was his only answer.

It was dark when we returned home and said good-by to Mr. Goldberg and his driver. Then Mama scolded me for talking so much. "But what did I do that was wrong?" I asked. And then Mama told me that Mr. Goldberg was blind. For years I thought I had made Mr. Goldberg feel sad by telling him to look when he could not see. Not until much later did I realize that he may have enjoyed my childish enthusiasm. Perhaps I had helped him see through my eyes.

Hunts Point

When I was about nine, the family moved a mile or so away from 165th Street to the Hunts Point neighborhood. This was 1927. My parents had relocated their store so we rented an apartment across the street. At night as I fell asleep I heard the ships' horns in the Sound. They sounded so far away, so filled with longing. The sound of the foghorns made me want to travel to faraway and unknown places.

On a hill over Hunts Point Boulevard, just east of our laundry store, were the remains of the "Dickey Estate." Or so we kids called it. Supposedly a wealthy family called "Dickey" had once owned that land. That may have been true because the remains of an ornate, horse-drawn carriage sat in the vacant lots. Often I climbed the steep hill with "kid" brother Lenny in tow. I loved to sit in the carriage and dream of long-gone days. Lenny found that boring. He was more into digging a hole in the ground and starting a fire to roast white potatoes.

To my delight I found other joys of real "country," hidden away near our Hunts Point apartment. The rows of apartment buildings ended short of the Gas Works. Nothing was built for blocks around. In one vacant lot, there were blackberry bushes and delicious wild strawberries. Pretty butterflies flitted around. After my cousin, the biologist, gave me a butterfly net, I started an insect collection. Sixty years later, on a return visit, there was still no construction there. Maybe the ground was too horribly polluted or too swampy.

In another part of this rare undeveloped area of the Bronx there was a cemetery dating to colonial times. The poet, Joseph Rodman Drake, was buried there. Chills came to my heart as I read the tender ages on some gravestones. I did not want to "prepare for death" as some of the stones instructed.

> Behold and see as you pass by
> As you are now so once was I
> As I am now you soon will be
> Prepare for death and follow me.

When I revisited the cemetery many years later, the poet was gone. The other burials remained in place although the grounds looked more neglected than ever. A more recent visit to the cemetery showed it has finally become a city park, named after Drake. The poet's body has been returned. A sign told me that a Weckquaesgeek Indian village called Quinna-hung had been on the site. In the late seventeenth century,

Thomas Hunt "acquired" the property. His mansion became a childhood haven for the poet, Joseph Rodman Drake. Born in 1795, Drake was a descendant of Sir Francis Drake, the British commander who defeated the Spanish Armada in 1533.

The sign did not explain what happened to the Weckquaesgeek Indians when Hunt took their village ground. But it did say that no trace was left of the African slave cemetery known to have been in Hunts Point. That was the first time I read of slavery in the Bronx. The city should locate those remains and give them proper respect.

Camp Kinderland and Camp Unity

I had another chance to enjoy "country" when I spent two weeks in Camp Kinderland in 1927 and 1931. The camp was operated by the left-wing International Workers Order. Summer camps for children and adults were a great achievement of the workers' fraternal movement. And at 18, I waited tables at the progressive adult camp, Camp Unity.

The next year I walked parts of the Appalachian Trail, especially Mount Tremper. I was not romantically involved with any of my fellow hikers. But there were a couple of men I liked a lot. Romance just did not happen. I laugh as I remember a challenging climb with my friend, Victor Teich. He set a good pace and of course I kept up. I was used to taking a break halfway up. But Victor said nothing when we got halfway up the mountain. So I said nothing.

It began to get hotter and hotter as we continued the climb. My backpack got heavier, and my clothes were wet with sweat. I just grit my teeth and thought, "Well if he is used to making this climb without a stop, I can do it too. I'm as good a man as he is, any day!" Finally, we reached the summit. He put down his pack and said, "That's the first time I climbed this mountain without a stop!" I could have killed him.

Almost 70 years later, I met Victor Teich again. During all those years, he remained active with the people's movement. Well over 80 years old, he had become a playwright and producer. Vic produced *The Empty Chair,* an award-winning play against the death sentence.

Pelham Bay

Pelham Bay was just a few subway stops away from our neighborhood. Five of us put in 25 cents each and we had a boat for the day. Best of all was Hunter's Island, a fairly short swim from City Beach. The rest of my life I kept looking for a nice island to swim to but never found the right beach again. We teenagers never ran into trouble in the bay, but I did as a child. Papa took my brother Lenny and me out on the Bay. A storm came up and Papa lost an oar! With just one oar, all he could do was turn the boat in circles. Since you're reading this book, you see that we were rescued and I survived.

It is amazing to me that I ended up spending most of my life away from the ocean. We do live near the great land-locked seas of the Great Lakes. That is not the same thing. But others in my family remained deeply connected to the ocean. My brother Lenny spent most of his life in the Merchant Marine. His ashes are scattered over the ocean that sustained him.

My husband Frank sailed the Liberty Ships in World War II. My oldest son, Carl, worked on ore boats while a graduate student. He said the sunsets on our inland seas are spectacular. My brother-in-law Joe Slifkin also sailed the seas as a deck hand in World War II. Only one son, Paul, carries on the family's maritime tradition, but only as a hobby.

Still, if I live to be 100, and I'm working on it, I will never forget the haunting sounds of ships' foghorns at night, nor lose the strong urge to go to faraway places.

Chapter 7

Organizing Laundry Workers
"Hey, CIO girl! We want a union, too."

I was probably born into laundry work. My parents worked in the "hand laundry" they "owned." In fact they owned almost nothing: a table-size electric mangle, some heavy gas-heated irons, curtain stretchers and clothes racks. Papa rented the store and he and Mama did all the work themselves. As I grew up, I learned to work the mangle and to mark and assort clothes. I even helped my father deliver bundles of clean clothes. So I quickly responded when, in 1933, the YCL asked us to help some laundry strikers.

On the picket line, the laundry workers were talking about sacrifices they had made to organize their industrial union. Two comrades had been killed in the struggle, they said. That made me sad but no less determined. I kept coming back to that picket line until the strike was won. The next call to help laundry workers came in 1937. The CIO's United Laundry Workers Union (ULWU) was in a big drive to organize the laundry workers of New York City. I was not quite 19, but they hired me as a full time organizer. Although I was a college student, I was familiar with commercial laundries. My age was not a problem. "Older" comrades showed me the way, especially Jessie Taft, now Jessie Smith. In 1937 she was all of 23 and had been an officer of a laundry union local. Some 68 years later, she and I were reunited when she read my story in the *Peoples Weekly World*!

Let's go back to the summer of 1937. The labor movement was exploding with the energy of hope. Conditions were ripe for a huge increase in union membership. Communist-led hunger marches to state capitals had aroused the fighting spirit of working families. The veterans' Bonus March to Washington, DC radicalized thousands more. In 1935, the Committee for Industrial Organization (CIO) formed and opened union doors to all workers in an industry. (In 1938, the CIO became the Congress of Industrial Organizations.) In contrast, the old American Federation of Labor (AFL) focus on craft workers had left out the millions who worked in mass production industries. These struggles, and passage of fair labor laws, created a pro-union climate. Meanwhile, the fight to save the Scottsboro Nine strengthened black-white unity.

Just write me out my union card.

Working for the CIO was a very different kind of summer job. In little over two months, our staff of 30 organized 20,000 laundry workers in New York City. CIO's newly chartered United Laundry Workers Union (ULWU) had to reach hundreds of plants scattered all around the city. The largest plants had 600 workers; most employed less than 100. According to the *Daily Worker*, predecessor of the *Peoples World*, the laundry union quadrupled its membership in two weeks. In June, 1937, they grew from 2,750 to 11,000 members.[4] Other unions grew just as fast or faster. For example, the United Auto Workers grew from 35,000 to 350,000 in one year.[5]

How did we organize so many in such a short time? The hardest part was running from plant to plant. None of us had cars. Once we reached the laundries, workers were very receptive. They wanted a union, and the law of the land protected their right to join unions. We organizers answered a few basic questions, then wrote out the union cards as fast as our pens could move. Miserable wages, long hours, hot heavy work, sexism and racism had ground the laundry workers down. But now they had hope because the CIO was organizing.

---

[4] The *Daily Worker*, July 2, 1937.
[5] The *Daily Worker*, July 19, 1937.

The basic organizing steps were simple. Hand out union flyers at the plant door as workers come in. Try to get names, addresses and phone numbers of workers who talk to you. Then make home visits. Or take a group to a nearby tavern after work for beer and talk. For me, that was a new experience. I don't think I had ever been inside taverns before. Talk to workers sitting outside the plant during the 60-minute lunch hour. Hand out union cards and sign up as many union members as possible. From those who sign up, form a union organizing committee. Try to have someone from every department. Today, these steps can take years. In the summer of 1937, it was done in days.

Of the 30 organizers on staff for the ULWU, half belonged to the Young Communist League or the Communist Party. They were totally committed to the union cause and willing to work unlimited hours, 16 or more a day. The organizer's pay was small, just $10 a week. As a child of the Depression, I could live on that. I lived with my parents and paid no rent. For a 40-hour week, ten dollars was less than the minimum wage of 35 cents an hour. It was a lot less than the minimum wage when you consider the hours. We organizers worked 60–70 hours a week. But we loved what we were doing.

Union organizing and civil rights

Overcoming divisions is the key to organizing. As an industrial union, the ULWU organized all laundry workers, whether they worked inside or outside the plant. Inside workers included maintenance and production workers. The outside workers were the drivers, white men with few exceptions. Inside workers were mostly women of color. My job was to organize the inside workers. The key workers, without whom the laundry could not run, were the kitchen workers. They ran the large commercial washing machines. Most were African American men. Kitchen workers proved to be very militant and among the first to sign union cards. That was true of African American laundry workers in general.

By 1937, African Americans had a lot of experience in fighting for their rights. The civil rights movement of that time fought to free the Scottsboro Nine and to stop lynching. African American workers had joined with white workers to fight hunger and evictions. They had answered the unemployed council's call, "Black and White, Unite and Fight." The unifying role of the Communists in these campaigns helped lay the groundwork for organizing the CIO. As a union organizer, I made house calls to laundry workers in Harlem. Suspicion changed to a friendly welcome when I said I was from the union. I thanked the unknown Harlem Communists whose work had opened doors for the union.

As I remember it, fear of joining a union was not a big factor then. Workers were not afraid because the U.S. government backed their legal right to join a union. But some were concerned about the sincerity of the union leadership. "How do we know they won't sell us out?" they asked. "That depends on you," I replied. "Workers can keep control of the union by being active. Go to the meetings and be sure that your leaders do what you want." I left it at that and got some good vibes in return.

Union-Friendly Climate, the Right to Organize

The Wagner Act (National Labor Relations Act) was passed and signed by FDR in 1935. It guaranteed the right to join a union.[6] In the six months after the CIO was launched on November 10, 1935, one million workers joined unions. Mass meetings in organizing drives often opened with a reading of labor laws that secured workers' right to join unions. That's how we did it in the CIO's laundry workers' campaign.

There was a union-friendly climate in working class neighborhoods. Joining a union to get better conditions was the talk of the day. The CIO and the civil rights movement united to fight for the New Deal laws that make up our "safety net." In addition to Social Security and unemployment compensation, it included the Fair Labor Standards Act that brought us the 40-hour week and a ban on child labor. Also, the Wagner Act

---

[6] Richard O. Boyer and Herbert M. Morais, *Labor's Untold Story* (Pittsburgh: United Electrical, Radio and Machine Workers, 1965), 291–295.

for labor rights was key to union organizing. It is true that blood was shed in bitter battles such as the 1937 Memorial Day Massacre at Republic Steel in Chicago and the "little steel" mills in Ohio. Still, most strikes ended in victory, encouraging more workers to join unions.

The new CIO needed thousands of organizers. Fortunately, there were a large number of seasoned organizers, ready to help. They had been trained in the struggles of the unemployed. Many were Communists and Socialists who had organized the unemployed councils and the workers alliance. These organizers became foot soldiers for the CIO and helped sign up millions of new union members.

On my way to the laundry I was organizing, I used to pass small manufacturing plants. In those days, workers had an hour for lunch. To escape the hot, steamy air inside the factories, workers often ate their lunch outside, in hopes of catching a cooling breeze. Word spread that the laundry was being organized. More than once, as I passed, workers would run out of a plant and shout at me, "Hey, CIO girl! We want a union, too." I was touched by their support but I missed the full significance. Joining a union had become the popular thing to do. These workers believed they had the right to a union, and to the better life that a union could bring.

Community support was very helpful to me the one time I went back on the decision I made at age six, not to fight with my fists. I had a fat armful of union leaflets as I walked through a residential street close to a laundry. The boss was ready for me. One of his women stooges grabbed the leaflets out of my arms, taking me by surprise. I must have stood there for a moment with my jaw dropping. But only a moment. "I'm going to get those leaflets back," I decided. So I chased after her, grabbed my leaflets back. The next thing I knew, we were both on the ground. That hurt my dignity a little. But I had saved the leaflets. People looking out of the tenement windows applauded. That helped my dignity a lot.

When the summer ended, I did not go back to college. The union work was too important and too exciting. Tens of thousands of laundry workers had joined, and now they wanted their first contract. But the Bronx Laundry Owners Association

Join the CIO! Cartoon by Peggy Lipschutz

did not want to negotiate with the militant United Laundry Workers Union (ULWU). The owners association claimed that they would negotiate only with a "responsible" union. Evidently they thought a "responsible" union would give the owners a better contract deal than they could get from the ULWU-CIO.

Meanwhile, the Amalgamated Clothing Workers of America (ACWA) had been eyeing the tens of thousands of laundry workers we had organized. So a deal was struck between the owners and the ACWA. ACWA took over the ULWU in an unfriendly merger that the laundry organizers were powerless to stop. The ACWA had played a key role in organizing the CIO and often took progressive positions on national issues. However, they were run from the top down, sometimes with an iron fist. We were soon to feel that fist.

At first, the change seemed to better my condition as an organizer. ACWA raised my pay from $10 to $19 a week. I bought my first suit! Soon after, however, all of us organizers were laid off. ACWA said they were laying us off until after the coming union elections so that we would not "influence" the results. Cut off from the workers during the crucial weeks before the union elections, many of the organizers never worked in the laundry industry again.

For the elections, there were two opposing slates. The ACWA slate included popular inside workers recently put on full salary by ACWA. Not only were they taken out of their hard, hot jobs, but their pay went from the $15 per week laundry pay to $50 per week regular staff pay. Their staff jobs included the use of a union car. In those days, car ownership among inside laundry workers was rare. With their pay tripled and the use of a car, the new staffers' loyalty to the ACWA machine was assured. Our independent slate featured rank-and-file workers with a record of union activism. However, the independent slate did not fully reflect the diversity of the inside workers, mostly African American and Latino. The independents were not really organized as a caucus. I am not sure they even had a complete slate. Of course, the ACWA slate swept the elections. A more experienced unionist would not have been surprised at the results. But I was devastated.

Commercial Laundry Work

Shortly after the elections, ACWA told us organizers that the layoff was permanent. But that was not the end of my commitment to laundry workers. Out of a job, I went out to find work in a laundry. Jessie Taft told me to stand outside her plant on Monday morning. Some bosses hired from workers who "shaped up at the beginning of the week." I got the job, my first in a commercial laundry.

Women did most of the work inside the laundries. We worked ten-hour days at the beginning of the week and eight or nine hours the rest of the week. Most were women of color, African American and Puerto Rican. I had a turn at almost every job inside the laundry.

Laundry plants, whether large or small, were organized on similar lines. It began with the "drivers" who picked up bundles of dirty laundry from individual customers and brought their loads into the plant. Inside work started with the markers who wrote the customer's name or number on hidden areas, such as inside shirt collars. In later years, pre-printed labels were clipped into place. Markers also assorted the linens and clothing and stuffed them into nets of "whites, colored or delicate." Marking was relatively light work but dirty. You can imagine how dirty. Or perhaps you can't. Take my word for it—it was disgusting!

The nets of assorted clothes were sent to the "kitchen" for washing. This was the heaviest end of the work. Only big, strong men worked in the kitchen. They shoved the filled nets into large, industrial-type washers. The washed, wet bags of linens and clothing were very heavy. They were hard to pull out of the large machines and the pace was fast. On traditional wash days of Monday and Tuesday, 16 hours of work a day was expected. Often, the men would stay overnight in the plant Monday and Tuesday nights. They tried to catch whatever sleep they could, stretched out on bags of wash.

From the kitchen, the wet clothes were dumped into hollow "shaking" tables. The shakers, mostly women, would pick up each wet piece and shake it hard to smooth out the wrinkles. The piles of wet laundry were placed over a horizontal bar in front of a very large mangle. Shaking was muscularly hard, but clean and relatively unskilled. I kind of enjoyed the exercise when I was on that job.

At the mangle, two women fed the shaken clothes onto the hot rolling web. Each grabbed opposite ends of sheets and tablecloths. Smaller pieces were a challenge because mangle feeders had to quickly cover the mangle web with the small pieces. On the other side of the mangle were the receivers who had to be very fast. They grabbed the sheets and folded them in time to receive the next output. On the folding tables, orders were kept separate, to be wrapped and labeled.

I tried working on the mangle where the feeder must keep the mangle covered with clothes at all times. To feed through without wrinkles, clothes and linens had to be properly stretched out. The mangle had two speeds, slow and fast. I tried to keep up, but a coworker said, "Beatrice has two speeds: slow and stop." So I became a "sleeve girl" in the shirt press department. I could do that quite well as I rotated between the hot sleeve forms and the steaming presses.

Sleeve Girl—A Hot Job

Everything past the shaking table was hot, hotter and hottest. Some laundries had almost no ventilation. It was not rare for workers to faint. I especially remember one hot summer when I was working as a sleeve girl. I probably worked on that job in the fall and winter too. But it was the summer I remember because it was so hot. The laundry was housed in an old, commercial garage and employed about one hundred workers, mostly women. There was little natural ventilation and I don't remember any fans. When the outside temperature rose above a humid 100^0 F, it was probably a steamy 20 degrees higher inside.

The sleeve girl got the shirt from the pressers. The wet shirt went to the collar-and-cuff presser first, then the back presser, and last, the bosom presser. The presses were all close together, putting out steam each time they came down on a wet shirt. My operation was last before the shirt folders. I used two hands to grab the shirt from the bosom-presser's stand. Quickly, I positioned the shirt on top of the two sleeve-forms. My job was to force the sleeves over the hot forms. There was no way to do that but lean between the hot forms as I pushed the shirt down. The sleeves were already steaming and drying as I raised my head. Then I pulled the shirt off the hot sleeve-forms, put it on a hanger and hung it on a rack. Last I used the hook tool that hung around my neck to button the front. By that time another shirt would be waiting for me. I had to keep up.

The hottest and steamiest job was operating the presses. My job was a close second. But at least it was clean, unlike my earlier job of sorting the dirty clothes. Normally, I sweat less than most people. On the sleeve job the choice was sweat or die. Of course there were those who sweated *and* died or at least passed out. I learned a lot about cooling down. Wet cloths around the forehead cooled the head and kept the sweat from running into your eyes. Wet cloths around the neck felt really good. And it was amazing how wet cloths tied around each wrist helped.

Yet and still, the sweat rolled down my body, down my legs and into my shoes. Puddles of sweat in the shoes were a weird sensation. "You have to drink water," the other workers reminded me. But there was little time. Then the boss got magnanimous. He began to pass out *free* salt tablets. It was amazing how those tablets kept down the aches and cramps that had annoyed me on the job. Probably someone told the boss he would get more work out of us to more than make up for the *free* salt tablets.

Finally, I reached the top of my trade and became a shirt folder. Many of the shirt folders were men because it was piecework and they could earn more. The shirt folder ironed the yoke and sleeve areas that the presses did not reach. Then he/she folded the shirt around a cardboard and slipped it into a large envelope. Before I became a shirt folder, I used to marvel how shirt folders' feet moved in an unconscious dance although the folding was done with the hands and arms. Strange thing! When I became a shirt folder, my feet began to dance on their own. Somehow, moving the feet fast helped me move my hands fast. If the iron lingered too long on the touch up, the shirt would be scorched. I am afraid I scorched my share until I learned.

The piecework quota for the day was 300 shirts, and I made my quota. But some did 500! Much smaller women than I were producing more than I could, no matter how hard I tried. I was never sure why but suspected that I was less desperate. Perhaps it was because I was not supporting a family at that time and had only myself to worry about. The wolf did not howl quite so loudly outside my door.

Last, the packers put everything together. The drivers, who started the process, finished it by delivering the clean and ironed laundry to the customer. They were paid commissions and made more than the inside workers. Some thought of themselves as small businessmen, soliciting new customers and collecting for the laundry service. A few were accused of having sticky fingers and not turning in their full receipts. Most were honest and hard-working and became good union members. They were members of the same United Laundry Workers Union as the more numerous inside workers. Among the union officers, drivers were represented beyond their numbers. The drivers, almost all white, rarely socialized with the inside workers who were mostly African American and Puerto Rican. Union events, however, were well integrated.

Of Toilet Paper and Tea

On one of my jobs, I noticed that there was no toilet paper in the rest room. I remembered the story about Lenin, the Russian Communist leader, and the right to drink tea. Russian workers in grim, nineteenth century factories used to drink hot tea at work. It was their only relief during the 12-hour day of hard labor. At one plant, the boss ordered an end to drinking tea at work. Outraged, the workers pulled a wildcat strike and won back their right to drink tea. At the time, some organizers thought that tea was not an important issue. Lenin replied, "If the workers want to fight for tea, then you fight for tea!" That story inspired me to fight for toilet paper. I came storming out to the work floor shouting, "There's no toilet paper. We want toilet paper." The manager came running with some waxed wrapping paper. Dead serious as I was, I still had to laugh. Wax paper was so inappropriate. But there were times when poor toilet facilities were not a joke.

At another Bronx laundry where I worked one summer, there were two women's rest rooms. I was told they used to be segregated, one room for white (European), the other for black (African American). The company cleaned neither room. The "white" rest room became filthy. African American women workers cleaned the other room themselves. So the white women began to use the clean "black" rest room. That ended segregation. On my part, I cultivated a strong bladder and tried to minimize my use of the rest rooms at work. Still, the rest room offered a few minutes rest, a rare chance to sit down.

(At least that was true for us women.) In the laundries, there was no such thing as a rest break.

Looking for a more permanent job, I went to the ACWA hiring hall. New workers then had a two-week trial period during which the boss could fire you without cause. In three weeks I worked on five different jobs. For no reason at all I was "let go" at each of these jobs. On some I lasted only half a day. I thought I had it made on the last job because I lasted until Friday afternoon of the second week. But a few minutes before 5 p.m. the familiar call came, "Beatrice, you are wanted in the front office." I knew what was coming: "You're fired!"

I did not know why I was fired. The company did not have to give a reason. Perhaps I had been recognized as a former union organizer. Even worse, it was possible that ACWA had notified the company, "We sent you a troublemaker named Beatrice Shapiro. Fire her!" In either case, I was out of a job. So I decided to go back to school. Tuition was free at Hunter College. The free tuition at city colleges was a victory won by New York labor years ago. At the time, we took it for granted. The free tuition is now long gone and these colleges have become expensive. Even with free tuition, I needed money to live. Sadly, my mother had died that year, and my father could not keep the family's apartment. Butch, my boyfriend, helped me survive. He was an employed commercial artist, a good person and loyal to the Communist movement. We drifted apart later and I don't remember why—probably just not enough mutual attraction.

In February, 1939, I graduated from Hunter College. The Depression was still on and did not end for many workers until World War II. For most Hunter College graduates, who were then all women, the only jobs were sales clerk positions at Macy's. But I did not have the clothing for that kind of job. My family was still on welfare and could not help me. Laundry jobs were available but I was on the "Don't Hire" list in the Bronx. Then some comrades in Brooklyn invited me to come there for a job. Progressives had won the elections in Local 328, and the Left had maintained its leadership. Just to make sure that the "Don't Hire" list would not catch up with me, I used my mother's maiden name, Chernin.

Big Move to Brooklyn

As Beatrice Chernin I returned to my life as a laundry worker at 35 cents an hour. It paid the rent for my furnished room, bought food if I did not eat too much, and rare, essential purchases of clothing. Moving from the Bronx to Brooklyn was very traumatic. I joked that I needed a passport to move to Brooklyn. There were some big differences. I moved from a congested tenement house neighborhood to a neighborhood with some single homes with backyard gardens. I rented a furnished room from some comrades who shared the rent for a single-family house. I loved the backyard and still remember it fondly. However, looking back, I wonder why I thought living in Brooklyn would be such a big change. The laundry work was certainly the same.

My first Brooklyn job under Local 328 was at Spartan Laundry. I was immediately active in the union and soon elected to the shop committee. That laundry was a new union shop in a newly-organized industry. The CIO Laundry Workers Industrial Union had been organized just one year earlier. The union won us a small raise and a big change in working conditions. With the union contract, you had dignity on the job. You could not be fired for refusing to go out with the foreman. But life-preserving needs such as good ventilation and rest periods were not yet part of our demands. All the workers on that job were young. It was not a job you could get old on.

Kicking Out the Gangsters

After a few months at Spartan Laundry, I was able to move on to the big time, the Brighton Laundry. That was the local's largest plant with 500 workers. The progressive leaders of Local 328 encouraged rank and file leadership. Among the rank and file leaders were women who had stood up to the "mob" and had run them out of the old AFL union. I marveled at their courage. Rose Polio, just 20 years old, was an outstanding leader among these brave women. When she asked me to run for educational director of the local, I agreed. Our slate was elected, but not without a vote-counting struggle.

Counting of the paper ballots was disputed late into the night. Hundreds of ballots remained to be counted. The counters locked up the ballot box in a warehouse and we went home to sleep. That proved to be a big mistake. The next morning, counting resumed. Hundreds of the remaining ballots were disqualified. These ballots had been spoiled by marking an "X" for six instead of just five delegates to the executive board. The sixth "X" on each spoiled ballot was obviously marked with the same pencil, different from pencils used on the rest of the ballot. The conservative opposition claimed victory in the election of the executive board. We appealed and the election was set aside. Months later, the ballot tamperers freely admitted the fraud. In the pre-morning hours they had opened the wood ballot box, changed hundreds of ballots and resealed the box.

In July 1939, new Local 328 elections were held to replace the stolen election of February 1939. I was among those elected to the new local executive board, as the local's educational director. As officers of an ACWA local, we received invitations to some lavish union functions.

I remember a big dinner given by the ACWA. It was a sumptuous banquet, the likes of which I had never seen before. On the table among other goodies were trays of nuts. I could not help but think, "So this is what they mean when they speak of a big meal as everything from soup to nuts." It was our dues that were paying for the luxurious spread. "Couldn't they give us a nice meal without going to so much expense?" I wondered. Of course the event was in a fancy hotel. Whatever I thought it cost at the time, I realize now that it must have cost more than I could have imagined. I am sure that each meal cost more than my week's salary.

Jim Crow in Washington, DC

One of the great benefits of working with the laundry union was the comradeship I shared with coworkers, especially my union sisters. At the Brighton Laundry, we had a good group of union-conscious women. I was one of six who got the chance to go to Washington, DC. We were a Brighton

Laundry delegation to the American Youth Congress (AYC) meeting with Eleanor Roosevelt. The YCL was an active part of AYC and helped us voice our concerns to Mrs. Roosevelt. I don't remember how we got there, probably on an AYC bus. Nor do I remember Mrs. Roosevelt's speech although I have read about it in history books. What I remember, as though it happened yesterday, were the hideous Jim Crow practices we experienced in the nation's capital.

We six young laundry workers came to Washington expecting an exciting time. We left after work and arrived in D. C. after dark. Of course we were tired but in high spirits. We were three African Americans and three of European descent. The Washington cab drivers were segregated so we hailed an African American cab driver. All six of us squeezed into his cab. Naturally, we did not have any hotel reservations. I had never stayed in a hotel. Probably my comrades were just as inexperienced. We asked the driver to take us to a reasonable hotel. It was in the white section of town. The hotel clerks looked at our mixed group and said, "No room." So we tried another hotel. And another. It was getting late. We were tired and frustrated. The driver said, "I can take three of you to one hotel and three to another." We did not agree. We refused to split up.

Finally the driver said, "Look, I can take you to a settlement house where you can all get rooms." The settlement house was in an African American neighborhood, and they took us in without question. We were very grateful; we had succeeded in staying together. The next morning we were invited to breakfast. What a glorious breakfast! It included delicious macaroni and cheese and fried apples, a new breakfast experience for me. All the standard items were also included: orange juice, bacon, scrambled eggs and home-made biscuits. We left fortified to listen to Mrs. Roosevelt on the White House lawn. On our return to Brooklyn, we felt even closer to each other and more united.

I had one other brush with the brutal reality of Jim Crow in our nation's capital. It was harder to take because I was alone and on a difficult mission. In the Bedford-Stuyvesant neighborhood of Brooklyn, I met William, a comrade from British

The business agent and shop committee of the Brighton Laundry. They won praise of officers for their good work for the union

Author, far left, with Brighton Laundry union committee

Guyana. He was sweet, poetic, romantic and perhaps a bit too good looking. We were sincerely in love for almost two years. There was just one problem. From time to time, he would come late to our dates, very late, hours late. The story would always be the same. He had been deep in a vital political discussion with a friend and lost track of the time. The discussion had always been aided by a bottle of something alcoholic. Sadly and reluctantly I realized that we could not go through life together with alcohol in the way. And so I told him, with affection but finality that we had to split up. Unfortunately, he had just been drafted.

William was sent to, or near, Washington, DC. He wrote a letter to me as though nothing had happened. Before he went overseas, I had to make clear that we had split. But I did not want to send a "Dear John" letter. Hard as it was, I thought I should go to Washington and do it in person. In Washington, I tried to get a taxi to take me to the address William had given me. First off, the taxis were still segregated. You either had to get a taxi for "whites" or a taxi for "colored." I was already upset by my delicate mission. There was a war on. African Americans and whites were giving their lives for democracy. And the capital city of our country was still segregated! That made me really upset. When I met William, he did not want to hear what I had to say. Perhaps it would have been kinder to lie but I could not do that. I saw William again, years later, at some national meeting of the CPUSA. By that time we were both married to somebody else. To my surprise, William asked, "Why did you break up with me?" He never got it.

Fighting for Union Democracy

The *Daily Worker* had extensive labor news coverage. That gave us some idea of what was going on outside our local union. But most of the time, we were entirely wrapped up in the fight around our local issues. However, what we could do locally was severely limited by national developments. In June 1940, the Smith Act passed, providing long jail terms for those allegedly "teaching and advocating the overthrow of the United States government by force and violence." The Act was part of a witch hunt against the Left but had bigger game in its sights. The main target of the red baiters was the Roosevelt administration and its labor-friendly legislation.

In later years, the Act was declared unconstitutional, but not before Communist leaders had spent years in federal prisons for "conspiring to teach ...." In 1940, the witch-hunters were stoking the fires. Those flames spread to our local and changed everything. Although the red baiters' fires were temporarily banked after the bombing of Pearl Harbor, those evil flames would be lit again after the war.

Since Local 328 was under attack by the ACWA machine as well as by the bosses, we had to fight for union democracy. When the "International" appointed our delegates to the New York State CIO convention, we were indignant. The union constitution called for election of delegates. We called an emergency Local 328 membership meeting. It was the evening before the convention. That night we elected our own convention delegates. I was one of those elected. We were not concerned that the convention site was over 300 miles away, in Rochester. But we had to get there before 10 a.m. so we could challenge the seating of the appointed delegates. Four laundry drivers and I left right from the Local 328 meeting.

The highway to Rochester went through the Adirondack Mountains. It was very foggy in the mountains, but we could not afford to slow down or wait for the fog to lift. In those days, cars had running boards. With a man on each running board to watch the road, and the driver peering through the windshield to see through the fog, we pushed on. They took turns driving. I was no help because I did not know how to drive. In fact, I remember only one inside laundry worker who owned a car. By morning, we came out of the mountains and the sun came out.

We reached Rochester just as the convention opened. The only open seats were in the back of the hall. We were barely seated when the motion was made to accept the credentials report. I had to act fast. "I object," I screamed. The convention was stunned. Screaming at the top of my then-strong voice, I strode down the aisle, shouting, "We were elected by a local membership meeting last night, according to our constitution. We demand to be seated! The delegates sent by ACWA were appointed, not elected by us."

I must have been a sight. No sleep all night, long hair streaming, shabbily dressed and couldn't care less and all of 21 years old. Bet my eyes were blazing. There was some kind of discussion on the floor. Before we knew what was happening, Mike Quill of the transport union was leading a huge crowd of delegates out of the hall to an already prepared meeting place. Evidently, a similar issue of union democracy was playing out on a state scale. But I will admit that I did not really know what was going on at the state level or inside other unions. Our focus was on our own Local 328 and our own fight for union democracy. Still, we Local 328 delegates felt quite heroic. At least I did.

Shortly after the convention, the ACWA leadership decided to rid themselves of the "troublemakers" of Local 328. In March 1941, charges were placed against our business agents Michael Coleman and George McGriff who were suspended, pending "trial." I worked closely with Michael Coleman but regret that I had little chance to interact with George McGriff, an African American business agent. McGriff was part of our rank and file leadership, but his shops were in an area of Brooklyn that I did not know.

The ACWA sent in enough staff with enough money to take the local over. They called a membership meeting after work that was not like any I had ever attended. Earlier membership meetings were attended by members who came on their own. They came because they had something to say or just wanted to know what was going on.

This meeting was different. Hundreds of workers had been bused in to the meeting by ACWA staff. The tactic was to shout down any supporters of the suspended business agents. I looked at these sister and fellow workers, low paid and overworked like the rest of us. What could I say that would reach them? This was worse than the Third Avenue El screeching overhead when the YCL held outdoor meetings. My first words had to win their interest. I shouted something like, "We're all here because our wages are too low and we can't pay our bills." The room quieted and for a couple of minutes people listened. "And it's too damned hot at work. Why can't they put some fans in?" Then the signal was given and the shouts and jeers started up again. Probably these workers were hungry and wanted to go to the free dinner they were promised after the meeting. That was another lesson for me in union politics.

The next step against Local 328 leaders was to put us on trial as "Communists." The "red scare" was an old weapon used against unions. The union organizing drives of 1919 had been followed by the Palmer raids of January 2, 1920. In the dead of night, the FBI arrested 10,000 in 70 cities. They were largely members of unions, many of them union officers. They, too, were charged with being Communists. Many were beaten, even tortured. Although over 80% were later released without charge, the repression set unions back 15 years. Unfortunately, some national union leaders gave in to the pressure of an early type of "McCarthyism."

Trial Lawyer—A New Experience

In April of 1941 the trial of our local officers was held before a committee representing the General Executive Board of the Amalgamated Clothing Workers. The committee of three included Jacob Potofsky and Frank Rosenblum, the top ACWA leadership, excluding only Sidney Hillman, We knew that the trial was a formality. The verdict was already written. Still, we wanted to make the most of any democratic opening available to us. We decided to be represented by one person to make a unified defense. Our "lawyer" had to be a member of the union. To my surprise, I was chosen. I would have chosen Julius Halpern, a more experienced leader. Perhaps our group thought a young shop worker would best represent our cause. While I felt honored to be chosen, I was worried. My only model of a lawyer was Perry Mason of the movies. He always won his cases by pulling a big surprise during the trial. What big surprise could I spring when the only "charge" against us was membership in the Communist Party?

Indeed, we did not go down without a fight. In a chilling preview of the McCarthy period, ACWA had bought some "witnesses." One was a driver who had been a personal friend as well as a comrade. For the sake of his descendants who may be honorable people, I will not mention his name. Some drivers used to get into trouble by spending their receipts on gambling, alcohol, or girlfriends. Then they would come up short when they had to settle their accounts with the owner of the laundry. We did not know that our friend was in trouble until ACWA put him on the stand. Later we learned that he had a gambling problem. He faced criminal prosecution, or at the very least firing, for not turning over money collected for laundry he delivered.

I did not do a "Perry Mason" type "turning of the screw" and expose his motive for testifying. I did not ask him what he had been promised in exchange for his "testimony," perhaps because that would not have been "nice." More likely, I didn't think of it. When he testified that he attended a Communist Party school and fingered other attendees, I asked him, "What did they teach you?" That seemed to make him squirm the most. He had to talk about work to strengthen the union and the fight for peace and against fascism.

The long and short of it was that they upheld the suspension of the officers and executive board of Local 328. As described in ACWA's *Advance*, the trial committee found that the "local

was under the complete domination of a small group of officers who respected only the policy and discipline of the Communist Party." We were expelled and the driver kept his job.
If he lost his boss's money again by betting on the horses, we
were not around for him to sell us out to save his skin.

What should we do? We held a very tense meeting of the
deposed officers and our close supporters. The members
still supported us. Should we split off, form an independent union and continue to fight for the membership? Older
leaders argued against this course. In principle, we oppose
dual unionism, they argued. From the practical viewpoint,
the laundry contracts were with the ACWA. If we split off, the
employers would declare the contracts null and void. We had
carried the fight as far as we could, some among us argued.
Then Rose, one of the Italian women who had founded Local
328, asked, "We stood up to the gangsters and drove them out.
What was the use of all of our fighting if it ends like this? Was
it all a waste of time?"

That question made us go back to basics. No, we agreed, it
was not a waste of time. We had won better conditions. Workers
had learned a lot about organizing. Some had learned to look
beyond their particular boss to see that exploitation was rooted
in the capitalist system. They could change bosses, but exploitation would continue. The whole system had to be changed.
That's why we wanted socialism, a system where key industries would be owned by the people and run by the workers.

Pearl Harbor Bombed

On December 7, 1941, the Japanese bombed the American
Fleet at Pearl Harbor. The United States was at war! To defeat
the Berlin-Rome-Tokyo axis, the U.S. became an ally of Great
Britain and the USSR. Red-baiting witch hunts were halted;
the government concentrated on stopping fascism and winning World War II. Despite undemocratic actions such as
our expulsion, ACWA leadership took progressive positions
on many issues. Frank Rosenblum and Jacob Potofsky were
staunch supporters of the war against fascism. Over the years,
I have had to work with more than one of their type.

Personally, I got over the expulsion of the democratically elected leaders of our union local. But one remark I neither forgot nor forgave. As our trial ended, Rosenblum took me aside and said, "Why are you so involved with politics? At your age, you should be thinking of getting married!"

Chapter 8

Working in a Machine Shop
What counts is winning the fight against racism.

Expulsion from the laundry workers' union meant expulsion from the industry, since we had won a union shop. Jessie Taft, my mentor in the laundry union, found a way to stay in the industry by working in non-union shops. Then she organized those plants. But most of the Communist laundry workers moved out to different industries. Perhaps many would have left the laundries anyway, as jobs opened up during World War II. I lost track of Jessie but asked about her a couple years later. "Oh, she married one of our best railroad comrades," a friend told me. Jessie Taft had become Jessie Smith. For many decades, Jessie Smith led the fight for tenants' rights in New York City. Rose Polio married Michael Coleman but that marriage did not last. I am sure that our brave Rose made her way in some other industry.

Although the war in Europe was increasing the demand for American products, factory jobs were still hard to get. I got one little job after another. I worked one week in a hat factory, another week in a pocketbook factory. It was amazing to me how much glue was used for those products. For a couple of weeks, I operated a machine that stitched together an endless cotton tape with a similar metalized tape. The end product was used to make wrappers for permanent wave curlers. Although the sewing machine had automatic feed, it was very low tech. As it was stitched, I pulled the tape forward about five feet and cut it. Then I ran back fast to catch the next length. The job was very athletic. I didn't mind; I just did not like the low pay.

Another little job was at the Eagle Pencil factory in Brooklyn. In one way it was easy. You sat on the job. I thought it was a luxury to sit on the job. I had not even realized that you could sit down and be paid. But it was hard enough in other ways. Our workday was nine hours. Of course, there were no coffee breaks. Coffee breaks as well as weekends off were victories won later by the unions. We just worked straight through until it was time for lunch. What if you had to go to the bathroom before lunch? You had to first check the lights. Above the bathroom door were three lights, one for each toilet stall. If the lights were all on, you were not supposed to go in. Each time a woman went into the ladies room she was supposed to turn a light on; then turn it off as she left.

The first time I used the factory bathroom, all three lights were out. I turned on one light and entered. To my surprise, I found the bathroom full of women and the air was full of cigarette smoke. Women had slipped in without turning on a light. They were taking a badly needed break. "Did you turn on a light?" the women demanded, as I walked in. "I'll never do that again," I promised.

Drill Press Operator

More jobs were opening up because of military orders. Finally, I landed a job at Dictograph, a Queens machine shop. They made Dictaphones, an early type of voice recorder. The skills needed to do the work were learned on the job. My first job was to hammer in small nails on terminal boards. After a full day's work, often more than eight hours, a person learns to hit the nail instead of the thumb. But at first the thumb took a lot of hits.

From hammering terminal boards, I moved on to the drill press department. For months on end, I drilled a hole through the head of steel bolts, all of the same type. The bolts were labeled "secret," but that was a joke. What could be secret about a bolt? By coincidence, I came across those bolts again on a later job. The bolt attached a label to radar training equipment. At that time, radar was "secret." But the bolts?

Eventually, the bolt order was filled at the machine shop. Then I was given telephone handsets to drill. They were molded of some plastic material. The technique was different from drilling steel. The molded material was delicate, easily fractured. I had to feel my way with the drill to avoid hairline cracks that would spread later. So I was careful. Working all day with no breaks except for lunch, I produced about 2,000 handsets. The coffee break had not yet been won for industrial workers. It was not yet one of our demands.

We had a big, mean, male foreman who did not know how to speak respectfully to the young women he supervised. If he had something to say to me, he would read out the number on my badge. "Number one thousand two hundred five, come here!" That got on my nerves. The work itself was monotonous. A robot could do it and today robots do such jobs. Calling me by my number just emphasized that for him, I was just a tool, not a person. One day I blew my top and told him as I jabbed at the name on my badge, "I have a name. Call me by my name, not my number!" So you could say the foreman and I did not get along.

The foreman decided that 2,000 headsets were not enough. He told me that I would have to produce more, or else. Dictograph was a union shop, so he did not spell out the "or else." But I was doing a good job, my very best. Didn't that foreman know that this was delicate work that could not be rushed?

I was angry. The juices began to flow in my body and I threw all caution to the winds. Grab the handset, bring the drill down, bear down on the drill, and put the handset in the box. Get a new handset, bring the drill down and repeat. The angrier I got the faster I worked. By the end of the day I had drilled 5,000!

The next day word reached me that the handsets had cracked. They never told me how many so I assumed it was all 5,000. I felt vindicated, although I hated the idea of so much waste. The foreman never said another word to me on the subject. He moved me to another department and I was out of his control. But I bet he never rushed another drill press operator doing a delicate job.

Punch Press Department

At the other end of the plant was the punch press department. Only men worked there. There was a war against fascism to win and I wanted to do more on the job. So I asked for a transfer to the punch presses. Even for 1941, those were ancient machines. To bring the press down to cut metal, the operator had to stand in front of the press and then grab both levers, one in each hand, and press down with his full weight. In a way, it was a macho job because it took strength. Needing both hands was a safety thing, I guess. It kept your hands out of the way when the cutting tools came down. But why was the press so hard to bring down?

I truly enjoyed that job, even ten hours of it. It gave my muscles a good workout, and I was keeping up with the men. The men considered the machines dangerous. Sometimes the presses repeated and came down on their own. The press was intended to cut metal but it could also chop off fingers or perhaps a whole hand. After two weeks, the men decided they did not want me there. They called my attention to a man who walked outside the plant almost every day at lunch time. "He used to work here," my co-workers told me. "One day the press came down on his hand and he lost four fingers." As I watched the injured worker, he seemed to lean to one side as he walked. "That's probably the side where he lost all those fingers," I thought.

The men in the punch press department could not stand the thought that I might lose my fingers. They asked the company to transfer me to another department. I did not fight the decision. To tell the truth, I, too, could not stand the thought that I might lose my fingers. The guys had been good union buddies. Otherwise, I might have fought their decision on principle. And perhaps I no longer enjoyed leaving work with all my muscles sore.

That's when I got my desire, a job in the lathe department. True, it was only on a milling machine, but the lathes were nearby. Perhaps, if I were lucky, they would let me learn. My buddy, Lois, had been hired after me. But she was ahead of me on the milling machines and "broke me in." My friendship with Lois helped me enjoy my all-too-short stay in the lathe department.

Hiring Lois signaled a victory for our union, known as UE, then short for United Electrical, Radio and Machine Workers of America–CIO. The company had been under pressure from the union to integrate their all-white work force. When FDR created the Fair Employment Practices Committee (FEPC) by executive order on June 25, 1941, it was a response to this type of community and labor pressure. It was also a practical measure because the large army draft was creating a shortage of labor.

At an earlier union meeting, a motion had been made to demand that the company hire African Americans. To my horror, there was a lot of opposition. It was a very tense scene. I was astounded when the maker of the motion, a union officer and comrade, withdrew the motion. "Why did you withdraw the motion?" I hotly demanded, after the meeting. "Well we wanted to prevent a negative vote. We could not afford to have the local go on record against integration. Next month, we will make sure that our supporters come to the meeting. Then we will make the motion again, when we will be sure of winning."

Peggy Lipschutz, Labor Education Fund

I learned a lesson that day that was never covered in any book on parliamentary procedure. I learned that what counts is not a "heroic" minority going on record for a principle, even if it leads to a defeat. What counts is winning the fight, in this case, the fight against racism. For the next meeting, the union leaders made a big effort to get the membership out. They had also done more to educate members on the need for unity. The motion to demand the hiring of African Americans won big.

When I left that machine shop, I took with me a lot that I had learned. Besides the many lessons in organizing, I developed some mechanical skills that were useful on future jobs. With World War II raging in Europe, the demand for labor had increased. Finally, my college degree meant something. I found a job as a junior electronics engineer. Technical work kept me employed for the next 20 years. In later years I would urge students not to give up their studies just because the job scene was discouraging. Learn! It may be useful later.

Chapter 9

Defense Worker in World War II
World War II could have been prevented.

Producing to Win the War

MY next job was titled "Junior Radio Engineer" at Emerson Radio. I moved to an apartment which I shared with some friends. The apartment was a short walk to Emerson Radio. Believe it or not, I woke up at 7:30 a.m., took a shower, dressed, ran a few blocks and punched in by 8 a.m. Then I spent a couple of minutes in the washroom to really comb my hair. Next, I ran down to the first floor coffee shop for a donut and milk. After that I was ready for a long day's work. We put in a lot of overtime, helping to win the war.

Yes, the U.S. was at war and the U.S. and USSR had become allies. That was after the Japanese attack on Pearl Harbor, December 7, 1941, and the Nazi invasion of the Soviet Union six months earlier. While the war was on, the U.S. government stopped its repression of the Communist Party. We laughed at the experience of one of my friends. The FBI had done one of its investigations on her. They asked her neighbor if they had seen anything suspicious going on in her apartment. "Oh no," the neighbor replied. "She is a good woman. She is a member of the Communist Party!"

American Communists were passionate about winning the war against fascism. As many as 10,000 volunteered for military service. More than a few died in battle. I could add to the list of comrades killed in World War II, those who died in Spain. In many ways, as I wrote earlier, the Spanish Civil War was the opening battle of World War II.

In the U.S., there were some who thought we were on the wrong side in World War II. To them, nothing was more important than destroying Communism and defeating the Soviet Union. The fact is that for three years, the Soviets were left to fight the Nazis alone on the ground in Europe. Not until the Normandy Beach invasion, June 6, 1944, did the U.S. and England open a Second Front in Europe. Every day that the Second Front was delayed increased the death toll.

I felt that I was helping to win the war by working in a defense industry. Could I say I was qualified to work in an electronics lab? Well, I had two hands, two eyes and I knew what a resistor was. The test they gave me was minimal. At the time I was hired, I knew almost nothing about electronics. Probably my machine shop experience was more important than my college degree in preparing me to be a model maker. But I had a willing heart and I learned quickly.

Working from a circuit diagram, the model maker built "bread-board" models for new electronic instruments. It was up to us to build a working model, starting with sheet metal and the parts. We had the run of the machine shop to bend the sheet metal to form a chassis, punch out holes for tube sockets and drill holes for screws and terminal strips. Then we mounted the tube sockets and terminal strips and wired and soldered the resistors, coils and condensers. This was before the days of printed circuits and transistors.

Organizing with UE

United Electrical Workers Union, UE, was organizing Emerson Radio. They had signed up most of the factory workers. The need for a union was easy to see. The company was making lots of profit guaranteed by the federal government. Still, they did not want to pay the workers a living wage. UE had not tried to organize the engineers, but they were willing to let us join. I had already negotiated a raise for myself. I hated having to do it on my own, but the war gave me some leverage. Emerson Radio hired me at 50 cents an hour. In two weeks I proved that I could do the job. So I went in to ask for a raise. "How much do you want," management asked. "One dollar an hour," I answered. The manager exclaimed, "That's double your pay!" But I would not budge and he gave in. All the other lab workers were underpaid, too. Henry, the engineer who was my project manager, liked the idea of being in a union. I believe he was making a big $50 a week as a graduate engineer. Together, we organized the department. The big day came when our negotiating committee went in to bargain for our first union contract. Henry and I represented engineering. To our surprise and disappointment, management refused to include the engineers in the contract. I can still see the big boss (I guess nowadays we would say CEO) giving this cynical excuse. "How can you include the engineers?" he said so smugly. "Engineers deal with intangibles!" For whatever reason, UE did not press the issue and we were left out. If we in engineering wanted a union, we would have to organize our own. That was our plan.

I hope the Emerson engineers did win union recognition. About that time, I gave in to my wanderlust and left the city. I had seldom wandered further from the Bronx than Brooklyn, except for a summer job at Camp Unity. But I had always wanted to travel. As a teenager, I had even hitch-hiked to Washington, DC for a youth rally one winter. I remember freezing in the rumble seat of a car for the three-hour drive. But basically, I seldom got out of the city.

Moving to Buffalo

It seemed the only way I could get to see more of the country was to move out of New York City. During World War II, when jobs were easy to get, I had the chance to relocate. "Go to Rochester, New York," some friends advised. Moving was easy. I packed my one suitcase, tied together my stack of books, and got on the train. I left behind my father, my brother Max and many friends. My brother Leon was already in the Merchant Marine, dodging the torpedoes.

It was my brother Leon who persuaded me to stay out of the armed forces. I told him I was considering enlisting. He told me, from what he had seen in Europe, women enlistees were just "officer fodder." During World War II, women were not used in combat. I did not mind being in a supporting service, but not that kind of service. Later I learned that Leon did not tell me the full story. Servicewomen in World War II made an important contribution to the Allied victory. My brother was just trying to keep me safe.

In Rochester, the Communist Party network found me a place to stay. I applied for work at Eastman Kodak, the main employer in town. At that time Kodak was non-union although unions had wide support in Rochester. Kodak offered me a job as an apprentice lens grinder at 50 cents an hour. I was excited about learning how to grind lenses. Rochester also seemed to be a pleasant city to live in. But I had left a job in New York City paying $1 per hour. So I decided to take the bus to Buffalo to see if I could do better there.

Buffalo, New York, was a hard-working industrial city with a lot to offer during World War II. The city described itself in business magazine ads as enjoying four seasons. Buffalonians put it another way: "Buffalo has two seasons, fourth of July and winter." In terms of weather, there was little to choose between Buffalo and Rochester. Both had harsh winters. Once in Buffalo, I applied at Colonial Radio, later part of Sylvania. They were making transmitters for the military. I was hired at once as a "junior engineer" at $1 an hour. That left me with little choice. I hopped back on a bus to Rochester. All my personal belongings went back into my medium-sized suitcase. Once again, I tied a rope around my books and grabbed it with my left hand. My right hand grabbed the suitcase. I was ready to relocate again.

I had wisely relocated to Buffalo in the summer time, when "the living was easy." But even in the summer, I had trouble understanding Buffalo weather. It took me many months, perhaps years, to remember that the temperature might be 80 degrees Fahrenheit in the daytime but could drop to 40 at night. I was often the only one on Main Street shivering in a sleeveless cotton dress at night. Everyone else, with any brains, was comfortably covered in a warm jacket. I had also heard about Buffalo winters, when cars and buses got stuck in the snow and everyone had to walk the remaining miles to home. That did not happen in my first year in town. Luckily, my first Buffalo winter was unusually mild. The next few winters gave me a good taste of the snow and ice that marked Buffalo's main season.

Bedbugs!

The Communist Party had an office in downtown Buffalo. That was my first stop. I could leave my suitcase there, look in the newspaper for "Rooms to Rent," and go out to get a room. I found a room on Porter Avenue near the Rainbow Bridge to Canada. Back at the Party office, I met a lot of interesting people. Although I had to report early the next morning for the new job, I stayed out late that night. Meeting people seemed more important to me than sleep. Tired and excited, I went to my new room, snuggled beneath the clean linens to get a few hours of sleep. But that was not to be. I felt one sharp stab and then another and said to myself, "Stop imagining things. Go to sleep." But then there was another and still another. I jumped up, quickly turned on the light and my worst fears materialized. The bed was full of bed bugs. Here and there were the telltale streaks of blood, my blood from the fresh bites.

Now there are some people who can sleep through bed bug bites. Bed bugs were then very common in New York City apartments, even in some high-rent areas. I know from experience. Unfortunately, their bites raise big welts on my body and I cannot ignore them. In my parents' apartment, we used to take the coil spring off the bed and doused it in turpentine. We even burned each coil with a match. But the bugs came back! In despair, I dragged some hard kitchen chairs into the living room. It was a hard bed, but the bugs didn't care for it either. Without the bugs I could get some sleep. But I had not expected biting bugs on Porter Avenue, then a rather nice street. What to do? I did need a couple of hours sleep and I could not get it there. So I packed my suitcase, shaking each piece of clothing to dislodge any traveling bugs. Then I headed downtown on the bus to the Ford Hotel and rented a room for about $2.50.

Junior Radio Engineer

The next morning, I hopped a bus north to Colonial Radio and went right to work. I was given a standard transmitter to take from test booth to test booth. The booths were operated by civilian inspectors employed by the army. My job was called "correlations," to make sure all the meters read the same, booth to booth. The army didn't seem to care if they had the correct readings, just that they all read the same. The transmitter weighed about 50 pounds. This was before miniaturization. As a woman, I felt I had to prove my strength. I declined the use of a dolly to wheel the transmitter around. Instead, I carried the heavy instrument chest-high to all the test booths. Maybe that's why I have a bad back now.

I tried but never succeeded in becoming active in the UE local at the plant. Most of my organizing work then was in the community. Hattie Lumpkin was my mentor for community work. We used to go door to door canvassing together. She was just so warm and so smart and so rooted in the community. After working with Hattie for a few months, I felt I had been in Buffalo for years. She had an open door policy in her home. Her house at 263 Watson Street was the center for community activists and Communists. Only two of her ten children had moved out and they lived just one or two blocks away. Cousins who had moved to Buffalo lived with her, too. Her daughter, Jonnie, became my best friend.

Win the War!—Our Priority

The first goal of the Communists in Buffalo, as elsewhere in the U.S., was winning the war against fascism. That was also the goal of the U.S. government. Winning the war was an all-class issue. There was supposed to be equality of sacrifice. What did the bosses sacrifice? Nothing! War contracts for companies were on a cost plus basis. The more the companies charged the military for their products, the greater the profit. The workers were making all the sacrifices. It was our men and women who were being killed in Europe and the Pacific. On the home front, we workers were patriotic, working as hard as we could while the companies made the profits. Meat, butter and sugar were rationed; wages and prices were frozen. Prices of necessities kept edging upward but wages stayed frozen. The class struggle never stopped but the union's hands were tied. Most unions honored the no-strike pledge for the duration of the war.

During World War II, the tax burden was largely shifted from the wealthy to the workers. Before World War II, very few workers paid federal income tax. The amount of income exempt from tax was relatively higher than it is now. Only one of my friends, an engineer, ever paid income tax. Now, even minimum wage workers have to pay income tax. On the positive side, labor made important gains during the war. Membership increased, and huge inroads were made against racism and sexism. There was practically no unemployment.

The fight against racism in the U.S. was one of the greatest contributions by the Communists towards winning the war. They had pioneered in the fight against racism in the '20s and '30s. In World War II, racism stood in the way of winning the war against fascism. To begin with, racism weakened the U.S. armed forces, still segregated in World War II. A segregated military, by definition, prevented millions of people of color from making their full contribution to winning the war.

I learned about the racism rampant in the U.S. Army from my friends, the Lumpkins. Racism endangered the life of Ozzie Lumpkin, one of Hattie's sons. When Ozzie was fighting in Europe, a German woman pointed Ozzie out and claimed that he had raped her. African American soldiers were being hanged every day on that kind of charge, according to Jonnie. Ozzie was saved only because his company commander came forward and said that Ozzie had not left the company at any time.

Jonnie Lumpkin, Fighting Racism at Bell Aircraft

On the production front at home, African Americans and other people of color had been kept out of many industries, especially those that paid a living wage. Those racist barriers had to be torn down. A serious shortage of labor had resulted from the drafting of millions of workers. The only way to relieve that shortage was to open industrial jobs to people of color and to women. In response to the emergency, President Franklin D. Roosevelt created the Fair Employment Practices Commission (FEPC). Fair employment became a requirement for federal contracts. Enforcement was often lax. My sister-in-law-to-be, Jonnie Lumpkin, led the fight at Bell Aircraft.

Bell Aircraft had assigned Jonnie to sweeping. The white women hired at the same time were given assembly jobs in production. Jonnie noticed that all of the African Americans at the plant were doing janitorial work. So she went to the United Auto Workers officers and told them, "Put me on production!" The chief steward told her, "Well, put on this steward's button, sign up members in the union, and give me their $1 initiation fee. Here's a contract. If a member has a complaint, write up the grievance, and we'll fight it." As Jonnie tells it:

> Black folks were eating outside at the railroad tracks. White folks ate inside at the lunchroom. One day the national anthem was played in the lunchroom and all the whites stood up. The blacks outside did not stand. So they called me in to ask why we didn't stand. I told them, "That's not my flag. The government's never done anything for black people."

By this time, Jonnie had joined the Young Communist League. She turned to them for advice on how to fight discrimination at Bell Aircraft. She also got support from the Buffalo Urban League and the NAACP. Letha Cloare of FEPC came to the meeting Jonnie organized. As Jonnie described it:

> So we set up a conference with the company about the segregated dining room and the failure to put blacks on production jobs. The company denied everything, but Letha Cloare stopped them. She knocked them dead, saying, "I'm as black as Jonnie. I've seen what's going on." (Cloare had a light complexion.) The next day 140 black workers were upgraded to production jobs. They put me in the gun room, me and seven southern whites.[7]

---

[7] Beatrice Lumpkin, *Always Bring a Crowd* (New York: International Publishers Co., 1999), 49.

The fight that Jonnie led against discrimination was part of the fight for the "Double V." The slogan was, "Victory against Fascism Abroad and Victory against Racism at Home." The entry of African Americans and Latinos into many industries was a gain that lasted years. Today, it is an endangered victory. Plant closings have hurt all workers but especially African Americans and Latinos. From what I see in Illinois and Indiana, African Americans are a much smaller percentage of the steel work force than from 1942 to 1980.

Full Employment and the "Work Ethic"

With full employment during the war, a previously unknown period of job and income security was sustaining working class Buffalo. Once racist barriers were lowered, job seekers, including the disabled, could find work. At Colonial Radio, in the women's washroom, I heard a worker say the unthinkable: "I hope the war lasts long enough so I can pay off my home." The other women moved away from her in horror and disgust. Most had friends and relatives risking their lives in combat. That incident made me feel very sad. Capitalism was a rotten system; it took a world war to provide jobs.

Full employment in World War II also knocked to bits some of the mistaken ideas about "work ethic." Unemployed workers had been criticized as lacking a good work ethic. During World War II, people who had been unemployed most of their lives made a complete change when they got a job at union wages. Consider my own experience. When I worked in laundries, I often took a day off to rest. I made so little money that it did not make that big a difference. But as soon as I started to make a living wage, I never took a day off from work. It would mean losing too much from my pay check.

The Atom Bomb

On September 2, 1945, the war officially ended, leaving 100 million dead according to some estimates. Vast lands were devastated. On V-J Day, we danced in the streets for joy that the killing had ended. We felt hopeful that a new era of peace had begun. But news reached us of a new weapon that the U.S. had dropped on Japan just before the war ended. We did not realize that our government had committed a horrible crime. I am ashamed to say that I believed Truman when he said the bombs were needed to end the war. It was years before we learned that Japan had already sent out peace feelers before the atom bombs were dropped. In fact, many say that the Cold War began with the dropping of atom bombs on Hiroshima and Nagasaki. As Curtis MacDougall explained in 1965:

> Few Americans ever learned that the Japanese government had sent peace feelers to the United States eight months before the bomb was dropped. Little by little, some Americans began to question the motives for dropping the atomic bombs. Robert R. Young claimed that the motive for the bombing was to put pressure on the Soviet Union. He was Chairperson of the Board of the Chesapeake & Ohio Railroad when he wrote this analysis: "We are kidding ourselves if we believe the atomic bomb was dropped [only] on Japan. There is evidence that fully eight months earlier, Japan was ready to capitulate. If the purpose of the bomb was to save American lives, then a fair warning before Okinawa would have saved more. ... No, the atomic bomb was dropped not militarily but diplomatically upon Russia."[8]

The political geography changed after World War II. In many countries, the people wanted socialism. Eastern Europe and China were able to move out of the capitalist orbit. Most African nations had won their political independence by 1960. But Western and Southern Europe seemed stuck with capitalism. That was true even though Communists had been

---

[8] Curtis D. McDougall, *Gideon's Army* (New York: Marzani & Munsell, 1965), 25. McDougall quotes from article by Robert R. Young in the *Saturday Review of Literature*, March 4, 1947.

the heroes of French and Italian resistance against the Nazi occupation. I wondered why French and Italian workers had not moved toward changing the capitalist system. Some friends from Italy explained it to me: no change of system was possible with the U.S. Army stationed in Western Europe.

Israel Established as a Jewish State

In 1905, the Zionist solution to oppression of the Jews was to leave Europe and the U.S. and go to Palestine. In contrast, my parents believed in fighting for democracy in Byelorussia, right where they were. They worked to bring about a revolution to get rid of the Czar. Their inspiration was the American Revolution that freed the American colonies from British rule. Unfortunately, the 1905 Revolution against the Czar went down to bloody defeat. My father, the revolutionary, was thrown into jail as I described earlier. After the revolution was lost, the Czar's government repressed civil liberties. My parents were among the thousands forced to flee.

My parents also supported self-determination for all countries, including Palestine. Before World War II, a democratic vote in Palestine would have resulted in a secular majority-Arab state. Religion would have been a private matter. In contrast, the Zionists wanted a clerical majority-Jewish state. Most survivors of the Nazi concentration camps wanted to leave Europe and come to the United States. I remember three boatloads of European Jewish refugees that tried to come to the U.S. when Truman was president. They were refused and turned around toward Israel. One boatload sank. That additional loss of life helped convince Jewish refugees to go to Palestine and give up on the U.S. as a destination.

Massive immigration had increased the Jewish population of Palestine to half the size of the Arab population by 1946. At that time, only 7% of the land was owned by Jews. Most Palestinians were farmers on their own land. The partition of Palestine in 1947, followed by driving Palestinians out of their ancestral homes, gave the Zionists what they wanted. By 1948, the majority living in Israel were Jews. In part, the Zionists won out because of worldwide sympathy with the Jewish victims of the Nazi Holocaust. The Holocaust led most Jews in the United States to passionately support Israel. Still, most American Jews continued to support progressive causes at home. But support for the Israeli government, right or wrong, led some American Jews into the reactionary camp on domestic issues too. That split continues to this day.

The Cold War

As the war ended, the class struggle in the United States again broke out into the open. Wages had lagged behind the price increases. Nor did wages reflect the increased productivity of American workers. A wave of "catch-up" strikes broke out in 1946 and 1947. In response, an unfriendly Republican Congress passed the Taft-Hartley Act in 1947. This Act gutted the 1935 Wagner Act which had outlawed unfair labor practices. Taft-Hartley authorized presidential injunctions against strikes and banned the closed shop and "secondary boycotts." It also allowed the states to pass right to work-for-less laws.

This was the domestic side of the "Cold War." Lasting damage from this period included the split in the CIO, likened to labor "shooting itself in the foot." Eleven of the most militant unions, with a membership of about one million, were expelled in an anti-Communist purge. In the '50s, the witch hunt took the noxious form of McCarthyism, a now discredited policy. But that hateful period did not end before thousands lost their jobs and innocent people went to jail. Thousands of good people were persecuted. A few, like the great actor John Garfield, committed suicide.

With World War II over, millions of active duty soldiers and sailors were returning home. War plants were shutting down. But rebuilding Europe (of course on U.S. terms) kept other American factories open. Unemployment had been brought from 14.6% in 1940 down to an all-time low of 1.2% in 1944–45. But it went up to 3.9% in 1946 and 5.9% in 1949. These figures do not count the millions of women forced out of the labor force when their war-time jobs ended.

Rosie the Riveter

"Rosie the Riveter" After the War

Whatever happened to "Rosie the Riveter"? Rosie was the symbol for the women who helped win World War II by taking factory jobs formerly done only by men. After the war, most Rosie the Riveters lost their jobs. Rosie was told she had to go back to the kitchen to open up jobs for the returning soldiers.

I know only a few hardy women who were able to keep their jobs in the steel mills. In the Buffalo auto plants, as I remember it, the UAW had two seniority lists. The first seniority list was for men. The second seniority list, for women, was placed at the bottom of the men's list. No woman, no matter how many years she had in the plant, could keep her job unless every man, no matter how new in the plant, was employed.

Not all gains made by women during World War II were wiped out. Consider the matter of clothing. Women had to wear pants on many factory jobs. After many women were forced out of their war jobs, the fashion bosses tried to get us back to dresses, long dresses at that. But many women, myself included, kept on wearing pants. Women who wear slacks today have Rosie the Riveter to thank.

During the war, dresses were made short and cut slim to save material. After the war, clothing manufacturers tried to get women back into an entirely new wardrobe. They came out with "The New Look" dresses with skirts billowing down to the ankles. It was a way to force you to buy a lot of clothes. I felt that they were trying to push me into restrictive clothing that our mothers had fought to liberate us from. But there were no other styles sold in the stores. "The New Look" made your old dresses and skirts obsolete. Finally, so many women complained that it was "The New Look" that became obsolete. Personally, I have tried to have the best of both worlds. Pants are warmer in the winter and dresses are cooler for the summer. Whatever the season, I resent the habit of making women's clothes without pockets to force you to carry a purse.

After the war, too many accepted the idea that women should leave their jobs to make room for returning soldiers. Racism was another side of the Cold War. After Roosevelt died in 1945, Truman allowed the FEPC to expire in 1946. But the "Double V" had not been won. Victory against fascism was completed, but victory against racism was facing setbacks. My friend and comrade, Jonnie Lumpkin, asked me to help her test racist hiring practices at the Fedders Air Conditioner plant. I did not really want the job because my daughter was just a couple months old. Jonnie did want the job. We both applied. They offered me the job. They told Jonnie, "Don't call us. We'll call you." Jonnie filed a complaint, but FEPC was on the way out and never took action on her case.

Class Struggle Continues

While many Communists were fighting and dying in World War II, Earl Browder, Party Chairman, decided that the Communist Party should be dissolved and become the Communist Political Association. As I wrote earlier, Browder claimed that capitalists had become "intelligent" during World War II. Therefore, workers should cooperate with the intelligent capitalists.

Browder's move was undone within a year. In April, 1945, the French leader Jacques Duclos sent a letter to American communists. In simple language, it explained that the profit system exploits workers and leads to class struggle. It has nothing to do with the intelligence (or stupidity) of the capitalists.

I cannot remember now how I swallowed the silly theory that some capitalists could become so smart that they would stop exploiting workers. Fortunately, a strong sector of the CPUSA leadership never swallowed the "intelligent capitalist" illusion. Led by William Z. Foster, leader of the 1919 national steel strike, they reorganized the Communist Party USA. I learned a lesson, too, from that experience. It was something like, "Don't believe in the tooth fairy." It will take more than a wave of a fairy's wand to eliminate the class struggle. First we'll have to eliminate exploitation.

Part 2
(On to 1965)

Chapter *10*

My Buffalo Family
*I was attracted by the warmth and the wisdom of the
Lumpkin family.*

Hattie and Elmo Lumpkin with their Ten Children

I came to Buffalo five years after my mother died. Her memory
was still fresh in my heart. Still, I did not think about her
during waking hours. But I often dreamed about my mother.
They were "wish-fulfillment" dreams in which the "mistake
about her death" was corrected. She was alive and I did so
many nice things for her, in my dreams. That dream persisted
for many, many years.

Although no one could replace my mother, my friend Hattie
Lumpkin had a heart big enough to mother us all. Hattie sort

of adopted me as she did so many other comrades who came to Buffalo alone. I was attracted by the warmth and the wisdom of the Lumpkin family as a whole. I did not know then that I would someday marry into the family. All the Lumpkin women have been a powerful force in my life. However, it took some years for me to earn my place in the family. After many, many years, they called me "sister." It was one of the greatest honors of my life.

When I first met Hattie, in 1943, she was already an eloquent experienced leader. With Hattie, I learned how to knock on doors to bring our message of two related struggles. We were fighting for justice at home, against racism. We were fighting abroad to win the war against fascism. More often than not, the door opened and they invited us to come in. We had many good discussions around kitchen tables. Sometimes, our new friends bought a copy of the *Daily Worker*, the Communist Party newspaper.

I worked with Hattie in the campaign to save the life of Willie McGee, sentenced to death in Mississippi. In 1945, Hattie told me about a similar case in Florida. A mother traveled throughout the state in a mule-drawn wagon, trying to raise money to save her son from the electric chair. She did not succeed in saving her son. And progressives did not stop the execution of Willie McGee, although large demonstrations took place in many cities. Still, our fight was not in vain. The lynchers were exposed, and the U.S. House of Representatives passed anti-lynching legislation. However, not until 2005 did the U.S. Senate apologize for failing to adopt an anti-lynching law for so many years.

Ma and Pa Lumpkin

To their ten children, Hattie and Elmo were known simply as "Ma" and "Pa." It is a great tribute to Hattie and Elmo that their ten children all survived to become strong, intelligent, caring adults. As parents, "Ma" and "Pa" provided more than just food, shelter and clothing. They instilled self-confidence in all of their children. It was a trait that could be traced back to Hattie's mother, "Ma Bess" Martin. The self-confidence was not based on pride or conceit. It was more a determination that they could do what needed to be done. I never heard them say, "I can't." That spirit inspired their son Frank when he was organizing workers. He worked to instill self-confidence and the feeling of power in the workers he led. After the war he became my husband. But I barely knew him back then. He was away in the Merchant Marine from 1943–1948. Besides, he was married to someone else at the time.

All of the Lumpkin women were strong, progressive and beautiful. Frank's sister Jonnie was my source for much of the family history that appears in this book. As I noted earlier, she was my best friend. I also have a special relationship with Bay, the oldest Lumpkin daughter. In recent years, I have become close to Bess, a younger daughter. There is a ten-year difference in our ages. But what's ten years, now that I am over 90? And we remember young, glamorous Gladys, who died too early. She dropped everything and came to Chicago to rescue my family when I was down with hepatitis in 1953. Who could have asked for better sisters-in-law?

The Lumpkin History

The Lumpkins trace their family back to 1861, to Sophie Lumpkin. She was a beautiful African woman, enslaved on a cotton plantation in Washington-Wilkes County, Georgia. Mr. Callaway, the plantation owner, had raped Sophie when she was only 16 years old. When Callaway learned that Sophie was pregnant, he made her "jump the broom" with (marry) Si, another enslaved African. In 1862, Sophie gave birth to Callaway's son and named him Frank. Callaway never acknowledged Frank as his son. But he did some big favors for him in later years.

After Emancipation, Si had to choose a last name. He chose Lumpkin, not the hated Callaway name. Si's stepson became the first Frank Lumpkin. Slavery had been abolished but it was replaced by sharecropping, near-serfdom. Sharecroppers were always in debt to plantation owners and not free to leave the plantation.

When the first Frank Lumpkin became 21, he told Callaway that he was ready to marry. An attractive Cherokee woman named Betty had caught his eye. Betty was already married and had four children. But that proved to be no obstacle. Betty's husband died in an unexplained plantation accident. Frank #1 was given Betty as his bride and 400 acres of farm land. Suspicions of foul play lingered for many years. Frank and Betty had four children. Elmo, their last child, became the father of the modern Lumpkin family. Elmo Lumpkin married Hattie Martin in 1911. He was 21 and she was 16.

Sharecropping and Lynchings in Georgia

Young Elmo and Hattie sharecropped on his father Frank's farm. They had six children, Wade, Bay, Frank, Ozzie, Jonnie and Elmo Jr. Frank would become my husband, 27 years later. Times were hard but there was something to eat. Cotton was the main crop but peanuts, corn and vegetables were also raised.

A white landlord's thieving ways took a tragic turn for Elmo's half-brother, Will Lumpkin. Will asked for his correct share of the crop. During the argument, Will called the landlord a liar. Elmo tried to get Will to leave town at once, but Will would not go. The next day, Elmo heard a gunshot. By the time he got there, Will was hanging dead from a tree. Eight little children were left without a father. Will's daughter, Lulamat, says they survived "in those hard, hard times" thanks only to help from Grandpa Frank and Uncle Elmo.

About 1922, the boll weevil hit the Lumpkin's cotton crop. Cousins in Orlando told the Lumpkins that there was work in the orange groves. Elmo, Hattie and their six children moved to Florida. Four more Lumpkin children were born in Conway, site of the orange groves outside of Orlando but now part of the city. They were Warren, Bessie Mae, Gladys and Roy. That brought the number of Lumpkin children to the nice round figure of ten.

The family had moved from sharecropping to working for wages. They were not any freer of racist violence, but as wage workers they had more rights. For example, Frank told me about working with a crew of orange pickers. The pickers followed the lead of a man they called "Live Wire." At one grove, Live Wire could not get the price the pickers needed for each box of oranges picked. At his signal, the whole crew walked off and started back to town on foot. Their protest paid off. The grower sent trucks to bring the pickers back and agreed to pay the price they had demanded.

The orange pickers fought for their rights despite the terror of the Ku Klux Klan. The Klan often marched through the African American community in Orlando. The African American towns, Rosewood, Florida, and Ocoee, Florida, were destroyed by white racists as shown in *Rosewood*, the Hollywood movie.

Frank loved to climb trees. The power company did not trim the trees that grew under the bare electric wires. Frank was 13 years old when he took a dare and touched a bare, high-voltage line. He had seen birds sit on the bare wires without injury. Of course, the birds were not grounded like Frank was in the tree. The powerful surge of electric current knocked Frank out of the tree. His friends' cries brought the local scoutmaster running.

The scoutmaster knew first aid and got Frank breathing again. But the surge of current had burned off joints of three fingers, including the right index (trigger) finger. There was no compensation from the electric utility in those days. Frank adapted his middle finger to take over the function of the index finger. After a while, he was a champion marble shooter again. But lack of his index finger disqualified him from many jobs and army service.

Bay Lumpkin—Where there's Life, there's Hope

Bay, the oldest daughter quit school early. She quit to take care of the younger children so Hattie could work and send the other children to school. In 1933, Bay married Taft Earl Rollins from Tallahassee. Taft joined the army in 1939 and was sent to Fort Bragg, North Carolina. Taft was returning from leave and did not know that a racist riot was raging at the bus stop for Fort Bragg. He stepped out of the bus and was bludgeoned to death by the race rioters. The Army sent Taft back to Bay in a box. The top of his head had been knocked off. Jonnie, Bay's younger sister, decided to leave the coffin open for the funeral so everyone could see what had happened. The army never investigated the murder of Private Taft Rollins. But the family and the community never forgot him. Bay went on with her life and lived with the pain.

Bay was and is my special friend. She continued her self-sacrificing family role for most of her life. She raised seven grandchildren and several of her great-grandchildren. At this point, I will get ahead of my story to write about a huge change that Bay made late in life. At 89, she put the remaining great grandchildren (all grown) out of her house. "Stand on your own feet," she told them. Then she had cataract surgery and called me in great excitement. "I can see, I can see!" she rejoiced. Soon she was driving again, lost weight, bought good clothes and decided to enjoy life. As she told me, she decided that she was a pretty good person. At 94, she joked that she was going to sue the hospital. "Why?" I asked. "Because I'm 94, and they can't find anything wrong with me!" So Bay is my proof that where there's life, there's hope. It is never too late to change.

Frank Lumpkin also quit school early, but he did make it into ninth grade, three years more than Bay. Much as he liked school, at fifteen he felt ashamed to be barefoot and shirtless. So at 15, Frank went to work full time. Even when he and his brothers were going to school, they still had to work in the groves. The school day ended early during growing season to leave more daylight hours for work.

The grove owners used their political power to stop passage of laws to end child labor. Congress had passed a Child Labor Act in 1918, only to have the Supreme Court declare it unconstitutional. The same thing happened under Franklin Delano Roosevelt. Not until 1938, after FDR threatened to appoint six additional judges, did the Supreme Court allow a ban on child labor (under 16) to stand.[9]

Racism Is Unnatural

Down the road from the Lumpkin house, the Harveys had two boys about Frank's age, Roy and Frank. They became

---

[9] *FDR's Fireside Chats*, Russell D. Buhite and David W. Levey, eds. (Norman, OK: University of Oklahoma Press, 1992), 120.

good friends. The family had a well-stocked tool shed. The boys and their friend Frank were allowed to use the tools. That began Frank's lifetime love of tools and machinery. But when it came time to go to school, the boys went different ways. Roy and Frank Harvey went to the white school, not that far away. Frank Lumpkin and his brothers and sisters had to walk past the white school and hike four more miles to the "colored" school. This experience convinced Frank that "Racism is unnatural." Seventy years later he was interviewed by Studs Terkel and told him the story. Frank was so eloquent that *the Nation* quoted most of the interview in their review of Terkel's book, *Race.*[10]

Frank was always optimistic that racism could be overcome. He had a ready answer to those who claimed it would take generations of education to overcome racism. His answer was based on his own experience in the "Great Migration" north. "Education can be overnight," he said. "That backward Southern white worker who gets on the train in the South has been using the 'n' word all his life. In 24 hours he's in Chicago and instantly learns not to walk around saying that word."

Migration to the North

War production was creating more factory jobs, even before Pearl Harbor. Wade Lumpkin, Hattie's oldest child, was the first to leave Orlando. He went to Buffalo, New York, where he was earning "big" money. Within a year, Hattie, Elmo, their ten children and their spouses, and widowed Ma Bess were gathered together in Buffalo. In time, the men all found jobs. Some of the women did, too. Wade, Frank and Warren became steel workers, Oz and his father Elmo became auto workers, Kiyer a packinghouse worker and Jonnie, an aircraft worker. Bay worked in the canning industry and Hattie worked summers as a housekeeper for rich families in Cape Cod. The three youngest Lumpkins were too young to work.

---

[10] Studs Terkel, *Race* (New York: New Press, 1992), 88–92. Interview with Frank Lumpkin. Reprinted in *The Nation*, April 6, 1992.

With the first few paychecks, Hattie put a down payment on an 11-room house at 263 Watson Street. Soon it was full. When cousins came and had nowhere to stay, Hattie made room for them. She told me that people criticized her for overcrowding her house. Her answer was, "No kin of mine will have to sleep in the street." After Hattie joined the Communist Party, her home was also the center for many activists, me included. We were new in town but with Hattie's help, we soon felt that we belonged.

It was Jonnie who brought about a radical change in the thinking of the Lumpkin family. Her first job in Buffalo was child care and housekeeping. She worked for two transit-workers who were members of the Communist Party. Jonnie found the goal of socialism very attractive. Yes, produce for people's needs, instead of for profits. Through Jonnie, the whole family was introduced to the labor movement. Hattie, Frank and Warren, as well as Jonnie, became Communist leaders.

Hattie became an outstanding community organizer. She was also well connected to her church. Whenever Hattie saw an eviction in her neighborhood, she went into action immediately. She sent her children around to call out the neighbors. The neighbors joined in to put the furniture back. Together, they returned the evicted tenants to their apartment. Usually, something would be worked out with the landlord so the evicted family could stay.

Bess

Bessie Mae—she has since citified her name to "Bess"—was different from her sisters and brothers. Severe asthma made her the only one of the Lumpkin children who was sickly and skinny. That won her special treatment from Hattie and Elmo. As a child, Bess adopted very high standards for order and cleanliness. Somehow, she had the energy and will to force those standards on the rest of the family. By the time she was eight she was helping with her younger siblings, Gladys and Roy.

Bess was the first in the family to become a white collar worker. Still in high school, she moved to New York City to attend a business school and become a secretary. As a skilled secretary, she staffed the office of the Committee to Protect the Foreign Born.

Patricia Jonnie Lumpkin

When Jonnie joined the Young Communist League in 1942, she was asked to recruit other members of her family. "There's one person you have to get," she told her fellow Communists, "my brother Frank." She said that Frank was always "teaching." I knew Frank as one of Hattie's ten children but we had little occasion to talk. Six years later, that would change.

Chapter 11

Single Parent

"Love! What's that got to do with it?"

Marriage, Motherhood and Divorce

Marriage, motherhood and divorce—I experienced all of that in Buffalo and in that order. Let's look at marriage and motherhood, since that came first. At Colonial Radio in Buffalo, I worked with civilian technicians who were testing radio transmitters for the Army. I especially enjoyed talking with an ex-farmer from Montana, Rod Mohrherr. Rod was exempted from the draft because of his poor eyesight. He had a degree from the University of Montana and was a self-educated electronics engineer. Rod was interesting and a very decent person. We were both alone in Buffalo, without family. We began to date, and a few months later we decided to marry. I was already 25 years old. That was considered kind of old to still be single.

There was no time or money for more than a trip to City Hall for the license. None of our relatives were in Buffalo, and there was a war on. Hattie Lumpkin and her daughter, Bay, accompanied us to city hall. They tried to fill in for my own family. And over the years, they became my family. Had it not been for Hattie and Bay, I would have felt quite alone.

After a few months of marriage I became pregnant. Colonial Radio did not allow pregnant women to work past four months of pregnancy. So I did not report my pregnancy for a few months. That allowed me to work into my seventh month. By the time I had to leave for maternity, I had worked for Colonial Radio for over one year. The union contract provided a week of vacation pay. But the company never paid me. In my ignorance, I thought I had forfeited vacation pay because I was not planning to return to Colonial Radio. When I learned better, it was too late to file a grievance. Workers get cheated so much. Although the contract was with the UE, a good union, the local leadership was weak. Colonial Radio, later bought by Sylvania, owes me one week's pay. With interest since 1944, that would be a tidy sum.

I don't know why I wanted to have children just as fast as I could, once I was married. But that's exactly what happened. However, I made very few preparations for the arrival of my first child. If anything went wrong, I felt I could not stand having a lot of baby stuff around and no baby. Maybe I was thinking of my mother's sadness on losing my brother soon after I was born. One thing was certain whether I thought about it or not. The baby would come when he/she was ready. Then I would do what needed to be done. And in due time, the baby did come. We named him Carl Joseph. I liked the name Joseph but I wanted him to have a one-syllable name like Carl.

I believe that the ease of birth is affected by the mother's cultural background. Later, I lived among Nisei women in Chicago and was surprised to learn that some never experienced pain in childbirth. (The Nisei are the first U.S.-born generation among Japanese immigrants). "Well, how did you know it was time to go to the hospital?" I asked in amazement. "You get a feeling, like you are going to menstruate," one tiny woman explained to me.

That approach to child birth was very different from what I heard as a child. My mother's friends enjoyed describing the details of their difficult deliveries. They seemed to try to outdo each other, talking about how much pain they had experienced. I was left with the thought that I owed a debt to my mother because she had suffered so much to birth me. It was a debt that I could never repay. In contrast, my contemporaries and I talked little about our childbirth experiences. The subject seldom came up. Still, the old wives' tales I heard as a child may have affected me. I certainly had a lengthy first delivery.

A Perfect Human Being

I remember very little of the prolonged delivery of my first child. No doubt, that was thanks to the painkillers. What I remember most was my amazement when the nurse showed me my newborn in the delivery room. I was surprised that my husband and I, ordinary mortals, could have produced such a beautiful, perfect human being. We took baby Carl home after the 10-day hospital stay that was standard then. I got up every couple hours to make sure he was still breathing. Before motherhood, I had always been a very sound sleeper. That changed after Carl was born. No matter how soundly I slept, one part of my brain remained alert for sounds from my children.

Fortunately, Carl turned out not to be as fragile as I had feared. I followed Dr. Spock's guide for child care after it came out in 1946. But that was too late for Carl, born in 1944. I followed the rules of an earlier generation. Put the baby on a regular feeding schedule and stick to it no matter what. Every four hours and that was it. Fortunately, Carl was a good feeder and it worked out. But I had so much to learn. I learned that you don't open all the drawers of a dresser and place an undiapered baby within firing range. That I learned the hard way. I learned that if the doctor says a child with a cold needs more humidity, it does not mean that you should turn your apartment into a rain forest. I had boiled so much water that the ceiling began to rain. They must have used good plaster in those days because the ceiling survived.

A late winter storm struck Buffalo when Carl was about seven months old. I had just weaned him onto a "formula" based on cow's milk. The snow was so deep that milk delivery trucks could not get through. But I had to have that milk. A mile away was the A&P, a large store with a supply of milk. So I strapped on my boots and asked a neighbor to watch Carl. The snow was waist-high, but I was young enough to enjoy the challenge. It would be days before the snow plows opened our streets.

As long as snow did not block the walks, I took my baby out. Baby carriages then often held groceries as well as the child. As the baby grew larger, we mothers would just shove the groceries over to make room for the child. But I did not realize that Carl was showing early signs of becoming a scientist. One day I left him in the buggy where I could see him and went into the bakery store. I made the mistake of having his back turned to me. Soon a small crowd gathered around him. That did not surprise me. After all, he was beautiful. Then they began to laugh. Now that puzzled me. When I got outside, I discovered that Carl was doing one of his first experiments. He had opened a carton of eggs, took an egg out, dropped it over the side, and studied it for a while. Then he returned to the package of eggs, took another one out, dropped it, and continued his study. The crowd was so entertained that nobody had thought to save the eggs.

Carl got to see much of Buffalo. We spent most of the day outside the apartment, as I pushed the baby buggy around town. It was good exercise, and he got the fresh air. In fact, a book on jogging suggested running with the baby carriage. That could burn enough calories to equal one piece of pie. So when I got bored with walking, I tried running. The upside of spending all that time outside was that my apartment stayed clean.

It was also a social experience. My good friend, Edna, had a baby boy about the same age. Edna and I would walk to our special ice cream shop, buy ourselves ice cream cones and double our pleasure. Over the months, our babies grew bigger. Then they began to look with great interest at the ice cream cones we were licking. Did I ever give Carl a taste of the ice cream? Not on your life! It wasn't good for him and I stuck to a very strict nutritional guide (for him).

My Second Child, a Girl!

On May 8, 1945, we celebrated V-E (Victory in Europe) Day. Germany had surrendered, Hitler had committed suicide, and Mussolini had been strung up by his heels. Fascism had been defeated in Europe. Imperial Japan still occupied much of Asia but we were optimistic that the war would soon be won. That was a good time for Rod and me to complete our family. And as soon as I could, I had another child. As luck would have it, the second was a girl. That gave me one of each. How nice!

Jeanleah benefited from my experience with Carl. And I had an easier time of it in every way. I got over thinking Carl was the most beautiful creature on earth because Jeanleah was just as beautiful. And I had to admit that my friends' children were lovely, too, even as lovely as mine. To me, nothing is more beautiful than a healthy baby.

Jeanleah was a very cooperative baby. Of course I gave her the credit, but it was really Carl who had educated me. He gave me the chance to do everything wrong, and I did. Based on my experience, I recommend that everyone should have their second child first. In many ways Jeanleah was ahead of her age. I am sure it helped that she had an older brother as a model.

Divorced and Back to Work

Father working, mother raising two fine children, one boy and one girl—what more could one ask for? Unfortunately that wasn't enough for me. I am sure I had loved Rod when we married but I had fallen out of love. I saw other marriages that were more the life style I had hoped for but could never achieve with Rod. Not that he had changed. And I had not changed. That was the problem; we were mismatched. We had a friendly divorce, and I had two little children to feed and no job. The war was over, and jobs were not that easy to get. Rod gave what child support he could afford but it was not much. There was no other man in the picture although there was one I had been eyeing (out of one eye). Any chance that he might become *the one* was literally drowned out. I had invited him to visit and accidentally poured two quarts of hot, boiling coffee in his lap. He took care to avoid my apartment after that and any further exposure to my defective coffee maker with the swiveling handle.

First I thought I could get by as a part-time waitress, as we called it then. After all, I had waited tables at Camp Unity. And I had learned not to stick my fingers in glasses of water that I was carrying to a table. But I was a long way from being a professional waiter, to use the modern, non-sexist term. I joined the union and was sent out on my first job the same day. My next job was in a downtown café outside the court house. I could have survived on the lunch tips I collected. They were pretty good. But I was only filling in for another worker. Naturally, as a union activist I thought I should attend the waiters' union meeting. When I arrived at the union headquarters, I thought I was in the wrong place. The large hall was almost empty. Four or five workers were seated together in the hall. They looked at me and I looked at them. "Is this where the waiters' union is meeting?" I asked. "Yes," they replied. I waited and they waited. Since I did not leave, they got up, went into the small, glassed-in office and had their meeting. They certainly did not invite me. That was the end of my waiters' union activism.

I decided to look for a full-time factory job again. The UE had organized the big Westinghouse plant, and there was a big struggle going on there. Naturally, I wanted to get in on the action. So I applied. With Emerson and Colonial Radio experience, I had a good background.

"No thank you," Westinghouse told me. Something gave me the feeling I had been placed on the "Don't Hire" list. But I didn't give up. I went to the state employment office. Yes, Westinghouse was hiring, and the state office could give me a referral. So I showed up again, this time with a referral to a specific job opening. "You are the most persistent girl I have ever seen," the employment clerk said. But there was still no job for me. Then I heard about one of our comrades who actually got hired. The "Don't Hire" list caught up with him just as he was putting on his safety shoes to work his first shift. The call came from the front office, and he was fired before he ever got out to the work floor.

Western Electric

I finally got a job as a machine operator in the Western Electric wire plant in North Tonawanda, just north of Buffalo. The company hired African Americans, but the town was infamous for its "all white" restrictions. It was said that no African Americans could stay in that town overnight. Western Electric had just defeated UE in a National Labor Relations Board election. The company brought in CWA (Communications Workers of

America) as the plant union. The plant produced wire for the telephone company.

I was 29 when I got that job and I was already a little old for the work. Most of the women were younger, more like 19. The job required both speed and stamina. It was almost impossible to keep up with the number of machines they gave us. Every finished spool of wire had to be labeled. Many of the younger women took blank labels home to fill them out so they could save time on the job. I refused to do that. It was absolutely against union principles!

My first job at Western Electric was to run a bank of insulating machines that spun cotton thread around bare copper wire. The machines were supposed to be automatic. "All" the operator had to do was to stop the machine when the feed spool of bare wire ran out. The operator pulled out the empty reel and put a new one in and threaded it through, Next, she braised together the bare ends from the new reel and the old reel. After checking to be sure the wire was threaded through, she turned the machine back on and made sure it ran smoothly.

Meanwhile, two other heads may have stopped. If the spool of insulated wire was full, it had to be removed and labeled. For those few, like me, who did not write the labels at home, it took another minute. We had 32 heads to run. To keep up, we had to move fast. We were not allowed to let the heads sit idle too long.

Even if we had any free time, it would have been very hard to talk to other operators on the job. The machines were very noisy. To talk to an operator and be heard, you had to put your mouth close to her ear. I did learn two valuable lessons in that department. The first was safety. I had the deplorable habit of lifting my right pinkie to balance my hand when I changed the spool of thread. One day the fast-whirling cup that held the cotton thread sliced some flesh off of my right pinkie. We joked that I had been imitating the gesture of fancy folks, pinkie up in the air when drinking a cup of tea. That job was anything but fancy. We wore safety glasses and ugly safety caps with elastic to keep our hair out of the machines. For those who set their hair, it was a perfect time to leave the curlers in, out of sight under the safety caps. Nothing like letting your hair set on the bosses' time. Most of us (not including me) left work with smartly styled coiffures.

For the number of women and men slaving away at the wire machines, there were a lot of men in suits walking around with pens and pads of paper—or just walking around. I am sure I was not the only machine operator who resented that. Just think of how productive we operators were to support all of those foremen, supervisors, efficiency experts, etc. (all white males). It was the time-study men I disliked the most. They hung around and were all over you with their stop watches and clip boards. That made me nervous and I began to work faster. But no worker in her right mind wants to use a faster-than-normal pace for time study. So I slowed down. Maybe I overdid it because the time-study men decided to leave. "We'll come back the next day," they warned.

Model Worker

I did learn that there are always better ways to do any job. Some workers are models of efficiency. These exceptional workers earned my highest respect. I observed and learned from my dear comrade, Florence Wachowski. Most of the operators, like me, were in constant, frantic motion, trying to keep up with the machines. But when you passed Florence's station she would be sitting, perhaps reading a magazine. All of the machine heads would be running and all of the wire spools were full. How did she do it? Florence had mastered that job and had not allowed the job to master her. I knew it was all in the timing. But I never learned her secret. I also remember Florence for the wise gift she sent us three years later, on the birth of my third child. We were broke, broke, broke. Florence sent her present in the form of cash. Her ten dollar check bought us food for one week.

After some months in the insulating department, I was transferred to the enameling department. To get there from the insulating machines, you had to walk through the braiding department. The braiding machines twisted several conductors to make up cables. It was the most disturbing industrial noise I have ever heard. I hated walking through the department and could not understand how people could work there all day. Compared with braiding and insulating, the enameling department was much quieter. It was also much hotter.

The enameling was done in ovens where the temperature was kept at 800 degrees Fahrenheit. Each operator had two low but huge ovens in front of her and two behind her. The ovens were about six feet wide and ten feet long. The feed/uptake end of each oven had 12 heads, for a total of 48 heads. Instead of cotton insulation, the wire was covered with enamel. The bare wire from a supply spool was fed through a groove with liquid enamel, then into the oven. It made several passes until the finished wire had enough coats of baked-on enamel. There was one big difference between my old job in cotton insulation and the enameling room. That difference could cost you your job.

For cotton insulation, the old wire was braised to the new wire and run until the spool was full. But in enameling, the old and new wires were never fused together. Instead, old and new wires were temporarily twisted (spliced) together. The old wire threaded the new wire through the oven's many passes. You were supposed to watch until the splice came out. Then the splice was cut and discarded. The old take-up reel was removed, full or not, and replaced with an empty spool. In the rush of keeping 48 heads going, the operator might turn her head and miss or forget the splice. That was cause to be fired.

Eventually, the company decided to get rid of me. They secretly cut open every spool of wire that I had enameled in two days. All my work and the value of those spools of wire were scrapped! I assume no splices-were found since I was not fired. Bernard, who carried out the company order to cut my reels (and told me about it), was my friend. He was an American Labor Party (ALP) activist. Thanks to Bernard, the company did not frame me with a bogus spliced reel. His solidarity meant a lot to me.

Child Care in 1947

Unfortunately, I had no relatives in Buffalo; I was on my own. I had nothing except two plump, lively toddlers. Whether they survived or not was strictly my business. The government could care less. Since I had to work, I needed child care help. When I started at Western Electric, my daughter was about 18 months old. She was a very bright and inquisitive child, probably as ready as many two-year olds. At that early age, she was already climbing out of her crib at night so she could take herself to the bathroom. But the minimum age for child care centers was two.

I hired a babysitter to come to my apartment while I worked. I earned about $20 a week and I paid the babysitter $10. On the face of it, it did not pay to work, but I thought the job promised more of a future than if I stayed home. From a newspaper ad, I found a young woman willing to cover for me while I worked 3:30 p.m. to midnight. Neighbors told me that she put my two toddlers to bed by 6 p.m. Needless to say, it was very hard for me to get up when the children woke at 6 a.m. It did give me a lot of time with the children, so I felt less guilty about working. We spent our mornings on trips around town, especially to the zoo. We made friends with the zookeepers who gave us updates on the big animals.

Finally, Jeanleah had her second birthday. There was no child care center near me but there was one on the way to the wire plant. That center was federally funded and affordable. It was set up during World War II by the federal government so women could fill the factory jobs left by men who were drafted. Luckily for me, the center was still operating in 1948. So Carl and Jeanleah started their formal education at a very young age. I changed my shift to the 7 a.m. to 3:30 p.m. shift. There was just one problem. The day care center did not open until 7 a.m., and I had to punch in before 7. Fortunately, some teachers came to work a half hour early and accepted my children. I was too desperate to worry that I was forcing teachers to work before their work day began.

Whatever the weather, I set off each morning with two precious bundles in my arms, each weighing over 30 pounds. I did not make them stand up and walk to the bus stop. That's because I felt guilty about waking them up so early. In 1948, they did not have two-seater strollers that let you wheel two toddlers around. Today, many strollers even fold and are allowed on buses and trains, in stores and museums. That's so much easier than carrying 60 to 70 pounds of little ones. I like to think that this victory is due, at least in part, to our fight in the 1930s and 1940s for women's rights.

Of course, my kids woke up once we were on the bus. When we got off the bus, we still had to walk across the prairie to the child care center. It did not snow every day in Buffalo, but it is the snowy days that I remember. Then, a fierce wind blew the snow in my face as I carried Jeanleah on one arm and pulled Carl along with the other. Bless those teachers! They opened the door, scooped up my kids, and let me run back to the bus stop. At least the bus ran often. Miraculously, I punched in on time, most days. I did have to miss a couple of days from work. Even healthy children will get sick. My foreman told me one day that if I was late or missed another day that I would be fired. I don't know how I managed, but I never came late again or missed another day.

Unless you have gone through it, you don't know how hard it is to be a single mother. It is especially hard if your family cannot help you. I lived through the Great Depression. That wasn't as hard on me because I did not have children to worry about. My diet was so poor after my mother died that I developed scurvy. That did not bother me. My doctor just gave me all the food samples he had and the scurvy went away. But not being able to give your kids basic necessities like a good diet—that really hurt. I did get a sewing machine but sewing was an area in which I had no natural talent. I learned to use the machine to take in Carl's clothing for Jeanleah. I was glad that Jeanleah was too young to care or to object. The sewing machine also allowed me to do big sewing jobs quickly, such as repairing worn out sheets. Just cut the sheet lengthwise down the worn-out center. Then sew the sides together to make a new, strong center.

The fight for good and affordable child care will always be close to my heart. I have never forgotten the walk across the snow-covered field with two plump toddlers in my arms. Good quality, affordable child care should be available for all children. It helped that my sister Western Electric workers were very supportive. They knew I was having a hard time managing all by myself with two toddlers. They asked me why I got a divorce.

"Did he beat you?" "No."

"Did he bring his money home?" "Yes. But I didn't love him."

"Love! What's that got to do with it?"

Western Electric Workers for Wallace with Paul Robeson. Author is second from right

Most of my sister workers were Polish and spoke English with a Polish accent. That puzzled me at first. There was a very large Polish population in Buffalo. But there had not been a recent influx of immigrants. As I later learned, my coworkers had all been born in Buffalo. They lived in a Polish-speaking neighborhood and attended parochial schools that were taught in Polish. So the Polish accent in their English was entirely a made-in-Buffalo product. None of my friends had seen the "old country." It was said that many in the Polish community had not even seen city hall, by far the most prominent building in Buffalo's downtown. That is how closed-in their home community was. I felt privileged to work with these loyal and honest women. My life was richer for knowing them.

Henry Wallace for President

Progressive workers at Western Electric were supporting the American Labor Party (ALP). In 1948, we organized a Committee to Elect Henry Wallace, the Progressive Party candidate for President. Our organizing was done on the shop floor, strictly rank and file efforts.

Henry Wallace had been U.S. Secretary of Agriculture from 1933 to 1940. He was Roosevelt's choice as vice president and was elected in 1940. Wallace supported FDR's policy of peaceful coexistence with the Soviet Union and other New Deal policies that benefited working families. But in 1944, Wallace was dumped in favor of Harry Truman as Democratic Party nominee for vice president. It was a step that led to the Cold War that broke out after World War II.

When FDR died in 1945, Vice President Truman became President. The "Truman Doctrine" launched the "Cold War" that soon erupted into a hot war in Greece (1947). Millions of people died in other hot "Cold Wars" since then, notably the Korean War and the Vietnam War. Undeclared, but deadly wars took many lives in Guatemala, Nicaragua and El Salvador, all a consequence of Cold War policies. It could even be argued that the Cold War led to the invasions of Iraq and to the great loss of life that followed.

In 1948, Henry Wallace agreed to run for president as a third party candidate. Progressives supported his campaign. As Curtis D. MacDougall summed it up, Wallace wanted to stop "a trend toward American imperialism in foreign affairs and destruction of the social gains of the New Deal at home."[11] The Wallace campaign on the Progressive Party ticket was the most important third-party campaign of my lifetime (to date).

A strong cultural movement was a prominent part of the Progressive Party campaign. Pete Seeger and Paul Robeson both made history when they performed at the Wallace rallies in Buffalo. Early in the campaign, Seeger sang at a rally held at Kleinhans Music Hall, near my apartment in Buffalo. It was standing room only, and we had to turn people away. Just a

---

[11] McDougall, *op. cit.*, 290.

few months later, a second rally was held in the same location. This time, the huge auditorium was filling more slowly. Some of the earlier support had melted away because many feared the election of the Republican, Thomas Dewey. Also, Truman had changed his campaign rhetoric to give "lip service" to Progressive Party program planks.

We activists were worried sick. We did not want Wallace to come to a half empty hall. Pete Seeger was supposed to sing a song or two before Wallace spoke. But we needed to stall until the hall filled. Seeger came forward and I thought he was very brave and upbeat. He sang and he sang and he sang, until the hall was as full as it was going to get. Everyone's morale picked up as Pete belted out one after another of the people's songs. I have loved him deeply, ever since.

We worked hard to bring in the Progressive Party vote. But when the count was in, we had only 1,150,000 votes for Wallace. Still, the campaign had achieved some very important goals. Before the Progressive Party entered the race, both Democratic and Republican Parties had planned to keep foreign policy issues out of the campaign. They did not succeed. Instead, Wallace made peace the central issue.

A very false picture of Truman as a friend still lingers in much of the labor movement. From what I remember, the opposite was true. Truman broke the post-war railroad strike of 1946 by threatening to draft strikers into the army. He tried to break the National Maritime strike by threatening to use the U.S. Navy as strikebreakers. Also, I believe that his hands were not clean on passage of the anti-labor Taft-Hartley law. It is true that he vetoed the law. Congress overrode the veto. Most Democratic congressmen voted for Taft-Hartley and failed to sustain President Truman's veto. As I saw it, Truman did not try to use his influence with Congress and allowed the union-crippling Taft-Hartley Act to become law.

Paul Robeson

For me in Buffalo, the highlight of the Wallace campaign was Paul Robeson's visit. I had heard him many times in New York City in Madison Square Garden. I can still feel the chills run up and down my spine as he sang. Paul's voice, full of love and struggle, of hope and righteous anger, moved my soul. But Robeson's huge presence loomed even larger in the Ellicott District of Buffalo. Early in the campaign, Robeson had pressed Wallace to make African American equality a major plank in his program. At Western Electric, we had organized a Wallace for President Committee. We were thrilled to have our picture taken with the great Robeson as shown above, on page 166.

Robeson's security team for the rally included all five of the grown Lumpkin brothers. As former boxers, Wade and Frank were especially valued for the security detail.

When Robeson arrived at the hall, it seemed the entire Buffalo police force had been mobilized to intimidate us. After Robeson had to run a gauntlet of Buffalo police, he said, "You should have let me know and I would have come prepared." He told us he had just come from the mine strikers' picket line at the Mesabi iron range. There he rode in a truck with the striking iron miners. Lining the road on both sides were the mine company's police, their guns drawn. It was not a surprise to hear that. Cold War policies abroad were being reflected in the greater use of violence against workers at home.

Lumpkin brothers, left to right, Wade, Frank, Ozzie, Elmo, Warren, Roy.

Chapter *12*

The Love of My Life

"There are so many beautiful faces."

AT a Buffalo fundraiser for the 1948 Wallace campaign, I became interested in Frank Lumpkin. At the time, I had no idea that he would become the love of my life. I had just quit my job at Western Electric because I had lost my child care. Our child care center was forced to close when federal funding was withdrawn. Fortunately, I had worked long enough to collect unemployment compensation. That could keep me and my kids going for a while. (Yes, the rules were more humane then.)

I vaguely remembered Frank from earlier visits to the Lumpkin family's home. But the year I came to Buffalo (1943) was the same year that Frank left for the Merchant Marine. Sixty years later, he told us about the discrimination he faced the minute he boarded his first ship. "It did not matter what I knew. I was black, so they put a shovel in my hands to feed the coal-fired boilers. They gave the white guy who signed on at the same time that I did, a notebook and pencil."

The next ship Frank sailed was oil-fired. His love of machinery made him a quick learner. In a couple of years, he moved up from fireman, oiler, to junior engineer. He liked the job and became what seamen called a "homesteader." He stuck with the same ship for many trips. But in 1948, when his ship was in Piraeus, Greece, the company sold the ship. Then the company offered to fly the seamen home, but they refused. These seasoned seamen, who survived years of sailing past bombs and torpedoes, claimed they were afraid to fly. Maybe they were afraid, but I doubt it. Their refusal to fly forced the company to send them back by ship. That way, the seamen continued to collect wages until they reached the U.S. Once off the company payroll, the seamen did not know where their next paycheck would come from.

Merchant seamen who served during World War II, like Frank and my brother Leon, did not receive veterans' status until 43 years after the war. One in twenty-six merchant seamen died in line of duty during World War II. That was a greater percentage of war-related deaths than any other U.S. service. Still, the Veterans Administration told me that merchant seamen are not eligible for any veterans' benefits. I hope they were wrong and that WWII Merchant Marine veterans can collect benefits, even if too late for Frank.

Frank and I "Engage"

The year 1948 was an opportune time for me to become interested in Frank. He did not have a ship to go back to. The very important presidential campaign of Henry Wallace needed his help. That kept Frank in Buffalo where I could get to know him better. And he was divorced and available. Our first chance to really talk was largely accidental, at a fund raising party. Unknown to me, Frank had gone to the party with a date. The host of the party was an amateur wine maker, and Frank was sampling the wines enthusiastically. That was the reason Frank gave me later for his date's leaving the party early, alone. As a Lumpkin, Frank was an automatic friend and we began to talk. I found him interesting but that was all. If he had had too much wine, I did not notice. I had come by bus and was glad to accept a ride to my apartment. We talked all the time, just friends.

Later that week Frank called to invite me to a movie. There was a French film in town that I wanted to see. Frank acted as though that was his choice, too. Little did I know that his taste went to westerns. The next week there was a party in Schenectady that I wanted to attend. He had a car and did not seem to mind the two hour drive (one way). I don't know what Frank saw in me. But slowly, I fell in love. He had an unexpected strain of poetry that drew me to his side. When he first stroked my face, he said, "There are so many beautiful faces." Had he told me that I was beautiful, I would have paid little attention. That's what all the men say at a moment like that. I was moved by the way he put it; we were part of a world of beautiful faces.

I was glad that Frank was interested in me and that he loved my children. After some months of dating, we decided to get married. I think it was his honesty and sincerity that first attracted me. And then he was so much fun to be with. He liked everything I liked, or at least put on a good show. I found out later that he really did not like the foreign films I liked. At least, he did not like them as much as I did. But he was very open-minded and ready to try new things.

After we were married, I saw more of Frank's most appealing trait: his love of his fellow workers. He really loved them, and he believed in them. He believed that workers had the power to change the world once they unite and learn to use their power. His mission in life, as he saw it, was to show workers they had that potential. Frank landed in the center of a big struggle that erupted in Buffalo.

Racism at the Buffalo Dock

In the summer of 1949, the Buffalo Communist Party initiated a protest against racism on a Lake Erie dance cruise ship. They had learned that single African American men had been refused admission. As demonstrators assembled, three African American men, members of Local 2603, United Steelworkers of America (USWA), bought tickets for the cruise. But they were barred from boarding. We demonstrators began to shout and boo. The police were called. One policeman began to drag a student demonstrator across the dock. Frank protested the rough handling of the student. The cop turned, let the student go, and brought his club down on Frank's head. As the blood spurted from Frank's forehead, his chief concern was that the blood was staining his only suit. As ill luck would have it, the suit was a light gray.

Frank's sister Jonnie spotted another cop aiming his pistol at Frank. Although eight months pregnant, she threw her arms around her brother's neck and began to scream, "Don't hurt him. That's my brother!" Her seemingly hysterical conduct may have saved Frank's life. Then the police arrested Frank, probably to cover up their crime of brutality. The student who was manhandled by the cop had disappeared in the confusion.

Frank was locked up after an emergency room doctor sewed up his forehead with five stitches. The charge was "interfering with a police officer making an arrest." Of course, Frank's brother Warren was documenting the scene with his camera. A few minutes later, Frank's father, Elmo, marched into the police station with the deed to their house. I was grateful and much moved. The Lumpkin house was home to at least 15 people. And Elmo was putting it on the line to gain Frank's freedom. That was Pa's function in the Lumpkin family?to work, bring home his pay, and come through for them in emergencies.

I was worried about Frank's head injury. On doctor's orders, I woke Frank up every hour, just to make sure he was not unconscious. I wasn't too sure what I was supposed to do if I could not wake him up. Scream I suppose. Luckily, Frank slept through the night quite well, even though I woke him up every hour. Although I did not get much sleep I was happy. Frank showed no symptoms of brain injury.

Ma Lumpkin Leads the Fight

The charge against Frank was only a misdemeanor. But a conviction could put him in jail for up to six months. We had to fight the charge while fighting to end discrimination aboard the cruise ship. Frank's mother, Hattie, swung into action. She was the Ellicott district chairperson of the Buffalo Communist Party. Hattie organized a labor/community coalition to end discrimination at the cruise ships. Fifty clergymen signed the coalition's petition to the state's attorney, asking him to drop charges against Frank.

Victory at the cruise ship came just before the trial opened. The boat company agreed to end racial discrimination on their cruises. USWA Local 2603 welcomed the agreement but warned that they would continue to monitor the boat company. They were still angry that three of their members had been denied entry to the ship. James Annacone, union leader and American Labor Party candidate for mayor, told the *Worker*, "Frank Lumpkin's blood-stained shirt is a warning that Jim Crow must always be upheld by the nightstick and the lynch rope. This unprovoked attack on a Negro worker is pure fascism."[12]

A respected civil rights lawyer, Thomas L. Newton, came out of retirement to take Frank's case. It would be *pro bono* (no fee). Newton asked for a jury trial. The student who had been manhandled by the police appeared as a defense witness. Community pressure was in Frank's favor. The police officer who had clubbed Lumpkin was already being sued for beating

---

[12] *The Worker*, August 7, 1949. Upstate [New York] edition, 2.

two African American women. Still, the State of New York pushed for a conviction. They brought in an African American prosecutor, a first for Buffalo.

The jury was all white. It was not a jury of Frank's peers, mostly business people and professionals. Many of us assumed that the jurors were prejudiced. Frank also feared that they would ask him about his professional boxing status. In New York, a boxer's fists had been ruled "lethal weapons." The prosecutor did question him about his fighting career. It looked bad for Frank. Joe North, the renowned reporter for the *Worker*, had already written his story. North's headline read, "All-White Jury Convicts Black Worker." But he had to tear up that story and write another one. The jury reached a verdict in just 15 minutes, a unanimous "Not guilty!" The audience broke into cheers. Strangers hugged Frank, and hugged each other, including some jurors. Our belief in black-white unity was reinforced.

Chicago, Next Stop

Once the trial was over, Frank and I were free to leave Buffalo. He needed a job, and there were none in Buffalo in 1949. The economy was in recession. We decided to move to Chicago. The saying used to be, "If you can't get a job in Chicago, you can't get a job anywhere." But in Chicago, apartments were almost harder to find than jobs. Some Buffalo friends, originally from Pittsburgh, came to the rescue. They had friends who were leaving their Chicago apartment to return to Pittsburgh. If we moved into the Chicago apartment before these friends left, the apartment would be ours. That meant we had to move fast.

All my previous moves had been simple, one stack of books tied with a rope, and one suitcase of clothes. My clothes would still fit in one suitcase. But this time I had two little children. The Chicago apartment was not big enough for all four of us to move in while our friends still lived there. It seemed a good time for the children to spend the summer on Aunt Lillian's farm in Montana.

With a preschooler in each hand, I boarded the train. In Chicago we changed to the famed Empire Builder that went through Montana. It was a long train ride, not exactly a vacation. Still, Carl, Jeanleah and I enjoyed the changing scenery from our coach seats. It was all new to us, a thrilling look at the mountains and plains of our huge country. There was even a glass dome-topped observation car where we could see the amazing star-studded night sky. In the day time, I got my first look at the western jack rabbits. By the eastern white cotton-tail standard, those jack rabbits were huge.

I lingered a day or so in Fairview, Montana, to make sure the kids were settled in. Lillian, Rod's sister, was a wonderfully efficient farm wife. I marveled at the way she casually made two pies for a church cake sale before she made breakfast and helped with the chores. She told me she used to work much harder when she worked in the fields, as well as doing the cooking for a bunch of hired "hands." The farm was near the North Dakota border in semi-arid land. Their irrigation system was well developed and allowed intensive farming. It seemed like a pretty good life to me. That is, if you didn't mind hard work and if the crops brought in enough to cover expenses. Rod once told me that he would have loved farming except for one thing. It was not an eight-hours-a-day job.

It was a long, lonely train ride back to Buffalo. Probably I should have been more worried about the impact of the separation on my children. But I had complete trust in Aunt Lillian. Back in Buffalo, Frank and I packed our few things and were soon in Chicago. We made a short trip to city hall, paid three dollars for a license and listened to a few words mumbled by the clerk. We were legally married. Our Chicago friends graciously allowed us to sleep on their living room couch for six weeks. Then they moved out and the apartment was ours.

It was time to bring my children home from their stay in Montana. Everything was going to be new to them, a new apartment and a new family forming. They were used to playing with Frank but now he was their stepfather. All would go well, I thought and hoped. All that was missing was money. Neither one of us had a job.

Chapter *13*

In Chicago, Fighting Racism
Chicago's segregated real estate is all about money.

With the Chicago apartment safely in our name, I went back to Montana to bring my children home. That took a big weight off my shoulders. It did not matter that we had no furniture and four quite large rooms to fill. All we had was the washing machine that Frank had shipped from my Buffalo apartment. A new friend in Chicago loaned us a sleeper couch for Carl and Jean. I bought a cheap mattress that we put on the floor for Frank and me. That was the last time that I used my bargaining skills honed in the East Bronx when nothing had a "fixed" price. They wanted $20 for the mattress, and I got it for $10. I still had a few unemployment compensation checks coming. We would make it.

Frank's daily job search came up empty. It must have been very hard for him. He had never had such a long stretch of unemployment. In hard times, it was often easier for women to find work. It did not take me long to find work as a wirer and solderer at the Motorola television plant on the North Side. At Motorola, I worked on an assembly line where I had plenty of company. You had to move fast, but that did not stop us from talking. After you memorized your 40 connections, you could work and talk. As long as you had someone to talk to, the day went quickly.

I wore a smock at work to hide my expanding waist line. Yes, I was pregnant. After a couple of months, the personnel department called me in. Somebody had noticed. They fired me for being pregnant. So I looked for another job and found

179

one right away as a typist at Spiegel. This time I wore a larger smock. I passed the typing test, just barely. I had never worked as a typist before. The job could hardly be called office work, more a production job. We typed only names and addresses, probably for shipping labels. Even with a looser smock, I was getting noticeably bigger in the middle. So Spiegel fired me. Fired again for pregnancy! There were no laws then to protect pregnant women from discrimination. When pregnant workers finally won rights on the job in the 1970s, I had special reason to rejoice. I lasted just two weeks at Spiegel but I did become a faster typist. That proved to be a useful skill in the years ahead.

Frank and I were down but not out. I had a couple of unemployment checks left in my purse. That was the rent money. As I walked home after dark one evening, a figure emerged out of nowhere. He grabbed my purse and ran away, down the alley. Although eight months pregnant, I could not let my last two unemployment checks disappear. So I ran down the alley after him, screaming, "Give that back." Fortunately, I could not catch him. That was one of the stupidest things I ever did.

To tide us over, I borrowed money from my family, something I had never done before. In time, the feds replaced the stolen checks. That was just another disaster that we survived. Paying for prenatal care was not a problem. I could not pay and I did not pay. I enrolled as a charity patient at the prenatal clinic at what was then a pretty good hospital, Michael Reese. From my Depression years, I had a lot of experience with charity medical care. The clinic was crowded and some of the staff were inconsiderate. I knew I had to put up with it but I did lose my cool once. We had waited for hours and got only curt answers when we asked for information. My patience gave out and I stormed out of the clinic shouting, "What do you think we are, cattle?" I know I shook them up, but that was little comfort because I was shaken, too.

Bundle of Charms

Paul Lumpkin was born in March 1950. I liked the name David but we wanted to name him after Paul Robeson. So he became

Paul David Lumpkin. Neither Frank nor I had middle names. Perhaps my children would find it easier to put in a middle name than write "none" on job applications.

Paul was born into a family that gave him lots of love. Even though Frank cannot carry a tune, he sang to his baby. Paul was Frank's little "bundle of charms." But we had little food in the house. Frank had returned empty-handed each day from his daily job search. One day he was so depressed that he spent his carfare on a movie and walked the five miles to our apartment. There were no jobs out there. The economy was still in the post-World War II recession. I was wondering how fast I could recover from childbirth and go out to find a job.

We did not starve because some of our friends helped us, even though we had not asked for help. Naturally, it was the poorest of our friends who saw the need. As they say, it takes one to know one. Eunice Torrienti brought us two bags of groceries. At that time she lived in the nearby Ida B. Wells housing project. Eunice earned the money to pay for our groceries by selling her breast milk. Florence Wachowski sent us ten dollars. As I wrote earlier, she was the model worker I had admired at Western Electric. The ten dollars bought some more groceries. The Salvation Army had sent us a housekeeper for a few days after Paul was born. But we were so poor that she brought her own brown-bag lunch. We could not get on welfare because we did not meet the residence requirement then in effect. But at least we had a place to live.

In some ways our apartment was better than any place I had lived in before. The rooms were much larger and there was a back door that opened into a paved yard. On good days I could put a playpen in the yard so Paul could be outdoors. There were some drawbacks. If the wind blew from the lake, all was well. If the wind came from the West, you would have to run inside and close the windows. A couple miles west of us were the stockyards. Back then, Chicago was the "hog butcher for the world." The smell wasn't pretty. Still, we began to love Chicago. As Carl Sandburg wrote of Chicago:

Hog Butcher for the World,
Tool Maker, Stacker of Wheat,

Player with Railroads and the Nation's Freight
  Handler;
Stormy, husky, brawling,
City of the Big Shoulders.

Unfortunately, our kitchen was right above the coal furnace. I was not aware of the danger to our health from the coal dust we inhaled. It was the dirt that I could not stand. Every three weeks, I had to wash our white polyester curtains or live with the dirty look. The white kitchen walls turned gray and had to be washed often. I got tired of all the washing, so I painted the kitchen walls and ceiling a dark green. Ugh! But at least I could not see the coal dust and just let the green get darker and darker. I did not let all that get to me. The only thing our family really wanted was a job for Frank.

Wisconsin Steel Chippers Wanted.

At last Frank had a job! He came home with the good news when Paul was just nine days old. Frank had seen an ad in the newspaper for Wisconsin Steel, "Chippers Wanted." He had chipped at Bethlehem Steel in Lackawanna and knew he could pass the chipping test. Frank chipped so well that the foreman tapped him on the back and said, "You have a job." Frank still worried that the company doctor would see that some finger joints were missing. But he passed the physical. Fortunately, the exam was so fast that they never noticed the missing finger joints. The company was hiring chippers but did not plan to keep them. When Frank asked for a locker, he was told he didn't need one. They said he would be there only one month. He worked there 30 years and one week.

The job changed everything. We could pay our bills. That allowed us to think of other things and enjoy the new baby. Our apartment had an open door, and friends dropped in any-time. My specialty was creamed tuna with peas and rice (with onions of course). It was good, cheap and could easily stretch to feed ten or twelve. We had a large living room and gave parties to raise money for our newspaper, the *Worker*. Frank was happy, working again. He loved to work and he loved his fellow workers. He expressed his joy with this little "back home" verse:

> All I want in this creation
> Is a pretty little wife and a big plantation.
> All I need to make me happy
> Is four little kids to call me pappy.

In midsummer of 1951, the fourth kid was born. We named him John Robert. John was named after Jonnie, Frank's sister and my best friend. She and her husband, Henry Ellis, had made the big sacrifice of giving up their jobs and leaving Buffalo to work for the Communist Party. The Party feared that the United States was going into full-blown fascism. They had asked Jonnie and Henry and many others to go "underground," as anti-fascists had to do in Nazi Germany. Jonnie became "Pat" and Henry became "Al" and they moved to Harlem. The names stuck. In later years, our son John could not understand how he could have been named after his aunt, since her name was Pat.

Lake Park Avenue—A Changing Neighborhood

Our apartment was located at 37th Street and Lake Park Avenue, a "changing" neighborhood. It was a great location. Venerable, still substantial apartment buildings lined our block. In the next block, there were historic Victorian mansions. Some apartments even had a view of Lake Michigan. The commute to the Loop, downtown Chicago, was only 15 minutes. When I rented our apartment, Farr and Associates Real Estate seemed happy to rent to me. They were not aware that they were renting to a mixed couple.

Chicago has long had the shameful reputation of one of the most segregated Northern cities. "Changing" neighborhood is a nice-sounding term used to disguise "white flight" and expanding ghetto. Even so, for a few years until white flight becomes complete, the streets of a "changing" neighborhood show a mix of people, "the way it ought to be." However, in my sixty years in the Chicago area, I have never seen a truly integrated neighborhood. A few higher-income areas around major universities may give the appearance of integration but it is more appearance than reality. Chicago's segregated real estate policy is all about money. On Lake Park Avenue, I saw how the realtors used scare tactics to induce white flight. After the white families left, the landlords rented the same apartments to African Americans at much higher rentals. Realtors got away with raising the rents because there was a big shortage of housing.

The housing shortage was compounded by racism. In much of the city, African Americans were denied the right to rent. Japanese Americans also faced discrimination in housing. When World War II ended, thousands of Nisei came to Chicago. They did not want to return to California where they had been removed during the war and forced into concentration camps. In Chicago, some Nisei families rented apartments on Lake Park Avenue.

The housing situation got worse when the big landlords saw a chance to make a quicker killing. Their frenzy for quick profits took a vicious form. Larger apartments were subdivided to make three or four one-room "kitchenettes." Nisei families and the remaining white families were forced out. The kitchenettes were then rented to African American families at a much higher total rent. Landlords collected the rents but made no repairs. In five years, the landlord got back his investment plus a huge profit. By that time, lack of maintenance and overcrowding had turned the building into a slum. The racists claimed "those people" ruined the neighborhood. The "city" found nothing illegal in this destruction of communities. Anyhow, it was widely believed that Chicago city housing inspectors were corrupt. The common belief was that the inspectors took payoffs. In return for payoffs, they let landlords violate the housing code in their rush for quick profits.

The apartments in our building were not that large and had escaped conversion to kitchenettes. Except for Frank, there were no African Americans in the building. Eight of the twelve apartments were rented to Nisei families. Farr & Co., our landlord, did not knowingly rent to African Americans. Other landlords on the block owned larger apartments. They did not want to rent to African Americans until the apartments were subdivided and they could increase their total rent.

Friends and Neighbors

I have many good memories from our four years on Lake Park Avenue. Our 12-apartment complex was a community of friends and comrades. I even kept my apartment door open, to make it easier to communicate. One day an FBI agent walked in to ask me questions about the Alexanders, who lived near the other entrance. I kept the apartment door locked after that.

The Tomsons on the third floor were also good friends. Goff, an engineer, helped Frank rebuild his car engine. Joan gave Jeanleah her first piano lessons. When Conrad and Naomi Komorowski moved out, they offered their apartment to Arlene and Lonnie Brigham, African American comrades. That gave us an in-house baby sitter, Arlene's son Donald. Arlene and I did a lot of things together. The Brigham family became our friends for life.

Above the Lumpkin apartment lived Toshiko, a Japanese war bride and a fascinating person. We called her Toshko. In Japan, she had married a Nisei soldier during the U.S. occupation. As a young lawyer, she was tapped by the Americans for the defense in the trial of Emperor Hirohito. In the Japanese press, Toshko took a lot of flak about the appointment that put her in the public eye. Only 25 years old, she faced prejudice as a woman and prejudice against her youth. In Japan, Toshko had heard that women were free in the U.S. The hope of equality made her look forward to coming to the U.S. with her husband. She told me how disappointed she was that American women were still so unequal. Toshko decided to become a journalist, got an MA in journalism at the Medill School at Northwestern University, raised her two daughters, and wrote for a newspaper.

I have great admiration for people like Toshko, who master a second language as an adult and write well in the new language. Joseph Conrad did it. My friend Toshiko Misaki did it, too.

Living among Nisei families was a rare opportunity for our family to learn about another culture. We formed close friendships with the Nisei families across the hall and above us. My friend, Caroline Shibata, showed me how to prepare a simple tasty Japanese dish. She knew I was not into elaborate cooking, so she showed me something easy. Just toast a sheet of dried sea weed over the gas burner and crumble the toasted sea weed over cooked rice. Her daughter, Josie, was the same age as Jeanleah and the two spent a lot of time together. I was pleased when Jeanleah asked for the *benjo*, the Japanese word for bathroom. She may not have retained any of the Japanese words she picked up. Still, I am sure that hearing another language helped her become a good language student.

Fight for Tenants' Rights

The Lake Park Avenue Communist Party club was a community resource. We got a call that tenants near the Illinois Institute of Technology (IIT) were refusing to move from their apartments. Their building was slated for demolition as part of a land grab by IIT under the excuse of "slum clearance." The landlord had turned off the heat although Chicago was suffering a deep winter freeze. We went over to the building to support the tenants' protest. In time, lack of water and heat forced the tenants out. Some moved into the lobby at city hall and camped there for days until the city found them housing. "Shorty" (Cliff) Howard and a couple of other friends slept in at city hall with the evictees. The rest of us camped there during the day.

Housing remained an urgent issue. When landlords supplied no heat, people tried to keep warm with dangerous space heaters. It was common to hear fire engines clanging through our neighborhood. A terrible tragedy highlighted the issue for the whole city. In the alley behind us, two single mothers with five children between them lived in a remodeled garage. The mother in charge left the house for a minute to buy some milk at the store around the corner. A flash fire broke out and five children burned to death. A hue and cry was raised against the mother. Nothing was said about the landlord collecting rent on an illegal structure, or the city inspectors who never condemned it.

The community was saddened and angry. The CPUSA club took the initiative to bring together a broad coalition. The coalition took the name, "Committee to Safeguard the Home against Fire." The committee's purpose was to prevent future fire tragedies and end the racist rental policies. Our goal was better enforcement of safety codes. This was my first of many experiences with coalitions in Chicago. It was a simple and powerful strategy. Bring together *everybody* who agrees on an issue, even if they disagree on other subjects. The pooled strength of the different groups can win on the issue that all the groups support.

If we waited until everybody agreed on everything, we could never move forward. There were selfish groups who wanted to "gain control" of a coalition even if that meant destroying it. Fortunately, we did not have that problem in the Committee to Safeguard the Home against Fire. We united Democrats, Communists, Republicans and non-political people. We included people of different religions and no religion. We were people of African American, Japanese and European descent.

Our landlord was as stingy as the rest of his kind. Our apartment was often too cold for a newborn baby. Frank was not going to let his baby freeze, so he loaded the coal feeder and got the furnace going again. All the apartments began to bask in the heat. That worked fine until the landlord padlocked the coal room. Our protests did not budge the landlord so there was only one thing left to do. Rent Strike! We learned from a long tradition of tenant strikes in Chicago. We notified the landlord that we were placing our rent money in escrow and would not pay him until he gave us some heat. I had never heard of escrow before, but it was a way of making sure the rent money would be ready when the landlord agreed to turn the heat back on.

In less than a week, Farr and Associates called our committee in to settle. I had never seen anyone like white-haired Mr. Farr. He looked as though he had been pressed between the pages of a book. All the juices were gone, and only the dry stuff was left. His voice came as though from miles away as he asked, "Are you impoverished?" We made it clear that we were not asking for charity. We wanted the heat we had paid for.

We got the heat. Winter was easier to take with a warm apartment to come back to after being out in the severe cold.

Willie McGee and the Martinsville Seven

Our Southside Party club made a big effort to save the life of Willie McGee. It was the same case that Hattie and I had worked on in Buffalo. McGee was an African American accused by his female employer of rape. Frank told me of a similar situation when he was a butler-chauffeur in Florida. A white woman, related to his employer, tried to entrap him. Fortunately, Frank recognized the danger and escaped the trap.

Together with some friends, we went to Congressman William Dawson to ask him to support Willie McGee. Dawson was only the third African American congressman elected in the U.S. since Reconstruction. The first two, Oscar de Priest and William Mitchell, were also from Chicago. Chicago has long been a leader in the fight for African American representation at all levels.

I believe that Dawson knew that McGee was innocent. But he was part of the Chicago political machine and he was not going to rock the boat. And he was very arrogant about it. "If you don't like it," he put it bluntly, "run against me." Dawson had just defeated Sam Parks, the Progressive Party candidate for Congress in 1950.

Willie McGee was executed in May, 1951. That was at the height of the McCarthy anti-Communist hysteria. Some "opinion-makers" claimed that McGee did not have a chance because Communists led the campaign to save him. But Communists also led the campaign to save the Scottsboro Nine in the 1930s. The Scottsboro Nine were saved. Other struggles that Communist helped to lead were also victorious. The difference was that people were more united in the 1930s than the 1950s. United, the labor-civil rights coalition won so much in the 30s—all the benefits we lump under the New Deal.

Sam Parks was a leader of the Packinghouse Worker's Union and a community activist. During the bottom of the McCarthy period, Parks organized an outdoor concert for Paul Robeson, right on 47th Street. The regular concert halls had refused to

Carl's birthday party, September 1950, photo by Jo Banks.

rent to the great singer. It was my second chance to be close to this great people's hero. He was an "All American" in many ways besides football (1918 and 1919). I am the proud owner of a photograph that Paul Robeson autographed. It shows a wonderfully mixed group of children, Japanese, African American and white, singing "Happy Birthday" to my son, Carl. Our little Paul, whom we had named after Robeson, was sound asleep and missing from the photo. But it was in his honor that big Paul autographed the picture.

Congressman Dawson continued to rule until his death in 1970. In 1971, Ralph Metcalfe, Olympic track star and anti-Hitler hero, was elected congressman. We supported Metcalfe's progressive acts but did not know him personally. After Metcalfe died, Harold Washington ran for Congress. We worked to elect him. We did know Washington personally. Harold knew everybody personally. That was his style.

Going back to Lake Park Avenue in the 1950s, we also worked to save the Martinsville Seven. The seven African American men, some of them teenagers, had been falsely accused of raping a white woman. They were convicted and sentenced to death. Protests erupted across the country and around the world. Our friend, Arlene Brigham joined a Civil Rights Congress delegation that met with the governor of Virginia. Arlene was from Mississippi; she knew the risk that she was taking by going to Virginia. Many others tried to talk to the governor. Still, he refused to grant clemency. The seven men were executed in February 1951. We called it a legal lynching.

Racist Riot on Peoria Street

In November 1949, I got an emergency phone call from my Party club. Aaron Bindman, an organizer for the International Longshore and Warehouse Union, was holed up in his house and needed help. Outside his house a racist mob was gathering, threatening him and his family with bodily harm. The night before, he had held a mixed (black-white) meeting in his house. The rumor went out that he was selling the house to a black family. But the mob had not yet jelled, and our caller thought they could be persuaded to go home peacefully. With a few friends, I rushed out to mingle with the crowd and spread the word of peace. We did not know that the police commissioner and the mayor had already been called but were "unavailable" to help.

END MOB VIOLENCE

ATTEND   MASS   MEETING

SATURDAY, FEBRUARY 23 - 6:00 P. M.

PLACE: BIG ZION BAPTIST CHURCH,
3027 SO. STATE STREET.

THE METROPOLE THEATRE STANDS AS AN ISLAND OF JIM CROW IN OUR COMMUN-
ITY. HOODLUM MOBS THREATEN THE LIFE AND SAFETY OF NEGRO PEOPLE WHO
CROSS THE 31ST AND WENTWORTH AVENUE MASON-DIXON LINE.

THIS MUST BE STOPPED!

Last Saturday night, when an interracial party led by the Civil Rights
Congress, entered the Metropole Theatre, mob violence shattered the peace and
quiet of Chicago's South Side as a band of hate-crazed white hoodlums made a
futile attempt to stop them.

Threats of physical violence, vile names, and assorted missels were hurl-
ed at the theatre which, the Civil Rights Congress contends, has long discour-
aged Negro patronage. Police guards and several riot squads were required to
escort the group to safety when they attempted to leave the theatre. The mob
had grown to several hundred raving maniacs during the time the group was inside the theatre.

The 2nd and 20th ward chapters of the Civil Rights Congress, under the
leadership of Mrs. Arlene Ward and Mrs Emily Freeman had been conducting a
campaign around the Metropole theatre for over a year, in an effort to guarantee the right of Negro people to enter the theatre. The violence flared as
a result of their efforts to enlist the aid of Negro and white people in the
community in breaking down the discriminatory barriers at the Metropole. Several Negro and white members of the 2nd and 20th ward chapters held an open-air
meeting at 31st and Wentworth on Saturday afternoon. They announced at that time
that they would be back that evening to attend the movie. When they arrived,
they were met by the mob.

THE NEGRO PEOPLE SEEK UNITY WITH THEIR WHITE ALLIES - NOT VIOLENCE.

BUT THEY WILL HAVE JUSTICE!

UNITE   AND   FIGHT!

Sponsored by: South Side Chapter, Civil Rights Congress
and Supporting Organizations,
3358 So. Parkway, Room 12 - KEnwood 6-9358,
Chicago 15, Illinois.

By the time we got there, fires had been lit in the street and stones were being thrown at the windows. I did talk to some women on the street, saying "Let's go home. We don't want any trouble." They seemed to agree. Suddenly a new element entered the crowd. The racist sentiment hardened. The crowd became a mob. The mob turned on the peace advocates and I became a target. Hate-filled faces jeered, "Rosie, why don't you go back to the University of Chicago!" The anti-black racism became mixed with antisemitism. Some shouted, "Hitler didn't kill enough of them!" Friends grabbed my arm and pulled me out of the crowd because I was prominently pregnant.

Probably I was lucky to get out unharmed. One of our friends was not that lucky. Dr. Sidney Bild, then a last year medical student, had also responded to an emergency phone call. He, too, was talking to people about going home, saying we don't want trouble. When asked, "What parish do you belong to?" Dr. Bild said, "None." That identified him as a non-mobster. A couple of mobsters attacked him and he defended himself. The police, who were idly standing by, arrested Bild. Then they took over the job of beating him. They threw him in the police wagon and beat him some more. At the police station they locked him up with three of his friends and four of the mobsters, all in the same cell. Meanwhile, the union organizer sat in his home with a loaded pistol in case the mob broke in. Fortunately, the mob did not try to enter. But every window was broken and the house was badly damaged. Soon after the riot, the Bindmans moved out. This excerpt from the Internet is quite accurate:

> The house on Peoria Street was one block south of the Visitation Catholic Church, one of the largest and most successful parishes in Chicago. In 1925, 1,575 children were enrolled in Visitation grammar school. It was the third-largest parochial school in Chicago. To the pastor, Rev. Msgr. Daniel F. Byrnes, the idea of Visitation as the center of the neighborhood was one which he was prepared to fight to save. The Catholic Interracial Council noted the large amount of Catholics participating in riots in Chicago and implored parish priests to preserve order. But immediately after the Peoria Street riots, Visitation's parishioners

organized the "Garfield Boulevard Improvement Association," with the intent of keeping the blacks out, and occasionally held their meetings in the parish hall. Monsignor Byrne, his parishioners would say later, routinely read the church boundaries at Sunday's Mass and promised to "buy up property before permitting Negroes to move in."[13]

"The Peoria Street riot in Englewood set precedence in racial conflicts to come because of its violence," according to *A Short History of Englewood*. They write that, "Police came under criticism for not breaking up the crowd earlier. When a member of the mayor's Commission on Human Relations contacted the Englewood Police during the riot, he was told that it was difficult for the police to disperse the crowds because they were neighbors."[14]

Metropole Theater Riot

Another complaint of discrimination plunged Frank and me into a huge anti-black riot in November, 1952. An African American couple reported that the Metropole Theater, on 31st Street near Wentworth, had refused to sell them tickets. The militant Civil Rights Congress decided to try to challenge the discrimination. They organized a mixed group to go to the theater together. About seven couples participated. We were admitted to the theater, one couple at a time. The film was a "western," Frank's favorite.

After some tension-filled minutes, we saw people running up and down the aisles, giving people messages. Then those people got up, in twos and threes, to leave the theater. Soon they began to leave in tens and twenties. We seven couples were the only ones left inside. I decided to go out to the lobby to see what was happening. The street was packed with the same hate-filled faces we had seen on Peoria Street. The crowd

13 http://people.virginia.edu/~mrs8t/englewood/peoria.htm., 11
14 *Ibid.*

was dense, maybe 500. There was no way we could leave with the mob blocking the entrance.

I returned to my seat with the news. The only calm face in our group was Frank's. He was enjoying his Western movie and refused to be frightened. Frankly, the rest of our group, including me, was scared. We were worried about how to get out without being beaten by the mob. Just then, we were surprised to see Arlene and Lonnie Brigham come into the theater. Unknown to us, a more tense drama had played outside the theater. The Brighams had come late but had not turned away when they saw the mob. A small number of police had also arrived. But they did nothing to break up the mob. Arlene saw an African American plainclothesman forced to draw his gun to protect himself from the mob. With incredible bravery, Lonnie and Arlene made their way through the white mob to join us. Arlene confided to me later that she had a bottle/can opener in her pocket. She did not hesitate to use it to make her way in.

When the large mob gathered so quickly, we assumed that it was organized by the local Catholic Church. Given the statements by Rev. Msgr. Daniel F. Byrnes of Englewood, that assumption was reasonable. Also, one of our own Lake Park friends may have inadvertently alerted the mob. Charles (Chuck) Freeman, an African American neighbor, was a true believer in black-white unity. He was also incredibly brave. With loudspeakers on top of his shiny new, green Kaiser car, Chuck drove up and down the streets surrounding the theater, booming out his message of unity. "White workers," he shouted, "come out and defend your black brothers. Black and White, Unite and Fight!" The white residents came out all right but it was not to unite with us. Every window in Chuck's car was broken. Bricks dented the sides. And Chuck had been so proud of his car! Miraculously, he was not hurt. Fortunately, none of us knew any of these details while we were inside the theater.

After what seemed like a very long time, two police wagons drew up to the back doors. I was disgusted that the police did not try to break up the mob. Instead, they took us out like convicts and stuffed us in two wagons. Later, historians would record the outcome. The Metropole Theater "incident" resulted in African Americans being driven back across Wentworth Avenue.[15]

Even with these personal experiences, we did not know the full extent of racist violence in Chicago. Arnold Hirsch wrote that "one racially motivated bombing or arson occurred every twenty days" in Chicago at that time. The army had asked for 12,000 tear gas and smoke grenades and 10,000 12-gauge shotgun shells "in the event of disorders in Chicago."[16] The Chicago city government followed a conscious policy of suppressing reports of racist violence. The newspaper owners fully supported the mayor in this policy. For example, the Chicago papers did not cover the infamous Cicero riot of July 10–12, 1951, until the third day, and only after images of the riot had already appeared on national TV.

With the anti-African American riots in Chicago, the McCarthy witch hunts and the Korean War, I felt that the country was going to hell. But when the civil rights movement of the 1960s and 1970s blossomed, our spirits picked up. Our struggles had helped lay the foundation for that great movement.

Summer Job on the Assembly Line

Our first summer in Chicago, 1950, was another chance for my two older children to visit Aunt Lillian on her farm. Our neighbor, Arlene Brigham, was ready to baby-sit for Paul who still fit in a basket. It was a good time for me to work for a couple of months and bring in some money. Frank and I were having so much fun raising baby Paul that we had decided to have one more baby. The cash I could earn would help handle the expenses for my fourth and last child. So I got another job on an assembly line, wiring and soldering tape recorders. On the line, I sat next to Maria, a Mexican American woman. Our conversation turned to food and budgets. Her food budget for the week was only $10! How did she do it?

---

[15] Arnold Richard Hirsch, *Making the Second Ghetto: Race and Housing in Chicago, 1940–1960* (Chicago: University of Chicago Press, 1998), note 88.

[16] *Ibid.*, 43.

For the next two months I heard her recipes. It all sounded very delicious and I took her word that it could be done for $10 a week. I am ashamed to say that I never tried to make her refried beans. There were two reasons for that. First, all of the recipes sounded like a lot of work. I was full of the spirit of women's liberation (and still am). Beans are good just stewed. Why go to the trouble of frying them, let alone re-frying them? The other drawback was Maria's frequent trips to the doctor. What was her trouble? Stomach problems!

In later years I had the luck to partake of my friend Juanita Andrade's Mexican cooking. I found out what I had been missing all of those years. And my stomach was just fine. In later years, Juanita reassured me when we needed to raise money for the Wisconsin Steel workers' Save Our Jobs Committee. I was agonizing about cooking hundreds of dinners. "Don't worry," she told me. "Everybody has talent. Mine is cooking. It will be all right." And the dinners always were a huge success. Unfortunately, her talent never rubbed off on me. I can do basic cooking, and that's where it ends. As a friend put it, I want no more than four ingredients in any recipe that I try. And two of them have to be salt and pepper!

Hospital Racism Kills

Soon after Arlene Brigham moved into our apartment building, she visited relatives in Mississippi. Arlene returned with her 13-year- old nephew, Sonny. Mozella, Sonny's mother, soon followed. Sonny started school in Chicago, and his future looked bright. An attack of appendicitis was promptly treated and the appendix removed. We thought that coming to Chicago had saved his life.

About one year later, Sonny experienced abdominal pain one morning. The pain became severe that night. Mozella and the Brighams rushed him to nearby Michael Reese Hospital. At 4 a.m. they returned. Mozella's screams woke me up, and I rushed out into the hallway. "Sonny is dead," Arlene told me, quietly. I wanted to scream, too. Nearby Michael Reese Hospital had turned Sonny away. They seemed more interested in his insurance (or lack of it) than in the sick child. "Take him to Cook County Hospital," they said. What they did not tell Arlene or Mozella was that Sonny had an intestinal adhesion, a dangerous post-surgery condition. At Cook County, Sonny waited four hours and died without being seen. Surgery could have saved his life. The emergency room doctors were working on a patient with extensive burns. No other physicians were available.

Sonny was not the first, and unfortunately, not the last child who died after being turned away by a private hospital. For our community of friends and comrades, the needless loss of our young friend left a wound that will never heal. Unfortunately, there was a sequel to this tragic story. An African American baby was taken to the emergency room of Woodlawn Hospital. The baby was very sick, but the hospital sent her away. The child died enroute to Cook County Hospital. The protest movement that followed did not go away. It continued under the leadership of Dr. Quentin Young and led to the founding of the Medical Committee for Human Rights. Legislation was won that makes it illegal for a hospital to turn away a patient in critical condition.

I met Dr. Young, hero of the "health care for all" movement, when I needed emergency care. But that story comes later.

Stockholm Peace Pledge

By 1949, the horrors of nuclear war had touched the conscience of people around the world. The Cold War was taking the form of economic blockades and preparations for war. In response, the World Peace Council was organized in Paris, in April 1949. Their committee met in Stockholm in March 1950, and launched the Stockholm Appeal:

> We demand the absolute banning of the atomic bomb, weapon of terror and mass extermination of populations.
> We demand the establishment of strict international control to ensure the implementation of this ban.
> We consider that the first government to use the atomic weapon against any country whatsoever

would be committing a crime against humanity
and should be dealt with as a war criminal.
We call on all men of goodwill throughout the
world to sign this Appeal.

Frank and I were among thousands of petition circulators
who brought in 1,350,000 signatures in the United States. Over
500 million people signed throughout the world. Support for
banning nuclear weapons was so strong on Chicago's South
Side that long lines of people formed, waiting to sign our petitions. In Buffalo, Frank's whole family circulated the Stockholm Peace Pledge. Every activist I knew and their friends
were working day and night to eliminate all nuclear weapons.

McCarthy Repression

The domestic atmosphere was also poisoned by McCarthyism.
The "red scare" was directed against liberals and progressives
in government, film industry and the labor unions as well as
the Communist Party. Good, decent people were hounded
out of their jobs. Some even committed suicide, for example,
the talented actor John Garfield. FBI agents were literally
jumping out behind every bush, as happened to me later in
Gary, Indiana. In Michigan, the six-year old daughter of the
Communist leader, Gil Green, was rejected by a progressive
summer camp for fear of reprisal from the FBI. When she was
finally accepted by a church-run camp, the FBI followed her to
watch her comings and goings from the camp baseball field to
the lake.

Despite the repression, we found a way to do political work
in the Lake Park Avenue neighborhood. Bernice Bild and I
would stash our leaflets inside the baby carriages when we
took our infants out for some air. Then we could pass out the
fliers, one at a time, without being noticed.

Recently I was asked, "What was it like to live under the
McCarthy witch hunts?" It was a period that made brave
people braver. At the same time, the repression made weak
people weaker. We defied the red scare to continue to work
for peace, jobs, democracy and socialism. But we paid a price.

Even people like Frank and me, who did not lose our jobs, felt the intimidation. We held our heads up high and attended a peace meeting. As you reached for the knob to open the door, a camera's flash went off in your face. We were advised to park a block or two from the meeting because the police were writing down the license numbers of all cars parked on the block. All your phone calls, whether to the doctor or your kids' teachers, were interrupted by obvious clicks. Even then, the FBI (or was it the CIA?) had technology to tap phones without making it so obvious. I suspected that they sent clicking noises to intimidate us and nobody was really listening.

Sometimes we may be thrust into situations where we have to take individual action. That happened to me at the corner of Cottage Grove and Pershing Boulevard, 3900 south. In the early 1950s, there was a lot of pedestrian traffic there. One afternoon, I saw two big cops manhandling a boy of about 13. As a mother, I had to do something. I'll admit that I got hysterical and began to scream, "What are you doing to that child!" A crowd gathered around us. The cops were white, and the child, as well as the gathering crowd, was African American. An angry mood was developing. The cops looked around at the crowd and at me. Hatred and fear showed in the policemen's faces. Then they let the child go. I felt the strength of the people. At a time of repression, our only protection is the support of people.

Smith Act Convictions

Hundreds of Communist Party members were indicted under the Smith Act between 1949 and 1957. Although the Supreme Court reversed some Smith Act convictions in 1957, it was too late for the top eleven national leaders of the Communist Party. They had already served five years in the federal penitentiary and paid heavy fines. They were convicted not of any actions but "conspiracy to teach" the overthrow of the government. In *The American Inquisition*, Cedric Belfrage explained why the conspiracy charge was used. "This "ancient British device was useful in cases where it had been decided to jail someone for his politics, but proof that he actually did anything might appear weak. He was then accused of talking about doing something, which the law rated as a more serious offense, and innocence of which was beyond proof."[17]

In this atmosphere of severe repression, the Communist Party made an understandable, but damaging mistake. They feared that a fascist dictatorship would soon come to power in the U.S. To prepare for this likelihood, the Party decided to build an underground structure that could continue to fight for people's rights even if the Party became illegal. The mistake proved damaging because good, active people were placed "underground," effectively out of action. For the Lumpkin family, it was a blow to their togetherness. Both Jonnie and Warren had gone "underground." Frank heard that his brother was somewhere in Chicago. Day after day, Frank cruised the streets hoping for a sighting of his much-loved brother. Warren did see his nephew's baby photo in the window of Jo Banks' photography shop. So he knew we were in town. But the two brothers did not find each other until some years later.

What was going on in the country that made Communists fear that the U.S. was going fascist? On the domestic scene, McCarthyite repression was raging. On an international level, the Truman doctrine led to the Cold War. In contrast to FDR's policy of peaceful coexistence with the socialist countries, the Cold War was dedicated to the overthrow of the socialist governments. The Cold War became hot during the Korean War, launched under cover of fighting communism. It lasted from June 25, 1950, to July 27, 1953. The invasion of Korea was just as unjustified and deadly as the later Vietnam and Iraq Wars.

My good friend and neighbor was one of thousands of Americans who suffered during the Korean War. Her husband had been sent to fight in Korea, leaving her and their little daughter without their breadwinner. Her husband had joined the National Guard to make a little extra money, never dreaming that he would be sent to fight in Korea. Fortunately he survived, but the war caused two to four million casualties. U.S. forces alone suffered 103,000 wounded, 36,516 deaths and

---

[17] Cedric Belfrage, *The American Inquisition, 1945-1960* (Indianapolis, Indiana: Bobbs-Merrill, 1973).

8,142 missing in action. In recent times, National Guard units are being sent to fight foreign wars again. As I write, Lumpkin family members have been sent to Afghanistan and Iraq.

Opposition to the Korean War was equated with being a Communist. In our Lake Park neighborhood, most sympathized with our call for peace. But fear silenced many who opposed the war. The McCarthy repression made people afraid that they would lose their job or even go to jail if they spoke for peace. Living through that time taught me the importance of democracy. We never should voluntarily give up our democratic rights, especially freedom of speech and assembly. That's why the Employee Free Choice Act is so important. It restores the right of workers to organize.

Back to Work in Electronics

John, my youngest, was all of 11 months old when I decided to work for a couple of months. I wanted to make some money for a family vacation. I used my electronics experience to get a job as a technical correspondent for Allied Radio. Paul was in a church-sponsored preschool, and Carl and Jeanleah were in public school. We found a loving home to provide day care for John. The Ketchum's home turned out to be too loving. When Frank picked up our son one afternoon, John told Mr. Ketchum, "Goodbye daddy." Frank's reaction was immediate. "Don't you know you just lost your job?" he said to Mr. Ketchum. By that time, John had reached two years of age, old enough to join Paul at the preschool. Frank lost no time in making the switch.

Had it not been for the sexism that challenged me on the job, I would have quit Allied Radio in two months as planned. Instead, I worked for them for 11 years. The department I had been hired into had been all male. The men had decided to freeze me out by not talking to me, except yes, no, or even briefer responses like a nod of the head. Otherwise, they seemed decent enough. It was obvious to me that they thought my hiring was a move to bring their wages down. Some weeks later, I got my chance to break through. I was alone with one of the men for a few hours, doing an inventory. "Look, Bob,"

I said, "you guys don't have to be afraid that I will bring your pay down. Tell me what you are making. If the company is paying me less, I will go in and demand a raise. And if I don't get it, I will quit!"

Bob did not tell me how much the men got. So I said, "OK, I'll tell you what I make." And I did. Bob still would not tell me how much the men were paid. A couple of weeks later, the supervisor told me that I should not have told anyone how much I was paid. Evidently, I was not bringing the wage scale down. I never did find out how much the others were paid. But after that day, the men began to talk to me. I considered that a victory for women's rights. It was not the right time to quit. Then I became interested in the electronics theory I was learning on the job. As long as I was learning, and received an average wage, it was a good job. So I did not quit after our family vacation. In fact, I worked four years for Allied Radio, left to work in Gary for U.S. Steel for two years and then returned to Allied Radio/Knight Kit for another seven years.

Julius and Ethel Rosenberg

On June 19, 1953, I got a phone call to rush down to the federal court building in downtown Chicago. We were part of a worldwide movement to save Julius and Ethel Rosenberg. A prejudiced judge had sentenced them to die in the electric chair after they were found "guilty" in a rigged trial. The charge was conspiracy to spy during World War II for the Soviet Union, a major ally of the United States during that war. Their real crime, in the eyes of the Cold Warriors, was their insistence that the trial was a political frame-up. The Rosenbergs refused to "confess," which meant giving more names for people to be prosecuted.

The execution was scheduled for the next day, the Jewish Sabbath. Religious people were objecting to an execution on the Sabbath. We had to hurry because the word was the execution might be done earlier. Arlene Brigham, her sister Mozella and three other women agreed to go. My daughter, Jeanleah, was only seven years old, but she wanted to go, too.

All seven of us squeezed into my little old car that got half way there and died. So we jumped out and hailed two cabs; one cab would not hold us all. We got there in time to join the protest, one of thousands throughout the world. As we marched with heavy hearts, the chilling news reached us. Instead of postponing the electrocution until after the Sabbath, it had been moved up. Julius and Ethel Rosenberg were dead.

My daughter was very upset. She pointed to a policeman on guard, "Mommy, the policeman is laughing." At the time, we did not know the full horror of this legal murder. The first jolt of electricity lasted fifty-seven seconds and failed to kill Ethel. She was re-strapped to the chair and given two more jolts before being pronounced dead. Ethel Rosenberg was the first woman executed by the United States government since 1865..

Chapter *14*

Evicted!
Landlords gave the Lumpkins a hard time.

IN 1953, we left Lake Park Avenue and moved to Woodlawn. The move was entirely involuntary. We were evicted! Rent control ended in Chicago on June 30, 1953. That very same day, the Lumpkins and the Brighams were served with eviction notices. With the end of rent control, tenants lost their protection from eviction. Farr and Associates said nothing about the rent strike, their real reason for evicting us. All they had to say in court was, "They are Communists," and the judge granted the eviction order.

Oh yes, we did more or less have an attorney. Irving Steinberg, that stalwart fighter for civil liberties, was not available. He found us a young, would-be civil liberties champion who was kind enough to take our case *pro bono*. This was during the worst of the McCarthy period of repression. It was just two weeks after the execution of Ethel and Julius Rosenberg. When the judge said, "Communists?! Eviction granted!" our attorney flinched. He murmured something but I did not hear it. Even if he had thundered in defense of our constitutional rights, it would not have stopped that judge. But I would have felt better about it. As it is, we lost in court without a real fight.

The next day, I was standing on the lunch line at Allied Radio. Workers were reading the *Chicago Tribune* and looking at me with that funny look. "Do you live at 3650 South Lake Park Avenue?" they asked. Our eviction case had made first page! The reaction of my co-workers to the eviction story was sympathetic. They knew that apartments were in short supply.

The shortage of housing during World War II had continued after the war. And my job was safe. Fortunately for me, Allied Radio was then owned by a Jewish family that respected their employees' First Amendment rights. The rumor was that these owners had actively opposed the execution of Ethel and Julius Rosenberg.

Evicted! With four kids.

Where was I going to find another rental that would take a family with four children? As luck would have it, I found an apartment in Woodlawn, another "changing" neighborhood on Chicago's South Side. The neighborhood was dominated by the nearby University of Chicago. It was "changing" to a poor African American community. The apartment was in a two-flat building. Two elderly white women, co-owners, lived downstairs. I told them that I had two children; that was only a little lie. I had only two children at home because Carl and Jeanleah were away at camp. It was seeing Frank that put the owners in shock. They would never have rented to an African American.

Our first few weeks in the new apartment were tense. The owners charged that we let the kids roller skate in the apartment. Frank went down to the owners to show them the little pull toys that the boys had played with. "We would never let our children roller skate inside the house," he explained. Whatever Frank told them, they ended up as friends. I was OK with them, but it was Frank they really liked. They relied on his help, and he was always glad to give it. Guess those elderly women had never really met an African American before. After we moved, they rented to another African American family.

We had an ongoing interaction with university faculty types during the year we lived in Woodlawn. Around the corner, the university had loaned a piece of land for use as a "tot lot" or play area for small children. We had two tots, so Frank decided to give the volunteers a hand. The volunteers were putting a fence across the front of the lot before they opened the area to children. Half a dozen university folk were digging holes for the posts. Frank moved forward to help. In a few minutes, Frank was doing the job himself, and the other six were standing around, watching in admiration. Frank and I got a big laugh out of that. Anyway, it was good to have a tot lot nearby.

Actually, in my 60 years of living with Frank, Woodlawn was the only place where we lived on the second floor. Coming from the East Bronx in New York, many-storied tenement buildings were the norm for me. But Frank's family had always lived in a house, even if only a farm worker's house that belonged to the plantation owner. "I don't like to live above other people," he told me. Still, he was not afraid of heights. Frank decided to put up a TV antenna on the slanted roof, two stories high. Since I was the one who knew how to wire the antenna, I needed to climb up there with him.

Frank extended the ladder to its full height, ending just under the edge of the roof. From the ladder, he grabbed the slanted roof and hoisted himself up. I merrily climbed up after him, but did not want to try hoisting myself over the edge of the roof. Still, I did not want to admit defeat. Just then, his big arm reached down. I grabbed it and he pulled me up. The rest was easy. Looking back, we both took an insane risk. Only years later did I hear Frank's story about his slide down a couple of floors after he lost his grip inside a brewery vat. Had I heard that story earlier, I never would have climbed to the roof on a ladder that did not quite reach the edge.

I could never have cared for four children and held a job without the help of my oldest child. When Frank worked days, Carl was in charge after I left for work. Jeanleah was not quite eight, and Carl was nine when we lived in Woodlawn. I did not think it a big thing to leave for work and count on them to get themselves to school. I would hesitate to do that now, but that is the way it was when I grew up. Paul and John were just four and two and a half years old. The preschool van arrived 15 minutes after I had to leave for work. I had them all dressed and fed before I left. I trusted Carl to take Paul and John down the stairs and into the preschool van before he left for school. Perhaps climbing up on the roof was not the biggest risk I took those days. Fortunately, we all survived.

Woodlawn

The Woodlawn and Lake Park areas have been gentrified since our time there, 1949–1954. Back in 1949, many Chicagoans still followed the country custom of shooting off guns to celebrate New Year's Eve. But Woodlawn was the only place we lived where we often heard shots when it was not New Year's Eve. After I heard the gunfire, I listened for police or ambulance sirens. Sometimes I heard the sirens after what seemed like half an hour. Sometimes I heard nothing more. At least on New Year's Eve we knew that the guns had not been fired in anger.

I thought of a friend on Lake Park Avenue who slept with a loaded gun under his pillow. One night he looked out of his second floor window and saw someone on a ladder, lifting the window. He pulled the gun out and shot through the window. Then he went back to sleep. His story worried me. I would not want to kill or wound anybody, even a burglar. I preferred to rely on a lock bolt that let the window open a few inches for air. It worked for me in the Lake Park apartment. As I was in bed one night and Frank was in the mill, I heard the window slide up and stop at the lock bolt. My heart began to pound. In a deep voice that I did not recognize I shouted, "Get the hell out of here or I'll call the police!" I heard nothing more and eventually went back to sleep. The lock bolt had done its job.

There were some good features to our Woodlawn location. We lived within walking distance of Lake Michigan beaches and the Museum of Science and Industry. Visiting the museum was a favorite treat for all the family, and absolutely free. Families like mine are now cut off from such wonderful opportunities. High admission fees have put the museums and zoos out of reach of many working class families.

In Woodlawn, we missed the community struggles that kept us busy for the four years we lived on Lake Park Avenue. The McCarthy repression had taken its toll. The movement did not begin to rebound until the '60s when freedom riders went into the Deep South to fight for "One person, one vote." One of Frank's brothers was "someplace" in Chicago. He had gone underground at the request of the Communist Party. After the Supreme Court threw out Smith Act convictions, some degree of freedom returned. One of the first things Frank did was to get together with his brother and his sister, Jonnie, who also had gone underground. They were very happy to live normal lives again. Neither one ever returned to live in Buffalo. Nor did we.

Trumbull Park

The year we moved to Woodlawn was the year of one of the worst and longest-lasting racist riots in Chicago. It was unleashed in Trumbull Park, in the South Deering neighborhood of Wisconsin Steel. African Americans on the

South Side wanted to rush to the defense of the families under attack. But the families who had moved to Trumbull Park were too far away from the black community. The McCarthy repression had weakened the movement. We were not strong enough to organize so long a march. And in 1951, the Chicago suburb of Cicero allowed racist riots to rage. The whole country watched the riot fires on national TV.

In a similar vein, Gerald Horne blames McCarthyism in his *Fire This Time: The Watts Uprising and the 1960s*.[18] He connects the lack of organization in the Watts uprising to the weakening of the Los Angeles Communist Party during the McCarthy repression. Not until 1966, thirteen years later, did the civil rights movement regain the strength to march to Cicero. That year, Frank and I marched with Rev. Martin Luther King, Jr. to Marquette Park in Chicago, another riot scene.

The Trumbull Park riot started when a racist mob tried to drive out an African American family from their apartment in the then new and desirable public housing near Wisconsin Steel. The riot began August 5, 1953, and continued for weeks. Four more African American families moved in and were met by a new round of violence. Frank London Brown was one of the new tenants. His novel, *Trumbull Park*, captured the heroism of the African American tenants.[19] They withstood bombs going off outside their windows every night, rocks thrown at their windows, and a barrage of insults. Again, the police made no attempt to disperse the mobs.

The racist violence at Trumbull Park spilled out into the streets around Wisconsin Steel. During these riots, African American steel workers had to drive through a barrage of stones to get to work. Some who were not lucky enough to have a car were beaten as they waited at bus transfer points near the plant. Two nearby taverns that served African American as well as white and Mexican steel workers were bombed.[20]

---

18 Gerald Horne, *The Fire This Time: The Watts Uprising and the 1960s* (Charlottesville, Virginia: University Press of Virginia, 1995).

19 Frank London Brown, *Trumbull Park* (Chicago: Regnery,1959).

20 William Kornblum, *Blue Collar Community* (Chicago: University of Chicago Press, 1974), 82.

The violence was kept going with money sent in by right-wing groups based outside of Chicago.

The mill itself was a safe haven. Many Mexican and white steel workers apologized to the African American workers for the violence they faced coming to work in the mill. They recognized that all steel workers had common interests and should support each other. But those who profited from racial division kept the violence going. Racism held back workers' solidarity for many years.

Dr. Quentin Young

In Woodlawn, I met Dr. Young as thousands had, as a patient. Now he is a famous leader in the fight for 'health care for all." I had a bad "cold," but it was not like anything I ever had before. When the fever first hit, it felt like I was a mouse and some huge cat was shaking the life out of me. I went to a doctor on the North Side who said I had "what was going around." After ten days I was so sick that I went to the nearest doctor I knew. He was out. Yes, I agreed to see his assistant.

The young doctor who rolled my eyelid down, and knew instantly what disease I had, said his name was Quentin Young. He did a urine test, shook the jar, saw the yellow foam and said, "You have hepatitis and must go to the hospital." "But doctor," I replied. "I have four small children. Couldn't I just take treatment after work?" Although Dr. Young was not tall, he drew himself up to his full height and solemnly told me, "Not under my care."

Then this doctor, who had never seen me before, offered to go to my home to explain to my husband why I had to be hospitalized. Having done that, he admitted me to Woodlawn Hospital. The next day he told me, "You are the last patient I was able to admit." He had spearheaded the protest against Woodlawn Hospital's refusal to admit a very sick African American baby. The baby died on the way to another hospital. Because of his stand against racism, the hospital had removed Dr. Young from their staff!

Somehow, Frank and the children survived my three weeks in the hospital. Frank's youngest sister, Gladys, came from

Gladys Lumpkin (right) with Stockholm Peace Pledge

Buffalo to help. Gladys, in my mind, was the most beautiful of the Lumpkin sisters. She was almost as tall as Frank, gracefully slim as a reed, and with the largest eyes I have ever seen. The photo for this section shows her collecting signatures for the Stockholm Peace Pledge. There was no medication for hepatitis in 1953, just bed rest, three weeks of it. Since I felt OK once I was put to bed, I had plenty of time to think. Other patients came and went in my room, all elderly women. For the first time in my life I thought about old age and how it ought to be.

Fortunately, there were some hospital workers who liked to stop and talk. There may be no cure for old age, we agreed. Still, there could be a cure for the emptiness so many old people felt. These discussions helped the time pass, and I learned a lot from the hospital workers. Also, I read to the point of eyestrain. A fellow-worker from Allied Radio had brought me a copy of Tolstoy's *War and Peace*. I read it all, page by page. When else could I have read over 1,000 pages of a novel?

Wisconsin Steel, the Social Side

The move to Woodlawn brought Frank closer to his job at Wisconsin Steel. That made it easier for Frank to bring fellow workers home with him. While I was at work, he and a buddy decided to try their hand at baking. The results were interesting. For one creation, they used a half cup of salt and one teaspoon of sugar. Just one taste and they knew they had made a bad mistake. Another time, they left out the baking powder. I didn't mind their messing around in my kitchen. But my hope that they would become accomplished bakers was not fulfilled. Their culinary skills remained at the level of warming up food on the salamander heaters in the mill.

Jose Andrade, Frank's partner and *compadre*, brought an ample supply of tacos, enchiladas, tamales and gorditas for his lunch in the mill. One morning, Frank brought home a bagful left over from the night shift. "What did you bring these for?" I asked sourly. But since they were there I heated some in the oven and tried one. "These are good!" I exclaimed. They were the work of Juanita Andrade, Jose's wife. After that, I looked forward to the leftovers from the mill. But I did not meet Juanita until the mill closed in 1980, many years later.

Emmett Paul was another good buddy from Wisconsin Steel and a good comrade. He had left Chicago and moved to nearby Gary. We visited his home and enjoyed the semi-rural location. There was room for children to run and play and some nearby woods to explore.

Emmett's TV set was not bringing in the channels. I had learned enough at Allied Radio to make the minor tuner adjustment that was needed. In gratitude, Emmett took one of the fat chickens he was raising and gave it to us, alive. There was a lot of excitement in the car on the return trip with four children and a live chicken. When we got back to Woodlawn, I wondered what Frank planned to do with that chicken. And when would he do it? The apartment had a long hallway running though it with bedroom doors opening on either side.

My daughter was especially tender-hearted about animals. "You're not going to kill it," she pleaded. Frank took the chicken to the kitchen, and the rest of us retreated to our rooms. But we opened our doors and there were four or five heads sticking out in the long hallway, hoping against hope. The dread deed was done and Frank cleaned and cooked that chicken. Nobody refused to eat it, but I would not want to repeat that experience. Frank was the only "country" person among us.

We kept up with the Emmett Paul family for many years. He and his wife retired to Guadalajara, Mexico, and we visited them there. On a later trip to Merida, Mexico, I was walking down a narrow street in the market. There I came face to face with Catherine Paul, Emmett's wife. And we didn't even know they had moved to Merida! The Pauls made our trip to Merida very special. This African American steel worker family found the culture of Mexico warm and inviting. They helped Frank and me feel that workers around the world are all connected.

Our 1953 visit to Emmett's house in Gary had planted a seed. In general, landlords had given the Lumpkins a hard time. Why not get our own house and move out of the city to Gary? The children would be free to play outside and I could have a garden. The train could take me to Chicago and I could still keep my job. On Frank's part, he did not mind the 14-mile drive from Gary to South Chicago.

We found a new, cheap housing development in the Wooded Highlands-Tolleston area on Gary's West Side. The prefab homes with composition-board sides were set on concrete slabs placed on the sand. The small homes sold for $7,500, with a down payment of $500. My hand shook when I wrote the check. It was by far the largest check I had ever written.

Chapter 15

Gary, City of Steel
We want water! We want sewers!

Our seven and one-half years in Gary, Indiana, 1954–1962, were formative years for the whole family. For the children, there was plenty of open space. No tall buildings blocked the view. Somehow it made me feel more alive to see the whole sky, not just a little patch between buildings. A strip of oak woods was just across the street. The woods ran along a ridge marking a prehistoric level of Lake Michigan. It was great for sledding. The kids gave the hills picturesque names like "Suicide Slope" and "Dead Man's Hill." Prickly pears grew in the sand. Wild asparagus for the asking sprouted all over in the spring. On the other side of the woods was Tolleston High School and Ernie Pyle Elementary, schools that seemed better than those we left in Chicago.

Tolleston was yet another "changing neighborhood." Almost all of the white families lived in homes of standard quality north of the woods. On the south side of the woods, our side, most of the homes were newly constructed "prefab" buildings. In twenty years they became slums. Most of the African American families lived on our side of the woods. There had been problems with racism at the school a few years earlier. Frank Sinatra, they said, came to Tolleston High School during World War II to help stop a racist riot. The school seemed quiet when we moved there in the'50s. But the tensions of a "changing neighborhood" were just beneath the surface. When my oldest son, Carl, went to class, other white children asked him, "When are you moving?" "We just got here," Carl replied. Almost all the men in our Gary neighborhood were steel workers. Almost all of the women stayed home, caring for the family and the house. I was one of the very few exceptions. For one thing, it was very difficult for the wife of a shift worker to work outside the home. More to the point, there were few jobs for women in Gary. There was one window-wiper factory in Gary that hired women. The wages they paid were too low to allow a woman to pay for child care. Besides, I never heard of any child care facility in our neighborhood. Next door to us, Mrs. Brooks took care of her grandchild while her daughter worked. Mrs. Brooks told me that she, too, had been raised by her grandmother. That was common in the South, she added. It was easier for younger women to find work.

The Sky's On Fire!

I kept my Allied Radio job in Chicago and rode in on the Pennsylvania Railroad Valparaiso Local. It did not take me long to learn how to sleep on the train. As soon as my head hit the back of the seat, I would snooze. In the winter, it was dark by the time I got home. One night I looked to the east and it was all afire. The night sky had turned pink. "Frank," I called, "there's a big fire out there." He laughed. "They're just pouring a heat of steel," he told me. Gary was truly a steeltown. Another night, though, the sky was ablaze in every direction. We stood and watched in wonder as bright yellow and green streamers shot down to the horizon. It had nothing to do with steel. My guess was that we were enjoying a rare visit of the Northern Lights to our latitude.

Our area was semi-rural. Early one Saturday morning, Mr. Fisher, who lived four blocks away, came a-knocking on our door. He wanted Frank to help him butcher a hog. Frank went with Fisher in a minute, like butchering a hog was the most natural thing to do. He did come back with some tasty pork chops. Another time he was called to use his country skills, the outcome was less to my taste. The kids had killed a squirrel with their BB gun. They had the nerve to bring it home, and

Frank had the nerve to dress and cook the varmint. I guess it made a tasty stew but I would have no part of it.

Art Adams, another family friend and Frank's Party comrade, had some experience with Gary's wild life. In his case it was rabbits. He tried to grow vegetables, but the rabbits ate them. "What did you do about that?" I asked, hoping to hear some useful tips. "I switched to a meat diet," Art said. Adams was a steel worker who helped make labor history. I did not know then that our friend had mentored people like the steel worker leader, Curtis Strong. Sometimes Art talked about the Memorial Day Massacre at Republic Steel. The Massacre occurred in 1937 when Chicago police shot into a peaceful crowd of strike sympathizers. Art told us about a famous reporter who was shot in the leg. She raised her dress high, and Art could see the blood spurting out of her thigh. That picture would not leave his mind and now it is fixed in mine.

The most countrified feature of our new neighborhood was the people. Almost all were African Americans originally from the rural South. People greeted each other on the street, and everybody knew everybody for blocks around. Frank leaned out of the window as he drove home so he could better greet passers-by. I will admit that I did not do the same. Some days, driving or walking home from the train station after a very long day, my thoughts were all on, "What am I going to feed my four kids?" Frank heard complaints about that. "Your wife didn't speak!"

Soon people found out how helpful a neighbor they had in Frank. If a neighbor needed a ride, Frank would jump out of bed, when he worked nights, and say, "Sure, Mrs. Taylor, I'll pick you up at the grocery." We had no public transportation and the nearest grocery store was a mile away. But I was too tender-hearted to interrupt Frank's sleep. So I walked the two miles from the train if I did not have the car. I did not mind the exercise. But on two occasions that I describe later, the walk did not go well.

We Want Water! We Want Sewers!

The city sewer system had not been extended to our area. We made do with septic tanks. Gary sits on the shore of Lake

Michigan, one of the world's largest reservoirs of fresh water. But we could not get any of it. The water supply was privately owned. The for-profit water company had no interest in bringing water pipes out to our thinly populated area. So we got our drinking water from wells. Our well water tasted fine. I thought if the city of Gary allowed septic tanks, it must be all right. I was a city girl and did not know any better. I had a lot to learn about the city of Gary as well as about septic tanks. Unknown to us, the wells were too close to the septic tanks. By the time we found that out it was too late. We had already moved in and signed our life away for a mortgage. No doubt, Frank and I would have eventually taken action on the issue of unsafe drinking water. But we ended up acting sooner, rather than later. It was the FBI that forced our hand. That was one time when FBI harassment had an effect opposite to what they intended.

We were in Gary only one month when Mrs. Bims called us about the FBI. She took care of Paul and John when Frank worked days. "Do you know any reason why the FBI is interested in you?" she asked. The call took me by surprise. My mind began to race a mile a minute. I quickly began to tell Mrs. Bims about our community activism. The FBI is trying to divide people and stop our community organizing, I added.

Frank and I realized that we had no time to lose. The FBI was trying to isolate us before we really got to know our neighbors. We had a pressing issue, the need for safe drinking water. There had been a case of typhoid in the area just before we moved in. So we invited the neighbors to a community meeting at our house. The meeting was well-attended, and we agreed to organize for our basic needs: safe drinking water and sanitary sewers.

Our first step was to take samples of the well water. We got sampling kits from the Gary Health Department. Then we canvassed the neighborhood and collected water samples. Only a couple of families refused to give us samples. They feared that if their water tested as bad, their homes would be condemned. The health department tested the water and gave us the results. At least 30% of the wells were contaminated by the septic tanks. My family was lucky—our water tested OK.

Our next neighborhood meeting decided to hold a rally where everyone could see us—outside city hall.

Fortunately, the Lumpkins were not the only experienced organizers on that committee. There was a pleasant surprise waiting for us on the day of the demonstration. We had prepared some hand-lettered signs to hold up with our slogans. But Katie Dowd had a better idea. She brought signs that literally spelled out our demands. Dowd's signs were large single letters. Put together, they said, "WE WANT WATER! WE WANT SEWERS!" And Katie came with two cars packed with 18 of her relatives. That was almost enough to hold up the letters. The *Gary Post-Tribune* took notice. Our picture made first page.

After our rally in 1954, we continued to attend city council meetings to keep up our pressure on city hall. The city of Gary said their hands were tied because the water plant was privately owned. The water company rates were very high. Still, we would have paid the monthly water bill. But we could not pay the thousands of dollars that the company wanted to bring water to our area. That left us with no choice but to drink well water, in many cases from polluted wells.

In 1958, George Chacharis became mayor. He was a former steel worker and sympathetic to our cause. Chacharis put an initiative on the ballot to allow the city to buy the water company. But the water company spent millions for deceptive advertising. Their slogan was, "Keep the politicians' hands out of our clean water!" I could not believe that we lost that vote. When Chacharis was sent to a federal jail on corruption charges in 1962, I was very suspicious. I still believe that his move for city ownership of the water company sealed his doom.

Yes, there was plenty of corruption in Gary, from the precinct level on up. I thought Khrushchev was talking about Gary when he pounded his sandal at the UN and said the U.S. government was based on gangsters. The whole political party rested on its precinct base. And everyone in Gary knew that precinct organizations were funded by payoffs from the rackets. Police and precinct captains were paid to look the other way when illegal drugs and prostitution came into the precincts.

We were still drinking the water from our well in 1962, when we left Gary. It took years to win our two demands: city water and sewers. About six years after our demonstration, the city brought sewers to Wooded Highlands. That made an immediate improvement in sanitation. Of course, the residents paid for it. Much later, water service was also extended. The main benefit of our fight may have been the lessons in organization that we learned. The way Frank put it was, "If you don't fight you know you will lose. If you fight there's a chance to win." For me, one of the best experiences of the water and sewers fight was meeting people like Katie Dowd, Mary Fisher and Joe and Fannie Norrick.

Katie Dowd, Mary Fisher and Joe and Fannie Norrick

Katie Dowd lived in the Small Farms area, just south of us. Small Farms was even more underdeveloped than our neighborhood. Many of the homes had dirt floors. "Worse than Mississippi," Mrs. Bims who came from Mississippi, told me.

As a teenager, Dowd took part in a historic uprising of cotton sharecroppers in Arkansas. It was a struggle that brought her to the attention of Eleanor Roosevelt, Dowd told me. She added, "Don't believe them when they say colored people can't stick together." Then she told me this inspiring story from the 1930s. Thousands of sharecroppers were being displaced by mechanical cotton pickers. These sharecroppers were given orders to move, but they had no place to go. Rather than waiting to be evicted one-by-one, they planned a bold, dramatic move. They hoped to focus attention on their demands and embarrass the government into finding them new homes. Their success depended on complete secrecy.

On their chosen night, 5,000 sharecropper families moved all of their possessions—big cooking stoves, animals, and all. They camped where the whole world could see them, along Route 66. Route 66 was then the main East–West highway from Chicago to California. The mass move took the authorities completely by surprise. Not one person of the more than 5,000 protesters had leaked the plan.

Mary Fisher also lived in Small Farms. She was one of the few people we knew when we first moved to Gary. In Chicago, Mary had worked with Frank in the steel workers club of the Communist Party. Fisher was among the many women who answered their country's call to work in the steel mills during World War II. She was one of the few women who held on to her job after the war. By definition, that meant she was tough. Frank held her in the highest regard. That's special praise by itself. In Chicago, she lived in Altgeld Housing of the Chicago Housing Authority (CHA). Frank used to say that she was the best community organizer. As he put it, "If someone burned a pot of beans in the project, Mary Fisher knew about it." That's the kind of organizing Frank taught me to love, personal and up close.

Joe Norrick was among the many coal miners from southern Indiana who moved to the northern part of the state to work in the steel mills. Along the way, Joe joined the Communist Party and met his second wife, Fanny Hartman. An electrician by trade, his real love was organizing and fighting for workers. Joe had a clear vision: the root of all evil was capitalism. Joe and Frank were friends and comrades on a gut level. Joe in the coal mines and Frank in the citrus plantations had come to the same conclusion. We have to change the system. To end exploitation, workers must run the country for the benefit of the people.

When we first met Joe, he and Fannie were living in East Chicago, near Youngstown Sheet and Tube where Joe worked. Then Joe bought some land in Gary. It was cheap because it was subject to flooding. The floods brought fertile soil, making good farm land. The old saying was true: you can take the boy out of the farm, but you can never take the farm out of the boy. Joe bought a tractor and planted everything good to eat. That was another level on which Joe and Frank had common roots.

Joe's speech was peppered with good, old-fashioned expressions from his southern Indiana farm background. A favorite was, "What's the hurry? You got ice in the wagon?" He also set a high standard for Frank to follow by building a three-bedroom home with his own hands. Without Joe's example, I doubt that Frank would have built our block garage, making it bigger than our house. For years the Norrick house was a center for rank and file steel workers. People enjoyed visiting the Norricks for good conversation and to admire the house that Joe built. We spent so much time visiting the Norricks that our children thought we were all one family. And we were.

I had met Fannie Norrick twenty years earlier in New York City. She was then Fannie Hartman, sharing an apartment with a famed organizer, Ann Burlak. The two seasoned organizers taught me some lessons I needed to learn. They seemed to think I was too serious. At 16, I was chomping my way through the Marxist classics and had picked up much of the old-fashioned book language. Fannie was blunt. She said I sounded like an old textbook. I did not remind her of it when we met years later, in Gary. But I never forgot it either. Hopefully her colorful criticism helped me clean up my language and talk regular talk. When I tried to become a writer, her advice helped me a lot.

We often had community meetings at our Gary home. My youngest child enjoyed passing around the cake that I had baked for the meeting, applesauce cake, I think. Of course I had another cake for my kids. Everyone at the meeting took a slice, and the plate became lighter and lighter. Finally, my child let out an anguished cry. "They're taking it all," he cried. Embarrassed, I brought out the other cake. I should have just laughed and let it go.

During the McCarthy repression, Joe Norrick kept us steady in rough waters. He helped us reorganize in Gary as we began to beat back the red baiters and the racists. In 1957, the Supreme Court threw out the second tier of Smith Act convictions. Rising mass protests, including the growing civil rights movement, helped write *end* to the McCarthy period repression but not before the McCarthyites severely damaged democracy. Our country has still not fully recovered.

Heart Attack!

Everybody thought of Frank as indestructible. Some even thought of him in terms of the John Henry legend. But as we know from the song, in the end the steam hammer did in John

Henry. One of the legends about Frank, a legend he cultivated, was that he did not need any sleep. He worked hard and he played hard. That did not leave much time for sleep. Card players, and he was one, are noted for losing track of the time. I think mostly he won. Frank told me once that he won a ring from Arlene Brigham's brother, a good friend. I made Frank give the ring back. Looking back, I realize that was dumb. Arlene's brother probably lost the ring to someone else. But I don't regret it. The ring was a present from his wife. I did not want something like that on our conscience.

Well one night Frank came home late, after we had all gone to bed. He was hungry and ate some lamb stew that I left out for him. It was winter time but the lamb stew was waiting in the warm kitchen for some hours. About 3 a.m. he woke up with a stomach ache and began to vomit. He lay down again but soon jumped up and began to jab shadow punches with his left arm. I guess he was trying to relieve the pain in his arm. I was alarmed and thought he had food poisoning. I called Gary Methodist Hospital but no, there was no doctor on duty. Don't bring him in! I called a couple of other hospitals in neighboring towns. They also claimed they had no emergency service.

Reluctantly, I called our own doctor, at 3:30 a.m. He said we could try ginger ale or similar drink to subdue the nausea. So at 4 a.m., I drove around Gary to find the ginger ale. At 7 a.m. Frank seemed better. So I did what we always did unless we were dead. And that is, go to work. As soon as I got to Allied Radio in Chicago, I called home. It seemed the doctor had been worried, too, and had made a house call to check Frank. "He said it was not so much my stomach as my heart," Frank told me. "He told me to go to the hospital."

I had just left our only car at the train station. Frank was off work, that day. "Take a cab to the station," I urged him. I left my job to start making my way by train and bus to the hospital in Hammond, where our doctor was on staff. Of course, Frank walked the two miles to the train station to pick up our car. Then he drove himself to St. Elizabeth Hospital. By the time I got there, he looked much better, but the diagnosis was confirmed. He was hospitalized with a heart attack, cardiac infarct. I picked up our car and drove home, to Gary.

The next morning there was a snowstorm blowing, and the road was icy. I decided to drive so I could see Frank at the hospital on my way to my Chicago job. I drove with great care until I needed to make a left turn. I turned the wheel slightly too fast and skidded across the road at a railroad crossing. I was bouncing across the bare rails, side-swiped a steel post and ricocheted back on the highway. Miraculously, I did not collide with another car. The only damage was a flat tire that I rode into the hospital lot. The little dent on the side of the car was hardly noticeable among all the other dents.

In four days, Frank was back at home, under doctor's orders to rest for four weeks. Before Frank went back to work at light duty, we got a second opinion from Dr. Quentin Young. He confirmed the heart attack and said that light duty would be OK. Forty years later, cardiologists could find no trace of the heart attack. One even made the snide remark, "What did they know in those days?"

However, the heart attack was a turning point in our lives. Frank quit spending as much time going to meetings in Chicago. Instead, he became more and more immersed in Gary politics. Local politics really appealed to him, so he became busier than ever. As for me, I quit my job at Allied Radio. I could not bear being so far from home in case of emergency. For six weeks I wrote ad copy for the *Gary Post Tribune*. It was fun, especially when a Goldblatts ad for shirts, 3 shirts for $1, was printed without the "r." When that job ended, I decided to do what everybody else in Gary did who wanted a job. I applied at the steel mill. U.S. Steel "big mill" and the tin mill did not hire married women. (Imagine!) But the U.S. Steel subsidiary, National Tube, did. With my technical background and basic typing skills, I got a job as a "metallurgical lab test report clerk."

Working in the Steel Mill

The first things I noticed when I reported to work at National Tube were the huge work areas and the relatively few workers per acre. I had been in a steel mill before when wives and families were given a tour of Wisconsin Steel. It was probably for the mill's 50th anniversary. But that was almost a joke. A green path had been painted on the concrete floor that touring relatives had to follow. Everything close to the path had also been painted green. Everything beyond the green paint was black with dirt and grease. Workers were laughing to the point of leering as each tried to spot his wife in the crowd. We visitors did not see much.

Frank working in Scarfing Dock at Wisconsin Steel, Chicago

My kids had toured the U.S. Steel's "big mill" in Gary on their 50th anniversary. That was an outright disaster. I heard that Paul had five or six of the free hotdogs and even more cokes with predictable consequences. He was one sick boy until he threw up. That made him feel better, if not the people around him.

But now it was me and the mill. So much space and so few workers per square block. What a difference that was from the crowded office at Allied Radio or the assembly line at Motorola! It made me think of my Marxist economics. All the profit of these big steel companies was being made off relatively few workers. How productive these steel workers were!

End of shift was the only time I got a sense of how many workers there were in the mill. They used to line up a couple minutes before punch-out time. We still used time cards that we had to punch and put into our slot on the punched-out side. Usually the test clerks were at the front of the line since we did not have to wash up. That was the fastest moving line of people any place outside of a professional track team. I had a recurring nightmare about that line. My fear was that I would drop my card at the clock and have to bend down to retrieve it. The momentum behind me would be so great that I feared I would be mowed down before the line could stop.

The office I worked in was right on the mill floor and it was old and out of date. But the job was very interesting. I learned a lot about metallurgy, working at National Tube. I was one of four women working for an engineer in charge of the metallurgical test reports. We answered phone calls asking if it was all right to use a certain lot of steel for a specific order. To answer correctly, we needed to know the chemical content and the physical conditioning of the steel. There was almost no job training, but a mistake could cost thousands of dollars. I am sure that such inquiries are now computerized.

I had always been interested in finding out what "stuff" is made from. With the job as an excuse, I enrolled in a physical metallurgy course at Purdue University Extension in Hammond. Metal alloys in general, and steel in particular, are fascinating, almost alive. It used to be said that metallurgists were half artists and half engineers. In those days it was true.

Alas, that department was quite isolated from other workers in the plant. I never found a way to break through as a union activist. I tried to interest my sister report clerks in attending a union meeting with me. They would not go, and I did not think I could do any good, alone. Looking back, I think I should have gone anyway. We were never encouraged to attend. An African American neighbor was a union steward at National Tube. Sometimes our paths would cross when I delivered the test reports. If he was alone, he would greet me cordially and ask about Frank. But if he was with other people, he would pass me as though he did not know me. I believed that the prejudice against my interracial marriage scared him.

After a couple of years, the mill entered a slow period. We went down to four days a week. Although the contract did not allow shorter than four-day weeks, we "voluntarily" went down to three days to keep all four women working. Layoff time is a terrible time in the mill (or anyplace else, for that matter). Workers are roaming all over the plant looking for someone they can "bump," someone with less seniority whose job they can take. Can you imagine how terrible it would be if there were no union? If foremen and managers could play favorites?

If I knew then what I now know about the steel workers union, I would have stuck with the job. But I felt my family needed more than three days' pay. So I used my days off to look for another job. Computer programmers were then few in number and were trained on the job. I applied for a programmer's position at Inland Steel. Personnel kept me there all day for a battery of tests. I felt I did well, and I could see that the hirers were interested in me. They knew I was already working at National Tube; that was in my favor. On the shelves of the personnel man who interviewed me was a book titled something like, "Reds in Steel." That did not bode well. Finally, he told me that I had done better on the tests than some they had already hired for the job. "But," he said with an air of finality, "you know you're a woman." Then, referring to my job at National Tube he added, "Count your blessings." Thus ended my chance of becoming a great information technology person.

A few months later, I returned to work for Allied Radio in Chicago. Frank's health seemed solid enough although he was back to sleeping just a few hours a day. He continued to smoke untold numbers of packs of cigarettes a day. It was as though the heart attack had never happened. The new job at Allied Radio was for a subdivision that made the Knight Kits. Like my job at Emerson Radio, I built and wired electronic equipment starting with a chassis and parts. But Knight Kits were designed for mass production. The chassis was already formed and punched. My job was to break down the construction into easy steps. I wrote a construction manual that showed how to assemble and test the kit. Along the way, I wrote a simple explanation of how the equipment worked. The company boasted that even a child could build the kits. I tried it on my children and made sure that was true. I really liked the job because I liked to build things and I liked to explain how they worked. First, I had to find out for myself how the circuits worked. That meant more studying and I enjoyed that too.

FBI and a Knifer, Lurking in the Bushes

One warm evening, before sunset, I was enjoying the long walk home from the train station. The sidewalks were deserted and peaceful. As I passed a weed-filled empty lot, a man startled me, jumping out from behind the bushes. "FBI," he said, "and flashed his badge." "Do you want to talk to me?" "No!" I shouted and kept on my way. Those were the bad McCarthy days. Another encounter had more dire consequences. But at least it was not government-sponsored. Still, I hold the government (and the system) responsible, at least indirectly.

I had left my car downtown for a minor repair. The shop was closed when I came from work in Chicago. It was a dark winter evening but not too cold. Instead of calling Frank, as the neighbors did, I decided to walk. I thought Frank was sleeping because he was on the night shift. Soon, I felt that I was being followed. Up ahead, there was a stretch of woods on either side of the road. I was not going into that more deserted area if someone was following me. So I turned to check who was behind me.

As I turned a man ran towards me, then lunged with a knife. It was so fast that I did not get a good image of his face. First he grabbed my purse. I did not let go, so he knifed me. In seconds he was slashing away with the knife, through my leather coat, about thirteen times. I fell to the sidewalk and thought I was dying. People a block away saw the attack and called the police. After an hour, or so it seemed, an ambulance came. The cuts were not serious. My leather coat had saved me. The knife, which was left behind, was a fishing knife, fortunately not very sharp.

"Be careful when you call my husband," I told the hospital staff. "He's already had one heart attack." When Frank took me home, the kids were already in bed. The next morning, at 4:30 a.m., Frank went to work. But first he loaded a pistol and put it under my pillow—just in case. I think I was more afraid of the loaded pistol than a return of the knifer. For years, I looked back over my shoulder if I heard footsteps behind me. It took some time, but I got over it.

Gary Schools

On the other side of the woods, next to Tolleston High School, was Ernie Pyle School for grades kindergarten through sixth. My daughter Jeanleah and oldest son Carl made a good adjustment to the Gary school. They liked it better than their old school in Chicago. Paul and John were still too young for school. But Paul had learned to print his name in the preschool in Chicago. Somehow, Paul got access to crayons while he was in Mrs. Bims' house for day care. Paul showed the whole world that he knew how to write by crayoning his name in large letters on the white siding all around the Bims' house. When I came home from work, the two boys were still scrubbing Bims' siding with scouring powder and wet rags. Paul had tried to blame it on John, but John did not know how to write. I guess the next time Paul tried an escapade, he did not sign his name to it.

Just about that time I made a trip to New York City. I wanted to visit my father, and I may have also had a meeting to attend. Frank agreed to care for the children, making it possible for me to leave. But there was a price I had to pay. When I returned, there was a trail of papers and junk that started one hundred feet away and went right up to the door. I opened the front door, and there was jelly on the door handle. Sand gritted the tile floor; each step went crunch, crunch. And from there it went downhill. Dishes piled the sink, and beds were unmade. Toys were all over. I tried to complain and was told, "What do you expect when you go to New York and leave me with four kids?" But the kids were fine. I guess, in the long run, that's what counts. But you couldn't tell me that at the time.

Soon enough, all the children were in school. That was convenient, just two blocks away if you cut through the woods. It was not a level two blocks. There were the hills to climb. I am sure that made the trip to school more fun. To relieve the overcrowding, a new K–3 school was built about a mile away. Whose kids were going to have to walk that mile? You guessed it. It was our kids, in the Wooded Highlands section of low-priced homes. The children from the other side of the woods, in the higher priced homes, could stay. This included some better-off African American families who lived in large, new, brick homes. One man even used a rider-mower to cut his not-that-large lawn. Some better-off, and to us rich families, were headed by doctors. The rest of the people with "money" were gamblers. I am not sure what lesson our children learned from the only career choices that they saw.

We did try to fight the transfer of our kids, or at least to get school bus service for them. But the community was divided, and we did not win. The nearby Tolleston and Ernie Pyle schools had a mix of white and African American children. The new Banneker School was100% African American, both students and staff. Paul and John were transferred to the new school.

Paul was watching some of the first televised protests of African American students barred from white schools in the South. "My school doesn't have enough white people in it," Paul wisely said. "Oh," I asked, "are there any white people in your school?" "Yes," he said. I had visited his class. So I decided to narrow down my next question. "Are there any in your class?" "Yes," he replied, "my teacher and me." I repeated the conversation to Frank. His take was that Paul's teacher would be "insulted."

The impact on our children of the racism in the media was deep and complex. One of our boys was snuggled in his daddy's lap watching a family situation comedy. Suddenly he exclaimed, "I want a white daddy!" My blood froze. Frank looked as though he had not heard it. I decided to rely on the deep love the son had for his father. "Do you want a different daddy?" I asked. "No!" was the quick reply. "I just want my daddy to be white."

This memory brings up the question people often ask me, and I shrug it off. They say, "Wasn't it hard for you?" They add that in 1949, the year of our marriage, there was much more prejudice than sixty years later. I can truthfully say that I never felt that I suffered as a result of marrying an African American.

Yes, there were hard stares. I brushed those off like water off a duck's back. I knew, deep down, that racism was so wrong and hateful. Those stares could not hurt me. Of course I was angry about any form of racism, including not being able to rent in some neighborhoods. That anger helped strengthen my determination to fight racism.

Frank's marriage to a white woman did create problems for his campaign when he ran for political office in Gary. But he never gave any ground to racist prejudice because he knew it was wrong. But it was hard to deal with the white principal of Ernie Pyle School. She sent word that she wanted to see me and came right to the point. "You have two white children," she scolded me. "You had no right to marry a black man!"

Her blatant racism outraged me. It still outrages me. But I controlled myself. She was holding my children hostage, and I did not want them mistreated. Neither the principal nor I gave any ground, and we parted as enemies. Fortunately, my kids' teachers were all very decent people. The prejudice did not carry over into their classrooms, as far as I knew.

Parent Teacher Organization

At Banneker School, we formed an unaffiliated Parent Teacher Organization (PTO). It really was strictly a parents' organization. The school did not provide us with any resources or leadership. Our PTO wanted to do something constructive for Halloween. We planned a Halloween fun fair with an entrance fee of a penny for each inch of waistline. We thought that would be fun and it was. For some unfounded reason, we expected the teachers to come and help. Of course none came; it was on a Saturday, their day off.

We had some games and refreshments ready and opened the door. We had expected 100 or 150 families. Instead one thousand children came. Their parents stayed home. Our committee had not realized that every child wanted to come because nothing else was going on. Since refreshments went fast and lines for the games were too long, the children began to run through the halls. It was a nightmare. Finally the principal came and closed the school. We learned more than one lesson that day on how schools run and how not to organize. Fortunately, there were no injuries and no destruction of school property. It was, without doubt, the biggest organizing fiasco of my lifetime.

Other projects of our PTO were more successful. We held Easter egg hunts for a number of years. After the children complained, I learned to make sure that my Easter eggs were truly hard. Our biggest success was our play for "Black History Week," the week of President Lincoln's birthday. By that time, I had been educated about black history by the African American Heritage Association, organized by Ishmael Flory. I don't remember the details, but I do know there were no kings and queens in the play. Yes, it is true that many African states were kingdoms before the European invasions, and that is important. It is important because it proves that most Africans lived in highly developed states. But for each king and queen there were thousands of serfs and peasants to support the monarchs.

In contrast, the play I wrote featured a cooperative African society where people planted their crops together and shared meat from the hunt. The play sparked my serious interest in African history. Ten years later, when I became a teacher, African history helped me teach mathematics.

Wooded Highlands Democratic Club

Clifford Mays, a friendly neighbor, had been the precinct committeeman forever. He raised dogs and gave our family our first dog, a beagle named Chi Chi. I did not realize what a good dog Chi Chi was, until we had other dogs. Although Mays was a good neighbor, as a committeeman he was just another cog in the machine. It was an unpaid position, but machine committeemen had other ways to line their pockets.

Frank decided to run for the job. For Frank, the cash flow was in the opposite direction; the money came out of his pocket to help people in need. The precinct committeeman was a very important position in the Gary communities. In hard economic times, for example during the 116-day national steel strike in 1959, the committeeman's recommendation got welfare checks for families to tide them over. When Frank was elected it was different. He recommended everyone who was in need and expected nothing in return. Many a time he took money out of his own pocket to feed children until their first welfare check came.

I don't remember that he spent money on his campaigns although each election was strongly contested. Campaigning was strictly door-to-door, talking to the voters. That was just the kind of work Frank loved. He personally spoke to every one of the 1,200 voters who lived in a big area with a lot of vacant land between houses. Out of this work he built a new community organization. For reasons that I don't remember, they adopted the name, "Wooded Highlands Democratic Club" (WHDC). Despite the name, they were strictly independent of the Democratic machine and city hall.

WHDC made a deal with a homeowner who had an unfinished second floor with its own outside entrance. In return for putting in a floor, walls, ceiling and washroom, the club got the use of the space for its center. Most of the members were steel workers, with a couple of auto workers and teamsters. Among them they had every construction trade that was needed. People put their full efforts into building their community center, even if it meant neglecting their own homes. Some of the best times of my life were spent at the WHDC, dancing to the jukebox. Ray Charles's "I have 50 cents more than I'm going to keep...let the good times roll," was a favorite. Food and drink were sold at very reasonable prices, and every cent was accounted for. Women were glad to go with their husbands to parties at the center. They said it was a place where men could go, have a drink and "not get into any trouble."

WHDC meetings were often educational, like all other projects that Frank organized. Frank invited a brilliant Nigerian friend, Chimere Ikoku, to speak at one of our meetings. Ikoku was completing his PhD in chemistry at the University of Chicago. His wife was also a student. The Ikokus spoke about the warm feelings Nigerians had for African Americans who visited as friends. One of our members asked a far-out question that astounded me. "What are you studying?" he asked Chimere. "Chemistry," Chimere replied. "Then how can you be talking about politics, when it is chemistry that you are studying?"

Mrs. Ikoku rose to reply. She was magnificent. She began with "Aristotle said," and continued, "If you want to know about medicine, ask a doctor. If you want advice for the market, ask a merchant. But if you want to know about politics, let any person speak because politics is everyone's business." I was impressed because nobody I knew quoted Aristotle. But I was more impressed by the power of her logic.

I have since heard that Chimere Ikoku moved up to a high position in education after his return to Nigeria. That was no thanks to the FBI that harassed him in Chicago. To his colleagues, our friend was known as a skilled diplomat who brought people together and smoothed out differences. Was he an anti-imperialist? Yes. Did that call for FBI surveillance? No!

Mrs. Ikoku's words about people's politics made a big impression on Frank and me. Politics, in the sense of public life, was Frank's "business." That was true for me, too. Before I was old enough to vote, I worked at the polls. That was the election for a second term for Franklin D. Roosevelt. The minimum age for voting was then 21, and I was only 18. As far as I can remember, I have worked on every election since 1936. Sometimes, there seemed no candidate worth working for, but there were always important issues to promote. David Orr, Chicago's progressive county clerk, did not hear Mrs. Ikoku. Still, he carried out her teachings. Orr brought high school seniors in to work as election judges, paid, of course. That reminded me of the Cuban practice. In many towns, the ballots are counted by students, guaranteeing the honesty of the count.

The WHDC taught us many lessons in community organizing. It was a center where people gathered and provided a ready-made mass lobby for good causes. We became a frequent presence at city council meetings, fighting for the sewers and water we lacked and for clean air. The city hall and the court house across the street were built in imitation Greek classic style. The large windows of the city council chamber gave a clear view of the evening sky, a sick yellow color. Just a few blocks away the mills were belching unfiltered smoke full of smelly gases. The mills were real, but the city council meeting seemed unreal.

I will never forget the arrogance of the U.S. Steel representative at one council meeting. We asked him, "Is there technology for the chimneys that could remove pollution from the smoke? "Yes," he replied, "but it is expensive." Then he added, "We are not going to do it unless you make us." He was so sure that the city council would not go against the company's wishes. Everyone knew that U.S. Steel controlled Gary's city council and more.

Soon after WHDC was organized, Frank asked me to put out a community newsletter. He always believed in the power of the press. Now I can add "editor" to my resume. Of course I was also the typist and operated the mimeograph machine. For those too young to have seen a mimeograph machine, it was a primitive printer with a roller that pushed messy ink through a typed stencil. However, I did have a staff of reporters and distributors. We named it the *Comet*, and it flew high for a few years. Of course, the mainstay of the newsletter was social news and reports of sickness, births, weddings and deaths. The *Comet* also educated the community on political issues, local, national and even international.

Integrating Gary's Beaches

In 1961, a long-simmering fight came to a boil. The issue was the right of African Americans to use Gary's Marquette Park Beach. An African American man was severely beaten at the beach as the police looked on. Frank read about it in the *Gary Post Tribune* and decided to check out the beach that same Sunday. Paul, John and I put our swim suits on, but Frank was fully dressed. Before I could get out of the car, Frank and the two boys rushed to the water. I had to run to catch up. The boys and I had a short swim in Lake Michigan's sparkling water. Frank stood guard. At the beach, the tension was thick enough to cut with a knife. On the way back to the car, we saw one other black family on the beach. They were peacefully eating a picnic lunch. "They are some brave people," Frank said in admiration.

Racist pressures have not let up in the many years since we left Gary. Gary has become a city in crisis since the loss of over 30,000 steel mill jobs. Unlike the Chicago mills that were leveled to the ground, most Gary mills are still producing lots of steel. They are doing it with just one fourth the number of workers, thanks to technological improvements. The huge loss of jobs and the exodus of most white families have turned Gary into the most segregated major city in the country and one of the most depressed. It hurts my heart to see empty lots turn to prairie on Broadway, Gary's "main drag." Big department stores, crowded with customers, stood on those empty lots in the 1960s. Gary is located on beautiful Lake Michigan, near the transportation center of the nation. To me, the city's depressed state is a damning indictment of capitalist greed.

Chapter 16

The New Cuba is Born
"Before the revolution, we lived like dogs!"

BY 1960, the long winter of the McCarthy repression was ending. Civil rights sit-ins were spreading all over the South and the border states. The steel workers' union had survived a 116-day national strike and had saved the integrity of their contract. Although the CIA overthrew President Arbenz in Guatemala in 1954, the Latin American revolutionary spirit was very much alive. I was excited by the 1959 revolution in Cuba. It was sounding more and more like the real thing. I wanted to go to Cuba and see for myself, before the United States cut off all travel. President Eisenhower had already put a partial embargo against trade with Cuba. If I was going to go, I had to hurry.

In June 1960, I got on a slow propeller-driven plane to Miami. The economy fare to Miami was $80 round trip. Another slow plane from Miami to Havana cost $40. The plane flew low enough to give a wonderful view of the Caribbean, turned gold by the setting sun. I have never seen a more beautiful sight. As it turned dark, lights sparkled like jewels on the little islands below us. It was quite dark when we landed in Havana's little airport.

My first stop was to change my dollars into pesos at the government bank. To my surprise, the official exchange was only one peso for one dollar. Well, I was not about to look for an illegal exchange, so I turned in my $40 for 40 pesos and hoped that was not as little money as it seemed. There were plenty of taxis outside the airport. But they wanted four pesos for the trip to downtown Havana. I noticed some Cuban workers waiting at the corner. I figured that they could not pay the four pesos either. Yes, it was a bus stop and the fare was only five centavos (five cents). It was the best bus ride I ever had and started my education about revolutionary Cuba. A friendly guitarist-passenger provided the musical background.

The bus passengers were curious about me. I managed to say, "I am the wife of a steel worker from Gary, and I came to see the Cuban revolution." A couple of bus passengers offered to help me find a hotel. I followed them across the plaza. It was the first time in my life that I saw a very different culture. Still, there was something familiar. It reminded me of the Spanish-speaking part of Harlem, but more so.

In the plaza, a squad of men in ordinary clothing were marching and drilling. "Who are they?" I asked. "Oh, they are *milicianos*," voluntary militia. Soon we passed women, drilling and marching. "They are *milicianas*." I was thrilled to see these liberated women. The people were in charge!

I noticed that all the stores were advertising familiar brands such as Singer sewing machines and General Electric refrigerators. I was in a different country but it seemed that the same U.S. companies owned everything. Later I learned that 90% of Cuba's foreign trade before the revolution was with the U.S.

Hotel Sevilla was 7 pesos ($7) a night. It was near midnight, so I booked the room anyway. In the daytime I would have to find a cheaper place. Of course I could have wired home for more money but I would rather not. My first thought in the morning was not, "Where am I going to stay tonight?" I had confidence that problem could be solved later. Instead I wanted to find one of the famous Cuban beaches and test the waters. Remembering my lack of concern, now I can only say, "How wonderful it was to be younger and confident!" I put my swim suit in a paper bag and set out to look for the beach.

Beaches for the People of Cuba

The clean, deliciously salty water made for a lovely swim. Watching the people was the biggest treat. People, especially the teenagers, seemed so happy and quick to laugh.

They joined hands in the water and laughed and sang. Later I learned that young people had just come out of a period of intense repression. Tens of thousands of teenagers had been killed by the Batista government before the revolution. Now they felt liberated.

At the beach I learned a lot. Before the revolution, the beaches had been reserved for tourists and rich Cubans, at least the white rich. Cubans had been barred from their own beaches. People's resentment was so high that the new government made beach access a priority issue. In the ten months since the revolution, they had developed a whole chain of beaches around the island, open to all at no charge.

The question of racism kept coming up. In Havana, I saw the racist housing pattern that the new government had inherited. Bathers on the beach assured me that the new Cuba opposed racism. "Fidel explained to us," they said, "All Cubans have African heritage, either directly from Africa or from Spain and the Moors."

When I questioned people on the street, not everyone supported the revolution. Tourism had dried up; those who depended on tourists were hurting. A man who owned a tobacco shop and a woman who had been a prostitute longed for the "good old days." Also, racism still lingered. A tobacco store owner was truly repulsive. He opened his shirt to show me that his skin was white although his face was tanned.

Our Revolution is Humanist

Walking in a park, I met a family of European Jewish refugees. I heard them speaking Yiddish, so I hurried to catch up with them. They did not know English, so we tried to communicate in Yiddish. They had found a new home in Havana after they escaped from Nazi-occupied Poland. They told me, "Wir sind mit die Regierung." (We support the government.) It was very emotional for me to find a common bond with this family, so far from their home and mine.

In the city center, a taxi driver offered to give me a city tour. "Yes, I am from the United States but, no, I cannot afford a taxi." Then I went on with my routine: I was a steel workers' wife from Gary, interested in learning about the new government of Cuba. I must have impressed him with my simple-mindedness because he made me an astounding offer. "I see you are a friend of our revolution," he said. "Come after work, and I will show you what our government is doing for our people." By then, he knew that I was happily married and not looking for a boyfriend. I thought he was sincere, too, and took him up on his offer. His name was Alfredo, and he spoke fluent English.

At 5 p.m., I returned to the taxi stand. Alfredo was waiting for me. We hopped on a bus that crossed the bay to East Havana. As we passed a big complex of new apartment buildings, Alfredo exclaimed: "See those new apartments. The government built them for working people!"

The bus route ended at a beach with new cabanas (cabins) scattered around. Alfredo asked a family of vacationers if we could see their cabana. The father of the family proudly invited us to come in. He was a worker, who had earned a week's free stay at the beach. Other working families were vacationing in nearby cabanas. The cabins were sparkling new with modern appliances and comfortable furniture.

I noticed the family's 14-year-old daughter scribbling notes as we talked. As Alfredo and I got up to leave, the daughter stood to read her notes to me. "To the people of the United States," it began. I looked behind me, and I was the only one from the U.S. standing there. "We, the people of Cuba, want to build a new and better life. Our revolution is humanist. We want to be friends with the people of the United States."

Tears came to my eyes. I promised to bring her message back to "the people of the United States." I don't remember the young ambassador's name. But I never forgot her moving message and the love for people that she poured into her words.

Even though my 1960 Cuban visit was so short, I wanted to take a look at the countryside, outside of Havana. The Tourist Institute suggested a trip to a tobacco cooperative. The cooperative farmers lived in new houses, built on the slope of a hill. One couple proudly showed me their tiled floors, the refrigerator and modern kitchen. Then the wife pulled out a photograph of the thatched hut they used to live in. "Before the revolution, we lived like dogs," she told me.

Havana Beach. 1960, 14-year old ambassador is seated
"Before the revolution, we lived like dogs!"

I think my guide took me to eight other homes. He tried to take me to as many as he could in an hour. At each home I was offered the traditional Cuban espresso coffee, brewed with sugar. The trouble is I was not a coffee drinker at that time, just an occasional cup of milk-diluted coffee. Still, how could I refuse such hospitality? So I drank them all. Fortunately, just as I felt my heart beginning to pound and my face turning red, I was rescued by the manager and his wife. It was lunch time and the most delicious meal I had in Cuba. After 48 years, I still remember the ham, a product of the farm cooperative.

Of course I did have some questions. The manager impressed me by asking that I write my questions. His answers were also impressive. I asked what percentage of the farmers had joined cooperatives. "About 10%," he said. The Cubans had learned from the Soviet experience and were not rushing the process. The revolution had brought agrarian reform. The big plantations were nationalized and divided up among the landless farmers. Before the revolution, these farmers had been low-paid farm workers, exploited by companies like United Fruit. Worst of all, was the "dead" season when there was no work in the cane. In the dead season, the workers had to find their own way to survive. Many children died in this dreaded period.

After they got their own land to farm, the new farm owners were given deeds guaranteeing their right to the land. Most were not ready to give up those newly-won deeds to form a collective farm. The collective farm had attractive services. They offered better housing, closer schools, medical care and a rich social life. Still, for most newly landed farmers, this did not outweigh the desire to own and farm your own land.

Among the collective farmers, there was a division of work. Every age group made some contribution. There was work to be done in the fields and later in the drying sheds. Grandmothers ran the preschools, freeing up the younger women to work in the sheds. The children's work was to study, something the new Cuba was doing in a big way.

The model tobacco cooperative that I visited was named after the Sainz brothers. The brothers were among the tens of thousands of teenagers murdered by the police just before Castro led the people's army into Havana. Señor Sainz, father of the martyred children, had been a local judge. He showed me the boys' room. The parents kept the room like a shrine, with student compositions still on the wall. Then he showed me a photo from a Miami newspaper. Two heads were circled—the military men who had killed his boys. The teenagers were killed as they were entering a movie house in the main square. When the first boy was shot, his brother rushed to his side. The soldiers shot him too. The boys' crime? They were teenagers, thus suspected of being supporters of the revolution.

On the return bus trip to Havana, my seat companion was a musician. I put my oversimplified question to him, "Do

you like the new government?" "Yes!" he exclaimed. "Why?"
I asked. Then he became agitated. "Why? Why? Do you see
those hills there? That's ours, ours, now. Do you see those
trees? That's ours, ours!" He was pointing to new plantings,
part of a huge reforestation project. The Spaniards had defor-
ested most of the hills. The U.S. companies got the rest of the
trees. The new Cuba was repairing the damage.

Could the New Cuba Survive?

Peasant rebels in Cuba, aided by striking workers, had
defeated the Batista dictatorship in 1959. But six years earlier,
the CIA overthrew the progressive governments of Iran and
Guatemala. The landowners had become very unhappy after
the Arbenz government of Guatemala nationalized the large
plantations owned by United Fruit, now Chiquita Banana.
Given that history, could the new, revolutionary Cuba survive?

"Yes!" said the Cuban newspapers. The Cubans based their
hopes on their creation of a new Cuban Army, devoted to the
people. They had dismantled the army of the Batista dictatorship. In contrast, old armies remained in place when Guatemala and Iran had elected progressive presidents. The CIA
had been able to subvert the generals of these old armies.

Soon after my visit in 1960, events moved very fast. Cuba
had nationalized the large plantations, many owned by United
Fruit Company and other U.S. based corporations. Plantation
owners were offered payment, based on the value that they
had declared for tax purposes. The U.S. owners claimed this
price was far less than the true value of the land. They did not
seem to mind admitting that they had defrauded the Cuban
government of taxes for many years.

President Eisenhower backed up the plantation owners
and tried to force Cuba back into the colonial mold. He cut
off the U.S. sugar quota that provided 95% of Cuba's sugar
market. Then he imposed trade embargoes that became more
and more severe. Finally, Eisenhower cut off all diplomatic
relations. Cuba then turned to the Soviet Union as its main
trade partner. From the revolution as "humanist," Cuba went
further and took a socialist path.

Chapter *17*

Working Class Suburb
Young people led the fight against racism.

Probably I would still be living in Gary if my job had stayed in the same place. But Knight-Kit/Allied Radio moved from their factory near Chicago's Union Station to Maywood, a western Chicago suburb. The move increased my daily commute to 50 miles one way. Some days I drove because public transit required so many changes, from train to bus. When I made it home, there were still four children to care for, meals to cook, laundry to wash and a house to clean.

Finally I told Frank, "Either I quit my job or we have to move. That was an easy choice for Frank. He did not believe in quitting a job. In the dead of winter, January 1962, we moved to Broadview, Illinois. Our new house was little over one mile from my job at Knight-Kit. But Frank's trip to work went up from 14 to 30 miles, one way. For the 17 years that we lived in Broadview, he never complained about the long trip to work. Never. But his heart still remained in Gary for years. Five years after we left Indiana, Frank went back to work in Richard Hatcher's campaign for Mayor. Hatcher was the first African American to be elected mayor of a major northern city.

It is always difficult to move in the middle of the school year. Had I known then what I know now, I would have waited until summer. Carl was a high school senior and Jean-leah a junior when we left Gary, Fortunately, it worked out. By that time, Carl had become a confirmed naturalist. At the new school, Proviso East, Carl was able to take more science courses. For the first time, he earned "A" grades and began to bloom academically. And Jeanleah continued to do well in her studies. I think there was more multiracial interchange at Proviso than in Gary in 1962. At the end of the semester, both entered Shimer College. Jeanleah, an excellent student, was granted early admission. Both continued their education up to the PhD level.

For my two younger children, the move to Broadview also seemed positive. Paul's natural leadership found many outlets in the Western suburbs. The very first week in the new school, he brought ten boys home with him. They played in our basement. We did not even have a basement in Gary. In no time, Paul was deep into the Roosevelt School sports program. John, too, did very well at the new school, especially in science. Both boys played baseball with the Little League and were active Boy Scouts. Frank had a lot of fun helping the Scoutmaster on some of their trips. But I had been raised to be skeptical about the Scouts. My parents thought that Boy Scouts were too militaristic. That was probably true at the time. Still, in our Broadview neighborhood, it was a good family experience.

Shopping, A National Pastime

Tommie Lee, Scoutmaster for the Broadview Scouts, was married to Maria, my friend and frequent companion. So what did working mothers do on Saturday mornings, after a long week at work? Go shopping, of course, looking for bargains for the family. Finding a "bargain" gave us a feeling of victory, as though we had defeated the "system." The high did not last long because most prices were so unaffordable. So there was nothing else to do but rush around to find the next bargain and get our next "fix." We knew every mall within a five-mile radius, and there were many. I can understand why some said that shopping was the leading sport of Americans in the twentieth century.

It must have been Maria's company that made the weekly shopping a fun experience. Sadly, I confess that I no longer like to shop. It seems such a waste of time. I buy the necessities. Frank and I kept the same clothes size all through the years. Our clothes did not wear out except for shoes. It was very different when we had children whose shoe size changed every few months. Children's clothes cost almost as much as adult clothing. Working families really need a family subsidy for each child to afford children's clothing at today's prices.

Frank Gets His Motorcycle, Kicks the Habit.

Frank had always wanted to have a motorcycle. I thought that as a father of four children, he owed it to us not to take the risk. It is hard to deny that motorcycles are more dangerous than cars. So he broke me into the concept piecemeal. He showed up one day with a three-wheeler. I admit that I took it around the alley once or twice, myself. Not a lot of time passed before he moved up to a real motorcycle.

My father visited us in Broadview soon after Frank bought the three-wheeler. Papa made the trip from New York City to visit us about once a year. At 87, he was still as daring as ever. He sat on the small trunk of the three-wheeler, no seat belt of course. Frank took him for a ride. On his return, Papa told me, "You know, I took a big chance." Now that I am 90-plus, I know about loss of balance. I could slap myself for letting Papa ride on the back of the three-wheeler motorcycle.

Hattie also came to visit us for a week. She drove all the way from Buffalo, New York. We enjoyed her visit and asked her to stay longer when the week was up. But she said she had to go. "If I stay any longer," she told me, "when I come home, a strange woman will answer my door bell and say, 'Who is you?'" Since she and Elmo were up in their 70s then, I thought that was very funny. However, I have learned more about life since that time. Hattie was a very wise woman.

Hattie sympathized with me when I complained about Frank's lack of interest in fixing up the house. "If you let him," she said, "a man will live in a tree." She gave me a lot of moral support. After all, she had been there, done that. When I was working hard on a job, taking care of four kids, doing the housework, etc., Hattie watched me and said, "You're just like I was." Of course I had only four, compared to her ten. But as she told us when we left Paul and John with her when they were two and four, "Nowadays, children take a lot more care." No doubt, the whole family gained from the extra hours I spent at home instead of commuting. I believe Frank added extra years to his life by making the move to Broadview. Free of the pressures in Gary, Frank quit smoking. A heart attack at the age of 37 did not convince him to quit. Nor did he quit when I nagged him for years after the heart attack. But in Broadview, he quit "cold turkey," as the expression goes. It was his decision, and I was careful to never question him on the subject. Frank left an open pack of cigarettes in his top drawer. He told me that he wanted to be sure cigarettes were within reach. I guess that assured him that it was his decision not to smoke them. It avoided the panicky feeling of being "out of cigarettes."

Perhaps nicotine addiction is like cancer. There are no cures, only remissions. For years after Frank quit, he had a recurring dream. In the dream, he smoked a cigarette and was very angry with himself. Then he would wake with a start, glad to find that it was only a nightmare.

Cold War and End of the World

Frank and I soon hooked up with a network of progressive people in the western suburbs. Some had been driven out of the Communist movement by the repression of the McCarthy period. A few were labor-based and others were religious activists. I enjoyed walking with Erica Marshall, younger than I, still with a baby carriage to push. We became part of the early peace movement to stop the war in Vietnam.

On October 27, 1962, it seemed the world might end. The United States Army had placed missiles in Turkey aimed at Moscow and other large Soviet cities. In turn, the Soviet Union placed missiles in Cuba aimed at U.S. cities. Cuba had already been invaded by a U.S.-supplied force that was defeated at the Bay of Pigs. And Cuba feared another invasion. President John F. Kennedy had issued an ultimatum to the Soviets. Their missiles must go, or else. The deadline was Saturday, October 27, 1962. If agreement was not reached before the day ended, the two nuclear powers could begin exchanging nuclear missiles and the human race could wipe itself out.

Force of habit carried me through the morning. After I finished my chores, I went out to walk with my friend, Erica Marshall. As usual, she was pushing a baby buggy. We tried to reassure each other. She echoed my thoughts. "As I made up the beds, today," she told me, "I wondered why I bothered if the world was going to blow up." As it turned out, it was just as well that we made up our beds. Kennedy and Khrushchev came to an agreement. Khrushchev agreed to remove their missiles. Kennedy pledged to remove missiles from Turkey and not invade Cuba.

At first it was hard to fight against the Vietnam War. I remember distributing Chicago Peace Council flyers outside a grocery store in Skokie, Illinois. The Peace Council was a coalition of Communists, union leaders. clergy and other religious, and whomever else we could get. Our flyers showed Vietnamese children, horribly burned by American napalm bombs. The shoppers were hostile. "Our soldiers would not do things like that," many said. We did not give up. As atrocities by the U.S. armed forces became known, and body bags returned by the thousands, the peace movement grew to gain majority support. We can take some credit for helping to end that war.

Fair Housing Fight in Broadview

Broadview was one of the working class suburbs just west of Chicago. Like Melrose Park and some other nearby towns, there was a substantial Italian working class population. They had little to say about how the towns were run. According to the rumor, "mafia" gangsters ran these suburbs. More than one notorious gangster lived in the neighboring town of Melrose Park. Racist divisions were even more intense than in Chicago. Once again, we had moved to a neighborhood that included both white and black families. But the truth was that it was yet another "changing" neighborhood. Roosevelt Road was then the "Mason-Dixon" line. We lived north of the line, in the small corner of Broadview that had a mixed population.

Our friend and comrade, Joan Elbert, told us how the May-wood neighborhood next to us went from all white to almost all African American in one short summer. In the 1950s, she, her husband and two children moved to Maywood. They were barely in the house when real estate agents began knocking on her door. "You know the colored are moving in here. Do you want to sell?" "No," Joan told them. "We just moved in," That did not stop the realtors. They came again, this time adding to the pressure. "Do you want to be the last white family on the block?" they asked. The Elberts would not be moved. But other families on the block were panicked into leaving. By the end of the summer, all the other white families had sold out, at depressed prices. African American families bought the homes at elevated prices. Once again, racist fear tactics put enlarged profits in the realtors' pockets.

We wondered why the vacant lot next to our Broadview house had an unfinished house foundation. We learned that an African American family had owned the lot. They tried to build there but were forced out. Other African American lot owners were refused building permits. It seemed that the village bosses had decided to stop black families from moving in. They made a deal with a developer to allow apartment buildings on the vacant lots in exchange for a promise to rent only to whites. The developer filed to change the zoning from single to multiple family units. We formed a civil rights organization to oppose the change. Our people fought bravely at a couple of tense village meetings.

As part of this fight, a courageous African American decided to run for the village board. But the board members were elected by a village-wide vote. Frank and I went into hostile territory to distribute his flyers. The police began to follow our candidate's car and stopped him for no reason. When the votes were counted, he lost as expected. Still, he had enough votes to win had the village been divided into wards. We were thrilled that our candidate received votes in every area of the village. We had friends in white precincts. We just wished we knew who they were.

Of course the fight did not have to stop there, but it did. We could have picketed the village hall and made our fight a public issue for the whole region. This was the early 1960s, and the civil rights fight was beginning to pick up steam around the country. Some African American neighbors were opposed to militant action. I can still hear their sad voices as they said, "We still have to live in this village *after* this is over." Fortunately, the experience did have some good results. Some of the teenagers in our neighborhood, white as well as black, went on to become progressive movement activists.

Young People Lead the Fight

A few years later, young people took up the fight against racism in the schools and park district. The youth section of the Maywood NAACP was fighting for a swimming pool for Maywood, the suburb next to Broadview. There was a swimming pool in another area, but children of color were not made welcome there. The fight was led by Fred Hampton, soon to become a national leader of the Black Panther Party (BPP). "Go slow," the community elders advised the young people. But they didn't listen. By that time my sons Paul and John Lumpkin were on the high school track team with Fred Hampton. They wouldn't listen either. The village claimed that there was no money for the pool. The young people marched down Fifth Avenue, the main drag. Somehow, store windows were broken. It became clear that the anger could not be contained. Then the village "found" the money for a pool.

The fight spilled over to Proviso East High School in Maywood when school officials refused to accept an African American homecoming queen. The Cook County sheriff's office declared war on the students. They mounted guns on the rooftops of homes surrounding the school. Inside the school, the police sprayed mace freely in the school corridors. The police claimed it was needed to control the students. They also claimed that mace was harmless. We know better now. One morning, as Frank returned from the night shift, his car was rear-ended by a sheriff's car. The deputy apologized; he was in a hurry to deliver a load of guns to sheriffs at Proviso High School. You can imagine how Frank felt with two boys in that school.

Two days later, Frank saw some high school students marching. They were protesting racism at the school and demanding an end to the sheriff's occupation of the school. Marching right up front was our son, John. Frank tried, but did not convince John that the most important thing was to get his schooling. John continued to fight for justice but he also continued to study.

The black student struggle that swept the campuses in the late '60s was trying to pry open university doors. Some elite universities opened just a crack, to admit just a few of the "best." A recruiter from the Massachusetts Institute of Technology (MIT) came a-courting John. No doubt that was because John had made the National Merit Honor list.

Once at MIT, John became interested in the Boston Black Panther Party. He became one of the cooks for the breakfasts that Black Panthers served to kids in Boston. With a number of young Black Panthers killed, we feared for our John's safety. But we did not tell him to quit their breakfast program. We knew the BPP was heavily infiltrated by the police; so we warned John to watch out for paid provocateurs. Police agents almost destroyed the organization from inside by urging terrorist actions. I doubt that our advice influenced John's actions. He always had a mind of his own. He had already decided to move in another direction. In 1970, he left MIT to study medicine and continued to fight for people's rights.

"For what I'm paying you, I could get a man."

My job at Knight-Kit/Allied Radio had brought us to Broadview. It lasted three more years. I liked the job because it was creative and produced a useful product. The company made kits that included parts and instructions needed to build your own electronic devices. As a technical writer, I produced the instructions manuals.

I thought I did a good job at Knight-Kit and gave the credit to my work experience. Every job I ever worked taught me something that I used on later jobs. Well, maybe with the exception of laundry work. Laundry work taught me to embrace wash-and-wear and let my iron rust. Laundry workers, on the other hand, taught me a lot, but that story is in an earlier chapter. My work in the machine shops taught me how to use drill presses, punch presses and a little about lathes. The jobs at Emerson Radio and Colonial Radio gave me some understanding of electronics. And the work at Knight-Kit taught me how to break down information into a step-by-step process that was easy to follow. The step-by-step idea was useful in my later work as a teacher. As it turned out, I was not to keep the Knight-Kit job forever.

When the manager of the instruction manuals quit, I was asked to take that job. That was the beginning of the end. I did not want to be a manager. I was not paid to be a manager. But my choice was to take the "promotion" or soon lose my job. I don't regret having accepted the manager's job. It gave me a peek into the training/brainwashing that low level managers endured.

We had compulsory (unpaid) weekly training sessions for one month. To soothe the pain, we were given a filet mignon dinner and tickets for two martinis. The first time, I gave away my two martini tickets. The second time, I gave one ticket away and drank one martini. The third time I drank both martinis and felt no pain. As I drove the few blocks home, my car was floating on air. I did not like that feeling one bit. For the fourth session, I went back to giving away both martini tickets. The content itself had a lot of truthful insight. Only the goal was wrong—to increase company profit, not to improve workers' conditions.

In 1965, three years after we moved to Broadview, the new president of Knight-Kit told me, "For what I'm paying you, I could get a man." And that is exactly what he did. One day, he called me in to tell me I was fired. A man I had trained took my place. Equality legislation was not in effect, and we did not have a union. There was nothing I could do. The firing was not a surprise, and I had made some exit plans. For over a year, I had taken evening courses to study education. I was planning to qualify as a public school teacher. But I was still short a few credit hours. So I needed to find another job until I could get my teacher's license. But first I wanted to go to a country I had heard so much about: Mexico.

Mexico

All my life I had wanted to travel. My wonderful trip to the new Cuba had sharpened my appetite. I had no job, and Frank could care for the kids for two weeks. The big kids would help. The only problem was money. If I took a bus, it would not cost that much. And I had learned to get by cheap on my Cuba trip. I bought a bus ticket to Mexico City, packed a few things in a slightly oversized hat bag and set off. The trip took two nights and the better part of two days. I managed to curl up and get some sleep. That was one of the times that short legs were an advantage.

In and around Mexico City, I came in contact with a vast new culture, the modern, and the ancient. It seemed that every time construction workers dug into the ground, they found remains of old civilizations. Just that year, the splendid Museum of Anthropology opened in Mexico City. The vast collection on display, artifact piled on artifact, was overwhelming. It was very emotional for me to see the people who came to see their own history. I was determined to learn more about the rich culture of the American peoples before Columbus.

Once back in Chicago, I found a job as a technical writer at ITT, International Telephone & Telegraph. When I passed the medical exam, I noticed that the bottom of the form had a scrawled comment, "Note, 46." Suddenly I realized that employers thought I was "old."

Then I saw an ad for a proof reader. It was a union job and paid a good hourly rate. I had done plenty of proof reading at Knight-Kit but this was different. It was display type, and I was not really qualified. It was also night work. That never agreed with me. After a couple of weeks I quit, to the foreman's great surprise. He thought nobody could afford to quit a job with such good pay. And he was right. But these temporary jobs had carried me through to the point where I had enough education credits to get my teachers' license. I had a job lined up at Crane High School for September. Also, I had just withdrawn my "profit-sharing" money from Allied Radio.

Frank and I decided to go on our dream trip, two months of camping in Europe. It was the chance of a lifetime. The youngest boys would come with us. I had, perhaps, too much confidence in the two older children. We left Carl, Jeanleah, and our dog, Guy, in charge of the house. Jeanleah had found a waiter's job, and Carl had a summer job in a local factory. They did well. The house was still standing when we returned in late August. Our camping trip deserves its own chapter. Our only regret was that the older children missed it. But they more than made up for it in later years. Both Carl and Jeanleah worked abroad and had the experience of immersion in another language.

We continued to live in Broadview for some years after our children had established independent lives. Frank did not seem to mind the 60 mile round trip on Chicago's congested highways. My daughter did stay with us for some months after her divorce. Her toddler son, Soren, was Frank's delight. And little Soren returned Frank's love. The police stopped Frank while driving around Broadview with blonde Soren sitting on the back seat. "What are you doing with that child?" the police demanded. "That's my grandson," Frank told them. "Your grandson!" the police exclaimed. "Just then Soren said, "Grandpa, let's go!" That saved the day. The cops failed to apologize but let Frank go on his way.

In 2007, Frank and I stopped in Broadview to check out our old home. Our old neighborhood appeared to be largely or entirely African American. Roosevelt Road was no longer the local "Mason-Dixon" line. That line had just been moved farther south and west. That so-called changing neighborhood had become de facto segregated as the real estate companies reaped the profits. But there's been a big change in the state's politics. Barack Obama, an African American, had been elected to the U.S. Senate, a huge breakthrough. When we lived in Broadview, I never thought we were just one generation away from electing a community-based African American as president of the United States. Now I know what can be accomplished in one generation.

Chapter *18*

Camping – From Yellowstone to Moscow
Hitler's "1,000-year Reich" lasted less than 12 years

Camping around the Great Lakes

IN our family, we were seasoned campers. How else could a steel worker's family of six afford to travel around the United

257

States? Basically, tent camping was no more expensive than living at home, except for the car expenses. And we had experiences that could not be equaled if we had gone the expensive tourist route. We usually set out in June, as soon as the kids' summer vacation began. We headed west for two reasons. The lack of rain made for more comfortable camping. And the grandeur of the western mountains drew us like a magnet. The simplest facts of nature amazed us city folks. I remember the first time we were away from the light of the cities at night and saw the starlit sky over the prairies. We were awestruck. The thousands of stars that shine on the planetarium dome were all really in the sky! We visited famous places: Mesa Verde with the Native American cliff dwellings, Rocky Mountain National Park with bears shaking the ice box at night, and Yellowstone Park with steam geysers popping on schedule.

Slumgullion Pass

Our biggest camping adventure was in a little known national forest. Frank used to like to go off the well-traveled road and, as he put it, "get lost." We were in Southern Colorado when he left the highway to follow an unmarked road. After a while, there was a sign with an arrow, "To Slumgullion Pass."

Slumgullion Pass was like the forest primeval. The six of us had it all to ourselves. There was water and a pit toilet. And we had enough food to stay for a few days. On the third day a Colorado camper came by and told us the story of Slumgullion Pass. He said it was the site of an ill-fated expedition from Montrose, Colorado, to Gunnison, Colorado. Alferd Packer led five gold prospectors through the mountains until a snowstorm trapped them in the pass.

Only Packer emerged next spring, well fed, leaving the gnawed bones of the prospectors behind. A trial was held and the judge found him guilty of murder. Legend has it that the judge cursed Packer as a depraved Republican, adding: "There were only five Democrats in Hinsdale County, and you ate them all!"

Tenting in France

By the time we decided to camp in Europe, we had a lot of experience in wilderness camping. June 1965 was the ideal time to go to Europe for a camping trip. I had lost my job at Knight Kit/Allied Radio and had collected my "profit sharing" money. It was enough to buy plane tickets for four. And I had a teaching job waiting for me when I returned.

Packing for the European trip was a challenge. We had to pack the tent, sleeping bags, Coleman Stove and two months of clothing for four people. Our baggage had to stay under 44 pounds each. Our budget was $100 a week for gas, food for four and camping fees. The new VW Squareback, waiting for us in Paris, cost $1600. Gasoline was the biggest expense with the price of gas $3.50 a gallon in Western Europe. Only in the Soviet Union and Mexico, was the price of gas comparable to the U.S., about $0.35 a gallon.

European camping turned out to be very different from our U.S. experience. By 1965, auto clubs in most of Europe had set up auto camps in many cities. To our surprise, most camp sites were near the center of town. Some were along the main river that flowed through the city. And the facilities were more developed than wilderness camp sites in the U.S. I have heard that has all changed.

It took ten days to get our Soviet visa in Paris. Of course, the days spent in Paris were not time wasted. We wandered everywhere and spent days in the Louvre. Finally, we got our Soviet visa and drove east towards the German border. The French countryside was pretty in an ordered kind of way. Neat rectangles of yellow and green formed a quilt work of farmland, like a calendar cover. We knew we were near the border when I heard German spoken in the villages of Alsace-Lorraine. I switched from my basic high school French to my basic high school German. It turned out that I did not know, whether in French or German, words for the most basic needs. For example, I needed a mineral oil laxative. How could I describe the purpose of mineral oil?

Frank had shown us how fellow workers told him to ask for eggs when he didn't know the language. He had us all laughing when he imitated a hen in labor delivering an egg.

But a dignified pantomime of the purpose of mineral oil was a challenge. I did know the German word for oil, *erl*. So I asked for "erl" at the *drogeria*. The clerk brought out cooking oil, kerosene and Mazola corn oil, one at a time. By now other customers had joined in the fun to help with the translation. "Nein," I said. Not for cooking, not for burning, not for eating; it's like medicine but not medicine. Finally they got the idea. *"für umkehren."* That sounded to me like "turn upside down and shake out the contents!" Sounded like what I needed. Everyone applauded. *"Danke schön,"* said I and paid for my mineral oil.

Germany

We crossed the Rhine at Cologne and knew we were in a different country. The delicious, light, French bread was no more to be seen. The dark, heavy German bread was good, too, but in a different way. We spent just one night in Frankfurt and pushed eastward to Nuremberg. A kind man led us to a big camping place, too dark to make out the details. We were the only campers there but too tired to care.

When we woke in the morning, the place looked strangely familiar. It was an abandoned stadium, overgrown with grass. A long reviewing stand ran across the front.

We were standing in the stadium of the Nazi Party, right on the spot where Hitler stood at the podium! Paul and John got an instant history lesson. Hitler's "1,000-year Reich" lasted less than 12 years, as the decay around us proved. Capitalism, too, would not last forever. As Frank always said, "Everything changes."

There was no speed limit on the famous (or infamous) Autobahn. Soon we reached Czechoslovakia, our first steps on socialist soil. When we reached Prague, we fell in love with the city. In 1963, there was an air of prosperity and well-being. Prague was lovely, its Gothic architecture unharmed by World War II. Our kids never tired of watching the little figures march out of the clock in the central square. In fact, we were having such a good time that we extended our three-day transit visa to seven days.

That gave us a chance to visit Ruth, a Chicago friend living in Prague. Ruth introduced us to the wonderful Czech roasted duck. She told us that Hitler had spared Prague from bombing, wanting to use it as a Nazi playground. In Prague, I was pleased to see that young women were working on non-traditional jobs, from electrical maintenance to installation of sewers. When Paul's "football knee" swelled up, we were quickly directed to an emergency clinic. Treatment was free, for tourists too. That was a pleasant surprise.

The Soviet Union

It was late in the day when we crossed into the Soviet Union at Uzhgorod. The camping looked tempting, but the Soviet visa called for staying in Lvov that night, and that's what we were going to do if humanly possible. The winding mountain road was narrow, making for slow going. Livestock crossed the road at will. I was driving when a white horse reared up suddenly in the headlights. Frank laughed. "Just like home in Georgia," he said as the animals crossed the road. This part of the Ukraine was returned to Soviet Ukraine after World War II, just 20 years earlier. The countryside was still underdeveloped. It was obvious that the Soviets could have used all of their resources right in their own country. Soviet aid to the countries of Africa, Asia and Latin America was true international solidarity. It came at some sacrifice of local Soviet needs.

Kiev

Kiev was a beautiful city with many tree-lined streets. The Soviet Union had the world's best camping bargain. Along with the night's camping permit ($5), came the services of an Intourist guide. In Kiev the guide was a daring graduate geology student whose name was Igor. Paul and John politely suppressed a laugh when they heard his name. Monster culture was then big in the U.S.; Igor was the name of a character in the Frankenstein movies.

Sometimes our Igor was too daring. He directed Frank to drive the wrong way down a one-way street near the sport stadium. The street was closed for a soccer game. The militia man on the street corner turned a vivid purple, blowing his whistle in protest. "Keep going," Igor calmly told Frank. "If he stops us, I'll tell him you're a visiting African prince." But in other ways, Igor was a model Soviet citizen, absolutely incorruptible. He refused to let us buy him lunch. "I am like a camel," he said. "I can go for long periods without food or water." Then he would insist that we see everything, so there was no time for lunch anyway.

Igor was not religious. But one of the first sights he insisted we see was the great cathedrals. Time after time, in the Soviet Union and Poland, we saw great architecture rebuilt after the Nazis had leveled it to the ground. These buildings had no military value but were destroyed in a deliberate attempt to erase people's history. In the Ukraine, the beautiful blue and white Orthodox churches of Kiev were bombed to the ground. The Soviet government rebuilt these churches and respected them as great works of art.

We were impressed by the amount of new construction all around us. I told Igor, "You have quite a few new buildings," He corrected me. "Not quite a few," he explained, "quite a many."

Camping in Moscow

Finally we reached Moscow. Again, we felt the ghosts of World War II all around us. The first year of the Nazi invasion, Hitler's army had pushed within 19 miles of the city. Nonetheless, the Russian people paraded in Moscow on November 7, 1941. They put on a huge celebration of the 24th anniversary of their revolution. Soviet troops marched in Red Square, in defiance of the Nazi offensive. Then they left the parade for the front lines. We felt both humble and proud to walk on the same ground. We were also very moved by a custom that Russian newlyweds practiced. After they said their vows, they placed their flowers on a memorial to the Soviet soldiers who died in World War II.

Any time of day, long lines stretched outside of Lenin's tomb. Our Intourist guides ushered us up to the front of the line. That was a courtesy, they explained. Tourists did not have to wait. I went in not knowing what to expect. Lenin's body was in a perfect state of preservation. The love that people hold for this modest man remains so strong that Russia's capitalist government is afraid to close Lenin's tomb.

I think of Lenin in the terms described by my Latvian friend, Ernest Amatneek, when we were students at James Monroe High School. Ernest's father was part of the Red Guard that was protecting Smolny Institute in the early days of the Soviet Union. Amatneek Senior was on guard as Lenin walked toward the Institute entrance. Lenin stopped at the gate to get out his pass. "Come right in, Comrade Lenin," Amatneek said with a big smile. But Lenin insisted. He showed his pass, just like everybody else. He wanted no special treatment.

Our Moscow experience was deepened by a chance stroll in front of the Metropole Hotel. A man from Ghana came up to Frank and said, "Hello brother!" George was an actor who had adopted Russia as his second (or third) homeland. When he heard we were from Chicago, he asked if we knew Charles and Margaret Burroughs. Indeed we did. They were dear friends. We met Margaret Burroughs soon after we came to Chicago. Charles and Margaret started the DuSable Museum of African American History with an art collection in their own home. As luck would have it, the Burroughs were also visiting Moscow.

For the rest of our time in Moscow, we were escorted by Charles, a graduate of Moscow University. He was born in New York, mostly educated in Russia, and had returned to the United States to serve in the U.S. Army during World War II. Charles interpreted the "Help Wanted" signs for us. They were posted all over the city. Unemployment was not a problem in the Soviet Union.

Byelorus Tractor

For our return trip, we headed west from Moscow and drove back to Minsk. In Moscow, Frank had asked to visit a steel mill, but that did not work out. Intourist knew that Frank worked for International Harvester, so they set up the next best thing. In Minsk, we were offered a tour of the Byelorus Tractor Works.

It was fortunate that we had an escort to the Byelorus Tractor Works because we would have missed it. The façade of the plant looked like a residential complex. Inside the plant, workers' comfort seemed a high priority. Drinking fountains offered a choice of cold water or seltzer

We must have arrived during a rest break. Nobody was working very hard. That started a debate within the family. Workers deserved to work without being pushed too hard. But it left us with an uneasy feeling, a feeling that they should have been working harder because they were working for themselves. Frank put it this way: "You have a responsibility to your kids, grandchildren, other people's kids. If you have knowledge, you have responsibility to share that knowledge. You can't take it easy."

Frank and I were both impressed by Soviet retirees who were not "taking it easy." Many were still working and collecting their pay and their pensions. Soviet pensioners could work as many hours as they wanted, at regular pay. That seemed an ideal solution to the problem of remaining productive in old age. But it was a solution that could work only under socialism, where the goal was human happiness, not profit.

I had the chance to revisit the Soviet Union 20 years later. Our camp was long gone, swallowed up by Moscow's expansion. I saw how much the economy had developed since 1965. But I did not feel the same sense of purpose that the people showed in 1965. Still I never guessed that Soviet workers would not fight to keep their socialist system. The loss of socialism led to one of the greatest population tragedies of all time. In Russia of 2006, for every baby that was born, there were ten deaths. Men's life expectancy dropped by 15 years.

Poland

When we left the Soviet Union and drove west to Warsaw, we saw only a few bombed-out buildings. They remained as museums. The rest of Warsaw had been rebuilt with amazing speed. Historic old Warsaw was rebuilt from the ashes with the aid of old photographs and drawings. The Poles had defeated the Nazis not only militarily but also spiritually. With Soviet aid, Poles had restored their history. The respect for history was a contrast to Chicago where historic architecture is being destroyed to maximize short-term profit.

Standing on the site of the Warsaw ghetto was a very emotional experience for me. In a neighborhood of new buildings, I used my poor German to ask a Polish woman, "Where is the Warsaw ghetto?" "You're standing right on it," she replied, and began to cry. I cried with her and felt bad that I had reopened a raw sore for this Holocaust survivor.

Crossing the Polish border, it took us just a few hours to drive across the German Democratic Republic (GDR) to West Germany. We camped in Frankfurt, in Heidelberg, then Lake Zurich in Switzerland. We were headed to Italy, then France and home again.

Italy

To get to Italy, we had to cross the Alps. I had the pleasure (or agony) of driving over the famous Matterhorn. I had heard so much about this fearsome mountain. It was true that the switchbacks were many and sudden. Still, I found it tame compared to some really hairy driving we had done in the American Rockies. There was a long and slow line of traffic ahead of me. All I had to do was follow the car in front of us. At last, we descended to the vibrant North Italian city, Milano.

From Milano, we made a side trip to Venice. Frank watched the gondolas glide by, but resisted renting one. Gondola rides were not in our budget. When the gondoliers saw Frank, they saw an oppressed person of color and a fellow seaman, not a tourist. They rose in their boats and gave him the clenched fist salute. It was a touching gesture of international solidarity.

Frank wanted to see Genoa again, a port that his ship visited after World War II. After a brief stop in Genoa, we were homeward bound, driving along the beautiful Riviera Road. Monaco lay like a sparkling jewel at night, sitting on the Mediterranean between Italy and France. Frank thought of going into the world-famous casinos. But he was dressed for camping, not the glamorous night life

Watts Burning!

Crossing Southern France, we decided to camp in Nice. We wanted to swim in the Mediterranean. Shocking news from home hit our eyes in Nice. The front page of every French paper had a screaming headline, "Watts in flames!" My hands shook as I bought the papers and read the dread news. We needed to hurry home to help the people who were trying to help.

Our last stop before Paris was at a rural camping place in southwestern France. We pitched the tent next to the fence at the far end of the grounds. Soon we were in a deep sleep. About 4 a.m., I heard heavy footsteps right outside of the back of our tent. A heavy body began to hit the tent wall. Then I heard loud roars, right in my ears. Frozen with fear, I shook Frank awake. "What is that," I whispered. "It can't be lions!" Frank listened and laughed and went back to sleep.

Again, there were some deafening roars. There was no more sleep for me that night. I was glad when daylight came. I got dressed and went outside. On the other side of the fence, I saw some cows chewing grass, just inches from where we had laid our heads. Those cows had bellowed right in our ears. No wonder it sounded like the roars of a lion!

The next day we were in Paris, back at Bois de Boulogne auto camp. Then we delivered our green Volkswagen Squareback for shipping to Chicago. The rest of our travel was by public transportation with the final luxury of a cab to the airport.. My thoughts were turning to my future life as a teacher.

John, Frank and Paul, left to right, standing at Hitler's podium, in the now dismantled Nazi Stadium, Nuremburg, Germany

Part 3
(1965–1986)

Chapter *19*

I Become a Teacher

Some students moved forward, leaving their messed-up past behind.

September 7, 1965, was my first day at Crane High School on Chicago's West Side. I will never forget that day. As an "FTB," a full-time-basis substitute teacher, I had my own classes for the entire semester. The student population was 98% African American, coming from the poorest part of Chicago. I met my first mathematics class with great earnestness. Whatever the lesson, the main point I tried to put across was that we would learn together. I gave the class a page to work on that I thought all could do. Then I asked the students to write their comments at the bottom of the work page. This class was called "Essential Mathematics 1." Only 30% of Crane's entering freshmen were allowed to take algebra, the normal freshman math.

The bell rang, and I hurried out to my next class on another floor. In the hallway was a scene like out of a movie. But these were high school freshmen, not longshoremen on the waterfront. And Marlon Brando was not there to advise me. Two boys were facing each other with knives drawn. Students were gathering around them. The knife holders looked tense and pale; the blood had drained out of their faces. I did not know them or any other soul in that building. I felt I should do something, but I didn't know what. So I continued to hurry to my next class. It has been on my conscience ever since.

Somehow I finished the rest of the day. I did not hear any ambulances or police sirens. There was nothing in the paper and no talk in the school of a knifing. Probably the students did what I had done—heard the bell and left for their next class. I never saw a scene like that again in 20 years of teaching. At home, I asked Frank what he would have done. He said without a moment's hesitation, "I would have asked them to give me their knives." "Did you ever do anything like that?" I asked. "Sure," he replied. Then I remembered a summer day when Frank had made a second circle around the full parking lot at Jackson Park Beach. He had seen a friend "who was about to get in trouble." The friend was gone by the time we re-circled. "My friend had a gun in his hand," Frank explained. "What would you have done if you had found him?" I asked. "I would have told him, Give me that gun! And he would have given it to me," Frank added.

At night after my first day of classes, I corrected the work pages I had collected from the Essential Math I class. One student had written, "F--- Essential Math. I want algebra." That student had my instant attention and sympathy. I talked to him after the next class. "If you want to learn algebra, I will teach you." He seemed interested and did some of the algebra work I gave him. Then he began to miss classes. Sometimes he came in reeking of alcohol and would put his head down on the desk and sleep through the class. After a few weeks, I did not see him anymore. He had quit school. A similar tragedy occurred in my home room class. Two of my students were identified by the school as superior students. I tried to give them extra encouragement. Before the semester was out, both had lost interest—big problems at home that were beyond my scope. Fortunately, some other experiences were more encouraging.

Of my five classes, one was an algebra class. That class was full of very bright students. I did my best but felt inadequate because the class remained unruly. Then the principal came in to evaluate me. I thought I had a different class. They were so attentive and so smart. They knew everything I asked them. The principal left impressed. I was, too. I had gained new insight into my students' strong sense of solidarity. I loved those students.

One of the best students in the algebra class was a white student from Appalachia. She quickly found solutions to hard "word problems." I thought she was gifted. On a hunch I looked up her IQ test score. It was 90, supposedly low normal. So much for IQ rankings!

Study? Hall

That algebra class was my best experience that semester. My study hall assignment was the worst. The study hall was held in the auditorium, along with a number of other "study halls." The light was not that good. Still, a few students actually studied despite the discomfort. But only a few.

The teacher's job was to ride herd on the students and keep them quiet. One day, I acted on impulse and provided the assembled study hall classes with some free entertainment. My only excuse is that the students were the same age as my sons John and Paul, who were 14 and 15 1/2. I often reacted to the students as I would to my sons. I called one student to come forward. Instead, he bolted and ran. Without thinking, I jumped to my feet and ran after him. The whole auditorium rose and cheered. "Look at Mrs. Lumpkin run!" The worst part was not my loss of dignity. It was my lack of speed. I was no longer fast enough to catch the student. I lost that race in more ways than one.

Another time I had more success in treating a couple of students as though they were my sons. Two boys in my division class were tussling. They were trying to rough each other up. I walked over and pulled them apart. Then I sent them back to their seats. After the period, a third student told me, "Mrs. Lumpkin, you should not have done that. Robert had a knife." I shrugged off the friendly warning. Still, I remembered it and recognized the good sense in the warning.

Of course, study hall also had a good side. I had one student who seemed interested. He came every day to both my study hall and my mathematics class. I learned to my surprise that he cut all his other classes. I was flattered. But in my sober old age I thought of a less flattering explanation. My time slots may have just been convenient for him.

The worst incident I had in the study hall carried a big price. It was a learning experience for me but at a student's expense.

272 JOY IN THE STRUGGLE

I was very new on the job. A student got up to leave, and I told him to come back. There, in front of all of the students, he defied my order to return. I reported him to the principal's office. I never saw him again, so I asked another teacher about the student. That teacher told me, "You hammered the nails in his coffin." It seems the student was removed from Crane and placed in some special school for "problem" students.

Crane must have had a "three strikes and you're out" rule. I felt terrible. Yes, I knew it was not I that put the student "in his coffin." It was the system. Still, it was a hard lesson. I learned not to report kids to the main office. It's like the lesson learned in many communities of color: do not call the police for anything less than homicide. The police may only make matters worse.

Leaving Crane High School

At the end of the fall 1965 semester, I got trapped by a "catch 22" regulation. I had been hired as an FTB substitute. My regular certificates, high school and elementary, were on their way. Unfortunately, my elementary school certificate came through first. The "catch 22" rule forced me to leave the high school and transfer to the elementary. That was a pity. I had made a good start in becoming an effective high school teacher.

My most difficult students took the news of my leaving the hardest. That class, labeled "Basic Mathematics," was really a dumping ground for disturbed students. They gave me a hard time all semester. Each day, I left the class on the verge of tears. But when I told them I was leaving, they cried. Then I began to feel ashamed. Until that moment, they were the one class I was glad to leave. Perhaps I had done more good that I had realized.

I was most concerned about the only young woman in that Basic Mathematics class. She had a big, disrespectful mouth, and mostly she disrespected herself. Some years later, I saw her again, this time at Malcolm X College. Jeanette had grown up and cleaned up her act, especially her mouth. She filled me with hope. I was happy to learn that some students were able to move forward and leave their messed-up teen years behind them. It taught me to never give up on a student.

Just a few blocks from Crane stood Manley School, then kindergarten to eighth grade. Despite the grim conditions at the school, there were some very good teachers. One had a fourth grade class made up of students with behavior problems. The first thing that teacher did was to improve the physical condition of the classroom, at her own expense, of course. She sewed curtains for the windows to soften the light. She brought in plants to put on the window sills and pictures to decorate the walls. As the students saw how much she cared, their behavior began to improve. She was a hero in my eyes.

Teaching Fourth Grade

At Manley, I took over a fourth grade class in February that had been without a teacher since September. Each morning started with an unpleasant duty. It was my duty to take away any candy that the children brought to school in the morning. For some, I knew it was their only breakfast. That was before the Black Panthers started their revolutionary hot breakfast program. I had 38 children in my class. I believe class size limit was then 32, still too large for fourth grade. The children were not even allowed a playground recess, just a class trip to the toilets.

Things can happen very quickly when 38 nine-year-olds are crowded into one room. I didn't even see what led up to a little boy banging a little girl's head on her desk. In minutes a big bump poked out on her forehead. It soon went down, but I sent a note home with the little boy. I wanted to talk with his mother. She did come in the next day. I believe the mother was doing her best. She referred to the growing civil rights movement (1966). "We are teaching our children to fight," she explained to me. I was astounded. "Fight for your rights, yes! But fight each other?" I asked. People need unity to be able to fight for their rights.

To tell the truth, I needed more unity in that classroom. Probably my hardest job, as a new teacher, was to get the students' attention. I had to work to restore some order in that class room. The substitute teacher had read his newspaper and let the kids run around as they wished all semester. I really sympathized with the nine-year-old boy whom I firmly, and I hope gently, returned to his seat. "Let me out of this zoo," he said. I remember the unhealthy texture of the skin on his arm. It was not the normal smooth skin of a nine-year- old. How bad his diet must have been to coarsen his skin like sandpaper! I was determined to teach the children what they needed to move up to the next grade. After great effort on my part, I had some success. But I was beginning to suspect that I was better at teaching high school than fourth grade. For one thing, although I am never sick, at Manley I was sick all the time. First it was flu that turned into pneumonia. Then a little scratch developed into blood poisoning. My body was trying to tell me something. Meanwhile my high school certificate came through. At the end of the school year, I transferred back to the high schools, this time at Austin High School.

The student body at Austin High School was about 80% white in 1966. Austin was then a "changing neighborhood." The students were not any smarter than the Crane students. Still, freshmen were routinely given algebra as their first course. At Crane, I was never asked for my lesson plans. But the principal did look at them at Austin. I tried to be innovative, but I soon learned better. My lesson plans were returned to me with the note, "Is this in the curriculum guide?" I soon realized that if I wanted to do my best for the students, I would have to keep two sets of books. One would be for the principal, copied straight out of the curriculum guide. The other would be for use with my classes, to give them what I thought they needed. This strategy worked. But keeping two sets of books meant twice as much work for me.

The rest of the school year went smoothly except for the big snows of 1967. The day before the winter holidays, the snow plow buried my car in the school lot. There had been racist incidents in this "changing" area. So I decided not to call on Frank to help me get my car out. Had I known that record snows were coming, I would have dug my car out then and there. If need be, I would have used my bare hands. But I did not know so I left my car and took the bus home. Record snows did fall and the streets around the school became waist deep in snow. I wondered how school could reopen because the fire department could never get through in an emergency. After ten days, the snows eased. Frank helped me dig my car out of the snow bank but it was never any good again.

From Margaret in my Fourth-Grade Class

At the end of the school year, a friend told me that the Chicago City Colleges (CCC) was hiring teachers. I applied and was hired by Crane Junior College, located in a wing of Crane High School.

Chapter *20*

Malcolm X College and Fred Hampton

"You can kill the revolutionary, but you cannot kill a revolution"- Fred Hampton

I reported to Crane Junior College in the same high school building where I began my life as a teacher. September 1967 was a very interesting time to come to the college. The black student movement was demanding Black Studies, and the Black Panther Party (BPP) was building its base in Chicago's West Side. Crane, originally known as Herzl Junior College, was the first of the Chicago City Colleges. Herzl opened its doors in 1911, in response to the demand of Chicago's labor movement and progressive educators. The goal was to provide the first two years of college to working class students. Tuition was free. In the Depression year of 1933, the college was closed in a cost-cutting move. Thanks to demands by organized labor and public figures like Clarence Darrow, the school reopened in 1934. The Jewish community was active in that fight, according to Harvey Echols, a fellow teacher at Crane College and a graduate of Herzl. Enrollment increased during the Great Depression although the budget was cut. In the years since 1934, the system expanded to seven colleges. Over 50,000 students were enrolled in college credit courses by 2008.

In 1967, the progressive white administration of Crane College was sympathetic to the students' demands. They were sympathetic enough to step aside when students demanded a black college president. That change came in 1969. I believe that the demand for representation was, and still is, a legitimate and important demand. But the students soon learned that "black" was not enough. Among both white and African American administrators, too many put their personal advancement ahead of community needs.

Black Studies had become a big issue at Crane Junior College. Many of the then majority-white teachers were sympathetic to the demand for Black Studies. But not all. The split may have been half and half. Students picketed the English teacher across the hall from me. She had refused to include *any* African American authors in her reading list. Still, some African American teachers told me not to be concerned about my classes. In their opinion, mathematics was exempt from demands for Black Studies.

I decided not to take the pass. It bothered me when some students said, "We are not good at mathematics. We are good at literature, law and verbal and visual arts." I had learned that Egyptian schools were already teaching mathematics 4,000 years ago. That tradition went way back in Africa. But I needed to learn more. I could not teach what I did not know. Where could I find the information I needed? That issue kept me busy for the next 40 years. Some of the fascinating information I found is outlined in a later chapter.

In the summer of 1969, half of the faculty transferred to other branches of the city colleges. Some who left did not want to add Black Studies to the curriculum. Others left because new positions had opened up closer to their homes. Among the newly hired teachers, a substantial number were African American. Because so many senior teachers had gone, newly hired teachers made up the majority at Crane. Most were excited about the promise of support for African American studies. But there were warning signs of problems ahead.

Warning signs included poor teaching conditions that worsened in 1969. Those bad conditions could be blamed, in part, on the lack of facilities in the old buildings. But poor administration was also to blame. Textbooks were not available, simply because the bookstore had failed to order them. I was determined not to let my classes get behind, so I wrote my own textbook.

Meanwhile, many more students were enrolling. Some of my classes were too large to fit into the classroom. Class size limits had been won in the first union contract of January, 1967. However, my class rosters far exceeded those limits. For example, my remedial mathematics class had 60 students. Before each class session, I had to scrounge extra chairs from the other rooms. We teachers put up with these bad conditions because it was supposed to be temporary. And there was a prize dangled before us that kept me going. That was the chance to develop ways to include African American culture in our classes.

In a remedial class, each student needs individual attention. How can you give personal attention to 60 people at once? I tried something new. First I gave a pre-test and found some students who were pretty good at the math. They probably did not need the remedial class. Then I divided the class in four groups and put a good student at the head of each. Of course I tried to make it up to the student leaders, give them extra attention and plenty of praise. That worked fine for about a month. Then the student leaders began to feel that they were working without pay, and they were. Whatever I tried, I could not prevent that class from melting away. At the end of the semester I passed everyone I possibly could, everyone who had mastered the minimum content of the course. I got the reputation of a good teacher.

At Crane Junior College I became a member of the Cook County College Teachers Union (CCTU), Local 1600 AFT (American Federation of Teachers AFL-CIO). It was a relatively new local and was forged in battle. Local 1600 had just won its first union contract the semester before I came to Crane. They had won it by defying a court-imposed injunction against their strike for union recognition. The strike leader, Norman Swenson, was sentenced to 30 days in Cook County Jail. Despite appeals, on November 30, 1971, Swenson had to go to jail and serve the 30 days.

The city college union was a very different scene from the huge Chicago Teachers' Union (CTU). In the CTU, there was little opportunity for new members like me to be active. In contrast, the union was wide open at the junior colleges. Much of the college faculty was also new when I started in September, 1967. So being new was not a barrier to union activism. I was quickly swept into action (or plunged in). Soon I was elected as a delegate to Local 1600's House of Representatives.

Student Power Grows

The Crane students had elected very capable Student Union officers. As a whole, the student body was more mature and more experienced than in typical colleges. Many Crane students wore Chicago Transit Authority or mail carrier uniforms, working full time jobs while studying. No doubt our most famous student was Fred Hampton. Other students became well known professionals. Stan Willis, student council president in 1966, became a lawyer. He was elected president of the Cook County Bar Association, an organization of African American lawyers. Among my mathematics students, Henry English went on from Malcolm X College to major in mathematics at a major university. He is the CEO and the driving force behind the Black United Fund of Chicago. Vernita Irvin completed her PhD and came back to teach in Allied Health at Malcolm X. Gide Colinet, a chemistry major, continued his studies and became a professor of chemistry at Olive Harvey, one of the Chicago City Colleges. Cynthia Henderson graduated from medical school and became a noted gastroenterologist.

In 1969, city college students pressed their demands so strongly that the faculty union had to pay attention. Local 1600's House of Delegates went into continuous session with student representatives. I don't remember that any agreement was reached, but their demands got a hearing from a very attentive audience. At Crane, African American students demanded, and received, a voice in the hiring and retention of teachers and administrators. At least they interviewed all faculty applicants as well as current teachers. Then they made recommendations about renewing annual teacher contracts. At the end of the semester, teachers who did not like student power transferred to other city college campuses. The teachers were able to move out of Crane en masse because college enrollment was expanding, creating many faculty openings. Sadly, that did not last; there are few faculty openings today.

In the heady, turbulent period of the late '60s, a new Crane College president was selected. Students and community participated in the choice, or so they thought. They interviewed three applicants referred by the Chicago City Colleges Board. One of the three made an instant hit with the students and community representatives. For each question he was asked by students and community people, he gave the exact answer they wanted. Then he would go a little further. The students were delighted. That applicant was Dr. Charles G. Hurst, Jr., a top administrator of City College in Washington, DC. The students believed Dr. Hurst was even more revolutionary than they were. They were convinced that he was the leader they were hoping for. And his first steps did not disappoint them.

Dr. Charles G. Hurst

Dr. Hurst became president of Crane College in February, 1969. Construction had already begun on a new building. A new name was also sought to reflect community values. Student and community activists chose the name of Malcolm X, assassinated four years earlier. He was a Black Nationalist leader known for his strong stand against racism and oppression. Conservative elements of the City College Board wanted the school named for Booker T. Washington. One of the first actions of President Hurst was to support the students' choice of Malcolm X. In the end, community support was decisive. Crane Junior College became Malcolm X Community College by a vote of a committee made up of West Side residents on October 29, 1969. Of course, the press gave all the credit to Dr. Hurst. As *Time* magazine put it, "After an eight-month battle with the board of the Chicago City Colleges, Hurst got Crane renamed for Malcolm X, raised the green, red and black flag of black liberation next to the U.S. and Illinois flags, and won the trust of Chicago's black radicals."[21]

No matter how radical student leaders were, Dr. Hurst seemed to be one step ahead of them. This process reached a critical point on the first anniversary of Martin Luther King's death. As the anniversary neared, there was a lot of tension on the West Side. It was only one year since Chicago's West Side went up in flames after Dr. King's murder on April 4, 1968. Whole areas were torched to the ground. In fact, forty years later, much of the West Side still stands desolate, nothing but weeds. Into the West Side tinder box, Charles Hurst threw a match. Early in April 1969, he delivered an explosive speech to high school students in the Crane auditorium.

I did not hear Hurst's speech, but I saw what happened after his speech. Our college shared a building with Crane High School. It was as though the whole auditorium full of students rose up and ran out to the halls, demanding justice. The police, it seemed to me, were glad of the excuse to go after the students. Reinforced with packs of dogs, armed uniformed police swept the high school halls. They drove the frightened youth first to

---

[21] "Education: Intellectual Black Power," *Time*, August 16, 1971.

one end of the building, then to the other. In a show of military force, a police helicopter swept over the Congress Expressway, along the side of the school. Then the helicopter landed in the school yard. I had the feeling that we were trapped, that the excessive police force was a warning of things to come.

I don't remember that anyone was arrested, just intimidated. For the high school students, it was another unwelcome reminder of the state of war between the police and West Side teenagers. After the police finished their military practice, the students went home and we went back to work. But nothing returned to normal. As I entered the Crane building a couple days later, I felt the electric tension. Four or five students were talking and looked up at me in a decidedly unfriendly manner. Just then, another student walked in, sized up the situation, came over and put his arm around my shoulder in a hug. The tension defused. That student was Fred Hampton, my friend and neighbor and leader of the Black Panther Party (BPP).

I remember another student activist, also a member of the BPP. He was an English literature student named Clifton Morgan, a fine young man. He liked to talk to us left-leaning teachers. Morgan had taken a new name, Babatunde Omowale, to show his pride in his African roots. He told me that the name meant "brother who has come back home" in the Swahili language. One day, Babatunde Omowale was found dead near the Illinois Central Railroad tracks, blown up by a bomb. The newspapers said police accused Babatunde of trying to blow up an IC train. That was totally out of character and against his principles of helping people. I was sad and shocked and fully expected a big investigation. But 24 hours later, the FBI announced that the case was closed. I grieved but also wondered, "What did they need to cover up that they closed the case so quickly?" I wish I knew the answer to that question. I swallowed my grief but never forgot. I hope some historian will dig up the truth about who killed Clifton Morgan/Babatunde Omowale.

Fighting to Save Free Tuition

Dr. Hurst continued to make news. The local press took a guarded position on him, which changed dramatically at the end of the year. On May 2, 1969, the *Chicago Tribune* quoted

Hurst as warning students in an assembly, "Outside forces are conspiring to destroy the Crane campus of Chicago City College." That was probably true because the West Side was the base of the BPP. A few days later, Hurst threw his support to a student trip to lobby in Springfield, the state capital. The students hoped to stop a bill to impose tuition for the first time ever in the junior college system.

I was very angry about the CCC board's racist move to impose tuition. (Everything in Chicagoland politics is affected by racism.) I felt personal anger because I had had the benefit of four years of tuition-free college education in New York City. I thought my students deserved the same opportunity. The Chicago City Colleges had been tuition free since 1911. During those years, the student body was predominantly white. That changed in the 1960s. Black and Latino students, largely excluded from higher education, began to demand open admission. Doors opened a crack. Most students of color were steered to the free city colleges. Then, as soon as the student body became majority non-white, the board of the Chicago City Colleges decided to impose tuition.

Tuition was largely a method of controlling college enrollment. Most Malcolm X College students got Illinois state grants that paid for their tuition. If the grants were discontinued, these students could not go to school. Working students did not receive these grants. For them, tuition was a heavy burden. Sure, the board said the tuition would not be much, $3 to $5 per credit hour. However, as we predicted, tuition has since gone up many fold. By 2008 it was $87 per credit hour with additional fees of $500 for paramedic and other courses.

In a historic betrayal, the CCCTU, AFT Local 1600, did not actively oppose the board's tuition proposal. The students did not have a chance. Unfortunately, this was not the first undemocratic move by the union leadership. I had already joined with other rank and file teachers to organize the Committee for Democracy and Action (CDA). CDA defended free tuition and won broad support. But we did not succeed in overcoming the lack of action by the union leadership. Some even claimed that tuition would bring in better students. Yet, some of these same teachers had enjoyed their own free tuition under "the GI Bill of Rights."

West Side Black Panther Party

Meanwhile, the Black Panthers were steadily building their influence in the community around Malcolm X College. Their free hot breakfast program was serving meals for some of the same children I had taught at Manly School. Without the Panthers' breakfast, these children would have come to school hungry, or at most, with a little candy for breakfast. The Panthers also operated free community health clinics where qualified doctors and nurses donated their time. This was the face of the BPP to Chicago's West-Side community, not the brandishing-of-guns image of the BPP founders in Oakland, California. The BPP was also into educating its membership. They had discovered Marx, Engels and Lenin. High school dropouts, who had never read anything harder than comic strips, were poring over this heavy and heady material. The Panthers were beginning to expand their program from fighting racism to ending capitalism altogether.

Frank and I had no illusions about the potential of violence from the police. Coming from different backgrounds, he and I had reached the same conclusion about capitalist state violence. He saw the Orlando police march under the white sheets of the Ku Klux Klan. At Wisconsin Steel in the 1950s, Frank saw the police stand by while racist rioters attacked African American steel workers. The same Chicago police force had killed ten steel workers and shot one hundred during the Republic Steel Strike of 1937.

On my part, I had seen New York City's "finest" mounted police use horses to pin strikers to the wall in the '30s. I saw the inside of a jail for no other reason than walking the Ohrbach's Department Store picket line during a strike. History taught us to expect police violence. But we were not prepared for the events of December 4, 1969.

"You can kill the revolutionary, but you cannot kill a revolution"

On December 4, 1969, while Fred Hampton and other BPP members were sound asleep in their beds and Mark Clark was on guard in the front room, a squad of Chicago police broke into their apartment. The police were armed with a submachine gun, shotguns and a map of the apartment showing the location of Hampton's bed. State's Attorney for Cook County Edward V. Hanrahan had ordered the murderous raid. The police fired up to 200 rounds into the apartment, enough to kill Hampton and Clark many times over.[22]

With the death of Fred Hampton, the freedom movement lost a young African American leader with the potential for national and international leadership. Fred had a working class outlook and lots of personal "charisma." His parents, Iberia and Francis Hampton, were long-time employees at the cornstarch plant in Argo, Illinois. Both were stewards, rank and file leaders in their local of the Oil, Chemical and Atomic Workers Union, now part of United Steel Workers. During summer vacations, Fred worked in the Argo plant and saw African American, Latino, and white workers cooperating to further the union.

Many have said that Fred was an eloquent speaker who had a lot of personal charm. That was true. But that is not what made him great. More important than charm was his total devotion to the "people." For him, the "people" began with his own African American people and extended to all who were exploited. He foresaw his death and said, "You can kill the revolutionary, but you cannot kill a revolution."

News of the killings stunned Chicago. The impact on the newly-named Malcolm X College had the intensity of an earthquake. The college was just a few blocks from the Panthers' apartment. I viewed the apartment right after the killings. The door looked like Swiss cheese. Thousands of us had lined up on Madison Avenue to see the apartment and show our solidarity. Then we marched to the funeral home, a silent, angry procession. It was hard to view the bodies of the slain youth leaders. They were the same age as my younger boys. Fred was my friend. I grieved for him and his family. Hampton's blood-soaked mattress and the front door riddled with bullets

---

[22] Howard Zinn, *Peoples History of the United States* (New York: Harper Perennial, 1990), 455.

are nightmarish memories that still haunt me. A couple of days after the police murders, the police blocked access to the site.

Hurst becomes the media's darling.

The day after the murders, Dr. Hurst called for the formation of "a young black army." He also talked about teaching students how to use guns. At the time, many used extreme rhetoric in their anger over the murders of Hampton and Clark. On December 11, the *Chicago Tribune* newspaper singled out Dr. Hurst for their attacks. They editorialized against Dr. Hurst for calling for a young black army and demanded that City College board chairman, Dr. John W. Taylor, do "something." Taylor quickly joined in to condemn Hurst's call to arms. It sounded as though Hurst's days as college president were numbered.

Strangely enough, in less than a month, the *Tribune* changed its tune. The paper gave page one placement to an article praising Dr. Hurst for "progress at the college." His radical rhetoric was excused as necessary to win the confidence of students and community. In all too short a time, the reasons for this quick turn-around of the media became apparent. We began to suspect that it was the FBI, not the student leaders, who had brought Dr. Hurst to the West Side of Chicago. By early 1971, he was the media's darling, first as chief strike-breaker in the teachers' strike, then as chief innovator of a scheme to replace teachers with computers. This scheme was immensely popular with big money media. It even brought Charles Hurst wide coverage by national media for educating students without all those pesky teachers. But it was a big bust from the educational point of view, as I will describe later.

Dr. Hurst fully exposed his true nature at the 1972 Republican Party convention. He became a leader of the National Committee for the Reelection of the President (Nixon). It was a dizzyingly rapid journey from supposed ultra-militant Black Nationalist to a leading apologist for Republican President Richard Nixon. Two years later, Nixon was forced to resign in disgrace. And Dr. Hurst had resigned as president of Malcolm X College in February 1973. There are some lessons in that.

Fred Hampton's hometown of Maywood was shaken to its roots by his murder. The Hampton family was well respected in Maywood, and Fred had many friends. Fred and his young friends had won their fight for a swimming pool in Maywood. The pool was already under construction. A motion was made in the Maywood Village Board to name the new swimming pool in honor of Fred Hampton. The board was bitterly divided, but ultimately voted that it be named the Fred Hampton Pool. There was solid support from the growing African American community in Maywood. Additional support by white progressives, notably Tom and Doris Strieter and Joan and Ted Elbert, helped tip the balance, and the Fred Hampton Pool stands for all to enjoy. But Rev. Strieter, who was a member of the village board, paid a price for his courageous stand; he lost his faculty job at Concordia College soon after.

Hanrahan Defeated. Hyde Elected Congressman.

Shortly after the murders, Edward V. Hanrahan, instigator of the raid on the sleeping Panthers, decided to run for Congress. He ran as a Democrat, and the district included Maywood, home of the Hampton family. Hanrahan lost the election. Normally Democratic Maywood had voted heavily against him. Hanrahan's Republican opponent, Henry Hyde, became congressman. The Hamptons felt somewhat vindicated. Unfortunately, Hyde went on to become a leading opponent of everything that Fred Hampton lived and died for. After the election, Hyde managed to get district lines redrawn to exclude African American voters. He knew he would never get their votes again.

In 1970, the families of Mark Clark and Fred Hampton, together with survivors of the police raid, filed a civil suit against Hanrahan and others involved in the assault. It took until 1983 for them to win a settlement. The civil suit was settled for $1.85 million, paid equally by federal, city and county governments. City and county taxpayers also paid two attorneys $2.2 million to defend Hanrahan and the police.[23]

---

[23] *Ibid.* 143.

The Panthers won another significant victory. Thanks to the example set by Black Panthers, the federal government has provided a school breakfast program since 1970. Many children, who otherwise would have had no breakfast, have benefited from the Panthers' initiative.

We always knew that forces larger than Hanrahan were responsible for the Hampton-Clark killings. Twenty-five years later, Paul Engleman in *Chicago* magazine, wrote this revealing report:

> State's attorney Edward V. Hanrahan claimed during a press conference following the raid that his men were victims of a vicious attack and managed to survive "by the grace of God." Hanrahan's account was the first of many falsehoods that would be told, repeated, and revised by law-enforcement personnel during the course of a police inquiry, a coroner's inquest, three grand jury investigations, a criminal trial, and at the time, the longest civil trial in U.S. history. It emerged that Hanrahan and the police were minor players in a larger production staged by the FBI, a secret counter-intelligence program—COINTELPRO—designed, in the words of J. Edgar Hoover, to "disrupt" and "neutralize" black groups and prevent the rise of a "messiah."[24]

Committee to Free Angela Davis

Soon after the Hampton-Clark murders, the Chicago Committee to Free Angela Davis was formed. She was a well-known Communist, feminist and African American revolutionary. Ronald Reagan, then Governor of California, wanted Professor Davis fired from UCLA. That happened in June, 1970. Two months later, a judge was killed in a botched attempt to free a prisoner. Angela Davis knew nothing of the shootout. Still she was accused of murder because a gun, registered in her name, was used in the shootout.

---

[24] Paul Engleman, "Night of the Hunters," *Chicago*, November, 1994, 101.

Of course, I was among the teachers and students who joined the Committee to Free Angela. We rented space at Malcolm X College to host a fund raiser for the defense. The night of the event, the door was locked. Sylvia Woods, the Committee's chairperson, tried to kick the door open. That kick was painful to her arthritic knee. But we got in and had a good fund raiser. Woods was famous as one of the three in the film, *Union Maids*. Twenty years later, she had lost none of her kick.

The Angela Davis trial for murder in 1972 drew world-wide protests. Many believed in her innocence. They thought she was prosecuted because of her beliefs. On June 5, 1972, the jury declared Davis innocent on all counts. Soon after she won her freedom, we hosted her at Malcolm X College. She had been in jail for 16 months until an international campaign won her right to bail. The racists and anti-communists made a big mistake when they arrested Angela Davis, we thought. The victory in the Angela Davis case strengthened the movement for peace and justice. Many new supporters had joined our ranks.

My Children, Anti-War Activists

About the time of the police murders of Hampton and Clark, the anti-Vietnam War movement was surging. Just months after Hampton and Clark were murdered, four students at Kent State were killed by the National Guard at an anti-war demonstration. Then two more students were killed at Jackson State. Many more were wounded. The college campuses had erupted in anger because President Nixon had lied about Cambodia. On April 30, 1970, President Richard Nixon admitted to the nation that U.S. troops were invading Cambodia. The U.S. had already bombed Cambodia without authorization by Congress. After the killings at Kent State and Jackson State, massive protests swept the nation's campuses. Many colleges closed, cutting the semester short. Students were sent home with a grade of "P" for Passing. My sons John and Paul were among those who came home. Neither John nor Paul returned to their universities.

At MIT, John had led a demonstration of thousands against the bombing of Cambodia. A member of the university staff, seeing John distributing anti-war flyers warned him, "You better watch out or they'll send you back to India." "But I'm from Chicago," John retorted. "Then they'll send you back to Chicago, and that's worse," the staffer persisted. Although John received credit for the year at MIT, he decided to leave that university. He had changed his goal from research science to medicine. As a medical doctor, John felt he could do more to serve people and change the system.

Paul was suspended by the University of Illinois because of his anti-war work. On May 7, 1970, we received a call that Paul had just been arrested. The day before, University of Illinois students had demonstrated against the bombing of Cambodia. Michael Parenti, a visiting professor from Yale and a peace activist, was brutally beaten and severely injured by police. Another teacher may have saved Parenti's life by throwing his own body over Parenti's prone form. Both teachers were arrested and held on $10,000 bail. That bail was double the bail for a policeman charged with "manslaughter" in the death of an African American youth one week earlier.

The day after Professor Parenti was beaten, Paul was arrested during a student rally protesting the attack on the teachers. He was held on $1,500 bail and charged with "interfering with an institution of higher learning, disorderly conduct and mob action." Paul's friends paid $150 to a bail bondsman to get him out. But the judge raised Paul's bail to $7,500. That was when we got the call for help.

It was dark by the time Frank and I reached Champaign. The police officer at the desk took 15 minutes to count twelve $50 bills while we agonized. Finally he agreed that the amount was correct and let Paul out. Paul's first thought was how to raise bail for another teenager still being held. Suspended from the University of Illinois, Paul moved to the University of Colorado in Boulder. Although he was there for two years, the only lessons that stuck were on skiing. He came home an excellent skier, not a skill in high demand in Broadview, Illinois. Paul tried different jobs until he became a railroad engineer on a commuter run. While his train sat in the station, Paul returned to classes at the Chicago campus of the University of Illinois and earned his degree.

My two older children had become anti-war activists in 1964, early in the war. At that time, it took a lot of courage. Jean-leah bicycled 80 miles of dangerous highway on a cold March day to join an anti-war march. Carl, my oldest, fought the draft call because he opposed the Vietnam War. He left graduate school to teach high school and get a draft deferment. Then the draft board called him up again, this time for induction. After passing the physical, the draftees were asked to step forward to be inducted. Carl refused. Although he remained "1-A," the draft board never called him again. In that, he was luckier than many other anti-war protesters. Many had to flee to Canada to avoid fighting a war they considered criminal. The U.S. lost hundreds, if not thousands of some of the best minds in our country. Jeanleah and Carl were lucky. They completed their PhD studies, she in theoretical computer science and he in biology. I am, indeed, a proud mother.

Author, Frank, their children, Jeanleah, Paul, Carl, John, and grandson Søren.

Chapter 21

Equality for Women—CLUW
Work classified as "women's work" paid less.

I have always fought for women's rights. Perhaps that began when I was five or six years old. Or perhaps it started earlier while I was still in my mother's womb. The year I was born, women still did not have the right to vote. They won it the next year. Clearly, there was a strong women's movement at that time. My mother would have been one of the supporters of women's right to vote. She was one of the first to cut her hair short and wear shorter than floor length dresses early in the twentieth century. Neither my mother nor my father ever told me that I could not do whatever I wanted to do "because I was a girl."

When I was about six, I was in a fist fight with a boy. It must have made a big impact on me. I never forgot that fight, even if I soon forgot what it was about. I closed my eyes and swung wildly. The grownups cheered us on. Unfortunately, nobody stopped the fight. "Jack Dempsey," some of the bystanders called me. "She's punching like a boy," others said. I took those remarks as praise.

Since I had my eyes closed, I never knew the exact outcome of that fight. But I did not see the little boy again. For some reason, I thought I had really hurt him, and that was why he was not around. So I decided then to never again get physical in a fight. But it left me with the idea that I was very strong, in no way inferior to any boy in strength. I spent a good part of my childhood trying to prove just that.

It wasn't easy. Sometimes the boys would not let me play their games. That just made me more determined. There wasn't a big choice of games in our neighborhood because space was so limited. We played stickball in the streets, dodging the cars. For those who have not had the pleasure, stickball is like baseball with a few exceptions. Instead of a bat you use a stout stick. Instead of a baseball you use whatever, usually a bouncy ball the size of a tennis ball. As for the bases, you improvised, depending on the width of the street. Instead of regular innings, you suspended the game when a car passed.

When we could use the cement yards behind the tenement buildings, we played handball and held relay races. I loved it all, especially handball. We didn't use the hardballs and gloves like the real players did. All our game required was just any bouncy ball and a blank wall, often labeled, "No handball playing here." In fact those signs helped us locate suitable walls for our game. In my pre-puberty days, I wore shorts in warm weather and kept my hair short. Sometimes people would call me a boy, and for some weird reason I was glad. Perhaps I did not want to hear, "You can't do that because you are a girl."

Blame the System

At the time, I was reading books way beyond my age. I read about prostitution and felt outraged that a woman would have to sell her body, even though it was not very clear to me what that meant. I liked to walk for miles, from neighborhood to neighborhood. When I saw a man pick up a prostitute, I felt bad because I could do nothing to help her. My strong feelings did not make me hate men. What I hated was that prostitutes did not have other options. With the Depression going on, that may have been true. At least, that's how I understood it. Also, I felt bad that my mother had to work in the family's hand laundry all day, standing on her swollen legs. But I did not blame that on my father. I blamed the capitalist system. Still, there were plenty of other things I did not understand.

From my reading and listening to adults around me, I had absorbed a lot of feminism by the time I was fourteen. I do not remember any arguments between my parents as I was growing up. Whatever their differences, they were probably not so big. We kids would probably have heard something in that small four-room apartment. This changed when my father had a major stroke. He became very hard to get along with. My mother took the brunt of his illness-induced bad temper. Of course, I sided with my mother. I thought she should not have to put up with verbal abuse. "Leave him," I brashly suggested. Mama's eyes filled with tears. "He wasn't like this before he got sick," she told me. That shut me up, and I felt a little ashamed. I felt more than a little ashamed as I grew up and learned more about strokes. I now know that bad temper is a common symptom after a stroke. Looking back, I think my mother realized that I was not that unfeeling for my father. She knew that I spoke out of a combination of ignorance, stupid smartness and love for her.

As I grew up, there were women and men who rejected the old concept of marriage. They rejected the idea that it was the wife's job to stay home to cook and clean and care for children, if any, while the man worked to support his family. They also rejected the idea that a woman should marry to get a good "meal ticket." They wanted to completely separate sex, and especially love, from any money arrangement. That was the rationale behind the "free love" movement of couples who lived together without getting married. I was a little too young to be interested in that movement. My interest in women's rights was more in equal opportunity for sports, education and choice of work.

When I joined the YCL, I was in an organization that championed women's equality. The huge advances of women in the Soviet Union encouraged us. When the women's liberation movement took off in the late '60s, I was more interested in "equal pay for equal work" than freedom from bras. Actually, I did not want to burn my bra because I am heavy-breasted and need a bra for comfort. Anyway, I later learned that bra-burning was a phony issue that the media had used to attack the feminist movement.

I was never confused about the source of sexism. The corporations that profit from inequality keep sexism going. An example of that was the two months of silent treatment that my male coworkers put me through at Allied Radio. As I wrote in an earlier chapter, it was hard to bear. But I knew that the men were afraid that the company had hired me, a woman, to lower the wage scale. The real problem was that companies paid women less for the same work. Also, work classified as "women's work" paid less, no matter how much skill or training the job required.

Coalition of Labor Union Women

I was one of many working women who sympathized with the women's liberation movement. From our work in our unions, we understood the profit motive that was behind paying women less. By winning equal pay, equal opportunity and respect for women workers, we could strengthen all labor, men included.

In 1973, seven women activists from seven different unions put out the idea of a union women's coalition. The seven included my good Chicago friends: Addie Wyatt, a packinghouse workers' leader; Clara Day, a teamsters' union leader; and Florence Criley, an electrical workers' leader. Soon they were joined by Barbara Merrill, a welfare worker and a founder of Black Labor Leaders of Chicago. Their work culminated in a national convention to form a "Coalition of Labor Union Women" (CLUW). The convention opened in Chicago on March 22, 1974.

Eight hundred women were expected but 3,200 came. Many were young; some like me, not so young. Almost all had come at their own expense. Some thought it was a near miracle that so many women participated. It was no miracle. The mass sentiment was there. Union women were fired up and "not taking it anymore." The ground work had been laid in well-attended regional conferences. I got into the action earlier in 1973, at the Midwest Regional Conference of Union Women. It was attended by 200 women from 20 different national unions and from 18 states. We wanted to fight for women's rights through an organization of our own. Men were invited to join too, to help fight for women's rights. My husband, Frank, was one of the first men to join CLUW.

The 1974 founding convention was tumultuous, at times almost out of control. The important outcome, to my way of thinking, is that we came out with an organization, the Coalition of Labor Union Women. That almost did not happen because a small but noisy group came with the idea of taking control of the new coalition. Of course, any one group "taking over" kills a coalition. A major difference between Teamsters and United Farm Workers also threatened to split the conference. That, too, was overcome. In her famous unifying, and stirring conclusion to the conference, Addie Wyatt brought it all together. She called for us to stand and join hands. It was very emotional. Then Wyatt led us in singing "Solidarity Forever" in a way that was seldom heard before. It became the trademark of CLUW conventions, a stirring finale.

Union women have gained a lot since that 1974 conference. We have moved forward on all of the four key goals that CLUW adopted: organize the unorganized, promote affirmative action, increase women's participation in their unions, and increase women's participation in political and legislative activities. In Chicago, in 2007, we added six women to the city council, including some active unionists. But some of that 1974 groundswell of enthusiasm and thirst for action has been lost. In the plague of factory layoffs, many of the younger women lost their jobs. When their employment ended, many lost their union membership. The labor movement lost these women activists. I thought that was a mistake, letting our unemployed members go. Fortunately, CLUW now has associate memberships so anyone can be a member.

Over the years, the CLUW membership has grayed, with few younger people joining. By the 2007 CLUW convention, I saw a change set in. A few of us old-timers were still there, including Joyce Miller, CLUW's second national president. But most of the old timers were gone, and a lot of new and younger women were coming forward. During the 2008 presidential election, a woman and an African American were the top two candidates for the Democratic nomination. We have grounds for optimism.

*Chicago CLUW members supporting plastic workers.
Author at right*

Women and Children

I strongly agree with women of all classes who protest the idea that women are just child-bearing machines (or sex objects). We have value as people, independent of our children and whether or not we have children. For women to live independent lives, we need to control when to have children. To me, it is obvious that reproductive rights, including birth control and abortion, are fundamental to women's rights. But it is too often forgotten that women's reproductive rights are also essential to the welfare of children.

Women who are worn out with too many or too closely spaced childbirths, or overwhelmed with a poorly timed pregnancy, cannot give their children the best care. The falsely named "right to lifers" oppose children's rights, just as they oppose women's rights. Proof of that is that the nation's chief anti-abortionist, George W. Bush, vetoed increased funding for SCHIP in 2008. SCHIP is the act that provides health care for children. As soon as President Obama took office, he signed the act extending SCHIP to an additional eight million children.

I think there is a close connection between children's and women's issues. The connection is societal, not biological. I think our social structures are decisive in creating the close bond between mother and child. This bond is strong cement, whether the child is adopted or a biological child. The social bond is in addition to the marvelous experience of giving birth to a live child. Before there was formula, there was also a year of breast feeding. Test-tube rearing of a fetus is still only science fiction.

Still, I can see the future of child rearing as a much more social activity. Both parents will truly share child rearing equally. Going further, I can see child rearing shared by a larger group beyond the biological parents. I can see each child as part of a larger family circle, beyond "blood" relatives. I hope that does happen because all adults should have the right to be involved with children. Also all children have the right to a large circle of adult support. But as things stand today, it is the mother, or grandmother, who has to give most of the preschool care. Unless the social system supports child care, either by paid leave or good early education, women cannot be fully equal and children suffer.

Dragon Dance for Affordable Child Care

In the years after CLUW was formed, children's advocates were pushing for more federal funding to create more affordable, quality child care. A pretty good child care law was passed by Congress in 1971, but President Richard Nixon vetoed it. In 1979, Senator Cranston introduced another child care bill. But he soon withdrew it, citing lack of support in Congress.

That made me mad. We should never give up just because Congress did not want to fund child care. All that meant was that we had to elect a better Congress. I was then the legislative director of the Chicago Chapter of CLUW. We drew up a short petition and planned to take it to the people. It asked Congress to pass a bill for federally-funded child care that was high quality and affordable. The response to the petition was enthusiastic. In Chicago, people lined up and waited for their turn to sign our child care petition.

Chicago CLUW took our petition campaign wherever people gathered. Support was almost universal. We made our weekly petitioning into a social event. First, we went downtown for an hour of petitioning. Then we'd meet for lunch and feel very good about what we were doing. In a few weeks we had gathered 5,000 signatures. It was just in time for the national convention of CLUW. With the permission of the national officers, we planned a dramatic presentation. We stapled copies of the petition end to end, making a long paper chain. As the convention opened, Chicago delegates marched in, holding the petition chain above our heads. It was something like a Chinese dragon dance.

Our dramatic entrance was a sensation. National CLUW went on record to introduce a new child care bill in Congress. Armed with the petitions, we visited Congresswoman Cardiss Collins. She set up a task force, including CLUW, to help her write a good bill. We kept the movement alive through the Reagan years and finally got a bill passed and signed in 1990. Even though the bill was watered down in its final form, it was the first time since World War II that the federal government accepted any responsibility for child care.

In a way, our child care fight reflected changes that would, in time, move the AFL-CIO to the left, closer to the people. In 1973, the AFL-CIO was stuck in the mud, not moving on workers' needs. Everything was done from the top down. Then union members began to find their voice through new coalitions such as the Coalition of Black Trade Unionists (CBTU), the Labor Council for Latin American Advancement (LCLAA), and the National Coordinating Committee for Trade Union Action and Democracy (TUAD). Our good friends at TUAD—Fred Gaboury, Rayfield Mooty, Debbie Albano and Adelaide Bean, along with *Labor Today* editors Jim Williams and Scott Marshall, helped bring these coalitions together. These labor coalitions, like CLUW, reflected the rising of rank and file union members. Without a push from the grass roots, too many unions would have sat out those years and waited for better times.

Growing pressure by union locals finally pushed the AFL-CIO leadership into action. In 1981, the AFL-CIO organized a huge Solidarity Day March to Washington. This was labor's response to Reagan's mass firing of the striking air traffic controllers. Estimates ranged from 500,000 to 750,000 marchers, the biggest labor action in years. The central demand was for jobs. Frank and I were there with the Wisconsin Steel Save Our Jobs Committee. We rode in the Danly Tool steel workers union bus with Joe Romano of the United Steelworkers. In Washington we met some of the Buffalo Lumpkins who had joined the march. Frank's brother Wade was there and his niece Robin.

CLUW'S American Family Celebration

In 1988, CLUW took back the high moral ground of family values by calling for an "American Family Celebration," on the Mall in Washington, DC. This celebration called for true family values: family and medical leave, quality child care, services for the elderly, comprehensive health care, equity and quality education, and economic justice.

Over 50,000 women, men and children came to the festive event. Tents with clowns, huge trampolines, games and music for the children gave the event a near-carnival atmosphere. But our purpose was dead serious. Reagan and the Republican ultra-Right had been using the cover of "family values" to roll back the rights of labor, women, children and people of color. By uniting the labor movement with the women's movement, CLUW advanced the true family values and exposed the Reagan hypocrites.

Since its founding in 1974, CLUW has succeeded in promoting more women to union leadership. In 2007, the AFL-CIO changed its convention rules to guarantee that more women and people of color are elected as convention delegates. However, plant closings and vast unemployment are eroding union membership and CLUW membership.

There has been a lot of discussion about loss of membership in organizations that depend on volunteers. Some people came up with theories and wrote books about a "change in culture." They observed that people don't go out as much as they used to. Television viewing, video games, long hours of work and unwillingness to volunteer were among the factors blamed. This was even before huge increases in the price of gas made every car trip a raid on the family budget. I will admit that I never bought these theories. But I had nothing with which to disprove them. That was before the 2008 presidential primary. Then more volunteers came forward than ever before.

Peggy Lipschutz, Labor Today

A Woman for President!

I was immediately attracted to Barack Obama in the 2008 presidential primary. We knew Obama as our Illinois state senator with a progressive record. For me, even more exciting than Obama himself, was the vast network of volunteers who came forward to elect him. I decided to visit the Obama volunteer center in Chicago to see how I could help. I was thrilled to see hundreds of volunteers, almost all in their teens or 20s. Some were at desks but most were sprawled on the floor in comfortable teenage positions. They were calling voters, talking into all kinds of phones and cell phones. When I left, the only other volunteer over 30 was leaving too. He was 58, and I was a few months short of 90. It felt so good to see a multitude of our successors.

I heard Obama speak out against invading Iraq before the war started. It was a nasty cold, windy day. In spite of the weather, Frank and I joined the march organized by the Hyde Park Peace Council. We still hoped to avoid the catastrophe of a U.S. invasion of Iraq. Our spirits were lifted when a state senator mounted the makeshift podium we had set up in the little park. That state senator was Barack Obama. After the disastrous war started, the most important issue for working families became, "End the war in Iraq." So when Obama entered the presidential primary, it was an easy choice: Obama for president!

But didn't I want a woman for president? Of course I did. For me, however, the issue never was choosing between electing the first woman president or the first African American president. I looked at two key issues. First was ending the Iraq war and changing the whole Bush foreign policy. The second was winning back labor's right to organize. I believe women's rights can best advance when labor's rights advance. As revealed in an AFL-CIO study, union women earned 32% more than non-union women. I thought that Obama had a better record on these key issues, so I was happy that he won the nomination. I was one of hundreds of thousands who gave their all to elect Obama. I did not know that I could still work that hard.

For both Clinton and Obama, the movements that gathered around them were even more important than the candidates. Many women became politically active for the first time because they wanted to see a woman in the White House. I will admit that I was surprised by a few personal friends who rushed to support Clinton over Obama because they so wanted a woman to win. After Obama won the nomination, my pro-Clinton friends lined up to help elect Obama. We were on the same wavelength again.

When I looked up "gender inequality" on the Internet, I found that women were not doing that well in the U.S. An international study reported, "U.S. slips in gender equality survey. One of the biggest surprises this year was the United States dropping from 23rd place in 2006 to 31st place in 2007's rankings. The U.S. now ranks behind South Africa, Cuba, Colombia, Bulgaria, Moldova, Lesotho and Namibia, and just one spot ahead of Kazakhstan."[25] To me it was not surprising that gender equality suffered under George W. Bush.

Katie Jordan, president of Chicago CLUW, and author,
1996 Democratic National Convention, Chicago

---

[25] *International Herald Tribune*, November 9, 2007.

Chapter 22

Teaching Truth
I could not teach what I did not know.

The 1960s student movement for African American studies helped inspire other student movements. There were demands for Latino studies, multicultural education, women's studies and more. All progressive movements of the time were demanding an end to the war in Vietnam. These student movements opened the door to rethinking the way world history was taught. Martin Bernal, author of *Black Athena,* has shown that the world history we teach in North America and Europe was revised about 300 years ago. It was rewritten to justify slavery and imperialism. In the revision, contributions to civilization by people of color were erased from the history books. Europe was credited as the primary source and center of the sciences and the arts. This exclusion of non-European history has been labeled "Eurocentrism," the false claim that all civilization began in Europe.

Back in 1939, when I got a BA in history from Hunter College, I had not learned about any of this. But by 1967, at Malcolm X College, I started to search for the true history of Africa. I read *The World and Africa* by W.E.B. Du Bois, one of the most famous members of the Communist Party USA. He fought all of his life for recognition of African and African American history.

My husband and I also worked with Ishmael Flory, chairperson of the Illinois Communist Party. In 1960, Flory organized the African American Heritage Association. They won official recognition for Jean Baptiste Pointe DuSable as the founder of Chicago. DuSable was the Haitian trader who settled in what is now Chicago in 1780. My association with Ishmael Flory and Margaret Burroughs alerted me to the need for African American studies.

Black Mathematics?

At Malcolm X College, the movement to include African American history was gaining momentum in 1968. I listened to student demands and tried to respond. Every teacher felt the pressure. I wanted to bring African and African American contributions to mathematics into my classrooms. But I could not teach what I did not know. I was looking for the sources of our school mathematics. In 1968, students at Crane/Malcolm X College pointed me in the direction of ancient Egypt. As part of their heritage, they featured ancient Egyptian themes in their murals. So I decided to learn about Egyptian mathematics.

I went through a stack of standard histories, reading about "Egyptian mathematics." What I learned surprised and delighted me. Ancient Egyptians had written mathematics textbooks as far back as 3,850 years ago! Unfortunately, many standard histories undervalue the Egyptian contribution. The most outrageous was a book by Otto Neugebauer, a prominent historian of mathematics. His evaluation of Egyptian mathematics was downright insulting. He wrote, "The role of Egyptian mathematics is probably best described as a retarding force on numerical procedures."[26]

Another widely read historian included the Babylonians in his put-down of the African and Asian pioneers of mathematics. Morris Kline wrote that compared with the Greeks, "The mathematics of the Egyptians and Babylonians is the scrawling of children just learning how to write, as opposed to great literature."[27] In all fairness, I should add that a few historians gave a more accurate assessment. I am especially indebted to Carl Boyer for his *History of Mathematics*, a very honest and useful text.

---

[26] O. Neugebauer, *The Exact Sciences in Antiquity* (New York: Dover, 1969), 80.

[27] Morris Kline, *Mathematics, a cultural approach* (Reading, MA: Addison Wesley, 1962), 14.

My next step was to read the mathematical papyri for myself (in translation of course). Their examples covered much of the school mathematics we teach today. That made me want to learn more about the people of ancient Egypt and why they needed all that mathematics.

Egyptian Literature

Luckily, I live just ten minutes away from the University of Chicago's Oriental Institute and their great library. Soon I was dishing out some of my hard-earned money for classes at the institute. When I started reading ancient Egyptian literature I really became "hooked." Much of it sounded as though it were written today, not 4,000 years ago. The relatively higher status of women in ancient Egypt attracted me. Egyptian women had the right to do business in the market place, to give witness in court, inherit property and even become pharaoh (king). Women in many parts of Africa enjoyed these rights, but they were rare in the Asian civilizations of the time.

Unfortunately, women enjoyed few rights in classical Greece. After Egypt came under Greek rule, the subservient position of Greek women clashed with Egyptian practice. Two different sets of laws about women's rights came into use. Egyptian women continued to enjoy many freedoms. In contrast, Greek women in Egypt had to live under restrictive Greek laws. For example, Greek women needed a male chaperon whenever they went out in public and women did not have property rights.

The moral values of ancient Egypt also sounded very modern, as did their human weaknesses. For example, in the 5,400-year-old tomb of a man named Sheshi, he made the case for favorable judgment on his after-life. He claimed to have been fair and considerate, to have spoken and repeated fairly and to have protected the weak from the powerful. He also claimed that he gave bread to the hungry and clothes to the naked.[28]

---

28 Miriam Lichtheim, *Ancient Egyptian Literature.* Vol. I (Berkeley: University of California, 1975), 17.

Pharaoh Hatshepsut by Margaret Burroughs

From the same period, a tomb inscription for Governor Harkhuf of Upper Egypt listed similar virtues. Harkhuf claimed he never gave a bad report of a man to his superiors nor deprive a son of his inheritance.[29]

Other writings also have a modern ring. Don't hang out at beer halls, they said. If you do, in effect, you will look like a beer barrel. Don't mess with other men's wives. "Become a scribe," they advised. It was the best trade or profession.

---

[29] *Ibid.*, 24.

Scribes were the people of learning and included clerks, letter writers, traders and kings.

For thousands of years, these moral values were respected in ancient Egypt. However, Egypt was a class society. As in our times, the powerful few often violated the moral laws. Tomb writings from the New Kingdom period, 3,500 years ago, detail some of the evil acts that were making the rich richer and the poor poorer. But evil men could not get into the Egyptian heaven. So the tomb owner declared his innocence before the god Anubis who judged such things. Here are a few samples:

> I have not robbed the poor,
> I have not killed,
> I have not ordered to kill.
> I have not added to the weight of the balance,
> I have not falsified the plummet of the scales.
> I have not taken milk from the mouth of children,
> I am pure, I am pure, I am pure, I am pure![30]

Also from the New Kingdom come perhaps the first love songs written and some of the most exquisite. These are sample verses:

> The wild goose soars and swoops,
> It alights on the net,
> Many birds swarm about,
> I have work to do.
> I am held fast by my love,
> Alone, my heart meets your heart,
> From your beauty I'll not part.[31]

> My body thrives, my heart exults
> At our walking together;
> Hearing your voice is pomegranate wine,

---

[30] Miriam Lichtheim, *Ancient Egyptian Literature.* Vol. II (Berkeley: University of California, 1976), 125.

[31] *Ibid.*, 190.

I live by hearing it.
Each look with which you look at me
Sustains me more than food and drink.[32]

This rich literature was new to me. It gave me more of a
feel for the people who developed so much of our school
mathematics.

Egyptian Numerals

Every time we use our modern numerals, we can thank the
ancient Egyptians and Babylonians. To record numbers, Egyptians used base ten numerals, the world's first decimal system.
They were the first to use ciphers, symbols to record numbers. For ten, they wrote ∩, instead of making ten tally marks,
1111111111. Place, or positional value, is the other great idea
needed for modern numerals. For example, the 3 in 309 has
the value of 300, or 3 times 100. Place value was first used by
Babylonians and a little later, by the Maya.

We must also thank the great Indian and Islamic mathematicians who came before us. Part of the great Indian heritage
was the use of a zero. For 309, Babylonians just left a space, as
in 3 9, but the Indians used a zero, as in 3 0 9.

Numerals are just the beginning of what we got from
ancient Africans and Asians. The classical Greek writers freely
admitted that they got their geometry from Egypt. Back in 1800
BCE, Egyptian geometry books taught formulas for areas of a
rectangle, triangle, equilateral trapezoids, and the volumes of
common shapes. They had also discovered the properties of
similar triangles and had a good approximation for pi.

Egyptian Zero

With the help of Frank Yurco, an Egyptologist friend, I found
evidence for an Egyptian zero. The authorities had claimed
that the ancient Egyptians never developed the concept of
zero .

---

[32] *Ibid.*, 192.

It is true that zero placeholders are not needed in the Egyptian numeral system. They wrote a number such as 2004 as we would write it on a check. They used 2 thousand symbols and 4 tally marks. But Egyptians did have a symbol to show a zero balance in bookkeeping. For example, if 52 loaves of bread came into the storehouse and 52 loaves were given out, zero was left. (52 − 52 = zero). The symbol they used was *nfr*, the word for beauty or "to be complete."

Zero (nfr) was used on construction guidelines to label ground level. These lines were painted on the monuments and are still visible at the Meidum pyramid, built 4000 years ago. Lines above ground were labeled 1 cubit above zero, 2 cubits above zero, and so on. Lines below ground were labeled with the number of cubits below zero. This was a very early use of signed numbers.

I had the proof that ancient Egyptians did have a zero symbol. The books that denied it were wrong. What should I do? Fight for the truth, of course. After many years of fighting, I was about to give up. Fortunately, my good friend Claudia Zaslavsky did not let me give up. She referred me to a respected journal with a progressive editor. They published my article with the evidence for the Egyptian zero.

After the article appeared, the earth did not shake. Nor did the walls cave in. In fact, I heard not one word from the "*Not Out of Africa* crowd." *Not Out of Africa* was a book of articles putting down efforts to restore African achievements to their proper place in history. Probably the *Not Out of Africa* agents never read my article. Somebody did read it though, because two other journals contacted me. They asked for more articles about the Egyptian zero.

Indeed, the story of abstract thinking goes back to much earlier times in African history. Africans were working an underground flint mine in the Sudan, 35,000 years ago. Sophisticated tools were made 90,000 years ago. People were drawing designs 77,000 BCE in South Africa and in North Africa (Morocco). Recent finds (2008) in Blombos Cave, South Africa, push the age of art back to 100,000 years ago. This evidence shows that abstract thinking began in Africa, with the beginning of Homo sapiens. By the time our species began to move out of Africa, they probably took an advanced tool kit with them. So all the textbooks that credit Europe as the birthplace of modern thinking will have to be revised!

A New Way of Teaching Mathematics

As I learned, I tried the new African material in my classes at Malcolm X College. It went over big. African American students were proud of the part that Africans had played in the origins of mathematics. Other students enjoyed it too. An unpublished study done by my colleague, Pat Flagg Poole, compared the responses of third grade students from different communities to African cultural materials for mathematics. Students from a 99% white rural school enjoyed the materials just as much as students from a 99% African American school in an impoverished suburb of Chicago. For some students, it changed the way they looked at mathematics. They began to see it as a human subject with a fascinating history that started in Africa and went back thousands of years ago. Humanizing the subject cut down on the fear that some students had about mathematics.

As I taught, I learned. I began to realize that racism had even affected mathematics textbooks. How could a textbook on math or science be racist or non-racist? To answer that question, just flip through any mathematics textbook. How many theorems will you find that are named after non-Europeans? Is that because all the theorems were first worked out by Europeans? It would seem so from our textbooks. But that's not the way it was.

For example, a fundamental theorem of geometry is named for Pythagoras, a Greek mathematician. But Pythagoras was far from the first person to relate the sides of a right triangle as $c^2 = a^2 + b^2$. Twelve hundred years before Pythagoras was born, Babylonians were using the theorem in Iraq. The theorem was known in India and proved in China hundreds of years before Pythagoras. Still, most students around the world, outside of China, think that this theorem was discovered by Europeans. Calling it the "Pythagorean Theorem" is just one example of attaching a European name to discoveries made by non-Europeans. There are more.

Any textbook that credits Europeans as the sole founders of mathematics is simply not teaching the truth.

I got more good material to bring to my classes from the mathematics of the Native Americans. I had seen the magnificent pyramids of Mexico. Where there were pyramids, there was mathematics. It did not stop there. I read about Chinese, Indian, Central Asian and North African mathematicians who brought algebra to higher levels. When I leaned about the navigation maps of Pacific Islanders and the astronomy of the Incas, I realized that all peoples had created mathematics.

Much of the traveling I have done in my lifetime re-enforced this conclusion. In Mexico, I saw the old Maya and Aztec cities, with layouts planned by their astronomers. In Bolivia, I saw 4,000 year old pyramids, aligned to line up with chosen stars. When I visited South Africa in 1996, I was near the cave where the oldest known numerical record was found, going back 37,000 years BCE.

This was information I had to share. So I decided to write.

Margaret Burroughs and Peggy Lipschutz

Author, Peggy Lipschutz, Margaret Burroughs on author's 90th birthday

I consulted my friend Margaret Burroughs, founder of the DuSable Museum of African American History. "Write something for the children," she told me. And that's how my first book was born, with more than a little help from Margaret. *Senefer, Young Genius in Old Egypt* brought the glad tidings of Egyptian mathematics to thousands of children around the world. Then I called on another friend, to help me reach the teachers. Reaching the teachers was key to reaching the children.

Peggy Lipschutz was another talented artist friend who sympathized with what I was trying to do. She had perfected a little known art form, the chalk talk. She used it to create powerful visuals that brought the message of truth and struggle to a huge audience. They say that every teacher puts on a performance to get her/his class interested in a lesson. Peggy and I certainly hammed it up with our chalk talk presentations.

Our topics included the "African Roots of Mathematics," the "Multicultural Roots of Mathematics" and sometimes we included the "Roots of Science." As I read a script, or just talked, Peggy drew a huge picture that told the story in vivid color. She used half-inch thick chalk on a three-by-four-foot board, large enough to engage an auditorium full of children or adults. Her wonderful sense of humor delighted the audience and helped me "lighten up."

In Chicago, African American mathematics teachers have been solidly supportive. Many opportunities were opened for me by Dr. Dorothy Strong, then director of the Mathematics Bureau of the Chicago Public Schools. Pat Poole, of the Illinois State Board of Education, opened many doors for me. With so much encouragement, I learned more and more. For forty years, I have continued to study, teach and write about contributions of people of color to mathematics and science. It's been a lot of fun, taking me to conferences around the United States, the Dominican Republic, India, China, Mozambique, Republic of South Africa, Guatemala and Spain. I met wonderful friends like Claudia Zaslavsky, Mariana Ferreira, Paulus Gerdes, Ubiratan D'Ambrosio, George Gheverghese Joseph, Arthur Powell, and Marilyn Frankenstein. .

Sadly, the public school opening to multicultural education proved short lived. From a promising beginning in the '70s and early '80s, there's been a big setback. Textbook publishers have backed away from multicultural content. They have responded to pressure from the Reagan-Bush ultra-Rightists against multiculturalism. Publishing is largely controlled by monopolies that do not want to offend the political right-wing gang.

What will it take for the truth to come out? Some will say that the issue is political. Of course it is. The idea that mathematics and science began *outside* of Europe knocks down one of the pillars of racism. I am convinced that truth will out, and help us change what we teach. At this writing, however, multiculturalism has been pushed to the back of the bus under the reactionary policies of Reagan and Bush. I think it will take a big resurgence of the civil rights and progressive movements to win a non-racist curriculum in our schools.

Peggy Lipschutz and author meeting with women of the ANC, Johannesburg, 1996

Meanwhile, I had to make a personal decision. I had retired from the classroom in 1990 for the second and last time. I could continue to work on multicultural education although no one would pay me for my services. But I would no longer have classes where students could benefit from and test multicultural materials. Or I could spend my remaining time directly in the political struggle. And as my husband Frank always said, "The system does not work. We must change it." I decided to put my time into changing the system. Younger people will pick up the multicultural research where we left off. They will restore our history so teachers can teach the truth.

Chapter 23

STRIKE!

There were many heroes among our Malcolm X faculty.

The Little Strike

With few exceptions, the Malcolm X teachers were union members. In the fall of 1969, the college opened with a mostly new faculty. Many came from jobs in the high schools where they had been members of Local 1, AFT. They quickly joined Local 1600, the Cook County College Teachers Union. College doors had barely opened when we were faced with a possible strike. I call it "The Little Strike" because it lasted only two days, and the issue was not a union contract or union recognition. In a way it was a rehearsal for a much bigger struggle that would face us in the next year.

The board of the Chicago City Colleges was getting ready to try to break the union. They began by removing two union leaders from their campuses and sending them to other campuses. No reason was given. The removal of union leaders, if left unchallenged, could weaken the union, frighten potential activists, and make it easy to deny a contract when that time came.

For the two days of the strike, no classes were taught at any of the seven city college campuses. After two days, the issue was sent to arbitration. Teachers returned to work, and classes resumed. The union won the arbitrations, and the transferred teachers were back at their campuses a few weeks later. But at Malcolm X, Dr. Hurst created a different dynamic. He was not yet ready to come out openly against the union. Still, he tried to keep the "We're all in this together," mystique.

318 JOY IN THE STRUGGLE

At our campus, he put it as Malcolm X College and the black community against everybody else. "Picket, if you must," he told the teachers. "But then let's come together as a community and make our plans." That was the gist of it, perhaps not word for word. After we came in for the meeting, Hurst asked one teacher to call together the African American teachers for a black caucus meeting. He asked me to call the white teachers together. I am embarrassed to admit that I fell into Dr. Hurst's trap although I knew better. I did it although I thought (and still think) that organizing as white teachers was wrong. But Charles Hurst was that persuasive.

Progressives have long recognized the value of black caucuses, Latino caucuses, or women's caucuses as a means of strengthening the fight for equality. That does not apply to a white caucus, in my opinion. Such a caucus, that excludes people of color, could have only a racist purpose. It is also misleading, I think, to speak of "the white community." White communities differ by class makeup and may have opposing interests. It all depends on whether they are working class, middle or capitalist class communities. And aren't they all-white because people of color are excluded? Besides the word "community" is being perverted. "They" now talk of the "intelligence community" and "the banking community." Are we now supposed to fall into the trap of honoring cutthroat bankers as "community organizers?"

In two days, the short strike was over and almost forgotten in the rush of events following the assassination of Fred Hampton and Mark Clark. Our student council leaders were busy on still another front, fighting the imposition of tuition. On their way to a student leadership meeting in Rockford, Illinois, the students made a wrong turn. Instead of going west, they went south. Not until they reached Pontiac, Illinois, did they realize their error. It was 2 a.m., so they pulled off the highway and fell asleep in the car. At 4 a.m. they awoke to police flashlights shining in their faces and the sounds of police dogs barking. They were arrested and charged with something. So we all put money in to bail them out and started a campaign to free them. The fight against racism was heating up.

Meanwhile the new building for the college was under construction. We had great hopes for the future. An excellent, mostly progressive, mostly young faculty worked very closely with student and community activists and with each other. I was one of the few "elders," already in my 50's. Few of us went home right after our classes. We hung around and exchanged ideas and plain communed with each other. We were African American, African, from the Indian subcontinent, Jewish of European descent, Southern white, Anglo, Chinese, Japanese, Filipina, Israeli. We lacked Latino faculty although perhaps 7% of the student body was Latino. On January 3, 1971, we were put to a test by fire and were not found wanting.

The Big Strike

In the last months of 1970, the CCC board refused to renew or extend the CCCTU contract. They wanted to gut our grievance procedure and increase the work load 25% with no increase in pay. The Board knew full well that they were forcing the union to strike. Chancellor Oscar Shabat had hired a union-busting law firm and got ready to try to break the union.

As Shabat expected, Local 1600 AFT voted to strike. On January 3, 1971, 95% of the faculty of the city colleges did not report for work. The teachers did not expect an easy victory. They had to defy a court injunction to get their first contract. And a 30-day jail sentence still hung over the head of the union president, Norman Swenson. It was a sentence he would have to serve later that year. Still, Local 1600 members were determined not to give up their hard-won gains.

I have walked many picket lines supporting other workers on strike. That was entirely different from being on strike myself. It is hard to describe the serious excitement that I felt on our first day on strike. There is no strike pay in the teachers union. But my anxiety was more than just loss of income during the strike. We worried that the colleges could be closed permanently. There is no law requiring attendance at community colleges as there is for elementary and high schools.

When you know your employer is determined to break the union, you need a plan to win. Our union chapter at Malcolm

X tried to prepare. I sought the advice of Jack Birch, a May-wood friend who was a long-time organizer for the United Electrical Union (UE). First, he said, make sure that you have an up-to-date address and phone list for all of your members. Strikers who do not show up to picket must be contacted right away. They may be working other jobs, true, but they may also be wavering. If the union does not contact them, they may show up a few days later as a scab. Birch also advised us to line up community support, including support from other unions. Solid advice. I pass it on for posterity.

Community Support

We had good grounds to ask for community support. In striking, we were also fighting for the students. Good working conditions for teachers mean good learning conditions for students. On this issue, however, we ran into conflict with the "business unionism" of our local officers, headed by Norman Swenson. They had already broken ties with the students by failing to fight tuition for the CCC. The conflict deepened when we offered Malcolm X students a "freedom school" as the strike dragged on.

Our freedom school was held in the Malcolm X strike head-quarters and helped build support for the strike. Some Local 1600 officers did not see it that way. A union "freedom school" was like scabbing, they claimed. The Swenson group claimed that we were no different from a plumbers' union. Plumbers would not provide services during a strike, they argued. For-tunately, most city college teachers supported community out-reach. In the next union election they elected the Malcolm X union leader, John Yeatman, as vice president of Local 1600. We could not win the local-wide election for president, how-ever, because the suburban chapters outvoted us. Suburban members were not aware of our issues.

Contracts should never expire December 31st. That might be all right for the Southern Hemisphere but not for the Northern Hemisphere, at least not for the Great Plains area. January 1971 brought record breaking cold to Chicago. For two weeks, it was below zero degrees Fahrenheit every day. When it went up to 20 above, we opened our coats. Normally, weather does not bother me, hot or cold. But never before did I try to stay out in subzero temperatures for a four hour picketing shift. I was surprised that we could do it. Of course, you learn to dress. Long underwear, for sure, two pairs of socks, heavy shoes, warm coat, fur-lined mittens and over the head and shoulders, a large wool scarf.

There were many heroes among our Malcolm X faculty. Weather-wise and other ways, Rhoda Olenick stands out in my memory. From my home in Broadview, Rhoda's home in Oak Park was on my way to Malcolm X.. Every morning at 7 a.m., I would pick up Rhoda for strike duty and she was ready. Rhoda was one of those people who cannot stand the cold. But she came anyway. And she came prepared. A really big battery was strapped to her waist and wires ran under her coat to small electric heaters in her mittens and in her shoes. We laughed, but it worked. Rhoda never missed a day of picket duty.

The strike went well at six of the seven city college campuses. Faculty support was solid, and there was no attempt to hold classes with scab teachers. But it was a different story at Malcolm X. Hurst decided to make a name for himself as the man who broke the teachers' strike. Only a few students were in the school, those on work-study jobs. Hurst staged a fraud, bringing these few students together in one classroom. Then he brought in the media to showcase his claim that classes were being taught at Malcolm X despite the strike. The media were glad to oblige. Every network carried the lie that the strike had failed at Malcolm X. Hurst added fuel to the fire by claiming, "All of the white teachers are outside, striking, and all of the black teachers are inside, teaching their students," and adding, "The strikers do not care about the education of black students."

John Yeatman

Hurst's claims about failure of our strike were exposed by John Yeatman, chairperson of the union chapter at Malcolm X. He was a biology teacher with the heart of a lion, the patience of an angel, and the class consciousness that comes from a long history of struggle. Other than that, he was a very quiet man. John Yeatman, with the support of other African American union activists, kept our strike ranks solid. They included Cathern Davis Flory, Harvey Echols, Judge Watkins, Andrietta (Chi-Chi) Ward, Jewell McLaurin, Martha West, Lula Rucker and others. Cathern and Judge moved up to higher union positions after Yeatman died.

After the strike, Harvey Echols was told by Hurst, "This college is too small for both of us. And I am the president." Harvey was forced to go to another city college to teach. There were a substantial number of teachers from India and China on our faculty. Baldeo Mohip, Dr. Dhaliwal and Dr. Syed were mainstays of our picket lines. Zenaida Bongaarts, a Filipina chemistry teacher, kept our spirits up with her wonderful pineapple egg rolls. Only one of the large number of Asian teachers scabbed.

In a strike or similar emergency, workers get to know all the other workers they never met before. We also met family members who came to help. I experienced that first at Malcolm X College and again when Wisconsin Steel closed in Chicago without notice. The emergency and our common cause brought us closely together. That was literally true when we huddled together in the freezing cold outside of Malcolm X College in 1971. The friendships we made then lasted for life. Wherever we are, we know we can call on each other if help is needed.

Tom Paine wrote that "These are the times that try men's souls." He was writing about the American Revolution. But it certainly applied to the teachers' strike at Malcolm X College. Out of the crucible of this strike, people of the purest metal were formed. So many ordinary people became heroes. Many had never expected to ever walk on a picket line. But they became educated overnight. We had a couple of staunch Republicans. One even ran for Congress on the Republican ticket. But when the issues became clear on the ground, they went with the union. I got the biggest kick when one political conservative asked a Teamster Union member not to cross our line. "AFL-CIO!" he shouted, as he pointed to the letters at the bottom of our signs. The truck driver turned his truck around and left. We all got an instant lesson in union solidarity.

We were very lucky to have a truly comfortable strike headquarters that became a second home during that critical period. One of our strikers, Rev. Gerald Forshey, made arrangements with a nearby Methodist church to use their large, carpeted, comfortably furnished facility. Cathern's husband, Ishmael Flory, brought his famous seafood gumbo. Zenaida Bongaarts brought the best Chinese barbecued ribs as well as her famous egg rolls. I probably brought ham and beans. That doesn't take too much imagination but it warms the stomach.. After picketing in the extreme cold, we could come to our haven and be well rested and well fed. Taking care of strikers' creature comforts goes a long way towards keeping up morale. The comfortable space made it possible to hold classes and conduct lively discussions.

Goons attack Our Pickets

Hurst's inability to split our strike ranks led to the use of other tactics. Somebody (guess who) hired thugs to come and beat up white teachers on our picket line. We figured that was the intent because all the teachers beaten were white except for Andrietta (Chi-Chi) Ward. We joked with Chi-Chi that the thugs mistook her because she was so bundled up. All of her face was covered except for her blue eyes. Despite our joking, we were furious that they had beaten Chi-Chi, the smallest among us. For us older teachers, it was as though they had beaten our daughter.

At the time the picket line was attacked, Cathern and I had just gone to strike headquarters to warm up after our picket shift. When word reached us of the attack, Cathern put her coat back on, called together all the strikers who were thawing out and said, "We're going back!" Without a second thought, we left the wonderful warmth and stepped out again into the frigid air. That day we had the largest picket line ever. The thugs did not come back. Not until 36 years later did I learn how these attacks were organized. The military arts teacher sent his students out to do the dirty work. A chemistry student,

Gide Colinet, heard the plans for an earlier attack. He notified Harvey Echols, and we temporarily pulled our line. Colinet saved us that day. He went on to become a chemistry professor and chair of the union at Olive Harvey College.

The violent attack on our picket line left scars that won't go away. Bart Maina, chairperson of the Biology Department, was one of the strikers punched by the thugs. He was a very principled man. Despite his beating, he returned to the picket line and was there every day until the strike ended. But he would never tie the picket sign around his neck again. The tie had made it hard for him to defend himself when he was attacked. Maina had been a soldier in World War II, serving under General Patton. He never lost his military bearing. After the strike, Maina fell victim to Hurst's war of nerves. Hurst sent a security officer to personally escort Bart to a room where Hurst was to meet him. Bart Maina stood at attention for one hour, waiting. Hurst never came, never apologized. The next week, Maina suffered a heart attack.

Some veiled threats reached me, too. My department chairperson cautioned me. He had "heard" that I was running a risk of "something happening to me." I don't think it was his intention to do the enemy's work. But that is how it is done, under the guise of friendship, spreading intimidating warnings. I was so angry that I sputtered, "You tell whoever said that to you that my husband is a professional heavyweight boxer. My sons are karate experts. And they are all good shots. Not to mention my brothers-in-law and nephews. They better not touch me because they will get more than they can give." As I write this I see that I mentioned only my male relatives. In fact, my sister-in-law, Jonnie, was the most formidable of them all. And I doubt that she ever handled a gun. Of course, my true protection was the people who were fighting together with us, students, teachers, other unions and community people. I wasn't scared, just angry.

Had we been better organized before the strike, we would have had a better idea of who might scab. Perhaps we could have talked them out of it. The American Federation of Teachers (AFT) does not have any strike pay. But help could have been offered to strikers with severe financial emergencies.

There is always an element of suspense on the first day of the strike. Will anyone go in? One teacher brought wood for our fire and walked the picket line with us for a few rounds. Then he went around the back of the building to go in and scab. The next morning he brought firewood again, but we told him what he could do with it. Actually, we told him quite gently, as one would explain to a three-year-old. Later in the strike, we would not have been as gentle.

Some scabbed out of fear that they would lose their job. Fear makes people irrational. I stood in the school driveway in one of our strikes when a fellow mathematics teacher drove in. He slowed down. I moved toward him to ask that he honor our picket line. Through the windshield, I saw a crazed look in his eyes. I jumped away from the car. He was going to run me over had I not got out of the way!

Violence, a Bosses' Tool

Some of the teachers from other countries were amazed that any teachers would scab. They were also surprised, and somewhat disappointed, that we allowed it. Teamsters who joined our line felt the same way. Violence had been used against us, but we knew that for us, violence would be counterproductive. We were determined to win the strike by keeping united and winning student and community support. But as the weeks dragged on, some began to lose heart. There was loose talk that the colleges would never reopen. We decided to strengthen morale by holding classes in labor history. Addie Wyatt was one of the labor angels who came to teach us. She tried to prepare us for compromises. She told us about the meat cutters strike, when Charlie Hayes, their leader, was fired. At the end of the strike, they got a contract but Charlie was not rehired. They had to go back without him. But in the end, the union prevailed. Both Addie Wyatt and Charlie Hayes rose in union ranks as international vice presidents. Hayes became my congressman, the only union leader in Congress. Frank and I loved Charlie.

Inspiring as Addie Wyatt was (and still is), we were thinking of winning, not losing. There was too much at stake, including the right of students to a college education. City-wide, the number of scabs remained small. Even at Malcolm X College where the pressure was greatest, 80% of the teachers stayed out during the five-week strike. We strikers at Malcolm X, thanks to our strong African American leadership, had defeated attempts to split the strike on racial grounds. We were proud to have played a key role in saving the union. If Shabat and Hurst had succeeded in breaking the strike at Malcolm X College, the strike could have faltered at the other six colleges.

Judge Cohen Writes Our Contract

Five weeks on strike may not sound long to steel workers who won a national strike that lasted 116 days. Five weeks certainly did not sound long to the Frontier Hotel workers in Las Vegas who were on strike five years before they won a union contract. And by 2008, the Congress Hotel strikers in Chicago had been on strike for more than five years. But in the city colleges, the loss of five weeks was putting the entire semester at risk. The pressure was mounting on our employers. The politicians who ran the city college system realized that they could not beat us back to work. So they did what union busters often do, they took it to the courts.

In the court of Judge Nathan Cohen, the CCC board did not get the injunction they wanted. They got something that may have turned out worse for us. Judge Nathan Cohen was heard to say that our contract had a lot of "fat" in it. He decided to "negotiate" our contract in his court. Swenson recommended that we go back to work while negotiations went on in Judge Cohen's court. A hot strike meeting, by a razor-thin majority, voted to go back. Basically, Judge Cohen would write our new contract. One speaker at our union meeting said about going back to work, "At least it will give us a chance to wash our long underwear. We can always go back on strike."

As any union activist knows, it not that easy to go back on strike. And indeed we did not. The contract negotiations under the judge's thumb, according to the official union web page, did not gut our contract. Many city college teachers thought otherwise. We did get a raise and kept our 12-hour contact load. The main thing we did not get was the "past practices" clause. That clause guaranteed that previous practices would be continued, even if not written into the contract. But it was only the past practices clause that prevented replacement of full-time teachers with part timers.

Some years after the 1971 contract, a hiring freeze was imposed. As full-timers retired or moved, they were replaced by part-time teachers. From a full-time faculty with just occasional "part-timers," part-time teachers now greatly outnumber the full-timers. The part-timers are fully qualified, but work for a mere fraction of a regular teacher's salary and no benefits. When part-time teachers asked to join CCCTU in the 1970s, Swenson told them they were not wanted. Since CCCTU represents only full-timers, its bargaining power has been greatly weakened. Students have lost access to their teachers since most of the faculty are part-time and seldom on campus.

Why did the teachers vote to accept the 1971 contract? In the most part they did not know what they were giving up. Our rank-and-file caucus, the Committee for Democracy and Action (CDA) did have members on the negotiating committee. These members tried to warn us. But little time was allowed for discussion of the contract. Printed copies of the changes were not available until the actual membership meeting that voted on the contract. That became the Swenson practice at future contract meetings.

I attended the end-of-strike contract meetings in 1973, 1975 and 1978. Contents of the contract were totally unknown to us. I could see stacks of contracts under the arms of the ushers. "May I have a copy?" I politely asked. "No," the usher replied. "My instructions are to wait until the meeting begins." The Swenson machine wanted the strike-weary teachers to ratify the contract before they found out what the board had taken away.

Barred From Campus

After the 1971 strike, John Yeatman, our union chapter chairperson, John Wenger, a grievance committee member, and myself, a union delegate, were "barred from campus." We were not allowed to teach our scheduled classes at Malcolm X College. Since we had valid contracts, they could not fire us at mid-year. They mailed us our paychecks. We turned that into a scandal, "paying teachers to stay at home when they were needed in the classrooms." In response to the protests, Dr. Hurst assigned us to teach, but at a college outpost. He continued to bar us from the Malcolm X campus. The outpost was at the Cabrini Green housing project, then notorious for its high crime rate. (I had some very good students in those classes.) But my husband laughed when he heard the news. "They really want to kill you," he said.

At the end of the semester, I was lucky. Of the three teachers barred from campus, I was the only one allowed to return to Malcolm X. I had just received tenure and could not be fired without cause. So I was back at the college in fall 1972. John Wenger accepted a transfer to Loop (now Harold Washington) College. Hurst had warned him that his life was not safe if he returned to campus. But the worst was yet to come.

John Yeatman didn't have tenure, and Dr. Hurst fired him. How could we go back to work and leave our union leader out on the street? Yeatman had just been elected city college vice president of our union local, beating Swenson's slated candidate. In response to the firing, there was an upwelling of support from rank and file union members. We created a fund to pay Yeatman's salary so his family would not suffer. Many of us put in $100 a month, a substantial sum for teachers on 1970s salaries. Sadly, the strain stressed John's heart to bursting, and he died in 1973. But he had the satisfaction, before he died, to learn that he had been reinstated to his job with back pay, as a result of our protests.

John Yeatman's premature death was a terrible blow to the Malcolm X faculty. For me, it was a searing, personal loss, like the death of a favorite brother. Our families had become close, too. As the union situation continued to deteriorate, we needed him so badly. His moral example strengthened us all. "John," I would smile, chiding him in my mind, "You had to go and leave us." Things had not yet reached the point where a scab from the 1971 strike could be elected to union office. But that would happen. It became a sad case of "shit rising to the top."

Cathern Davis Flory

Cathern Davis stepped in to lead the union chapter on campus after the premature deaths of John Yeatman and Bruce Hayden. Hayden, hired soon after the strike, had reinforced the African American leadership on campus. I gave Cathern my whole-hearted support as did Beth Lehman, chapter grievance chairperson. Beth was another pure-hearted person. Our faculty was rich with good people in those days. It did not matter that we suffered repeated attacks from corrupt bosses. As long as we had so many good friends, and student support, we could stand up to whatever they could dish out. Beth went on to law school, part time. So we had a grievance chairperson with legal training. In time, she graduated from John Marshall Law School and left Malcolm X College to practice law full time. However, our circle of friends remained intact, wherever we went.

Like Beth, Cathern Davis Flory was a major influence in my life. Cathern was a highly moral and extremely brave person. She also had a strong sense of drama and an absolutely magnetic presence. Her proud posture, mature bright eyes and strong features fit well with the beautiful African clothing she wore. When Cathern and I visited Tashkent in Soviet Central Asia, there was an international movie festival going on. People thought she was a visiting African movie star. They flocked around her and asked for her autograph. At our dinner table, admirers sent her a bottle of wine. They knew she was somebody important. And they were right.

Teachers followed Cathern's lead at Malcolm X College because they respected her. They appreciated what she had done for the school. Cathern promoted the study of African history and appreciation of African cultures. The walls of the college were adorned with wonderful pieces of art that she brought back from annual trips to Africa. Her thrust was always to promote unity, rather than division, between white and African American teachers and students.

Davis was married to Ishmael Flory, chairperson of the Communist Party of Illinois. Although she never joined the Party, she was a strong supporter of socialism and the Soviet Union. Great leaders such as W. E. B. Du Bois and

Paul Robeson stayed at her home. She had a special friendship with Margaret Burroughs. Both Margaret and Cathern set me on the path of using African cultural materials in my teaching. It has been a path of struggle but also added to the joy in my life.

Educational Genocide

During the Nixon years (1969–1974), the national policy on junior colleges changed. Looking back, the new policy was a cynical response to the demands for which students of color were fighting. Students had been demanding access to a college education. They won admission to the buildings. But they were told to lower their expectations. The Nixon policy aimed to limit community colleges to "post-secondary" education, instead of the first two years of college. Watering-down of community college education began in 1970. That year, the Carnegie Commission issued a report on community colleges. In effect, the Nixon-Carnegie policy was:

1. Allow African American, Latino and low-income white students into the community colleges.

2. Change the mission: Instead of two years of college followed by transfer to a four-year college, give them "practical courses." To accelerate this change, funding preference was given for vocational and other non-college credit courses.

John Yeatman took the lead in exposing The Carnegie Commission Report. He called the Report, "Educational Genocide." I wrote a similar article, "The Community Colleges, A Promise Betrayed," for *Political Affairs*. A longer treatment of the same subject is in the book, *A Dream Deferred*, by Steven G. Brint and Jerome Karabel.

The limited number of mathematics offerings was an example of watering down the curriculum. In 1970, Malcolm X College offered only high school level mathematics courses. Students who moved on to a four-year college found themselves far behind. After Dr. Hurst became president, poor administration created other road blocks.

I needed help and moral support. So I told my husband what a big mess the college was in. "What should I do?" I asked. His reply was simple. "Teach them," he said. Frank always had a way to get to the heart of the issue. Pat Ellis, my sister-in-law, added similar advice. She said, "Teach with examples. Always start a topic with 'For example.'"

Looking back, it is easy to put the blame for the downward spiral of educational standards on our weak citywide union leadership. That would be wrong. It is true that the Swenson leadership did not fight to keep free tuition. It is true that they abandoned union democracy. But the Swenson faction did not create the attack on education or the attack on the teachers' unions. Nobody in the union had applied for or granted an injunction to stop our strikes. Nobody in the union had put the local president in jail, not once, but twice. Nobody in the union wanted to cut back the academic classes. In even a bigger sense, not even the Shabats and the Hursts were the main enemies of students and teachers. For that, we would have to look at the Nixon administration and the corporations they represented. They were carrying out a policy to underfund and downgrade the community colleges.

In 1966, Local 1600 had blazed the way for other college and university unions. Faculty and students were working together. We were building a true community of learning and struggle for justice. But in the 1980s, the local had sunk so low that scabs from the 1971 strike were made officers of the union chapter. By 1982, the loss of union spirit affected the moral fiber of the faculty. When I left Malcolm X in 1982, the faculty had voted out our stellar union chairperson, Cathern Davis. Instead of Cathern, the chapter elected a person of questionable character who was fired "for cause" a few years after. What happened in between to make such a big change? That is a question I thought about a lot, over the years. It's a process that's hard to explain.

The easiest, but not best, explanation is corruption. Local union officers were corrupted by the extra money that came with their office. To hold those offices they sacrificed union democracy. Instead of democracy, officers practiced business-type unionism. In business unionism, members pay dues and officers provide service. Don't let the members know too much. Otherwise they may run against you and win.

I saw that type of thinking in action after John Yeatman died. Our rank and file caucus ran another Malcolm X teacher to fill John's position as local vice president. He lost. Later he told me he had learned how to get elected. It was simple. If your side loses, just switch sides and run on the other slate. He did, and was elected. Not too long after that, we were both at an AFT convention. AFT had given up the secret ballot for election of their national officers. The same local vice president returned the ballot I had signed and said, "You voted for the wrong candidates." I refused to change my vote. "You will never be a delegate to another AFT convention," he gently warned me. We were still friends. He was just carrying out orders.

I think we have to look at the bigger picture to understand how we sank so low. Local 1600 led the fight for college teacher unionism in 1966. That was the same time as the rise of the civil rights movement, the upsurge of the women's movement and the Latino rights movement. By the end of the '70s, however, anti-labor attacks were increasing. These anti-labor attacks accelerated with the election of Ronald Reagan. He fired over 11,000 striking air traffic controllers, and their union was smashed. Reagan carried on a sustained attack on the government's civil rights apparatus and greatly weakened affirmative action. Racism and attacks on labor went hand in hand.

Meanwhile, the fear factor worsened with the closing of steel mills and factories all over the country. The old AFL-CIO leadership was incapable of leading a fightback. Without a fightback, fear spread. I believe it was fear that led Malcolm X College teachers to make such a poor choice in their union election. Fortunately for the AFL-CIO, progressive leaders won the 1995 AFL-CIO elections. They have been leading labor's fightback since that date. But the early 1980s under President Reagan was a very grim time for working families.

Time to Quit

In 1982, I could have collected my helpful City College salary for another six years. But I felt that it was time to quit. The closing of Wisconsin Steel in 1980 was placing other demands on my time. Frank was organizing thousands of workers who had been left with nothing, not even a union. Their one-company union folded after the steel mill closed down. In 1981, Frank led three busloads of Wisconsin Steel workers to put their case before Congress. They made history. But I could not go because I could not leave my students. The steel workers did not need me to help plan their strategy. But I was always being called on to help write a press release or a leaflet. The Wisconsin Steel workers were keeping me too busy to hold a full time job. With 17 years as a teacher, I could still collect a small pension. The Social Security I had earned in years of work in factories and labs, could keep us going as retirees. So I quit the City Colleges, only to return to teaching at a later date.

CCCTU, Local 1600, a Twenty-first Century Update

In 1973, 1975 and 1978, the Chicago City College board forced a strike each time the teachers' union contract expired. Twice, negotiations ended up in the courts. In 1978, Mayor Bilandic mediated the strike in two all-night negotiating sessions. Each time, raises were negotiated. But the clause protecting past practices was never regained. Then for 22 years, contracts were renewed without a strike. Oscar Shabat was gone. The new chancellors, and there were several, made few changes.

In 2004, the board forced the teachers into a strike again. This time, the union made a huge concession. They accepted a two-tier work load in the contract that ended the strike. Future teachers would have to work a 15-contact-hour week while teachers already hired could keep the 12-hour load. To those who fought the two-tier work load, Swenson had a simple reply, "I don't represent the people who are not yet hired." However, everybody lost the 12-hour load after the 2006 strike. Starting in 2008, all city college teachers had to work the 15-hour load. In effect, class size limits have also been lost. Everyone is paying a big price for the failure to organize both full and part time teachers in the same union.

I don't like to end a chapter on such a negative note. And I don't think the story ends here. Teachers who are now part-timers will join the full-timers to rebuild the future Cook

County College Teachers Union. In 2006, there were many examples of this type of solidarity. Many part-time teachers honored the picket line during the full-time teachers' strike. Almost all of the striking part-timers were fired, but the fight to reinstate them continues.

Mrs. Hortensia Allende, widow of President Allende, with two Malcolm X College unionists, the author and Beth Lehman, Chicago, December 1973

Chapter 24

Socialist Cuba

The Cuban people won my heart.

Frank and I have learned so much from our visits to countries in Latin America, Africa and Asia. Wherever we have gone, we found that working families want the same things: peace, full employment, a living wage and a better life for our children. We have seen for ourselves that the workers' struggle is international. To win, we need to follow Karl Marx's advice, "Workers of the world, unite!"

Ruth Lipschutz and author, taking turns, mixing cement with Venceremos Brigade, Cuba, 1983

The Cuban people won my heart when I first visited in 1960. So in 1983, soon as I retired from Malcolm X College, I volunteered for the Venceremos (we will win) Brigade. In 1983, in Cuba, the Brigade helped build new housing. We did some touch-up cement work in a new apartment building. My job was to sift the sand used to mix the cement. I enjoyed shoveling the sand and tossing it through a big sieve. The exercise helped the arthritis in my back, and I felt I was helping Cuban families who would live in the apartments.

Fighting the FTAA, from Chicago to Cuba

Author's son, Dr. John Lumpkin to Fidel Castro's left. Gov. Ryan, Illinois, standing behind Castro

Altogether, I have made six visits to Cuba and look forward to a seventh, some day. In 2001, Frank and I attended the 18th Congress of the Central de Trabajadores de Cuba (CTC or Cuban labor federation). On the way to the airport for the Cuba trip, we made a stop at a Chicago steel-spring plant. The plant was moving operations to Canada and Mexico, under provisions of the North American Free Trade Agreement (NAFTA). Over 1,000 protesters marched in front of the plant. "FTAA (Free

Trade Area of the Americas) would be NAFTA on steroids," the steel workers warned. Almost three million workers in the US have lost their jobs due to NAFTA. The impact on Mexico has been even worse.

The international session at the CTC Congress focused on the need to stop FTAA. I was among many from the U.S. who had put our names in to talk. To my surprise, I was among the first called to speak. When I got up to the platform I looked across and saw President Fidel Castro looking my way. My hands began to shake. I almost lost it. After 30 seconds, which is a long time if you're standing at a podium, I pulled myself together. "FTAA was also a threat to steel workers in the U.S.," I said, describing the Chicago steel workers' demonstration we had just attended. Then I mentioned the "Charleston Five" case and the longshoremen's union's call for international solidarity. The Charleston Five, four longshoremen and one checker, had been slapped with riot charges after 660 police attacked their picket line. I was still shaking when I went back to my seat. One sweet friend from Minnesota reassured me, "Fidel was taking notes when you talked." "That was probably just to record the phone number of the longshoremen's union," I replied.

Cuban Steel Workers

While in Cuba, Frank and I visited the steel workers union in Havana. We asked about job security, women in the mill and health and safety. Ramon Cuellar led the discussion. He talked about production figures. Their steel output hit a low of 90,500 tons in 1993 after the dissolution of the Soviet Union. It recovered and reached a record 300,000 tons in the year 2000.

But we had asked about the workers, not about production. The Cuban unionists thought it was obvious that workers' conditions depended on production. Whatever the Cuban steel mill produced was for the benefit of the workers. We and they lived in very different systems.

About women workers, we were told, "There are many women working in the steel mills. They work as engineers, technicians and supervisors." In response to my question,

Cuellar said that women did not do the heavy jobs in the mill. The CTC had already told us that women made up 44% of local union presidents, 60% at the municipal level and 38% of the national executive board of the CTC. The Cuban steel workers described some of the family services that their plant provides. When school is out for holidays or summer months, workers can bring their children to the plant for supervised trips and activities. The plant has its own beach and cabins for workers selected by the union or recommended by doctors as in need of a beach-vacation cure. The mill has a free clinic, including dental services, for its 1,200 workers and the community. The mill's cultural center includes a theater; sports facilities feature a professional quality baseball field, basketball courts and gyms. Wrap-around services make a community strong.

There are seven air-conditioned dining rooms in the mill. Most workers live close enough to bicycle to work. For those who live farther away, the mill provides special bus service at a cost of a few cents. The plant provides work clothes and free laundry service. In fact, Cuellar told us, the workers can bring their clothes from home to be laundered. A barbershop is part of the mill complex.

Still at every turn, even as visitors, we could see the harmful effect of the U.S. blockade of Cuba. Although production had recovered at the steel mill, less-strategic factories remained crippled by a lack of supplies caused by the blockade. Workers and farmers of both countries would benefit from an end to the blockade.

Mexico is another Latin American country that Frank and I visited several times. And it is home to great Native American civilizations. From the top of the Pyramid of the Sun near Mexico City, we could appreciate the vast size of the pyramid and the city that surrounded it. The pyramid was about 65 meters high (213 feet) with a square base measuring 215 meters (705 feet).

But we could not get lost in the glories of the past. Some days we passed protest marches of poor farmers carrying red and black flags. The marches were usually around election time. "The police don't dare attack them during election time," friends explained to us. The farmers' struggle continues to this day. It has become an even grimmer fight since the NAFTA trade treaty was signed. Ruined peasant families have flocked into the big cities, swelling Mexico City to over 22 million people. Many other millions, driven by hunger, cross over or under the border to work in the U.S. In the U.S., NAFTA has caused many factories to close, laying off their workers.

FTAA and the Miami Gestapo

On November 20, 2003 we went to Miami with the United Steelworkers for a huge demonstration to stop FTAA. We got a preview of what a police state in the U.S. would look like. It was scary.

It was a work day, but the city had shut down. The mayor of Miami had mobilized his entire police force and those from surrounding cities. Dressed in full riot gear, they blockaded the streets and lay in wait for us. We were tens of thousands of union members and thousands of young people. Thanks to our demonstration, delegates of countries who expected to sign the FTAA treaty were not able to meet. They stayed in their hotel rooms and eventually went home—without a treaty!

After we marched into Miami without incident, we rallied in a stadium while the march continued. It was good to see Frank's brother Warren and his wife Frances with the Orlando retirees. But it was hard to hear because a couple of police helicopters flew low overhead, trying to drown out the speakers. The rally over, we went to a high point to watch the end of the march.

Things turned ugly. Thousands of young people were marching in peacefully. Suddenly the police started beating students and arresting some. Then the police began to harass us retirees. Our hotels were about two miles away. The police refused to let our buses through. Then they herded us, including people with canes and crutches, down the street and away from the buses. We had no alternative but to walk the two miles. I was appalled and disgusted by the police cruelty. But our sacrifice was not in vain. Together, we had prevented the signing of FTAA.

Some years have passed and the FTAA has not been signed and probably never will be. The political situation in South America has changed in favor of regional cooperation rather than domination by the United States. Coalitions of leftist parties have elected presidents in Venezuela, the ABC countries (Argentina, Brazil and Chile) and Bolivia, Ecuador and Nicaragua. The dictatorships in Uruguay and Paraguay have been toppled. Cuba still stands strong. This is a time of hope.

Author dancing with oil worker, Cuba 2000, Joy in the Struggle

Chapter 25

People's Power in Chile
"You see, Beatriz, wherever you go in this world, you have family."

Frank got 26 weeks of vacation at Wisconsin Steel in 1973. That was a once-in-five-years deal that the United Steel Workers union won from the steel companies. The original demand had been for a shorter work week.

Frank's extended vacation came at the end of May 1973; my summer vacation had just begun. There was enough time to do something extraordinary. We decided to take a bus down the South American stretch of the Pan-American Highway, from Colombia to Santiago de Chile. I did not suspect that I would witness the most dramatic events of my life. It shifted the whole focus of my political life for the next ten years.

I was eager to revisit Chile so Frank could experience the hopeful changes I had seen. His insights would make the experience more meaningful for me.

Popular Unity

It was June, 1972 when Beth Lehman and I first visited Chile. Beth was my Malcolm X colleague and sister teacher unionist. We were swept up by the mass enthusiasm of the workers for the Popular Unity government headed by Salvador Allende. Allende, a socialist, was democratically elected president in 1970. He was leading the drive to take back Chile's natural resources from the foreign corporations. Homes for working families were being built, and three-fourths of the unemployed had been put to work. To build their country, workers and students were donating their labor, doing *trabajo voluntario* (unpaid, voluntary labor).

At the Santiago office of the educational workers union, Beth and I met highly committed teachers. They were giving their all for the education of workers and their children. Their commitment helped us understand the revolutionary process going on in Chile. I wanted Frank to see it too. The very next year, he and I took off for South America.

The cheapest way to get from Miami to Santiago de Chile was to fly to Colombia; then take a bus at the border with Ecuador. The bus was designed to squeeze in as many short people as possible. I had just enough leg room, but Frank's long legs pushed his knees into his chest for the whole trip. He never complained.

The oppressive nature of the Ecuadorian government of 1973 was painfully clear at military check points. There were many. The bus had to stop, and we all got out, dragging our luggage. Soldiers roughly searched the passengers' belongings. Finally, we made it to Quito.

Quito is blessed with one of the most beautiful natural settings of any city. On every side were mountains, cloaked in soft green. The Native American origins of Quito were visible in the walls and old buildings near our hotel. Down the street, stood a massive wall made of huge rough-faced stones. The uneven edges fitted snugly together without mortar. It was a fine example of Inca or Aymara stone work.

Most beautiful of all were the people. But we were saddened by the sight of whole families laboring as "humans of burden." Men, women and children, they walked bent over with packs on their backs, bigger than they were. Like other places with poor living conditions, there was the ever-present smell of stale urine in the streets. Quito was surely a much cleaner and happier city before the Spanish conquest.

After a day's rest in Quito, we were back on a bus to Santiago. We still had to get to Peru, ride the whole length of that long country (2,757 km), then another 2032 km inside Chile.

In Peru, we stopped for lunch at a restaurant perched up on a hill above a rare stream of water. I must say that our bus driver knew the best restaurants for our meal stops. The food was always good and reasonable. I still remember the meal, a mild white-fleshed fish, potatoes and salad. The fish was so good I thought it was fresh-caught from the river below.

After the meal, we had the funniest experience of any trip. There was no toilet on the bus. Naturally, after eating and before re-boarding the bus, we looked for the toilets. Signs on the wall pointed to *Servicios higiénicos-hombres*, and for women, signs pointed the other way, *Servicios higiénicos-mujeres*. So I rolled up the legs of my blue jeans, just in case the "hygienic services" were leaking. I went one way, and Frank went the other way. But we didn't find it and decided we had made the wrong turns. We tried again and this time I persisted. I followed the arrows which directed me outside the building. There were other women squatting in the sand, making use of the "Servicios higiénicos." At that point I joined the other women and hoped the fish we ate were not from the stream below.

Chile

The next day we knew that we had made it to Chile. Long lines of people waited to buy cigarettes and bread. Many believed that the shortages had been deliberately created to destabilize President Allende and his Popular Unity government. Popular Unity was known as Unidad Popular (UP) in Spanish. UP was a coalition of an umbrella-type Socialist Party, the Communist Party and some smaller, religion-based, social democratic parties.

Chilean presidents were usually elected with a plurality, not a majority. Allende was elected with 36% of the votes, more than some other presidents had won. He went ahead with the Popular Unity program, hoping to pick up support. They nationalized the copper mines; copper was Chile's main export. The vote in the Congress was unanimous. Allende also began a land reform, breaking up big plantations and distributing the farms to landless farmers. Mine owners were compensated. But the compensation was based on the value declared for tax purposes. The owners, many from the U.S., were furious. They had undervalued the mines for years and cheated the people of Chile of needed tax income.

Finally, we reached Santiago. It had been a long journey by bus. For our return, we planned to fly back from Santiago to Bogotá. That proved to be impossible. Much had changed in one year. The country was in severe crisis. The Nixon policy of destabilizing the elected government was taking its toll. The workers, young people and farmers who had received land in the reform were still the backbone of the UP. Working families had benefited from gaining union rights, more public works jobs and better schools for their children. The UP vote went up from 36% to 44%, a rare mid-term improvement.

From the very beginning, terror tactics were used against the Allende government. In 1971, General Schneider, commander-in-chief of the Chilean armed forces, was assassinated. He was killed by thugs from Patria y Libertad, an ultra-right organization. General Schneider had strongly resisted pressure to prevent the inauguration of Salvador Allende, winner of the presidential election. Not that Schneider was an Allende supporter, but he was determined to uphold the constitution. Schneider was replaced by General Prats, another defender of the constitution. When some tank commanders made the first armed attempt against the government in June 1973, Prats disarmed them. His quick action prevented a massive death toll.

After the military coup on September 11, 1973, Pinochet forced General Prats out of the country. Pinochet's secret police (DINA) followed Prats to Argentina and murdered him and his wife. Generals Schneider and Prats were exceptional commanders, widely recognized for their intellectual achievements, Schneider was a painter, and Prats a writer. Three years after the coup, the Chilean terrorists came to Washington, DC and murdered Orlando Letelier and his U.S. associate, Ronni Karpen Moffitt. Letelier had served as Ambassador to the United States, appointed by Salvador Allende. (Ultimately, a U.S.-born DINA agent, Michael Vernon Townley, Chilean Army Captain Armando Fernandez, and two anti-Castro Cuban exiles were convicted for these assassinations in U.S. trials spanning 1978–1990.)

The whole rule of law had broken down in Chile in 1973. Fascist-minded judges were setting assassins free, although they had been caught firing into union and student offices. These judges were in office for life and were accountable to no one.

The leading newspaper, *El Mercurio,* was owned by the vice president of Pepsi Cola, Augustin Edwards. It was, and perhaps still is, a conduit for CIA funding. *El Mercurio* published calls for the overthrow of the elected Allende government. The government closed down the newspaper. Then courts acted fast and ordered the paper reopened. Naturally, newspapers in the United States hailed the reopening as a victory for freedom of the press. The government of Richard Nixon and Henry Kissinger was working to hasten the violent overthrow of Chile's elected government. The U.S. denied Chile normal commercial credits and applied other sanctions. Chilean industry began to grind to a halt for lack of replacement parts. The economy, which had grown during Allende's first year, plunged into crisis.

Right-wing Violence

As we roamed the streets of Santiago, Frank and I saw bands of paramilitary punks, part of the fascist "Patria y Libertad." They were openly drilling in the streets just a few blocks from the government center. Some were thrill-seeking sons of the rich. Others were "lumpen" elements, not people who worked for a living.

Twice, organized workers went on general strike to stop a military takeover. On June 15, 1973, the Central Unica de Trabajadores (CUT) called workers out to the city center to protect government offices. In a heavy downpour they came and saved the country. For hours, the streets looked like a battleground, but government buildings, workers' offices, and newspapers were secured. To stop the fascist drive, CUT called a general strike for June 21st.

We witnessed the huge demonstration in support of the government on the day of the general strike. People came on every kind of vehicle they could beg or borrow. The entire fleet of garbage trucks had been mobilized by the garbage workers' union. The trucks were piled full, layer on layer of demonstrators. Every other kind of work vehicle came, also loaded with workers. It was a maximum effort by the workers.

After the general strike of June 21st, things seem to turn around. The country gained a few days of relative peace. Frank still wanted to see the steel mills, over 200 miles from Santiago. We took advantage of the lull to hop on a bus for Concepcion on June 27th.

Steel workers of Huachipato

Early the next morning, Frank and I took a city bus toward the Huachipato steel mills near Concepción, 500 kilometers south of Santiago. The mills had long been run by Bethlehem Steel but had been built with the aid of government funds. The UP government nationalized the plant. From town, we took a taxi right to the mill gate.

"What Party are you with?" the guards asked at the mill gate. I tried to answer in my poor Spanish, or Castellano, as they called it. What should I say? We were not authorized to represent anybody. So I spluttered, and said I had written some articles for the Communist newspaper, the *Daily World*. That was enough information for them.. In a few minutes we were on our way to one of the most moving and inspiring experiences of our lifetimes. We were led to the office of Arturo Contreras, leader of the Communist steel workers of Huachipato. When I explained that Frank worked at Wisconsin Steel in Chicago, Contreras was delighted. He said they had received many delegations but no actual steel workers.

In a little while, Contreras got tired of talking to Frank through me. "Why don't you speak Spanish!" he demanded. Frank replied that he didn't talk English that well, and the Chileans understood. Chilean steel workers, also, had limited access to education. But they hoped that would all change with the UP.

Coworkers of Contreras took us for a short tour of the mill. From my time at National Tube I recognized some things in the mill. Huachipato, like Wisconsin Steel, was an integrated mill. Iron ore and coke came in one end and steel rolled out at the other end. Perhaps they made their own coke. Soon Contreras joined us and said, "All steel mills are the same. What you want to do is meet the workers." Frank agreed. For the next ten hours, that's what we did. We were in and out of workers' homes, with Contreras's small house a home base. We were also in and out of cars, three different ones borrowed for the occasion. Of one car, the driver proudly declared, "This car is in the service of the revolution." It rained and it poured, but we hardly noticed.

Among the headquarters we visited were the offices of the Communist Party of Huachipato. The large poster on the wall called for the basic virtues: *Honor, Deber y Luchar* (Honor, Duty and Struggle). In the U.S., that would have been called "corny." But it brought tears to my eyes. The Young Communists had similar priorities. Their slogans any mother could love: *Estudiar, Trabajar y Luchar* (Study, Work and Struggle).

As the day rolled into evening, and evening into night, Contreras asked if we liked sea food. He invited us to a little repast at a local restaurant. We walked in, and twenty people were waiting, all Communist steel workers. It was like a fairy tale, and the best part was it was true. We talked and sang all night. And we all ate the local seafood and drank the mellow Chilean wine. The beer is smooth, too. We all felt pretty good. As we shared in the international exchange and comradeship, one of the younger steel workers said to me, "You see, Beatriz, wherever you go in this world, you have family."

"You must go to Lota and meet the coal miners," they told us. Compañeros in Santiago had also talked about the coal miners of Lota. They were the most solid, the most heroic, the most revolutionary of all. Perhaps their solidity came from the conditions of their work. The Lota coal mines extended out a mile underneath the ocean. Workers depended on each other for safety, for their very lives. The steel workers made a phone call, and it was all set up. Our first stop would be the Communist Party office in Lota. It was past midnight. Our friends took us back to the hotel and wished us a good trip to Lota. We tried, but never learned, if they survived the coming horrors.

Coup Attempt in Santiago

We had finished our breakfast when we got the news. Fascist army commanders had mutinied in Santiago. Frank and

I decided to return to Santiago immediately. On the train we got the good news. The coup had been crushed. But the tone was grim at the Communist Party office. The attempted coup had revealed how well entrenched the fascists were inside the armed forces. The Communists were working feverishly to stop a more massive attempt to overthrow the government. It seemed to me that they were also preparing for the worst. If a military coup/golpe overthrew the elected government, the Communist Party was ready to work underground and continue the struggle.

The political situation had become too menacing for Frank and me to stay. But the airport had closed, so we had to wait. I sent a couple of news stories to the *Daily World,* but we did not know how else to help. Every day the economic situation in Chile got worse. Hyperinflation had set in. While United States corporations were turning the screw on the Chilean economy, they were funding Allende's opposition. The heavy hand of the Nixon administration was known to all in Chile. It gave rise to a bitter joke:

"There can never be a coup in the U.S." "Why?"
"Because there is no American Embassy in the U.S.!"

Graffiti began to appear in Santiago with the one word, "Jakarta!" That was a deadly threat. Just six years earlier, right-wing military had killed a half million people in Jakarta and other parts of Indonesia. Other Chilean graffiti was just as deadly, "All Marxists Must Die!"

Since there was no date certain for the reopening of the airport, we decided to return the hard way, again on the bus. Frank and I made it back to Arica, on the border with Peru. There was a crowd in the bus terminal; many were desperately trying to get out of Chile. I tried once again, in broken Spanish, to negotiate two seats, but bus after bus left without us. Finally, Jorge Valdivia, a Peruvian in his twenties, came to our aid and got our tickets. We boarded the bus with a new friend. I will never forget his kindness. I still wanted to take Frank to Cuzco and Machu Picchu. But Frank wanted to keep going north as fast as possible. He did not plan to stop until we reached Broadview, Illinois. Within the week we were back home.

September 11, 1973

On September 11, 1973, the Chilean Navy, after maneuvers with the U.S. Navy, began the military coup against the elected government of Chile. President Allende was killed, and General Pinochet declared himself president. Thousands of workers and students were murdered, their bodies piling up in the morgues. Bodies were floating in the Mapocho River or simply laid out on the streets. Many more thousands "disappeared." Some were found years later, buried in mass graves. Others were dropped by helicopter into the ocean and never found. Hundreds of thousands fled the country, perhaps one million.

What could we in Chicago do? Progressives in Chicago were deeply traumatized by the murder of Allende. They were outraged by President Nixon's role in bringing the military dictatorship to power. Even worse, the Chilean military had attacked the dream of peaceful change of the economic system. There was an emergency need for solidarity aid to the Chilean people. The Communist strategy in such emergencies is to build the broadest possible coalition to work on the issue. We consulted our comrade, Sylvia Kushner of the Chicago Peace Council. The Peace Council agreed to send out a call for solidarity actions.

We made a special appeal to the U.S. labor movement because the Chilean trade unions were the heart of Popular Unity. The response was gratifying. Union after union passed resolutions for the restoration of democracy and labor rights in Chile. One way I thought we could help was to bring these labor statements together in a compelling format. Peggy Lipschutz, the great movement artist, came to the rescue. With brilliant cartoons and layout, Peggy put together a booklet that "read like a comic book." That statement was coined by a labor leader, and I took it as highest praise. The booklet, *Solidarity with the Unions of Chile*, was widely distributed at union gatherings to receptive audiences.

Committee to Save Lives in Chile

In the days after September 11, 1973, *Life* Magazine showed gruesome, detailed photographs of the bodies of young workers and students piled up in the Santiago morgue. The bloodletting sickened all of us. Saving lives in Chile became the most immediate issue. Through the Chicago Peace Council, we brought together a coalition that formed the Chicago Citizens Committee to Save Lives in Chile. It was chaired by Ernie DeMaio, district director of the United Electrical Workers (UE).

Our first big move was to organize a rally to welcome the widow of President Allende to Chicago. Father Bill Hogan and other clerical members of our committee secured the indoor stadium of De Paul University for the rally. It was early in December, and the temperature hovered around 0^0 Fahrenheit. I knew the rally would be big when people came an hour early and waited in the bitter cold. We expected 1,000, and 4,000 people came. Our committee was overwhelmed. We did not have enough members to handle the collection, my only such experience in my lifetime as an activist.

On the personal side, the visit with Mrs. Hortensia Bussi Allende was a moving experience. I was very proud that my son John was part of her security team. As the wife of a physician, Mrs. Allende took an interest in John, then in medical school.

The Communist Party of Chile continued to function underground although hundreds of its leaders were killed or "disappeared." One of its first acts was to help the other UP parties reorganize. Given the intense rivalry among the parties, that seemed surprising. Still it made a lot of sense. Especially in underground work, coalitions were important. The underground asked us to send delegations to Chile that included legislators. Delegations from the U.S. and other countries could pressure the junta to stop the killings.

Just a couple of months after the rally with Mrs. Allende, the Chicago Citizens Committee to Save Lives in Chile sent twelve Chicago-area leaders to Chile. Our committee made the travel arrangements to Santiago for February 16–23, 1974. Delegation members paid their own way. The delegation included two local legislators: Anna Langford, veteran Chicago City alderman, and Doris Strieter, village board member in Maywood. Abe Feinglass, UFCW international vice president and Ernie DeMaio, UE district director, brought a strong labor voice. Academics included Geoffrey Fox, University of Illinois, Chicago; Father Gerard Grant, Loyola University, Chicago; George Gutierrez, Northern Illinois University and Joanne Fox Prazeworski, University of Chicago. From religious organizations were James Reed, pastor of the Parish of the Holy Covenant United Methodist Church, Chicago; Jane Reed, of the board of Church and Society, United Methodist Church, and Dean Peerman, managing editor, *Christian Century*.

The twelfth and most poignant of all was Frank Teruggi, Sr. He was on a special mission. Teruggi wanted to find out who had killed his son, Frank Teruggi, Jr., during the coup. When he returned, he said that his questions had been answered. He believed that his son had been detained in the National Stadium and murdered there, probably "fingered" by the U.S. Embassy.

The delegation spent one week in Chile. They gave a dramatic report on their return. Over 800 Chicagoans paid admission to hear their report and to support solidarity with Chile. For those who could not attend, Peggy Lipschutz and I produced an illustrated booklet with the highlights of the report.

As the years rolled on, the long night of the military dictatorship persisted. In the first years after September 11, 1973, Chicago became home to about 300 Chilean refugees. Doris and Rev. Tom Strieter of the Chicago Citizens Committee to Save Lives in Chile were leaders of the church-based movement to sponsor the refugees. Sarah Staggs, John and Pat Coatsworth and Doris Strieter were among those who organized mammoth concerts by famous exiled Chilean musicians: Quilapayun, Inti Illimani, and others. The audiences filled the huge auditorium of the Medinah Temple.

Our committee also sponsored the Chicago premiere of *Missing*, attended by the star of the film, Jack Lemmon. That 1982 film centered on a father's search for truth in the murder of his son, Charles Horman, during the 1973 coup in Chile. Our committee raised what was a lot of money for us. Much of the money we raised went back to Chile, to help organizations fighting the dictatorship.

In 1980, my own family went through a disaster, the closing of Frank's steel mill in Chicago. Our Wisconsin Steel Workers

Save Our Jobs Committee got a lot of support from activists in the Chile solidarity movement, especially the Barrientos, Coatsworth and Feinglass families. Nery Barrientos, a Chilean refugee, even dusted off his guitar, and Lucy Barrientos raised her lovely voice in song, to help us raise money for "Save Our Jobs." While my heart was always with the Chile solidarity movement, the fight of the Wisconsin Steel workers took up more and more of my time. I was happy that Sarah Staggs, Doris Strieter, Joan Elbert, the Coatsworths, Sylvia Kushner and other friends kept the solidarity movement going strong.

Inside of Chile, the struggle against the military dictatorship kept growing. Finally, in 1988, the movement for democracy forced the dictatorship to hold a referendum on Pinochet's rule. He lost. An election was called for 1990. It put an end to the dictatorship. But Pinochet retained power as the head of the armed forces. The pre-Pinochet constitution was not restored. That left the Pinochet constitution in force. The restrictions on unions remain in effect to this day. State terror has ended, but workers are still fighting to regain their democratic rights.

Miracle or Mirage?

In 2006, Frank and I made another trip to Chile. Starting with the modern airport, I could hardly recognize Santiago. Whole areas had been transformed with tall, new, modern office buildings of steel and glass. When we took a bus to visit Nery Barrientos in Viña del Mar, the new highway was smooth and multi-lane. The bus itself was ultra-comfortable with room for passengers with long legs. We were looking at the misnamed "Chilean Miracle," for which the "Chicago Boys" took credit. The "Chicago Boys" were neo-con economists from the University of Chicago, followers of Milton Friedman.

Greg Palast exposed the "Miracle" as a mirage. After nine years of Chicago-style economics, Chile's industry keeled over and died. GDP dropped by 19 per cent for 1982 and 1983." At that point, the "Chicago Boys" went home.[33]

---

[33] Greg Palast. January 18, 2011. http://www.gregpalast.com/miracle-cure-but-the-medicine-was-bright-red/.

Palast credits state ownership of the copper mines, nation-alized under Allende, for pulling Chile out of deep crisis. Pinochet had been afraid to touch state ownership of copper although he privatized everything else. The big increase in copper prices funded some of the new highways that impress tourists. But what about the people? Palast cites some alarming statistics.

Frank Lumpkin helping Volodia Teitelboim celebrate his 90th Birthday, Santiago, Chile, 2006

"In 1973, the year General Pinochet brutally seized the government, Chile's unemployment rate was 4.3%. In 1983, after ten years of free-market modernization, unemployment reached 22%. Real wages declined by 40% under military rule. In 1970, 20% of Chile's population lived in poverty. By 1990, the year "President" Pinochet left office, the number of desti-tute had doubled to 40%."[34]

Nancy Diaz, a retired professor of French studies, told us about the real conditions that tourists don't see. "Poor people from the slums outside Santiago don't even come into the

---

[34] *Ibid.*

city," Diaz told us. "The police don't want them here and they harass them." We asked where the slum residents worked. Diaz replied, "They work for low wages in factories outside the city. And many are unemployed."

Frank and I were lucky to have picked a good time to revisit Chile. We were just in time for Volodia Teitelboim's 90th birthday dinner. We had met Teitelboim on our earlier trip to Chile. It was wonderful to meet him again. The birthday dinner was just a few days after Michelle Bachelet became the first woman president. Hope was in the air.

José Cardemartori, Minister of Finance under Allende, Susan Borenstein, leader of Chile Solidarity in U.S., Author, Ana Recabarren[35].

35 Ana Recabarren continued fighting for justice although her husband, son, daughter and daughter-in-law were killed by Pinochet police.

Chapter *26*

Steeltown—A Good Life?

It was not easy being the wife of a steel worker.

United Steelworkers protesting President Bush's invasion of Iraq.
Women of Steel: Blanca Morales, Author, Sue Maroko

Travel and our community work as Communists enriched our family life. But on a daily basis, the Lumpkin family lived pretty much the same life as the steel worker families around us. We all went to work to support our families. Thanks to the union, we earned enough money to raise our children to become productive members of the community. To Frank, the job meant even more than that. He loved working in the mill. In part, that was because he loved working with machinery. The larger part was his love for his fellow workers. Like his fellow workers, Frank went to work well before shift time. He did not like to rush. There would be enough rushing when shift began.

The time before the shift was social time, talking in the locker room. The conversations covered many topics, from ancient Egypt to current political elections. More than once, Frank's first quest when he came home from work was to look for a book. He wanted a book on the subject they had debated in the mill that day. Frank was either trying to prove a point or find more information. Information was ammunition for the next day's debate in the locker room. The discussion often continued around the salamander where they heated their lunch.

From a story Frank told me about Phil, I gained some insight into what the job meant to many steel workers. Phil was forced to retire when he reached 65. He had worked at Wisconsin Steel mill for 47 years. The day after he retired, he came into the locker room to talk to his buddies. When they went out to start their shift, Phil took a shower, dressed and went home. The next day he came in and did the same thing. The day after, it was also the same. Finally the company barred him from entering. They claimed their insurance did not allow retired workers to come into the plant. Stories like this changed my understanding of work. I had thought work was something you did only because you had to. Frank showed me that there was joy in work. The job was much more than the paycheck. It was the worker's identity, her contribution to society and a source of pride.

When Wisconsin Steel closed, people talked about losing "good" jobs. What was good about working in a place that was hot, dirty and dangerous? The easy answer was, "the pay check." After the mills closed, the only jobs they could get paid only half their steel worker's pay. Those jobs were in a far suburb, and the commute was expensive. "And they expect you to set up your own machines, too!" exclaimed one of the newly unemployed Wisconsin Steel workers. Steel worker's pay took care of a family's minimum needs. That was impossible on $4 per hour, less than half the pay. Another benefit lost in the plant closing was union protection. The union made the huge difference in working conditions. I never heard anyone say the steel mill was a good place to work before the CIO organized the mills. The talk used to be more like, "I don't want my kids to work in the mill."

Before the Union

I heard a lot about conditions "before the union" from Russ DePasquale. He was one of the Communist leaders I met in Buffalo in 1943. DePasquale helped the CIO organize Bethlehem Steel in Lackawanna, New York. After the CIO won a contract, Russ was elected president of the union local at the mill. Before the union, his job in the mill was extremely hard and heavy. At the end of the shift, he did not have enough strength left to walk across the street to his car. He had to sit down on the street curb and rest first. When he made it to his house, he rang the bell for his sister to help him up the stairs. And he was only 19 at the time and strong as a bull!

Then the company fired him for organizing. But they had to call him back because nobody else was strong enough to do his job. DePasquale told me that after the union won a contract, the company put three men on his job. Each worked twenty minutes on and forty minutes off each hour. I cannot forget the stories he told about hard times in the 1930s. His baby was sick and needed some medicine. Russ took the prescription to the drug store although he had no money. The pharmacist said, "You've already run up a big bill."

"He looked at me, and I looked at him," Russ said. "Then he gave me the medicine. I must have looked like I would kill for the medicine. The truth is I don't know what I would have done, had he *not* given it to me."

Before the union, hiring for the mill was done from a "shape-up." Men lined up at the gate and the foremen felt their muscles. The men felt like cattle at an auction. Then the foreman would point and say, "You, you and you. That's all for today." Those who did not get the nod left with nothing to bring their families. It was said that you had to slip the foreman some money or other present to get hired. Abolition of the shape-up was a priority demand of the workers.

Wisconsin Steel was no different. There had been a mill at 106th Street and Torrence Avenue since 1875. The first steel mill built in Chicago was at that site and was called Brown's Iron and Steel Company. In 1905, International Harvester bought the mill from Brown. Why did Harvester name the mill Wisconsin Steel? That's an odd name for a mill in South Chicago. According to the official company history, it was cheaper to incorporate in Wisconsin. It was all about the company making more profit and paying less tax. Since that time, many generations of families worked there. One brother recommended another brother for a job. When the mill closed, all the brothers lost their jobs at the same time. One could not help the other.

Many nations contributed workers for Wisconsin Steel. They came from Ireland, Germany, Poland, Serbia, Croatia, Italy and other places. Mexican workers joined the work force, starting in the 1920s. They had worked on the railroads and traveled with their jobs to Chicago. Some stayed, got jobs at the steel mills and sent for their families. But no African Americans were hired at Wisconsin Steel for almost 40 years. In other South Chicago steel mills, African Americans made up over 23% of the work force. The long-time Wisconsin Steel company practice was "divide and rule." As the superintendent of Wisconsin Steel stated in the 1930s, "I will not have Negroes in the plant."[36] During World War II, Franklin D. Roosevelt set up the Fair Employment Practices Commission (FEPC). FEPC forced Harvester, owner of Wisconsin Steel, to start hiring African Americans. Fair employment was a condition for receiving federal contracts during World War II.

---

[36] Horace B. Davis, *Labor and Steel* (New York: International Publishers, 1933), 33.

Frank admired the first African Americans hired by Wisconsin Steel. Their courage was still legendary when Frank started there in March, 1950. "They sat down while they were waiting for steel." he told me. Before that, Wisconsin Steel workers were afraid to be seen "sitting down on the job." "After a while," Frank added, "other workers began sitting down if there was no steel to work on. The company finally put in benches for them."

I could relate to that story because I had worked as a waiter, formerly called "waitress." Even if all customers were already served, we had to stand. Never get caught sitting down! Some might say that's not a big thing, but it is, if you're standing on your feet all day. Your feeling of being a wage slave is reinforced when the boss says you have to stand just because he says so. In the day-to-day battle between workers and bosses, it makes a big difference if you don't have to be afraid of being fired without just cause. On most jobs, it was the union that made the difference. At Wisconsin Steel, workers did not have union protection. The company had succeeded in keeping out the USWA, United Steelworkers of America-CIO. They put in a one-company union and kept a real union out by paying the same wages and benefits that USWA had won. That "bargain" set the stage for a later tragedy.

During World War II, the shortage of labor gave workers more leverage. Our friend Ed Sadlowski, the steel worker leader, told me that workers could go from mill to mill and get hired immediately. That was a time of full employment. In fact, that was the only time, since I began working in 1933, that there was full employment. Full employment, to me, means having a job for everyone who wants to work. What a lousy system capitalism is, that it took a World War to have full employment! It's even worse than that now. The wars since World War II have failed to supply more employment. During the Vietnam War there were many unemployed, and during the Iraq War, the country plunged into a serious recession.

Racist Barriers on the Job

When Frank started working at Wisconsin Steel in March 1950, about 30% of the workers were African American. Another

40% were Latinos, mostly Mexican. Still, the company's racist "divide and rule" practices continued in another form. For example, Frank applied for a job in the mill's steam power plant in 1950. With years of work in ship's engine rooms, he was highly qualified. But the foreman told him right out, "We don't have any colored in this department." I heard the same story from another Wisconsin Steel worker who wanted to be a diesel mechanic. He decided to spend his own money for diesel mechanic school. Eventually, he broke through the barriers and was promoted at Wisconsin Steel. As a diesel mechanic, he was one of the few to find comparable work when the plant closed.

The racist divide was deepened by real estate practices in the Wisconsin Steel neighborhood. For years the area was restricted to "white families only." By 1950, some Mexican families had moved to the South Deering area. Still, not one African American family could rent or buy in that neighborhood. In 1953, four African American families moved into South Deering. They rented apartments in the relatively new and desirable public housing in Trumbull Park. A vicious white riot was organized, as described in a previous chapter. But inside the plant, workers put racial apartheid aside. The work, itself, called for cooperation and respect among the workers.

Steel Worker's Wife

It was not easy being the wife of a steel worker. In the first place, if you lived near the mill, everything got dirty faster. In our first Chicago apartment, I had to wash the curtains every three weeks. As I write this, I am looking at drapes that I have not washed for 18 months, and they look fine. So it's not that I'm particular. But after three weeks near the mills in 1950, the curtains were heavy with soot. That was before we knew the damage that soot did to our lungs. At least we could wash the curtains.

The extra cleaning was not the hardest part. The hardest part for me was trying to have a "normal" family life while Frank was changing shifts every week. It was hard to impossible to gather all family members together at the same time. Children go to school on the day shift. For the children, as a minimum, the steel worker's wife prepared three meals between 7 a.m. and 6 p.m. When the steel worker worked 3 p.m. to 11 p.m., another meal had to be served about midnight. In those years I always worked days, so getting enough sleep was a problem. Or else I left the meal out for Frank to warm up. That was dangerous and may have had serious consequences. I have always suspected that a lamb stew I once left out for Frank spoiled before he got to it. Food poisoning could have induced the heart attack that Frank suffered in 1955 at age 38.

In many ways, the "midnight" shift was the worst. Frank never complained about it, not once. But the wife's job, when she was home, was to keep the kids quiet so dad could sleep. Since I worked during the week, I worried about that only on weekends. Frank slept only in bits and snatches during the day. Paul and John took advantage of the time after school and before I got home. They could ask their dad for anything while he was sleeping, and he would always say, "Yes." It is easy to see why most steel workers' wives stayed home and did not work.

Holidays were the hardest part for me as a steel worker's wife. Neither Frank nor I came from families that had made a big thing out of the holidays. Frank often said that Hattie and Elmo had nothing special to give their ten kids for Christmas, maybe a piece of fruit. They lived in a plantation worker's house in Conway and later rented a four-room house in Orlando. There was no room big enough for twelve people to eat at the same time. So the pretty picture of a large family gathered around a dinner table was not possible.

That was also true for my family; tenement apartments were small. Sometimes we did go to my aunt's large apartment for Passover Seders. But that was not our nuclear family gathered in closeness, like the Hollywood ideal. My mother insisted on cooking big Sunday dinners, her only day off from the laundry. But I do not remember big dinners on the holiday. So I tried to supply for my kids what I believed I had missed. I tried very hard to have extra special dinners with Frank, me and our four kids on the national holidays, and Jewish and

Christian holidays. I never believed we had to be believers to celebrate a holiday.

That was all good and well. I could knock myself out, stuff a turkey, fix the trimmings, and bake some pies. But when would we all sit down together and ceremoniously devour the good food? Too often, Frank was absent. On his part, it was hard to get into the holiday spirit while he was holding a chipping hammer or behind a scarfing torch. I never quit trying to have a big holiday dinner. Sometimes I succeeded. Still, there was something much worse than having to work and missing the holiday with the family. That was having the day off, and the next one and the next, because there was no job.

Frank, with grandmother, mother and father,
Buffalo, NY, another steeltown

Chapter 27

Annihilation of Wisconsin Steel
"If you can't find a leader, be a leader."

IN another book, *"Always Bring A Crowd"—The Story of Frank Lumpkin, Steelworker*, I wrote about the Wisconsin Steel workers' lengthy struggle for justice. Here I give just a short account in terms of my personal experience.

On Friday, March 28, 1980, the steel-town life I described above came to a sudden halt. The mill where Frank worked for 30 years closed without notice. Frank came home from work Thursday saying, "There's a rumor that the mill is closing." The next day, the workers found the gate padlocked. Suddenly, 3,400 workers were out on the street, no job, no health insurance, no pension and no closing benefits. An open hearth worker summed up the feeling of the workers: "I felt like they lined me up against the wall and shot me." To make things worse, there was no union to help them. The company union closed its doors when money from dues check-offs stopped coming in.

In some ways, the 1980 closing of Wisconsin Steel struck southeast Chicago harder than the Great Depression of the 1930s. In the '30s, the steel mills banked furnaces and laid off the workers. But the mills remained standing. Hope stayed alive. In contrast, Wisconsin Steel was not just closed in 1980. It has been totally destroyed, annihilated. The prairie has taken over, as it has at nearby U.S. Steel, Republic Steel and Acme Steel. The Wisconsin Steel shutdown was only the first in what became an avalanche of steel mill closings in Chicago.

364 JOY IN THE STRUGGLE

When Wisconsin Steel first closed, we did not understand what had happened. In time we learned that we were victims of corporate fraud. In 1977, International Harvester, owner of Wisconsin Steel for 75 years, dumped the mill. They wanted to avoid paying pensions and closing benefits. The way they did it was to "loan" a tiny company the money to "buy" Wisconsin Steel with its 3,400 employees. The company, named Envirodyne, was just a shell. It was owned by a couple of engineers and had less than 20 employees. In less than three years after the "sale," Wisconsin Steel went bankrupt. Harvester thought they were in the clear. And they would have gotten away with it, had it not been for Frank Lumpkin and the Save Our Jobs Committee.

Frank was 64 when Wisconsin Steel closed. For a year I had been after him to retire. When a half ton of steel broke his foot, I took the injury as a warning. "Get out," I begged him, "While the rest of you is still in one piece." Good thing Frank did not listen to me! When the plant closed, he came forward to give leadership to thousands of Wisconsin Steel workers, left with nowhere to turn. As he put it, "If you can't find a leader, be a leader."

Within a couple weeks of the plant closing, Frank began to organize the workers' fightback. He started with fellow workers from the scarfing dock, meeting in the basement of our home. Soon men from other departments joined to form the Wisconsin Steel Workers Save Our Jobs Committee. The company told them nothing about the closing. Not one word. Just don't come in tomorrow— maybe never. So the committee's first job was to try to find out what was happening. Would the mill reopen? Would the company make good on their last paychecks that bounced? For lack of a real union, workers began to flock around Frank and the Save Our Jobs Committee (SOJ).

Save Our Jobs Committee

Save Our Jobs (SOJ), as it was called in Southeast Chicago, became well known throughout Chicago and beyond. I never saw a group of workers learn so fast. Aside from Frank, few

Wisconsin Steel workers had ever carried picket signs. But when television cameras turned their way, they picked up their signs and held them high. Then Wisconsin Steel workers began marching all over Chicago. In time they became the most experienced picketers in the city. Every year, for 16 years, they picketed the mill on the March 28th anniversary of the closing. Every year, they picketed the International Harvester stockholders meetings. They did not even change their signs. Year after year, the signs read "We want justice," or "Harvester, pay us our money." All they had to do, as the years rolled on, was paste a new number on the signs: "Waiting 1 year, Waiting 2 years, Waiting 3 years, … Waiting 16 years." The final settlement checks, from their last employer, came just two months short of 17 years after the mill had closed.

There was an important side benefit of the Save Our Jobs struggle. Their fight for benefits helped save the community from demoralization. Thousands of workers learned the value of solidarity. It was a beautiful thing to see and be part of. Many steel worker wives told me that they were glad that their husbands were going to Save Our Jobs meetings. "It keeps him out of the tavern," one said. "It gives him something to do," another added. As the support for our cause grew, many Wisconsin Steel workers began to realize that they were making history. They felt that they were fighting for more than just their own family. And that made them proud.

Community organizations of all types helped Save Our Jobs continue the fight for justice. This support was crucial when we needed to send three buses to take our case to the floor of Congress and to the Pension Benefit Guaranty Corporation (PBGC). The small storekeepers, beauty salon owners, even the local banks, all contributed thousands of dollars to send the buses. Local churches opened up their doors and their hearts to Save Our Jobs. Uniting the community rolled back some of the racism that had divided the steel communities. That was especially true on the East Side.

Chicago's East Side was home to many steel workers, then all white. For almost a century, real estate interests had prevented families of color from locating there. I was a poll watcher in an East Side precinct when Harold Washington ran for mayor in 1983. Washington won that citywide election. But in the precinct I watched, like most on the East Side, he got only 5 votes out of the 325 cast.

These racist prejudices were overcome when the Wisconsin Steel workers began to fight for justice. Workers saw the need for unity. Frank and I drove to the East Side one afternoon, at the height of the SOJ struggle. Frank had been reluctant to go because of the area's racist history. But he got a very friendly reception. Workers came over to ask, "How are you, Frank? How's our case going?" The racists did not show their face.

Frank helped win union support for SOJ, and that was not easy. In the past, Wisconsin Steel workers had not supported the United Steel Workers of America (USWA). Frank and his friends tried, but never succeeded in bringing in a real union. Under the company union, Wisconsin Steel worked full blast during national steel strikes. After the strikes, the Wisconsin Steel workers pocketed the same raises the union won. That was all past history. The company union disbanded after the mill closed. It was the new Save Our Jobs that was fighting for workers' rights. For progressive leaders of USWA, it was a question of principle. They ended up giving full support to SOJ. That solidarity paid off for the union, too. Save Our Jobs brought massive support to the union's picket lines and rallies.

Until their mill closed in 1980, some of the Wisconsin Steel workers thought they had a bargain in the company union. In the end, they realized they had made a mistake. With a real union, the company could not have closed without paying workers their closing benefits. Some thought that the company had paid off the president of the company union and its attorney, Ed (Fast Eddie) Vrdolyak. I, too, suspected a payoff.

I don't have the proof, but I believe the proof is still out there, someplace. In those years, Ed Vrdolyak was a powerful Chicago Alderman. He became infamous in 1983 for leading the racist attack on Harold Washington, Chicago's first African American mayor. Incredibly, Vrdolyak eventually pled guilty to defrauding a school of millions of dollars and was sentenced to 10 months in prison. According to the prosecutors, Vrdolyak has been repeatedly disciplined by the Illinois Supreme Court for unethical conduct as a lawyer. The 3,400 Wisconsin Steel workers were not his only victims.

After a year of SOJ demonstrations, mass picket lines, press conferences and mass attendance at bankruptcy court, Frank found a lawyer willing to take the workers' case. Many lawyers had turned Frank down. Finally, talented Tom Geoghegan, of the well-known labor law firm of Len Despres, stepped forward. Geoghegan said he could not say, "No," to Frank Lumpkin. Not until seven years later, were Geoghegan and Despres compensated for their work and expenses. They were true heroes to the Wisconsin Steel workers.

Although Save Our Jobs did not save the steel workers' jobs, they won important victories. Geoghegan had sued International Harvester, the long-time Wisconsin Steel employer. In 1988, eight years after the closing, Harvester was forced to pay close to $15 million to 2,700 hourly Wisconsin Steel workers. That was just a fraction of what the company owed the workers. Still, the settlement money saved many homes from foreclosure. Workers were also glad that the company did not walk away without a scratch after trying to dump the workers' pensions.

Then SOJ sued Envirodyne, last employer of Wisconsin Steel workers. At the end of 1996, Envirodyne settled with SOJ for another $4,000,000. They should have paid much more, but the court allowed them to declare a phony bankruptcy. In fact, Envirodyne had become a Fortune 500 company, leveraging the money they got from the phony Wisconsin Steel sale. They could well have afforded to pay us. As Frank often said, "It was legal but not just," and, "Bankruptcy laws were not written for the workers."

Women of "Save Our Jobs"

Save Our Jobs could not have stuck it out for so many years without the support of the steel worker families, especially the spouses. That is where I tried to help. Often, I could not help in the day-to-day actions and decision making because I had to work. I did write press releases and leaflets, even booklets presenting our case. But my main contribution, I believe, was bringing the wives together, making Save Our Jobs a family affair.

In organizing the Wisconsin Steel Workers Women's Committee, I followed Frank's model of unity. Every activity equally involved Latina, African American and white women. Some of the women already knew each other from their church work or from the community. But most of us had not met the other Women's Committee members before. As we worked together, we gained respect for each other. And with respect came love.

The Women's Committee started out with our specialty, food. Save Our Jobs expenses were minimal. Our office space was donated, starting with the Lumpkin house. Our first real office was donated by State Representative Miriam Balanoff. Next, we had donated space above Roma's Restaurant on South Chicago Avenue. Then we moved to the USWA's Hilding Anderson Hall where we stayed until we won our court suits. Even our furniture and file cabinets were donated, thanks to the Community Renewal Society. Still, we had to raise money for the telephone bill, printing flyers, and fees for copying legal documents. So we decided to give a dinner to raise money. USWA Local 65 donated their hall, and all the food was donated. To make it affordable for jobless steel workers, we sold dinner tickets for $3.00. Would you believe that we made $3,000?

All of the TV networks had come to film the event. They could not help but focus on the collection of colorful gelatin desserts, a Mexican tradition. Their attention was also grabbed by the folklorico dances performed by Nancy Andrade's seventh grade class. Nancy is the daughter of Jose Andrade, Frank's partner at the mill. There were many proud families when footage of our dinner-rally appeared on TV network channels. Cable was new then but we even appeared on the start-up channel, CNN.

In a few months, the Women's Committee followed up with another dinner that netted $2,000. Over the years, the dinners became annual affairs. After 16 years, we were still giving dinners. Most of us were content to just eat and listen to the music. I was among the few who still got up and tried to dance. Our

Women's Committee branched out to action beyond fund raisers and cooking the food. More women began to march and picket with the men.

Switching Gender Roles

The mill closing was hard on the men. Perhaps it was even harder on the women. Many who had never worked outside of the home began to look for paid work, no matter how low the pay. For example, my friend Carmen had six children. That was enough work, right in the home. But her husband's unemployment compensation ran out, and they had to go on welfare. She felt it was like selling herself into slavery, the questions you had to answer.

Finally, there was no other way. As Carmen put it, she had occasionally worked outside the home before. But now it was like, "Hey, you're not going to make it unless you find some work." Carmen made the rounds of local stores until she got three days' work a week. After her first day at work, Carmen came home from work to find the breakfast dishes still in the sink. Husband and children were lounging in front of the TV set, and nothing had been cooked for dinner. "That's not what I do when you go to work," Carmen had to tell her husband.

With husbands unemployed and their wives working, a degree of role switching took place It reminded me of the film, *Salt of the Earth*. (I watch that film again and again; it's such a good women's rights movie.) It was comical the way Ray Gutierrez described his situation. His wife got a job at Goldblatt's Department Store when Wisconsin Steel closed. So Ray had to stay home with the kids. When his wife came home from work, he met her at the door. As they kissed, he told us, he bent one leg back, as the wives do in the movies.

Where Did All the Workers Go?

When Wisconsin steel closed on March 28, 1980, there were 3,400 on the payroll, 2,700 of them hourly workers. Many left Chicago in 1980 in the hope of finding work elsewhere. Some may have been lucky, but most came back to Chicago empty-handed. Most of the Wisconsin Steel families stayed right where they were. Only a few found comparable jobs, in other mills or working for Chicago Transit Authority. They were the lucky ones with specialized skills. In time, most of the younger workers found other work but at much reduced pay. That left over half of the work force, 40 or 50 years old, as the long-term unemployed.

A Save Our Jobs' officer, Wayne Schwartz, had been a mill electrician. The sudden closing of Wisconsin Steel left his family without health insurance. Since his wife was taking cancer treatments, Schwartz had to have health insurance. In the private market, it cost him many thousands a month. He and his electrician partner, Carl Dutko, tried to get odd jobs in their trade. It did not go well. They worked in private homes and ended up not being paid. Then they worked as low-paid security guards. Benjamin Muñoz, another Save Our Jobs leader, found work in factories that were not union and paid low wages. When he became old enough for a pension, Muñoz became one of the volunteers who staffed the Save Our Jobs office full-time.

After unemployment compensation ran out, our families became desperate. We fought together with other workers and won an extension of unemployment benefits. But the extension ran out after six months. Many had no choice but to go on welfare. Some fathers moved out of their homes so their wives and children could get welfare. Families would meet in the park so dad could see his children. Hungry families needed help, so Save Our Jobs opened up a food pantry. Families lined up in the street and waited for food, even during heavy rains. More and more workers died. The funeral announcements kept pouring into the Save Our Jobs office. We tried again and again to get those statistics, but the company would not release the figure. Some committed suicide; we don't know how many. There were also more reports of families breaking up. What made things worse is that other mills began to slow down or shut down, too.

Rank and File Leadership Style

"Save Jobs Committees" had started in 1979 at Pittsburgh mills but disbanded after a year or two. They had organized massive protests, but could not keep the movement going. In contrast, the Wisconsin Steel Save Our Jobs Committee was active for 17 years, from 1980 to 1997. How was Frank able to keep SOJ together for so many years?

There were favorable factors that helped. First, Chicago is a union town; the United Steelworkers gave SOJ a home. The Wisconsin Steel workers also had the support of progressive public officials. These included Congressman, and later Mayor, Harold Washington; State Representative, and later U.S. Senator, Carol Moseley Braun; Congressman Gus Savage; State Senator Richard Newhouse; and State Representative Miriam Balanoff, followed by her son, Clem Balanoff, Jr. Consumer organizations such as Illinois Public Action Council, now Citizen Action of Illinois, gave important support. The rank and file labor monthly, *Labor Today*, and its editors Fred Gaboury and Scott Marshall, gave SOJ national coverage. Environmental, civil rights and women's organizations also supported SOJ.

Wisconsin Steel workers in Washington, DC

Two very important factors were Frank's leadership style and the brilliant legal work of Tom Geoghegan. Both Frank and Tom understood that continued SOJ activism helped pressure the companies to settle our court suits. Frank believed in rank-and-file leadership. The SOJ membership made all the decisions. Many new rank-and-file leaders were encouraged to come forward. There were 35 executive board members listed on the SOJ letterhead. Wisconsin Steel workers, racially divided by the company, united behind the multiracial leadership of SOJ. It could not have been done without full equality inside the movement.

I believe that Frank's social vision, his Communist beliefs, strengthened his faith in workers. For him, the biggest part of the Save Our Jobs victory was the empowerment of his co-workers. He told Tom Geoghegan that the fight would have been worthwhile, even if they had not won the money. Geoghegan was puzzled. But I think I understand. Frank's goal was to unite and educate workers to end exploitation, to end capitalism. He often told me, "The system (capitalism) does not work." His goal was a system that puts people before profits—socialism. Everything that united workers and built their fighting strength was a step towards a better system. Besides, Frank enjoyed every day of the fight. He loved watching his coworkers grow in the struggle.

Luckily, I was off work when Frank led over 1,000 workers on a march to the Economic Development Administration (EDA) office. As the biggest creditor, EDA had just acquired the Wisconsin Steel mills and the 280 acres on which it sat. The federal government owned the plant. The workers were demanding that EDA open and operate the mill.

We were received by a visibly shaking, frightened EDA director. I am sure he sent our message to Washington. But Ronald Reagan, the newly elected Republican President, had no plans to operate a nationally owned steel mill.

I was working so I missed the Wisconsin Steel workers' bus trip to Springfield, the state capital. There, workers were greeted and escorted by State Representatives Carol Moseley Braun and Miriam Balanoff. Most of all, I was sorry not to go with the three busloads of Save Our Jobs members who went to Washington, DC in 1981. In DC, they were given one hour of time on the official Congressional Agenda. As the Wisconsin Steel workers sat and applauded in the galleries, they heard a half dozen Illinois Congressmen praise their efforts. One was Harold Washington, soon to be elected mayor of Chicago. That was all recorded in the *Congressional Record, U.S. House of Representatives*, April 9, 1981.

From the Capitol, SOJ marched to the Pension Benefit Guaranty Corporation (PBGC). With so many congressmen supporting the workers, PBGC opened the purse strings and began paying the insured amount of the pension. Sadly, laws and regulations have changed since 1980, making things even harder for workers. Under the George W. Bush presidency, many who lost their jobs in plant closings lost years of their pensions. There were so many thousands of bad regulations under Bush that it will take years to change them.

Underestimating Workers

Among workers, there is a deep reservoir of leadership potential. I saw it with Frank when the mill closed and the company union quit. Frank rose to the occasion. Just ten years earlier, I had seen it at Malcolm X College when John Yeatman came forward to lead the union in a crisis. Then I saw it again when Yeatman died. Bruce Hayden came up from the rank and file and picked up the torch that Yeatman had carried. Those experiences convinced me of the potential of rank and file leaders.

There were some who made the mistake of thinking that I was masterminding the SOJ movement. That was wrong. Those friends underestimated the ability of workers to become leaders. In particular, they underestimated the leadership capacity of African American workers like Frank, who dropped out of high school to work full time. As a side issue, they also misunderstood the relationship between Frank and me, as though I were the "brains" of the family. Of course, our children never made that mistake. I never wanted a "brains" competition in our family; I didn't want to lose. Also, children are more apt than adults to judge people for what they are, not for a piece of paper that reads, "College Degree."

The underlying issue, I think, is leadership style. Working class leaders are not necessarily the greatest orators among the workers. The great orators often become preachers. I found a remark by "little Manuel," Frank's coworker, very revealing. Manuel told me, "Frank surprised me. He was always so quiet in the mill." It was true that Frank did not make long, flowery speeches. But when he sent out a call to organize after the mill closed, workers responded. They responded because Frank proposed action and convinced his coworkers that they had the power to win.

Summing it up

The closing of Wisconsin Steel and the long fight to pay the workers' benefits was a turning point in my husband's life. Our lives were so intertwined that it became a turning point for my life, too. Two and a half years after the mill closed, Save Our Jobs was requiring my full-time attention. So I took early retirement. But after five years, I was ready to go back to work. The city college job was gone, but high school teaching jobs were available. I continued my volunteer work with the steel workers, but on a part-time basis.

Part 4
(1986–2008)

Chapter *28*

Bowen High School
Chicago teachers, my heroes

MY return to the high school classroom led to one of my most productive work experiences. Thanks to the civil rights movement, school administrators allowed the use of multicultural materials in the classrooms. That gave me an opportunity to impact the Chicago Public School curriculum. I introduced some contributions to mathematics by people of color, especially those of Latinos and African Americans.

I started my return to the high school classroom with a few days of on-call substitute teaching. A few days were enough. It was an invaluable experience. I saw a cross section of Chicago high schools. In my first two days at Kenwood High School, I experienced the sublime. Even the food in the teachers' lunchroom was almost good. My schedule included a French class. I remembered enough to attempt to teach French. It was all so very, very "advanced." In the lunchroom, the geology teacher explained to me why the earth's magnetic poles switch about every 5,000 years. How nice.

The next two days were different. I was down in the basement with much larger classes in "Essential Mathematics." That proved to be not so sublime. The students did not like it, and neither did I. Nor did I like the racist patterns in the Chicago schools. The French class, a high-school level subject, was filled with mostly white students. Essential Mathematics, a remedial level class, was African American except for one student. I realized that Kenwood had two schools in the same building. I had experienced the same thing with my own children at Proviso High School in Maywood.

One of the two Kenwood schools offered many opportunities. The other was segregated, with little chance to advance. Essential Mathematics was designed for students who scored low in mathematics. Many had developed an intense dislike for the subject. So CPS made the class twice as long, so students could have twice as much of what they did not like. What was CPS thinking? That these students were slower so they needed more time? From what I saw, the students were not slow at all. That was not the problem.

I had one positive experience in those Essential Mathematics classes. It was my introduction to rap as an art form of the people. One of the students, trying to put the substitute teacher down, began to rap. I had never heard such a free flow of poetry in a classroom before. I was pleased and amazed. Probably the student was amazed, too, because I called him up front to perform for the class. That shut him up. But others were not so easily intimidated. They gladly volunteered until I was forced to cut it off and get back to the lesson. There should have been some way to turn some of that creative energy to learning.

My next gig was at King High School. When they told me it was library duty, it sounded like a choice assignment. Fine, I could help students find books, work on reports, or even help with homework. Once there, I was shown where to stand and survey my charges. Nothing happened. I guess that was good but I did not feel that I was doing my job. So I asked a couple of students if I could help them. They seemed surprised. I saw a student with her head down on the desk, resting in her hands. I should have remembered that I had done the same thing as a high school student, because of lack of sleep. But it seemed more than not enough sleep. "Are you all right?" I asked. She looked up, seemed annoyed and declared loudly, "I'm pregnant." I did not have a reply for that.

Finally, another teacher on library duty asked me what I was doing. I said that I was trying to help students who were working on reports. Or helping students find the books that they needed. That turned out to be the wrong thing to say. My colleague gave me a disapproving look and patiently explained: "That's not our job," she told me. Our job, as she explained it, was to keep law and order in the library. Englewood High School was my next call to substitute. I was assigned a typing class. How hard could that be? I don't even remember if the class was co-ed. An incident among the young women in the class crowded out any other memory.

One student had just returned to school after a two-week suspension from school. Everything happened so fast that I never saw what triggered the upheaval. Next thing I realized, the returning student was on the floor, on top of another student. One second later, all of the students rose from their seats and divided into backers of one student or the other.

The commotion ended in a flash, just as it had begun. An administrator came into the room, removed the student who had just returned from suspension, and the class settled down. The next day, I was sent to the special education rooms. It was explained to me that the regular teacher was wonderful. He had taught the students chess. That was my assignment, to let them play chess. I let them play chess.

Bowen High School

Somehow, these substitute teacher gigs were not working out as I had hoped. If I wanted a chance to teach, I needed my own classes with the same students every day. So I got a job at Bowen High School as a full-time-basis substitute teacher. Bowen was next to Bessemer Park, a short distance from U.S. Steel's Southworks. The neighborhood surrounding the school had been made up of neat, well-maintained steel workers' homes. That changed in the early 1980s. Street gangs had become a problem. The gangs were made up of young people who felt that their future was gone after the mills closed.

I knew I was nearing Bowen High School when I was two blocks away. As soon as I passed the telephone company building, the graffiti began. Nor did it stop at the school building itself. Graffiti all over the school building was a bad omen, I thought. Once inside the building, I was invited into the principal's office. A mural, painted on the wall of his office, showed the pouring of a heat of steel. But steel was no longer being poured in the mills near the school. I looked out of the window at the steel workers' homes that faced the school. The mills were down, but the people were still there. Their children would be my students, and I was determined to do my best for them.

My Bowen schedule included some "good" classes. I was lucky. Because I had a degree in history and political science as well as math, I got a civics and an economics class as well as three mathematics classes. It was interesting trying to teach "civics" to 38 students, including 12 labeled "special ed." I should have filed a grievance since the class size limit was 32. My big concern was to help the "special ed" students.

The mislabeling of students in our inner city schools as "special ed" is a major scandal. It is a crime that cuts short the educational development of tens of thousands of students. "Over 50% of our students are 'special ed,'" a "progressive" teacher once told me. I was shocked. My friend had swallowed this racist classification. By definition, "special ed" students cannot make up the majority of students at a neighborhood school. Indeed, some of my civics students labeled "special ed" were very good students.

Soon after my arrival at Bowen High School, I asked about the computer lab. "It's closed," I was told. During the summer, someone had broken into the school and shot 13 computers. "In the heart?" I wondered. Did the vandal come from one of the steel worker families that lost everything when the mills shut down? Perhaps the vandal blamed technology for the mass unemployment in steeltown. Then I realized that we cannot look into the heart or the brain of the vandal(s). It could have been an ex-student with a grievance against teachers or administrators. Meanwhile, we had no computer lab.

When I saw the movie *Stand and Deliver*, I truly sympathized with Jaime Escalante. But I could not rise to such great heights. Escalante became an exceptionally gifted teacher even though his school's computer lab was wrecked. I was not that exceptional. I had a life and a family outside of teaching. Nobody made a movie about me, and not all of my students went on to college. Still, I like to think that I was a good teacher, although not superhuman.

As a union activist, I was encouraged by the thinking of my economics students. To actively engage them, I divided the class into two informal debating teams. We debated current economic topics. My students were strongly and instinctively pro-union. Naturally, that pleased me. But on foreign policy issues, I was surprised by the lack of interest. The year was 1987, between the Vietnam War and 9/11 at the World Trade Center. However, it was the height of the Cold War. The huge military budget was hurting our economy. The nuclear war danger remained high. I tried to stir up some interest in foreign affairs but continued to draw a blank. Except for Mexico, all other countries seemed too far away.

About half of the student body was African American. The other half was mostly students of Mexican descent. But my honors classes, much like the French class at Kenwood High School, had very few African American students. A lack of unity between the two communities made it hard for parents to improve the school. Some outside organizations worsened the situation. They provided buses to bring parents in to vote in the elections for the local school council. An all-Latino school council was elected. They were all good people. But they did not have the strength that a united council could have delivered.

The Teachers, My Heroes

Unfortunately, the principal had ties to neither of the two school communities. He remained holed up in his office. It seemed to me that he had given up on the school. Students roamed the halls with no purpose, entering class late or not at all. Inside my classroom, I can truthfully say that some learning went on. Not enough. Outside the classrooms, it was sheer anarchy in the halls. The school administration looked on helplessly, or they did not care. I don't know which; the effect was the same.

Then the teachers got tired of administrative inaction. They took matters into their own hands. They became volunteer hall monitors. A teachers' committee set up study rooms for students who were late to class and were found wandering in the halls. Another committee drew up a schedule to make sure that hall monitors' posts were covered. But it came at a cost. Teachers gave up their badly needed free time.

I was very proud of my sister and fellow teachers. Their organization and sacrifice made the plan work. Bowen High School changed overnight. I did not know it was the same school. Classes were not disrupted by latecomers, more students were in the classrooms, and the halls were quiet and orderly. The teachers showed that it could be done. No support or even recognition came from the school administration. After a few months, the system began to break down for lack of support. Substitute teachers took over classes when teachers fell ill. These substitutes could not be asked to give up their free periods. After two months, the teachers were worn out. They needed their prep periods. Chaos returned to the corridors. That's how it was until one of the teachers moved up and replaced the retiring principal.

The street gangs that flourished after the mills closed were a big problem. One of my students was afraid to leave the classroom at the end of the day. He opened the door, stepped out, and ran back in. I offered to escort him out, but he declined my offer. I did not know exactly who or what he was dodging. Gang pressure seemed the logical explanation. This tension continued for a week. A couple of weeks later, everything seemed to have changed for him. He looked different, perhaps paler. I had to admit, though, that he seemed more relaxed. My guess was that he had joined the gang. I felt that the school had failed him, but I did not know what more I could do.

One of my most frustrating experiences at Bowen was trying to keep standards high for my advanced algebra class. By coincidence, my grandson was taking the same class at a suburban school with high academic standards. My students were as smart as those in my grandson's class. I was determined to keep up with the best, to give my students the same material that my grandson was studying. At first, it worked. Then it became impossible. There were just too many classes either shortened or canceled altogether. At the least provocation, or so it seemed, class time was cut, or the day ended at noon. We began to slip behind. I still managed to put across the minimum content that my students needed to go on to a higher mathematics class. But I was not able to give them the same enriched content that my grandson was getting.

Multicultural Standards

By Peggy Lipschutz, from author's Senefer and Hatshepsut.

My work in multicultural mathematics proved very helpful in high school teaching. Years earlier, I had teamed up with artist Peggy Lipschutz. She gave chalk talks that brought to life the ancient Egyptian mathematics and pyramids. We also talked about the Mexican pyramids and the Maya and Aztec mathematics. Dr. Dorothy Strong, Director of the CPS Mathematics Bureau, saw one of our shows. Strong was a founder and past president of the Benjamin Banneker Association, an "Equity Leader in Mathematics Education." She called me to the CPS central office to help write standards that included multicultural mathematics. That was one of the most stimulating periods of my life. At night we worked on materials and standards for all the Chicago Public Schools. The next morning, I was back in the classroom, testing our new materials with my own class. I did not get a lot of sleep. That did not matter. It was a wonderful opportunity to learn and to teach. Students in my classes were proud to learn that their ancestors included some of the earliest mathematicians. Students of European descent were also fascinated. They were learning a part of history that had been hidden from them.

Soon after we completed our Chicago standards, a large Texas school district produced theirs. They had copied, word for word, some of the multicultural standards that I had written. Some Chicagoans were annoyed, but I was pleased. Plagiarism of a writer's work is the greatest compliment the writer can get. Besides, I wanted our multicultural standards to spread far and wide. That was my goal—to promote the fight against racism and find a better way to teach.

The Candidate's Wife

During my time at Bowen, SOJ achieved its greatest victory. The $15 million settlement from International Harvester made Frank a hero to many in South Chicago and the South Side of Chicago. Friends and comrades suggested that Frank run for state representative. The goal was to strengthen the movement for political independence. So Frank ran as the candidate of the Independent Progressive Party, a new party created for that campaign. That cast me into yet another role in life, "the candidate's wife."

Many steel workers were active in Frank's campaigns of 1988, 1990 and 1992. We had a large audience for our program on the big issues of the time. But we did not have the money to beat the Stroger machine. That type of victory will come later, as labor strengthens its independent political role.

Chapter 29

"Always Bring A Crowd!"

I wrote it for all of our children and their children.

IN June 1990, there was a staff cutback at Bowen High School. My low seniority at Bowen put me among the teachers "excessed" out. For the fall semester, I was hired at George Washington High School on Chicago's East Side. I continued my "second job," as a teacher-writer for the Chicago Public Schools.

Washington High School was right across the street from Republic Steel. In 1937, the police killed ten steel workers on that site, during the Little Steel Strike of the CIO. It is known as the "Republic Steel Massacre," or "Memorial Day Massacre." Few at the school were aware of this labor history. There was certainly just as little awareness of African American history.

One day, I wore a Benjamin Banneker Association button with Banneker's picture on a postage stamp. He was the African American astronomer/mathematician who created the outline for the new capital, Washington, DC. Some students asked me, "Who's that?" "He's Benjamin Banneker," I explained, "a mathematician and astronomer." "I didn't know there were any black mathematicians," the students said. I am sorry to say that teachers told me the same thing. After that, I made sure to wear my button every day.

My Second Retirement

About Thanksgiving 1990, I decided to take my second, and final, retirement. I kept getting colds that would not go away.

And I wanted more time to work with SOJ. They were suing Envirodyne Company, their final employer, hoping to win another big settlement. Retirement gave me more time with the women in SOJ. We were all proud that together we were making history. I realized that it was time to record that history. Frank's methods of organizing could be useful to other workers in battle.

"Always Bring a Crowd," the story of Frank Lumpkin, Steelworker

Someone needed to write a book about the Wisconsin Steel workers. Part of the story had already appeared as chapters in other books. Tom Geoghegan, the SOJ attorney, wrote a beautiful chapter about SOJ in *Which Side Are You On?* The chapter was titled, "Always Bring a Crowd," after one of Frank's favorite sayings. That was the inspiration for the title of the book I eventually wrote. Another well-known book about closed mills centered more on European ethnic communities. We wanted to give full coverage to African American and Latino steel workers, as well.

Who better than one of us to write our story? I decided to try. My first efforts gave a detailed record of how the plant closed. Then I listed each step in organizing SOJ. Next, I wrote about each SOJ campaign with names and dates, all in order. I passed around a few chapters for comments. Nobody seemed to find it interesting, including me. So I thought it over and looked for a different approach.

People are interested in people. Could I tell the Wisconsin Steel workers' story through a book about Frank? From the members of SOJ, we had heard other interesting stories. Could I put those stories together? I had never written that kind of book.

How do you write a "real" book? And how could I write about Frank's early years when I had never been to Washington-Wilkes County, Georgia? Frank had not been back there in 45 years. It was a long drive, but we saw no other way. So we jumped into our car and set out. Frank had a cousin who was still in the town. Her family would help us fill in the blanks.

In *Always Bring a Crowd*, I described how we made that long trip and knocked on the door at the address we were given. "Come right in," they said and welcomed us warmly. We talked with them, on and off for two days. Only after we returned to Chicago did we learn that we had visited the wrong house. So much for Southern hospitality!

Church, School, and Cemetery

So there was nothing to do but make another trip. We went to Orlando first so Frank's brother Warren could take us to the right house. Their real cousin, Lulamat, treated us royally. She was on the same street, two blocks away from the false Lulamat. How could we know that the street numbers went up, and then they went down again? Washington-Wilkes County seemed to have changed very little over the years, but of course it had. Otherwise it would not have been safe for Frank and me to have gone together.

Warren took us to the church that served the community where Frank was born. The church is located in Hilliard Station, just outside of Washington-Wilkes County. Attached to the church was their school, one room for all class levels. Behind the church was the cemetery. Stone markers stood over the more recent graves. Beyond the markers, there extended a mass of unmarked and neglected graves. Buried there were hundreds, perhaps thousands of enslaved African Americans. It was they who picked the cotton that enriched the plantation owners, the Callaways. I felt the generations cry out, the suffering and the joys of the people buried in this neglected slave cemetery.

In these unmarked graves were my husband's and my children's ancestors. How did Frank feel? He looked glum, but said nothing. Warren said only, "It's a shame. These graves should be respected." There lay victims of the holocaust that depopulated Africa. Africa lost 100 million people to the slave traders. To date, that Georgia cemetery, where African holocaust victims lie in unmarked graves, remains unrecognized.

Listen to the Workers

I think the better parts of the book about Frank came from listening to the workers. There were a good number of poets among them. Some of the "interviews" I recorded were sheer poetry. And the workers had so much to say, jokes included.

I decided to keep the text at a sixth or seventh grade reading level so all could read it. I thought college graduates would not object if the book was easy to read.

Neglected gravesites of enslaved Africans at Hilliard Station,
Washington-Wilkes County, Georgia
(Headstones mark 20th Century burials)

Chapter 30

Heat or Eat?

"Peoples Energy and Enron lined their pockets with money that consumers should never have paid; money that was made illegally."

IN the winter of 2001, the gas bills for heating our homes went sky high. Working families were hard hit. Some on fixed incomes faced a choice of "heat or eat." People were angry when they saw their huge gas bills.

We were up against the biggest corporations. It would take a really big movement to bring our gas bills down to what they used to be. So on February 7, 2001, our Southside Communist club talked to our coalition partners and together we acted fast. Within a week we had a rally of 130 people to demand lower gas prices.

What caused the spike in the price of heating gas? We agreed that it started with the deregulation of gas wells, beginning in 1978 (President Carter) and continuing in 1985 (President Reagan). Without the restraint of federal regulation, gas suppliers were allowed to create an artificial shortage. Then they charged whatever they wanted and blamed it on "supply and demand."

Federal re-regulation was needed. But meanwhile, we had to stop service cutoffs for those who could not pay the big gas bills. Illinois law forbids shutting off heating gas between October First and April First. However, once the gas company cut off a family's service, no law required that it be turned back on the next winter. Every winter, some whose gas had been shut off froze to death in Chicago.

On February 13, USWA locals and Save Our Jobs co-sponsored a rally that formed a new coalition, "Angry Utility Consumers." Leaders of USWA locals, Save Our Jobs, Chicago CLUW, the Free Salvation Missionary Baptist Church, Saint Bride Roman Catholic Church and many block clubs were included.

The next month (March) we brought a busload of protesters to a demonstration against Peoples Gas, a company owned by Peoples Energy. The company claimed they were not profiting from the rise in gas prices. At a later date, the Illinois attorney general proved the company had lied. Peoples Gas was forced to pay back the overcharge to their gas customers. The March demonstration was organized by Pat Quinn, later elected Illinois lieutenant governor. Other community groups came from Bridgeport, Back of the Yards (stockyards) and South Austin.

People waited in line to sign our petitions. We had 7,000 signatures asking for rollback of the price increase, re-regulation of gas wells and no shutoffs of gas service. But April 1st was fast approaching, when Peoples Gas could legally cut off service. Some thought the number of families with past due gas bills was as high as 40,000.

Just before that deadline, we called a demonstration against gas shutoffs. All TV networks showed our demonstration on the evening news. What should be our next step? Our 7,000 petition signatures should gain us some leverage. Where would it do the most good? Congress has the power to roll back the gas rates. State legislators can stop the gas company from cutting off service. Aldermen could put pressure on both state and federal governments. So we made enough copies of our signed petitions to present at all levels of government.

By this time, many organizations had come together to speak out against high heating gas bills. Frank and I attended a strategy session called by Rev. Dr. Al Sampson, a prominent church activist. As we came in, Sampson said, "Brother Lumpkin is here! I must be doing something right!" In campaigns to follow, I heard Frank acknowledged by famous African American leaders. Frank's great moral force was recognized again and again.

City Council Resolution

The campaign got very interesting when we took it to the local level. We visited Alderman William Beavers to discuss a moratorium on gas shutoffs. Beavers was well known as a Daley machine politician. Still, he responded favorably. He agreed at once to put a resolution on the floor of the Chicago City Council. The resolution passed unanimously! Unfortunately, the resolution had no binding power. We heard that the Illinois Commerce Commission (ICC) and the state legislature did have that power. On to the ICC!

Our coalition joined with Rev. Al Sampson and Pat Quinn to present combined petitions with 12,000 signatures. We asked the ICC for a 150-day moratorium on gas shutoffs. But the commission failed to act. They seemed more concerned about protecting People's Energy profits than saving people from freezing to death in the coming winter.

Our next target was the U.S. Congress. Congress had the power to re-regulate gas and make the price of gas more affordable. We met with Congresswoman Jan Schakowsky and her staff. They told us that the Government Accounting Office (GAO) was investigating the huge hike in gas prices. They said the GAO already had proof that suppliers deliberately withheld gas to make the price go up.

With the help of Chicago CLUW, we took our petitions to Congressmen Jesse Jackson and Bobby Rush in Washington, DC. Jackson agreed with our demands. Rush did not comment on our petition; re-regulation seemed a hot button issue for him.

Corporate Crooks, Capitalist "Morality"

In the summer months of 2001, anger about our gas bills waned. For the next few winters, the price of heating gas dropped from the high peak of 2001. We felt vindicated when the City of Chicago and the State of Illinois sued Peoples Energy for fraud. The suits led to a settlement of $100 million, paid to the consumers.

In a press conference announcing the state suit, Attorney General Lisa Madigan said, "We allege that from 1999 to 2002,

Peoples Energy and Enron lined their pockets with money that consumers should never have paid—money that was made illegally. .... The transactions are very complicated, but the reason behind them is very simple: Peoples Energy wanted to generate profits they were not entitled to under law, so Peoples Energy devised and carried out a scheme with Enron to do so."

Chapter 31

Living While Old Under Capitalism
How to make old age part of living, not just dying

I grew up with little or no contact with old people. Of my four grandparents, three remained in Byelorussia. The fourth came to the U.S. when he was up in his 70s and did not survive long. My contact with him was limited, and there was a language barrier. No old people lived in our East 165th Street apartment building in the Bronx. As a matter of fact, there were not so many old people alive. When I was young, I never expected to live long enough to get old. When warned to slow down, to stop "burning the candle at both ends," I brushed off the warning. I felt that if I lived to be 40 that would be long enough. As for our middle years, I have noticed that most of us are too busy making a living and trying to survive to think about old age.

But at 36, something happened that thrust the old age question right in front of my eyes. I was hospitalized with hepatitis. The standard treatment in those days was hospital bed rest for three weeks. My roommates were all elderly. I began to think a lot about old age and how to make it part of living, not just dying. I felt sad, not because my roommates were dying; it was more because they were not living and seemed to have nothing to live for. The women were existing, but without joy or sense of purpose.

One of the hospital maintenance workers often dropped by to talk.. We talked about old age and how it could be different and better. We agreed that it was important to remain truly alive until we died. The key ingredient, we thought, was work, and to continue to play a useful role in society. But suppose we wanted to work part time while we collect our full pension. We should be able to do that, perhaps four-hour days, or two-to-three-day weeks. And if we did not want to work on our old jobs, there should be other opportunities.

Eleven years later, in another country, I saw an answer to this problem. A family camping trip in 1965 took us to the Soviet Union. Everywhere, we saw old people working. The newspaper vendors, the sausage sellers on the street, the clerks who registered us at the camp sites, they were all past retirement age. "How much are you paid?" we asked. "We get our regular wages," they replied, "according to how many hours we work." "We work only as many hours as we want," they added. "What about your pension?" we asked. "Oh, we get that too!"

"That would only work in a socialist society," I thought. "You have to have full employment and a shortage of labor. Otherwise the grandparents would be taking away their grandchildren's jobs." The lack of democracy did in the former Soviet Union. But one thing they did right was to allow old people to collect their pension and work.

In pre-capitalist times, extended families had jobs for everyone to do. That included the elderly, as long as they were not too frail or sick. But there is no room for old people in the small "nuclear" families of our modern society. In most cases, older people now have to go out of the home to contribute to society. And we have no jobs that I know of, where the boss tells a retiree, "Work as many hours as you want, and we'll pay you per hour. And of course, you collect your pension, too."

Personally, I had a really bad experience trying to work and collect my pension, too. It ended up with my having to pay back all of my pension for a year and a half, about $25,000. But a little service credit was added to my pension base. That raised my pension more than $100 a month. Disregarding inflation, I figured that I would have to live another 18 years to get back the money I had to return. Well, at this writing, I have made it. Of course, if I consider inflation, I have not caught up yet. Maybe never.

Save Our Jobs Fights On.

My second and final retirement came around Thanksgiving, 1990. At 72, I was ready to become a "senior citizen." But I had to wait until early 1997. That's when the Wisconsin Steel fight ended and the last settlement was fully distributed. The Save Our Jobs Committee continued its monthly meetings until 2001. These meetings had become part of the lives of the Save Our Jobs activists. The meetings themselves had become more social and educational, less about Wisconsin Steel and Envirodyne. Still, we continued to be a resource for the steel union (USWA), the general labor movement, Citizen Action and the peace movements. They would call the Save Our Jobs Office for help. We were always glad to join their picket lines and demonstrations.

Senator Richard Durbin and author at Alliance for Retired American rally against privatizing Social Security, 2009

Sometimes we were a dramatic presence at picket lines. That was true at a steel workers' picket line at O'Hare Airport, supporting embattled steel workers in Mansfield, Ohio.

By that time, many Save Our Jobs members were showing signs of old age decline. Frank and I marched as always. I may have felt pain in my joints, but I smiled and did not show it. But other Save Our Jobbers were making a much bigger sacrifice. They were limping with canes, pushing walkers, hopping with crutches and taking a few minutes of essential rest on folding chairs.

But the biggest hit of all was Tom Fineberg on his scooter. Tom had a really bad hip. His other hip was still serviceable. He figured out a way to keep his independence and still get around quickly. Put the leg attached to the bad hip on a scooter step. Push hard with the good side still on the ground. And roll with his white hair flying! Few could keep up with him. Tom and his scooter were a sensation.

When Save Our Jobs disbanded, we formed a new organization to fight for the rights of retirees. We kept the respected initials and let them stand for "Seniors Organized for Justice." I had wanted the name, FIRE, for Fighting Retirees. But the majority ruled, and SOJ lived on in a different format.

Alliance for Retired Americans

In 2001, the national AFL-CIO helped establish the Alliance for Retired Americans (ARA), a progressive retiree organization. Frank and I attended the founding convention, representing SOJ. We paid our own fare but stayed with son Paul in Washington. ARA opened its arms to community groups, too. SOJ, the retiree group, had found a new home! By 2003, we were in the middle of a huge, nationwide fight to stop President Bush's "Medicare Part D" giveaway to the big drug companies. It was a fight that took us into senior centers, "golden age" lunch rooms and senior housing.

Ever since Medicare became law in 1965, the congressmen who voted against it have tried to gut and subvert it. They hated Medicare because they saw it as the first step to health care for all in the U.S. But it took the evil genius of George W. Bush to undermine Medicare under the pretext of expanding it. The Bush wordsmiths named it the "Medicare Modernization Act." It was supposed to add prescription drug coverage to Medicare. In reality, the act was a cynical scheme to raise the price of medicine and increase the profits of the big drug companies. A delayed bomb hidden in the act was a plan to privatize Medicare, starting in 2010.

At age 80, Frank and I were lucky and did not need any medicine. That changed. By 2003, I was put on Fosamax to rebuild bone density. The lowest price I could find was $17 a pill. Yes, it was just once a week but $17 for one pill! I took the first pill after drinking coffee one morning. Then I read the instructions. "Take on an empty stomach." Otherwise the pill would not be effective. I had just wasted $17. I wanted to stick my hand down my gullet and retrieve the pill!

Then Frank needed a couple of pills that ran over $300 a month. That meant that he would fall into the "donut hole" in late summer. In the hole, Frank would have to pay full cost for his medicines. That was no accident; big increases were built into the law. The law *forbade* Medicare from bargaining for lower prices. In contrast, the Veteran's Administration can bargain for lower prices and pays 40% less.

Don't call me "cute"

I responded when ARA sent out a call for our prescription drug horror stories. I ended up getting my picture in the *Chicago Tribune* and the Joliet newspapers, one photo uglier than the next. For some reason, good photographers are very fond of my wrinkles and other visible signs of weathering many battles. With their good equipment, photographers are able to capture every telltale skin fold.

Of course, there is another, perhaps better way to look at these wrinkles. Older is beautiful! That's probably true past a certain age. I may have passed that certain age. Young women are beginning to call me "cute." I try to accept it graciously, in the spirit in which it is intended. But I don't exactly like it. I would rather be thought of as formidable in the fight for people's welfare and human survival.

The big drug companies make the 19th and 20th century robber barons look like small change. An August 2007 ARA report, "How the Drug Industry Profits from Pills," predicted that medicine sales for 2007 to 2017 will gross $1.2 trillion. "Big pharma" spends only 13% for research and development. But 17% was pocketed as pure profit. Where did that profit go? Much of it went for obscenely inflated salaries for drug companies' CEOs. Here is a partial list for 2006, as noted in the AFL-CIO 2007 Executive Pay Watch Database: Wyeth $32.8 million, Johnson & Johnson $28.5 million, Abbot Laboratories $26.9 million, Pfizer Inc. $19.4 million, Eli Lilly and Co. $15.2 million, Merck & Co., Inc. $10.2 million, Bristol-Myers Squibb Co. $ 9.7 million.

Author, Harriet Glover, Juanita Andrade of Seniors Organized for Justice Supporting locked-out AK Steel Workers

Chapter 32

Sixty Years with Frank
I liked him as well as loved him.

I married Frank because I loved him, and he loved me and my kids. I knew that marrying into the Lumpkin family was a wonderful opportunity. But it was also a challenge. The family had very high standards that I would have to live up to. I tried to earn my place in the family circle. The Lumpkins were a strong family and embraced each member in a tight circle of love. Their love did not stop there; it flowed outward too. Their love embraced all working people, especially those who were fighting for freedom.

Over the years, many have asked me, "Wasn't it hard to be married to a black man in 1949, with all the open racism of that time?" "Not at all," is still my ready answer. Frank and I worked well together. We enjoyed doing things together. We shared the goal of getting rid of capitalism. Fighting racism was a necessary first step to changing the system.

At this writing, Frank and I have been married 60 years. Younger people often ask me, "How did you stay together so long?" For some reason, I am always mildly amused when asked. I certainly don't feel that we have any special advice to pass on. We certainly both had plenty of faults. Probably it took me 60 years to curb my sharp tongue, at least a little. I also hope I have learned to curb my frowns and withering glances. If Frank had to put up with that, no wonder we never had any arguments. Actually, I would list that as his main fault as a spouse. He would not stay and argue any disagreement to a resolution. But there were so many common faults that he did not have.

The biggest fault he never had was that he never, never, never made any demands on me to do domestic chores. In terms of the traditional wife's role of cook, I did tend to fall into that role. That was especially true since I worked days, and he did rotating shifts. But he never, never demanded food. If I had cooked, fine. If I hadn't, he scrounged around the refrigerator and "made do" without complaining.

Eventually we worked out a division of labor. If it was a matter of building something, or fixing a car, Frank was right on the job. In Gary, he built a three-car garage with porch. That made up for living in a tiny house without a porch, basement or attic. The Gary house was tiny, but we made it into a jewel that would never need painting. Frank applied wood paneling to two bedrooms and the living room. Nine years later, the house was torn down—to make room for an alley, the city said.

Washing dishes was something I quit asking Frank to do. He did it so well. First he boiled the water. Then dishes were washed in boiling water. Then more water was boiled to rinse the dishes. Finally, they were truly sterilized with more boiling water. Hours later, when Frank finished washing the dishes, the whole kitchen was germ-free. As he told me, they did not have a hot water heater in their house in the orange groves. Every bit of hot water they used had to be heated on the stove. I respected the process. But I did not want to spend more than 15 minutes on dishwashing, so I did it myself.

Money

Over the millennia, most societies have taken a serious view about the issue of money in marriages. The ancient Egyptians did a pre-nuptial contract that stated exactly what goods were brought into the marriage. The woman got her part back if the marriage did not last. Today, only a few very rich people do marriage contracts, but many think it is a good idea. Frank and I never talked about money before we got married. That was easy. We didn't have any. Although Frank had worked since he was 16, we got together at the one time he was unemployed and broke. I had just left my job at Western Electric. Unemployment compensation kept us going, but it wasn't enough money to argue about.

Frank's approach to money was simple. It did not interest him. It was only good for one thing—spending. My ideal was that husband and wife should work out the money together. That did not happen. There really was no need to worry about money. By the time basic bills were paid, clothes bought for four growing kids, food on the table and supporting the good causes, the money was gone.

Frank's great sense of humor kept us going. It was just the kind of humor I liked, insightful and never mean-spirited. His generosity was also very attractive, even if hard to live with at times. Since money didn't mean anything to him, he was not slow to give it away. As a precinct committeeman in Gary, he recommended families to receive state welfare. There was always some delay between applying for welfare and receiving benefits. If Frank saw hungry children, he was not going to wait. He reached in his pocket and shared what he had.

That was especially true in 1959, during the historic 116-day national steel strike that stopped everything in this one-industry town. It was only just that Frank should share what he had. Through no fault of his, Wisconsin Steel worked during the national steel strikes. We were one of only three families, for blocks around in Gary, who were still getting a paycheck. The other two were an auto worker's family and a truck driver's family. All of our other neighbors were on strike.

There was another side to Frank that some did not know. It was part of what made it possible for him to last 17 years in the protracted fight around Wisconsin Steel. Frank was a deep thinker, a real worker-intellectual. He enjoyed reading books on political economy and philosophy. It was slow reading, but that's what he liked. For his 6 a.m. shift, he would get up at 4 a.m. so he could read for an hour. The deeper and more difficult the book, the better he liked it. Few people knew that he also enjoyed reading poetry. The poet Lonnie Nelson realized it and gave him a book of her poems. Frank enjoyed her book and read her poems again and again.

Strongest Man in the Steel Mill

For many years, Frank was the strongest man in Wisconsin Steel. At least that was true on the billing dock, a department of around 300 men. His strength must have contributed to his self-confidence. It certainly contributed to my feeling of safety when I was with him. I naively put us into potentially dangerous situations on our travels. We had a lot of fun poking around in dark streets and alleys in countries we visited. Later I learned that was not a good idea. Actually, it would not have been a good idea in Chicago, either. Muscular strength does not prevail against guns.

Of course, raising our children was our greatest joy. Our children go through so many interesting stages, all of them lovable. I am not romanticizing; child care involves a lot of work and trouble. But after the work was done and the troubles resolved, I forgot about the hard part. What I remember is that raising our children was so much fun. I have come to believe that everyone should have that experience. Of course, not everyone can physically reproduce. And future societies may decide to limit population growth. What I predict for the future are family circles, friends and relatives, that help biological parents raise a child.

I have sometimes wondered, "Why have I been so lucky that I was able to keep my eyes on the prize?" Some who were Communists and helped build the unions have dropped out of the worker's movement. They remain sympathetic but have lost their focus. I like to think that I would have stayed the course on my own. I'll never know. Married to Frank, I kept moving toward "the light at the end of the tunnel." We lived among workers who kept us focused on the workers' cause and gave us hope for humanity. Our hope is based on the strength of "the people united." They have the power to create a society free of exploitation.

On a personal note, some have asked me for my formula for continuing to live while old. I have only one suggestion: stay active with people of all ages in working for a better world. Care about the whole human family, not just your own relatives. There are so many fascinating changes in the works. We can do it if we work together. And exercise.

*Author, left front, in zumba class at South Side YMCA.
Instructor Alisa is front center.*

Chapter 33

Living and Loving with Alzheimer's Disease

Bea: "*We had a long, good life together.*" – *Frank:* "*It's not over, yet!*"

Frank was already 80, and I was 78 when the Wisconsin Steel workers got the last settlement from Envirodyne at the end of 1996. We had done a lot together and looked forward to doing more. Then things happened that were not in our plan.

Many of our friends were also old. One by one, they began to die. Cancer was the grimmest reaper. Of course there were strokes and other afflictions. The disease I knew less about was Alzheimer's Disease (AD). It got my dear mother-in-law, Hattie. But she died from a stroke before her AD became severe.

AD was a disease that people did not advertise. They covered it up, like something shameful. The statistics are sobering. It has reached five million in the U.S. Unfortunately, other countries are also not spared. There are 16 countries with longer life expectancies than the U.S. The more old people, the more AD. Does it have to be this way? I doubt it. It's all a matter of priorities, whether you put dollars into science research or the war machine. Still, I cannot say I gave the subject a lot of thought—until it struck home.

When I first met Frank, my best friend was his sister Jonnie. Jonnie married Henry Ellis and was later known as "Pat" Ellis. Pat's religion was *love,* and her church was the Communist Party. She was made of pure gold and was blessed with the gift of oratory. For those she thought were hurting the workers' cause, she also had a store of fire and brimstone and knew how to use it. When Hattie Lumpkin (Ma) died, Pat took over as leader of the extended Lumpkin family. As Pat neared 80, illness laid her low. It threw us all off balance, because her love helped sustain so many of us. She had some heart problems. The doctors fixed her heart with a pacemaker. Arthritis gave her pain so she took pain pills. Then it became clear that there was another problem, something for which there was no cure. Pat had AD.

After a few years, Pat needed more help than her husband, Al, could give her. That's when I learned about nursing homes. Pat's nursing home was only a mile from our house so we visited several times a week. The nursing home workers did their very best, I thought. But the resources were so meager.

The lack of resources was obvious in terms of the food. I never saw anything that could be called "dessert" at that nursing home. After two years, as she neared the end, Al came down with AD too. He managed to hide it for a long time. I got calls from the police two times when Al was found wandering on Chicago's South Side. Finally, the Department of Aging took over and placed him in a nursing home.

When we visited Al one Sunday evening, it was like a scene from the "insane asylums" of the eighteenth century. People were wandering around aimlessly. Others were calling for help, but nobody answered. I could see only one aide on the floor with about 40 patients. Fortunately, Al did not need any help that evening. But I cannot erase that desolate scene from my mind. Our elders deserve better than that.

Some years earlier, my son Dr. John Lumpkin had gone into public health work. He became well known for forcing some bad nursing homes to clean up their act. I would hate to think that conditions deteriorated again after he was no longer on that job. Long term care is not just a retiree issue. Millions are in long term care residences and many are cared for at home.

In 2008, I was elected Illinois secretary of the retiree organization, ARA. At a press conference with Senator Durbin (D-IL), we protested cuts in federal aid to nursing homes. Most nursing home patients are on Medicaid, paid for by state and federal funds. Underfunding of nursing homes is one of the saddest features of our broken health care system.

AD, the Memory Eraser

When Frank forgot a lengthy repair to his car, I was afraid something terrible was happening. Car repairs were something he took very seriously. So we went to the Rush "Memory Clinic" for advice. A senior doctor made the diagnosis: mild AD. Patients can live from two to 20 years after the diagnosis, he said. Since Frank was 80 at the time, and they said he could live to 100, it did not sound too bad. And at first it wasn't bad. Life was almost normal for a number of years.

A couple of years after Frank's dreadful diagnosis, we drove to Washington, Georgia, and then on to Orlando, Florida. Frank did most of the driving. He also flew alone to meetings in New York and participated meaningfully. Frank was able to function independently. I did begin to hire plumbers and carpenters for some of the work he always had done himself. But by that time he was in his middle 80s and of an age where he should not need to do that kind of work.

The first big changes occurred at night. Frank began to have occasional nightmares. He would wake up in a start, with his fists swinging. A fist connected with me once. The blow was weak, blunted by sleep, and no harm was done. But Frank was horrified when he learned what had happened. He said we had better sleep in separate beds. That sounded reasonable, but it did not come to that.

One day we were on Commercial Avenue, driving home. A detour took us down a side street. On the side street, Frank pulled the car to the curb and asked me if I minded driving the rest of the way home. That's when I realized that Frank was losing the map of Chicago that had been imprinted in his brain. He knew the well-traveled path from home to his office. But once off the path, for detour or other reason, he was lost. What a frightening feeling that must have been!

What love alone could not do, AD brought about. Frank and I became an inseparable pair. If you saw one, you saw the other. Before AD, Frank and I took some separate vacations. Often, meetings or conferences took us in different directions. As the disease made slow inroads into Frank's brain, safety issues dictated that we stay together. But we kept moving, trying to keep a step or two ahead of the disease. And move we did, out of the house every day, whatever the weather.

We went to every picket line and demonstration for the good causes we believed in. Naturally, we went to every steel worker's action within 50 miles. We supported laundry workers organizing with UNITE, hospital workers marching with AFSCME for union recognition, and the Congress Hotel strikers with HERE. We joined many peace and justice actions. On some Sundays in bitter weather, both Frank and I stood with "Not in My Name" on Michigan Avenue to join Jews who were opposing the Israeli occupation of the West Bank and Gaza.

We marched on Commercial Avenue with Centro Communitario Juan Diego against Bush's war in Afghanistan. We marched in Chicago's Hyde Park on a cold day to prevent a war in Iraq. That's where we heard then State Senator Obama speak against invading Iraq. Of course, we never missed demonstrations in support of universal health care, to protect Social Security from privatization, or election rallies against Bush policies.

Frank and Beatrice Lumpkin at Chicago rally to save SS from privatization

What about the days when we did not march and did not have a political meeting? From our South Shore Chicago home, it is an easy drive to Chicago's major museums. I bought memberships in all three. Sometimes we walked three to five miles on the lake front. We kept on the move. I was afraid that if we stopped to rest, AD would catch us.

Traveling Abroad with AD

Frank and I continued our annual vacation trips for 11 years after his diagnosis of AD. In 1997, we visited Senegal during February, African American History Month. In 1998, we went to Cuba with the US/Cuba Labor Exchange. Everything with Frank was still pretty normal. I had also planned to attend the First World Congress on Ethnomathematics in Granada, Spain. Ordinarily, I would have gone by myself. But I did not want to leave Frank alone for ten days. We had a beautiful trip,

The next year Frank and I went to La Paz, Bolivia. La Paz is one of the most beautiful cities on this planet. As the AD was slowly changing Frank, he began to walk behind me, rather than at my side. He claimed he was protecting my rear. On the streets of La Paz, pedestrians did not seem to have the right of way. When I heard agitated cries from the crowd, I turned to see Frank sprawled out in the street. The car involved had sped away. I rushed to his side. Was he hurt? No. In a flashback to his athletic past, Frank saw the little car coming at him and pushed hard on the fender. That diverted the car and sent him sprawling to the ground. Nothing was hurt but his feelings and a torn pants leg. So we both survived.

We did not quit traveling but switched to escorted groups. It just seemed the safest way to go. Group travel took us to Cuba and China in 2001, the Galapagos Islands, 2002, Vietnam in 2003, Venezuela and Cuba again in 2004. It all went well even if Frank did not always distinguish between China and Vietnam, or Mexico and other Latin American countries. But in 2006 we made one last trip on our own, to visit friends in faraway Chile. In Santiago,

I had one of the most frightening experiences of my lifetime. I was sure it would be the last time that Frank and I could travel out of the country. That proved to be true. The hotel room I had booked on the Internet was large enough to get lost in or lost out of. After the 11–12 hour flight, we fell into bed, exhausted. After four hours of total unconsciousness, I realized that Frank was not in the bed. I called him. No response. Then I checked the bathroom, the closet, even under the bed. No Frank. I immediately had a vision of him walking down the boulevard, barefoot, a head taller than most of the people on the street, not knowing one word of Spanish.

Frank Lumpkin, center, with union members, Dakar, Senegal

In a panic, I began to throw my clothes on, while I suppressed my sobs. Then I thought of calling the front desk. I made myself understood, because I heard the welcome words: *No se preocupe, señora.* (Don't worry ma'am). I guess he saw Frank, dressed in pajamas, on his way out. Frank had turned the wrong way when he walked out of the bathroom. Once in the hotel corridor, all the doors looked the same.

Frozen Glaciers in Bolivia, a 2 Hour Bus Ride From

Sun in the Tropics

Something similar but not quite so scary had happened right in Washington, DC. Frank and I were attending the annual convention of the ARA. We cut costs by sleeping in our son Paul's apartment. With Paul and his wife, Dugan, we were watching a rented movie. Halfway through the movie, I noticed that Frank was gone. Then we split up, some by elevator and Dugan by the stairs. The desk clerk in the lobby had not seen Frank. Just then, Dugan called. She had found Frank in their underground garage, looking for his car that was back in Chicago.

Driving with AD

As far as I know, nobody has ever recovered from AD. The disease does its damage by destroying cells in the brain. Most of us think of memory loss as the main symptom of AD. Sadly, memory is just one part of what AD patients lose. Control of the muscles is also involved, and that can mean anything from inability to walk and incontinence, to difficulty in swallowing food.

The area in Frank's brain that controls driving a car must have been spared. In all those years, he never had an accident. Before my 88th birthday, I went to take my annual road test. Frank was almost 90. He came along because I did not want to leave him alone. When I stepped up to renew my license, Frank stepped up, too. "Oh no," I told the clerks. "He can't get a license." The clerks looked at me; then they looked at him. They were probably thinking, "What's wrong with her? Why is she trying to stop this fine-looking man from getting his license?" Frank passed his vision test and passed his road test. He had a valid license!

Then one day in May 2007, he slipped out again. When I looked out the window, the car was gone. Our neighbor helped me look for him. No, he was not at the union hall, not in McDonalds, not at the Walgreen lot, not at the senior center. Much as I hated to do it, I called the Chicago police. Just then, my cell phone rang. It was the St. John, Indiana, police. They got my cell phone number from Frank's ID bracelet. St. John is a town of about 5,000, east of Schererville, Indiana. "Are you Mrs. Lumpkin? We have Frank Lumpkin here. His car broke down on Indianapolis Boulevard." They had towed the car to the police pound.

Another neighbor came to my rescue and drove me to St. John. It turned out that the clutch had suddenly gone out on our car. Otherwise, with a full tank, who knows where it would have ended. Frank told the St. John police that he was returning from a conference in Detroit. The three-block tow cost $120. Other than that, Frank was free to go. I was glad to hear it because Frank had gone out without his wallet. He was driving without the valid license secured over my objections.

Now I had to do something to guarantee that Frank would drive no more. So I had a hidden switch put in the ignition circuit. I did not know that the two of us would have only a few more weeks to enjoy our life together. And enjoy it we did. On May 19, 2007, we rode the SOAR bus for the steel workers' lobbying day in Springfield, Illinois. It was a great trip. At the end of the month, we were part of the 70th anniversary commemoration of the Republic Steel Massacre. As I sensed the end of our time together, I thought of all the good things we had done. "We had a long, good life together," I said to Frank. "It's not over, yet!" was his cheerful reply.

But six weeks later, our life together was over. It was a series of infections that sent Frank to the hospital. After a week in the hospital to knock out the infections, Frank went for rehabilitation to the best nursing home we could find.

Where Are the Men? The People of Color?

The first thing that strikes the new visitor to a nursing home is, "Where are the men?" In the highly recommended home that Frank went to, the big question was, "Where are the people of color?" Both answers are grim. Women greatly outnumber men residents, because the men have died off. The answer to the second question has two parts. The first is racism, the extreme segregation of Chicago neighborhoods. The second part is also racism, the lower incomes and lack of pensions for people of color. The better nursing home was far from free.

The big question was, "Who's going to pay for it?" Some friends asked me, "Doesn't Medicare pay for nursing home care?" The short answer is "No," although they do pay for rehab (rehabilitation). After the first hospital stay, Medicare paid 100% for 20 days of rehab. For the next three weeks, I had a co-pay of 20%. When the bill for the rehab came, I was shocked. My co-pay came to $120 a day! Then rehab was over, and we had to pay the full price of nursing home care, $7,000–$8,000 a month. And that's what I did for a couple of months. I would have had to sell our house to continue at that rate. Then where would I live? Anyway, nobody is buying houses. And at $7,000–$8,000 a month, what I could get out of my house would soon be gone.

It is Medicaid that pays for poor residents' care. But Frank and I had small pensions and Social Security. Technically, we were not poor. Fortunately, Illinois extends Medicaid to nursing homes for people with average retiree incomes. Our state is one of only 13 that have such laws. Instead of $7,000–$8,000 a month, I began to pay $2,000, and Medicaid paid the balance, at a reduced rate. The $2,000 a month was still a large sum, but I did not have to sell my house. At least not yet.

My sister-in-law Bess faced a similar situation. But she lives in Arizona. Unfortunately, that is not one of the 13 states that help spouses pay for long term care. In Arizona, she was told that Medicaid would not help her pay the nursing home until she had sold her house and spent all but $2,000.

The rehab center got Frank back up on his feet. I spent much of the day with him, and we did a lot of walking outside the nursing home. They had live entertainment a couple of times a week, vaudeville acts and musical performances. With a catchy tune going, Frank and I got up and danced. In fact, Frank was so mobile and physically able that "rehab" discharged him after one month. Then he moved to the Alzheimer floor where they claimed their activities would help maximize his abilities. I actually looked forward to the move. Instead it turned out to be a nightmare.

Alzheimer's Floor, a Nightmare

First, Frank was one of the few African American patients at the nursing home. He has always related well to people of all colors. The same may not have been true of some nursing home staff. In the dining room, they put Frank in the corner, with this back to everyone else. Their excuse was that his reflux (food coming up) might disturb other patients. Then the staff decided that psychotropic drugs were needed to calm Frank down. The ordinary dose did not quiet him sufficiently, so they sent him out to the emergency room of the local hospital for further sedation.

I was at Chicago's Bud Billiken Day parade when I got the call. I found Frank splayed out in four parts on a gurney, each hand tied down and each foot tied down. A mask was over his face. "After we tied him down, he spit at us," ER staff told me.

At my request, they removed the mask and Frank became calm. "There are bad people out there," he told me. "They're trying to help you," I replied without much conviction. He had not eaten all day, so I was allowed to bring him food. After he ate, they tied him back down on the gurney. "I want you to stay with me for 17 years," Frank told me.

We waited and waited and waited. The psychiatrist they were waiting for never showed up. At 10 p.m. that night, staff shot a powerful dose of some drug into him and shipped him back to the nursing home. At the home, they got a doctor's permission to hugely increase the dose of the psychotropic drug. I think it was doubled. After a few days of heavy drugging, he was keeling over, putting his head down on the table. Back to the hospital!

Frank lay in the hospital bed for a couple of days with an IV going, but no medication. They had both of his arms tied down, day and night, to prevent him from removing the IV needle. Then it was realized that he had pneumonia, so antibiotics were added to the IV fluid. After eight or nine days, the pneumonia was knocked out, and physical therapists came in. Surprise, surprise. After more than a week of being tied down, Frank could neither sit up nor stand on his feet. On his butt were a couple of nasty sores. And it was in that condition that he spent the rest of his life.

Frank returned from the hospital in such poor shape that hospice care was recommended. Hospice care has helped many families in the final months of the illness. The hospice team includes a doctor, nurse, certified nursing assistant, social worker, and a coordinator who come to the nursing home or the patient's home. Their mission is to provide comfort for the patient and help to the family. Funding for hospice care is provided by Medicare.

Admission to hospice is restricted to patients expected to die within six months. That six month estimate is the doctor's best guess. But at the time Frank was placed in hospice, the Bush administration was cracking down hard on cases that ran over six months. So the hospice kicked Frank out in a few weeks when he improved slightly. When his condition went downhill again, he was readmitted. I thought that they might have to kick him out again. Frank was a fighter and did not surrender easily.

Although in hospice, Frank continued to know me and friends and family. He greeted me with a kiss and a wink. Frank spent much of the time of my visit looking intently into my eyes. And I looked into his—so close and so sad.

A Better Way

It was inspiring to learn that Canada has a more humane and efficient way to pay for long term care and other health care needs. In 1971, the Canadians won health care for all. Knowing that they did it encourages me to believe that we can do it too in the USA. Lynn Williams, retired president of the United Steelworkers, described the care his mother got in a Canadian nursing home and the benefits of health care for all: "My mother lived in a nursing home for the last ten years of her life and it cost only the difference between a double room and her single."[37] I wrote the above before President Obama signed the Patient Protection and Affordable Care Act. At last, we are on the way. But we still have a long way to go.

We all know that we will not live forever. Death at an advanced age was not scary to Frank or me. New life is born as old life dies. Our immortality, Frank and I believed, is in helping new life flourish. Frank's teachings live on. In large part, that's why I am recording these memories.

---

[37] Lynn Williams. January 18, 2011. http://www.huffingtonpost.com/lynn-r-Williams/rebuilding-the-labor-move_b_84295.html.

YCL at Bud Billiken Day Parade, 2002

Chapter **34**

Postscript
Our replacements have arrived!

Peace Vigil

IN October 2008, I rode the Obama bus to campaign in Merrill-
ville, Indiana. My favorite campaign slogan was "We are the
ones we were waiting for." I felt good to be part of the "we."
The young people on the bus were a perfect cross-section of
multiracial Chicago, a total blend of purpose and dedication.
My heart sang; our replacements had arrived!

Meanwhile, Frank spent the campaign in the nursing home.
I talked to him about Obama every day. I knew he wanted to

know. But I could not tell if the news was getting through to him. The day after the election, the first page of the *New York Times* carried Obama's picture and his name in three-inch letters. I showed it to Frank. He looked at it, hard. Then he drew his right arm out from under the covers, bent it at the elbow and raised his clenched fist high!

Postscript

On March 1, 2010, 7 AM, I got the call from the nursing home, "Frank passed." An outpouring of love and support from family and friends sustained me.

Every citywide and local newspaper wrote articles and editorials praising Frank's leadership. WTTW, Chicago's public TV station, replayed their video of Frank at the closed Wisconsin Steel mill. It was proof that Frank's message lives on.

We organized two memorials for Frank at union halls. The first was across the street from the site of the Memorial Day Massacre at Republic Steel. Steel workers packed the hall. They had worked with Frank and continue to support labor's cause. The other memorial was at Workers United. Arrangements were made by CLUW to honor Frank, a long-time member of CLUW. Public officials spoke, including two members of the U.S. Congress, a city alderman, and a resolution from the Illinois State Assembly was read.

Music was supplied by members of Frank Lumpkin's family. Sons Paul and John sang a Frank version of the labor classic: "I dreamed I saw Frank Lumpkin last night, alive as you and me." Niece Nicole Parrini sang Amazing Grace and nephew Rev. Vincent Teague sang His Eye Is On the Sparrow. Comrade Reverend Tim Yeager played a bag pipe salute as Frank's ashes were buried at Forest Park (Waldheim) Cemetery, next to the Haymarket Martyrs' Monument.

There was poetry in Frank. It was part of what brought us together. There was poetry in Rev. Tom Strieter's eulogy at Workers United. I give some excerpts from Strieter's eulogy. Martin Luther King called himself a "drum major for justice." Strieter applied the same title to Frank.

From Rev. Strieter's Eulogy

Throughout history there have been drum majors: The Hebrew social prophets who cried out for the oppressed—the widows and orphans and disenfranchised—and condemned the oppressors. Amid the struggle, they looked forward to what they called "the Day of the Lord," to that time when there would be justice and peace and equity.

The Carpenter from Nazareth was a drum major for what he called "the reign of God." He said it was breaking through into the present, changing the order of things. It was turning the tables against political oppression—"throwing down the mighty from their thrones and exalting those of low estate," and bringing an end to economic oppression—"filling the hungry with good things, and sending the rich away empty."

This was a vision of the revolution of peace and justice and equality in the here and now. But in that struggle, he was crucified by the power of Rome for "stirring up the people."

There was another Hebrew prophet, Karl Marx—a drum major in the struggle for economic and social justice, with the vision of a classless society: "FROM each according to his ability; TO each according to his needs."

Cuba, 2000. Joy in the Struggle

Frank Lumpkin, too, has been a drum major—in his own time and place. How fitting that his ashes blend together with the Haymarket martyrs. For the ongoing struggle and the vision also is Frank's legacy.

Author with 3 grandchildren. Joy in the Struggle

Bea and Frank, Forbidden City, China. Joy in the Struggle